Polarization and Democracy
in Latin America

Polarization and Democracy in Latin America

Legacies of the Left Turn

SANTIAGO ANRIA
AND KENNETH M. ROBERTS

THE UNIVERSITY OF CHICAGO PRESS   CHICAGO AND LONDON

The University of Chicago Press, Chicago 60637
The University of Chicago Press, Ltd., London
© 2026 by The University of Chicago
All rights reserved. No part of this book may be used or reproduced in any manner whatsoever without written permission, except in the case of brief quotations in critical articles and reviews. For more information, contact the University of Chicago Press, 1427 E. 60th St., Chicago, IL 60637.
Published 2026
Printed in the United States of America

35 34 33 32 31 30 29 28 27 26   1 2 3 4 5

ISBN-13: 978-0-226-84760-3 (cloth)
ISBN-13: 978-0-226-84762-7 (paper)
ISBN-13: 978-0-226-84761-0 (ebook)
DOI: https://doi.org/10.7208/chicago/9780226847610.001.0001

Library of Congress Cataloging-in-Publication Data

Names: Anria, Santiago, 1982- author | Roberts, Kenneth M., 1958- author
Title: Polarization and democracy in Latin America : legacies of the left turn / Santiago Anria and Kenneth M. Roberts.
Description: Chicago : The University of Chicago Press, 2026. | Includes bibliographical references and index.
Identifiers: LCCN 2025039139 | ISBN 9780226847603 cloth | ISBN 9780226847627 paperback | ISBN 9780226847610 ebook
Subjects: LCSH: Polarization (Social sciences)—Latin America | Democracy—Latin America | Political participation—Latin America | New Left—Latin America | Latin America—Politics and government—21st century | Latin America—Politics and government—20th century
Classification: LCC HN110.5.Z9 P573 2026
LC record available at https://lccn.loc.gov/2025039139

♾ This paper meets the requirements of ANSI/NISO Z39.48-1992 (Permanence of Paper).

Authorized Representative for EU General Product Safety Regulation (GPSR) queries: **Easy Access System Europe**—Mustamäe tee 50, 10621 Tallinn, Estonia, gpsr.requests@easproject.com
Any other queries: https://press.uchicago.edu/press/contact.html

TO OUR MENTORS—EVELYNE HUBER, JOHN D. STEPHENS, RICHARD FAGEN, TERRY LYNN KARL, AND PHILIPPE C. SCHMITTER

Contents

List of Illustrations   ix

INTRODUCTION   Democracy and Polarization in Latin America   1

CHAPTER 1   The Left Turn, Democracy, and Dynamics of Polarization   16

CHAPTER 2   The Social Democratic Left and the Conformist Temptation   45

CHAPTER 3   The Populist Left and the Autocratic Temptation   86

CHAPTER 4   Comparative Perspectives: Argentina, Ecuador, and Uruguay   129

CHAPTER 5   Latin America's "New" Polarization: A Multidimensional Approach   174

CONCLUSION   Polarization, Democracy, and the Leftist Dilemma   198

Acknowledgments   215
Appendix   219
Notes   223
References   235
Index   275

Illustrations

FIGURES

Figure 1.1: Mapping the left's democratic imaginaries onto Dahl's two dimensions of polyarchy / 25

Figure 1.2: Political polarization, 1900–2022 / 34

Figure 1.3: Polarization: spatial and institutional dimensions / 37

Figure 1.4: Axes of political contestation / 39

Figure 5.1: Political polarization, 1980–2020 / 178

Figure 5.2: Polarization of society, 2000–2022 / 180

Figure 5.3: Political polarization (1980–2020) and social polarization (2000–2020) / 181

Figure 5.4: Left-right self-placement, 1995–2023 / 184

Figure 5.5: Relationship between participation and left-right self-placement (six countries) / 191

Figure 5.6: Ideological self-identification and participation curves / 191

Figure 5A.1: Relationship between participation and left-right self-placement (individual countries) / 220

TABLES

Table 1.1: Presidential elections and reelections of left and center-left candidates in Latin America, 1998–2015 / 18

Table 1.2: Changes in the Gini index of inequality in Latin America, 2000–2016 / 37

Table 5.1: Ideological self-placement and political engagement / 190

Table 5.2: Ideological distance polarization in presidential elections / 193

Table 5A.1: Ideological self-placement and political engagement (controlling for income) / 221

Introduction

Democracy and Polarization in Latin America

The democratic regimes installed across Latin America in the late twentieth century proved surprisingly resilient (Brinks et al. 2014; Luna and Rovira Kaltwasser 2014; Levitsky 2018), given the region's historical track record of political instability and pendular swings between democratic and authoritarian modes of governance. Contemporary democracies in the region, however, are almost everywhere facing great challenges. Processes of democratic erosion or "backsliding" have led to increasingly authoritarian regimes in Venezuela, Nicaragua, and El Salvador, and several other countries—including Brazil, Guatemala, Ecuador, Bolivia, Honduras, and Peru—have had to counter serious autocratic threats. Democratic regimes have also become increasingly polarized over the past decade in a growing number of countries, with acrimonious conflicts among rival political elites and, in some unlikely cases, widespread social mobilization and mass protests against the established order—what are sometimes known as social *estallidos*, or "explosions." In much of the region, mainstream political parties have been eclipsed by new and more radical contenders while historically centrist parties have weakened or collapsed. Anti-incumbent voting and volatile swings of the political pendulum between leftist and rightist governments appear to be hallmarks of the region's "new normal."

This book examines the roots of this volatility and polarization, which have been heavily conditioned by the political conflicts engendered by democratic challenges to Latin America's historically entrenched social hierarchies and inequalities (Hoffman and Centeno 2003). These challenges found expression in the unprecedented political shift to the left—the so-called left turn—experienced in much of the region in the early twenty-first century. The conflicts associated with challenges to those hierarchies and inequalities contributed to the turbulent demise of the left turn and a conservative political backlash in a number of countries. To develop this argument, we analyze the formative experiences and institutional contexts in which both populist and social democratic lefts (Lanzaro 2014) rose to power in Latin America, and the nature of the social and political conflicts unleashed by their quite different approaches to the classic dilemma of the left in power—that of reconciling political democracy with ambitious social and economic reforms.[1] We deploy a comparative analysis of two populist lefts (Venezuela and Bolivia) and two social democratic lefts (Brazil and Chile), along with secondary analyses of their leftist counterparts in Argentina, Uruguay, and Ecuador.

Together, these comparisons help to explain the distinctive types of political failings or defects to which the populist and social democratic lefts were prone and the reasons for their respective patterns of political demise in the 2010s. They provide insight into why Latin America's left turn ended as it did in different countries, with (often short-lived) conservative restorations between 2015 and 2020. They also help us understand how the left turn continues to shape contemporary political dynamics in the region, with democratic orders that are increasingly polarized along both socioeconomic and cultural axes of conflict, and with a variety of new (and sometimes old) leftist parties alternating in power with conservative and, in several cases, far-right rivals.

Our analysis suggests that nearly all our comparative cases became highly polarized during or after the left turn, with the partial exception of Uruguay. While polarization was hardly surprising in countries like Venezuela and Bolivia, where new populist lefts confronted the entire political establishment (see Handlin 2017), it was much more puzzling in Brazil and Chile, where social democratic lefts made explicit efforts to moderate their stands, build broad and multiparty governing coalitions, and contain polarizing dynamics. Polarization, however, took different forms and followed different sequences in distinct national contexts, and it arguably produced different effects, even within these two subsets of cases. Acute polarization, for example, contributed to democratic backsliding in Venezuela and a gradual descent into authoritarian rule, whereas in Brazil and Bolivia it posed serious threats that democratic regimes have, to date, been able to withstand. In Chile, polarization helped spawn but then neutralize efforts to dramatically expand social citizenship rights under democracy, leaving a political stalemate in its wake.

A central goal of this book is to explain why and how the general pattern of deepening polarization has developed and played out differently across the region, with strikingly diverse implications for the stability and character of democratic governance. There is, then, a central paradox at the heart of this book having to do with the unexpected character of the polarized endings that our four primary cases share—and the diverse pathways and causal processes that produced variation within this shared outcome. Through a comparative historical analysis of the formative experiences shaping the populist and social democratic lefts, and the institutional contexts in which they rose to power, this book develops an original theoretical framework for explaining common patterns as well as variation across cases.

Polarization is hardly new in Latin America (Sarsfield et al. 2024), and it is surely not unique to the region. Indeed, it has become a central theme in scholarly debates over the threats to democracy on the global stage and contemporary patterns of democratic backsliding (Levitsky and Ziblatt 2018; McCoy and Somer 2019; Haggard and Kaufman 2021; Lieberman, Mettler, and Roberts 2021). In Latin America, the political instability and democratic breakdowns of the 1960s and 1970s were often attributed to class conflicts—in particular, elite reactions to the political mobilization of working and lower classes—and post–Cuban Revolution ideological polarization between proponents of capitalist and socialist models of development (O'Donnell 1973; Linz 1978; Valenzuela 1978).

Not surprisingly, then, theorizing about the region's so-called third wave of democratization (Huntington 1991) in the 1980s and 1990s often highlighted efforts to temper political conflicts and defuse polarizing dynamics. Dominant approaches treated democratization as an institutional compromise between rival political elites (Rustow 1970; Przeworski 1991), and they expected social actors, such as labor unions and protest movements, to relinquish the political stage to more established institutional actors as democracy took hold. For example, in their influential study *Transitions from Authoritarian Rule: Tentative Conclusions About Uncertain Democracies*, O'Donnell and Schmitter (1986, 55) argued that social mobilization would push forward democratic transitions, but they assumed that the "popular upsurge" would be "ephemeral," giving way to more institutionalized forms of political contestation as elections were scheduled, parties reemerged, and rival elites negotiated mutually restraining "pacts" to reduce uncertainty and keep democratic competition bounded. The goal of these pacts was to bring an end to authoritarian rule and establish minimal standards for electoral democracy. Typically, negotiated pacts required moderation and compromise by rival actors both within the regime and among regime opponents, and they contributed to the demobilization of some of the civil society actors that had pushed for democratization (Karl 1987).

Years later, Mainwaring and Pérez-Liñán (2014, 58–59) argued that democratic competition had been moderated during the third wave by traumatic experiences with military repression and hyperinflationary pressures that tempered expectations and transformed actors' preferences. These authors attributed the unexpected resiliency of Latin America's third-wave democracies to these processes of ideological moderation and political depolarization, which fostered the construction of a normative consensus for democratic governance in the 1980s and 1990s. In turn, the ideological hegemony of the Washington Consensus (Williamson 1990) for free-market or "neoliberal" development models within technocratic policymaking circles provided an economic complement to this democratic political convergence (Weyland 2001), a trend made all the more compelling by the leading role of historical labor-based populist or center-left parties in the implementation of neoliberal reforms in a surprising number of countries (Stokes 2001; Roberts 2014). Elite consensus around free-market reforms reduced the political space for democratic actors, especially left-wing parties and their social bases, to advance radical or redistributive socioeconomic agendas (Fishman 2018).

Contemporary forms of polarization, therefore, signify a dramatic change in Latin America's political landscape from the era of convergence in the late twentieth century, and they pose significant challenges to the dominant modes of theorizing about the region's third wave of democratization. These challenges invite renewed inquiry into the underlying causes and consequences of political polarization. As we will explain, they also call for a reexamination of polarization's complex and even contradictory relationship to political democracy.

Democracy and the Paradox of Polarization

Polarization is a complex, multidimensional political phenomenon by which society is sharply divided into conflictual and mutually antagonistic political camps (Mason 2018; McCoy and Somer 2019; Sarsfield et al. 2024). As defined by McCoy et al. (2018, 18), polarization is "a process whereby the normal multiplicity of differences in a society increasingly align along a single dimension, cross-cutting differences become instead reinforcing, and people increasingly perceive and describe politics and society in terms of 'Us' versus 'Them.'" It exists when major political rivals are far apart in their ideological identities and programmatic stands on salient economic or cultural issues—what can be thought of as ideological distancing or "spatial" polarization (Roberts 2021). Polarization also has an "affective" dimension—which may or may not map onto stark ideological differences—related to emotional feelings or attitudes when there is mutual distrust and dislike between major political adversaries (Iyengar et al. 2012). In Sartori's (1976, 126–145) pathbreaking work, polarization was not simply a function of ideological distancing; it also entailed the presence of "antisystem" parties that denied the legitimacy of the regime in place. In related terms, recent scholarship has emphasized the polarizing effects of political rivals waging conflicts over the basic institutional rules that regulate political contestation under democracy (Levitsky and Ziblatt 2018; Roberts 2021; Schedler 2023) or denying the democratic legitimacy of other actors.

On the supply side, polarization may be driven by the top-down strategic behavior of political elites who seek to demarcate and mobilize their followers by delegitimizing or even demonizing opponents. Elite actors who flaunt democratic norms and procedures in pursuit of their political objectives are especially polarizing. At the mass level, or the demand side, polarization may reflect strong differences of opinion or deep political divides between different social groups within a given society, such as those based on class, race, gender, religious identities, geographic region, or ethnicity (see Mason 2018). It can also be fostered by patterns of social mobilization and protest around highly salient and contentious issues—what has come to be known as "contentious politics." McAdam et al. (2001, 322), for example, see polarization as a recurring, interactive process in episodes of social mobilization and political contention that involve a "widening of political and social space between claimants" and "the gravitation of previously uncommitted or moderate actors toward one, the other, or both extremes." Where mass protests mobilize new actors into the political arena around grievances or claims that lie outside the established agenda, some measure of polarization is underway (Tarrow 2022, 10).

In recent times, polarization has seemingly become a convenient shorthand for much of what ails democracy in Latin America and beyond.

Excessive, or what McCoy et al. (2018) call "pernicious" polarization, can generate severe conflicts that paralyze democratic institutions or, worse, threaten their very survival when political antagonists cease to process their differences by mutually recognized democratic means (see Haggard and Kaufman 2021; Schedler 2023). As Svolik (2019) demonstrates, polarization can make citizens more tolerant of democratic transgressions by the political parties or leaders they support. The greater the antipathy for a rival political camp, the more inclined citizens may be to restrict those citizens' democratic participation—or exclude them altogether.

As this book demonstrates, however, caution should be exercised in assessing the implications of polarization for democratic governance. It cannot be assumed that polarization is intrinsically and inevitably threatening or degrading to democracy. A certain measure of polarization, or conflict, is arguably *healthy* for democratic politics, as it can encourage party building (Levitsky et al. 2016) and more programmatic (as opposed to clientelistic or personalistic) forms of partisan competition (Kitschelt 2000). Polarization can enhance democratic accountability by forcing parties to stake out meaningfully different positions on salient issues, respond to the interests of different types of voters, and develop name-brand loyalties among citizens who care deeply about major policy issues. Scholarship on both Europe (Mair 2013; Berman and Kundnani 2021) and Latin America (Roberts 2014; Lupu 2016) has thus warned about the unsettling political effects of democratic competition that has been drained of its substantive content—and, therefore, of meaningful conflict—by the programmatic convergence of mainstream political parties.

Especially in contexts of egregious social and economic inequalities, some measure of polarization is virtually inevitable when underprivileged groups pressure democratic regimes to adopt public policies aimed at redistributing income, power, or resources. That is surely the case in Latin America, where contemporary class inequalities are overlaid onto racial and ethnic hierarchies implanted during the colonial era and where patriarchal traditions cut across class distinctions (Hoffman and Centeno 2003). As Huber and Stephens (2012, 10–11) remind us, redistributive policies, or any measures to level the social playing field, are far from automatic under democracy; they are the fruit of political action grounded in the organizational power of popular constituencies in both civil society and partisan spheres of representation. The social and political mobilization involved in the development of that organizational power covers a wide spectrum of collective action, from strikes, protests, and other forms of contentious politics to party building and electoral participation in more institutionalized arenas of contestation. Whether led by working and lower classes, subordinate ethnic or racial groups, women, or sexual minorities, these mobilizations invariably challenge established social and political hierarchies. They are routinely perceived as threatening by those occupying more privileged rungs on the social hierarchy, or simply those accustomed to the traditional social order.

Conservative political backlashes, or countermovements, are thus a routine, though surely unintended, by-product of progressive movements to reduce social and economic inequalities (see Borges et al. 2024), as the US and European experiences readily attest (McAdam and Kloos 2014; Bustikova 2022). The prevalence of these backlashes suggests that polarization is likely to be an inherent risk assumed by those who dare to challenge existing power relationships, and managing that risk is a paramount concern. It follows that an absence of polarization in a highly unequal society may not be a marker of a healthy democracy; it may reflect, instead, stifling patterns of political domination that normalize the existing social order or block underprivileged groups from organizing to contest it.

Perhaps it is not surprising, then, that a long tradition of scholarship, drawing from a range of different theoretical perspectives, has traced the very origins of modern representative democracy to political conflict, gridlock, and polarization—not a shared civic culture or a normative consensus on the public good. In Dankwart Rustow's (1970) classic formulation—which heavily influenced a generation of scholarship on third-wave transitions (see O'Donnell and Schmitter 1986, 38)—democracy consists of a set of conflict-regulating institutions that are explicitly designed to allow hostile and distrustful political adversaries to coexist within the same political community. It is, in short, an institutional compromise whose genesis is in a "hot family feud" (Rustow 1970, 355) between bitter antagonists who may well prefer a different political order but cannot impose that order on their rivals at acceptable costs of repression or violence. Democracy's essential institutional arrangements—such as iterative cycles of competitive elections, the rule of law, minority political rights, and horizontal checks and balances—help secure this compromise by lowering the stakes of political contestation, lengthening actors' time horizons, and regulating political conflicts that might otherwise spiral out of control and culminate in political violence (see Przeworski 1991). They are, by design, mechanisms of depolarization.

Political conflict—in particular, class and distributive conflicts—also play a central role in the gestation of democracy in both microanalytic rational choice accounts (Boix 2003; Acemoglu and Robinson 2009) and more sociological macrostructural explanations (Rueschemeyer et al. 1992). In these approaches, distributive conflicts are a product of social and political mobilization from below, by workers or other "popular" constituencies, who challenge elite control over material resources and political power. Given the potential for polarizing distributive conflicts to culminate in either social revolution or elite-based authoritarian backlashes—both of which entail high risks and high costs—democracy can emerge as a type of institutional compromise to credibly share power and resources while limiting the scope of change. Building on these insights, Haggard and Kaufman's (2016) careful empirical research demonstrates that class-based distributive conflicts are common, but they are hardly a necessary condition for transitions to democracy in the modern world. Even where distributive conflicts are negligible, however, the origins of democracy can often be traced back to intraelite conflicts that were addressed through the introduction of democratic institutions, much like the class conflicts analyzed in the earlier works (see also Madrid, 2025).

Taken together, this scholarship suggests that conflict and polarization are not always or necessarily inimical to democracy. To the contrary, polarization is often the very source and motivation for democracy and a principal justification for its core institutional innovations. High levels of ideological and/or affective polarization are compatible with democratic governance so long as rival actors are willing to subject their dueling interests and preferences to the bounded uncertainties of democratic contestation and find reassurance in democracy's conflict-regulating properties. Crucially, this requires that democratic antagonists practice what Schmitter and Karl (1991, 82–83) labeled "contingent consent"—in essence, a willingness to accept the verdicts of democratic competition and adhere to its established rules so long as rival actors do the same, recognizing the ongoing or iterative nature of democratic contestation on a level, institutionally bounded playing field.[2] Polarization becomes a threat to democracy only when it serves as a pretext for one side or the other to break with this contingent consent by violating basic democratic norms and procedures in pursuit of unilateral partisan advantages.

The challenge, of course, is that contingent consent to an institutional compromise is difficult to construct and sustain among antagonists who share a mutual distrust. Rustow's (1970, 358–360) confidence that political learning and habituation will generate democratic norms endogenously to help secure an institutional compromise rings hollow in an era of rampant democratic backsliding undertaken by elected officials (Bermeo 2016;

Haggard and Kaufman 2021). An institutional compromise may be especially elusive when political power is imbalanced rather than gridlocked—as we will see in the analysis herein of the populist-left cases in Venezuela, Bolivia, and Ecuador—or when the social landscape is highly unequal, as it is throughout Latin America (although it is less egregiously so in Uruguay). Extreme, historically entrenched social and economic inequalities make it harder to reach the kinds of mutually acceptable social truces between competing interests that can reinforce adherence to a democratic institutional compromise (Sandbrook et al. 2007). Such truces were integral historically to the social democratic class compromises that induced socialists in northern and western Europe to break with Leninist revolutionary currents, become integrated into democratic capitalist orders, and play a central role in the development of redistributive welfare states in the middle of the twentieth century (Castles 1978; Przeworski and Sprague 1988; Berman 2006). They are much harder to construct in contemporary Latin America, given the tighter global market constraints on the region's open, commodity export–based economies, with high levels of capital mobility, lower levels of industrialization, segmented and informalized labor markets, less densely unionized work forces, much weaker party organizations, and deeper racial and ethnic underpinnings of the class structure and social hierarchy.

Latin America's more severe economic inequalities can magnify—and sometimes radicalize—bottom-up political pressures for redistributive reforms and increase the likelihood of elite backlashes against higher taxation or potential threats to property rights (Boix 2003; Acemoglu and Robinson 2009). Likewise, social mobilization for equal rights by women and indigenous communities in Latin America poses basic challenges to culturally ingrained status hierarchies that are often fiercely defended by those accustomed to positions of power or privilege. Profound inequalities help explain why Latin America has a long tradition of radical social and economic reforms implemented by left-leaning authoritarian regimes able to concentrate powers and cut through the institutional constraints of democratic checks and balances (Albertus 2015), as well as a tradition of right-wing authoritarian regimes that repress popular social and political movements advocating for redistributive reforms (O'Donnell 1973; Remmer 1989).

For leftist parties committed to reducing economic and status inequalities in Latin America, therefore, liberal democracy offers both opportunities and constraints—and a relatively narrow but ill-defined band of maneuvering space to navigate between them within the institutional boundaries of a democratic order. As our case studies demonstrate, efforts by the populist left in Venezuela, Bolivia, and Ecuador to redefine and relax those institutional boundaries were intrinsically polarizing, and they contributed to the tragic demise of democracy in Venezuela and to its unsettling in Bolivia and Ecuador. Although a venerable scholarly tradition suggests that more moderate and accommodating strategies are likely to achieve greater success and sustainability (see Weyland et al. 2010; Huber and Stephens 2012), our analysis of Brazil and Chile reveals some of the limitations of the social democratic approach, and we ultimately conclude that the approach warrants a more sanguine assessment. Chile's social democratic left bent over backward to avoid polarization by accommodating elite interests and strictly adhering to democratic rules of the game, but this cautious approach set the stage for massive social protests demanding more extensive reforms and, ultimately, a far-right backlash aimed at defending the institutional and economic legacies of the Pinochet military dictatorship. Brazil's social democratic left also adopted an accommodative strategy to minimize opposition and maintain economic stability. It largely (though not completely) avoided mass protests from the left, but it still encountered a virulent far-right backlash with marked authoritarian tendencies.

Uruguay's social democratic left came closest to navigating the shoals in a durable and less polarizing manner, in part, as we show, because it combined a legislative majority with strong grassroots participatory channels that helped keep the party leadership accountable to its social bases even while moderating its programmatic stands. But Uruguay's redistributive pressures were also less acute, given the country's relatively strong welfare state tradition, less extreme social and economic inequalities, and greater public role in the provision of social services. As such, our approach recognizes the significance of underlying structural conditions and constraints, even if it highlights the relative autonomy of the political sphere (see Collier and Collier 1991) and the importance of political agency.

Although deepening polarization became the norm outside of Uruguay, our analysis demonstrates that the timing and sequencing of polarization differed across the populist-left and social democratic cases. Polarizing dynamics were present at the outset of the left turn in the populist cases, as a logic of polarization was deeply embedded in the broader systemic crises that spawned a new left and ushered it into power (see Handlin 2017). By contrast, the social democratic lefts took office through routine democratic alternations and sought to contain polarizing dynamics, but in Brazil and Chile, polarization intensified near the end or the aftermath of the left turn itself. As we explain in chapter 1, these polarizing dynamics were conditioned by political vulnerabilities specific to the two different types of left and the contexts in which they ascended to power—what we call the "autocratic temptation" for the populist left and the "conformist temptation" for the social democratic left.

To be sure, deepening polarization and the eventual demise of the left turn were also related to policy and performance failures on the part of leftist governments. The generalized failure of the left to devise effective and progressive responses to the problem of rising crime and citizen insecurity bred widespread discontent that conservative and far-right political actors could channel through appeals to law and order and harsher policing methods. Similarly, corruption scandals and the failure to craft economic growth models less dependent on volatile commodity export markets opened the door to political backlashes. These backlashes took a severe toll following the demise of the global commodity boom that had heightened citizens' expectations during the heyday of the left turn (Campello and Zucco 2020). In the Chilean case, a reluctance to break with neoliberal market orthodoxy by strengthening social citizenship rights created vulnerabilities to an outflanking on the left by student-led social protests and a new left partisan alternative with movement origins.

It is important to recognize, however, that deepening polarization was not simply a reaction to the failures of the left or to those of democratic regimes more broadly. The conservative and far-right backlash that has been integral to polarization dynamics in the region is also a response to some of the achievements of the left turn, and of the region's democratic regimes, in promoting new forms of social equity and inclusion (Kapiszewski et al. 2021). Although many of these achievements have been modest, women's and indigenous movements have worked within democratic regimes to claim new rights and advance equity-enhancing reforms. The patterns of social mobilization that made these limited gains possible inevitably politicized new dimensions of conflict, thus activating right-wing civic and political networks through churches, parties, and conservative civil society groups (Mayka and Smith 2021; Borges et al. 2024).

Given these dynamics, some degree of polarization may be a natural sequel to the late twentieth-century institutionalization of democratic contestation on Latin America's highly unequal social landscape—and to the inevitable, and surely essential, efforts to make democratic regimes responsive not just to traditional elites but also to the full range of societal interests. The challenge, then, is to find more effective and constructive ways to contain and manage this polarization within democracy's conflict-regulating institutions. The chapters that follow chronicle the diverse efforts of leftist parties and governments to navigate this institutional terrain while advancing objectives for more or less radical equity-enhancing reforms.

Overview of the Book

To develop our theoretical claims about the importance of formative processes and institutional contexts for shaping the profiles of different leftist currents, we use a process-tracing approach—an approach that is particularly well suited for linking causes to outcomes (George and Bennett 2005; Beach and Pedersen 2013)—and paired cross-national comparisons. In selecting cases, we have chosen paradigmatic examples of each type of left—Brazil and Chile for the social democratic left and Bolivia and Venezuela for the populist left. Comparisons across these sets of cases allow us to examine different types of left turns and the roots of polarized conflict both during and after the left turn itself. We highlight meaningful parallels and contrasts between cases through a "paired comparison" approach with theory-building purposes (Tarrow 2010). While paired comparisons are valuable for deriving analytical leverage and teasing out differences across pairs of cases over long periods of time, case narratives are helpful to understand how specific processes unfolded and to identify variation within each pair of cases. To gain further analytical leverage and increase the number of observations, and thus strengthen the evidentiary base for causal inference, we also develop broader cross-national comparisons. These include the cases of Argentina, Ecuador, and Uruguay.

Differences across and within the two types of left mattered not only for how they governed but also for the way the left turn ended, with polarization as a central consequence of the overarching process. A comparative analysis helps to identify the mechanisms that led, across two quite different sets of cases, to broadly similar outcomes—the demise, at least temporarily, of leftist projects to deepen democracy, and the onset of acute political polarization, albeit with different effects. This is, then, a study of different cases that follow distinct paths toward similar though not identical outcomes. To explain why and how the general pattern of deepening polarization has emerged and played out differently across the region, and to identify the different mechanisms that triggered polarization, "contextualized comparisons" (Mahoney and Rueschemeyer 2003) using a comparative historical approach are fundamental. This approach allows us to trace the origins and causes of political outcomes that are harder to observe in a single case while still preserving illustrative case detail. To track ideological polarization and emerging lines of political conflict at the elite and mass levels, on both economic and cultural axes of contestation, this comparative analysis draws on secondary sources, a combination of quantitative indicators, and public opinion data to study the complex interplay of elite and mass-level political dynamics.

Our analysis begins in chapter 1 by placing the left turn in a broader historical perspective and examining the formative experiences and institutional contexts that shaped Latin America's populist and social democratic lefts. These formative experiences and institutional contexts created markedly different conceptions of democracy within the two lefts, and they heavily conditioned their respective strategies for pursuing ambitious social and economic reforms within democratic institutions. They also gave rise to distinct political vulnerabilities—the autocratic temptation for the populist left and the conformist temptation for the social democratic left—that weighed heavily on their respective dynamics of political polarization. The dynamics of polarization along both economic and cultural axes of political contestation are then explained, along with their elite and mass-level manifestations.

Chapters 2 and 3 provide a comparative analysis of Latin America's populist and social democratic left turns and how they came to an end. Taken together, they identify the political conditions that constrained the left's ability to "deepen" democracy, as well as those that ushered in its political demise, setting the stage for polarized politics even where the left turn itself was not highly polarizing. While chapter 2 focuses on two paradigmatic cases of the social democratic left (Brazil and Chile), chapter 3 focuses on two paradigmatic cases of the populist left (Bolivia and Venezuela). Each case narrative covers a long historical arc, tracing the formative experiences that shaped the character of the main leftist party, the pathways they took to national political power, the institutional contexts in which they governed, and the dynamics of polarization unleashed by their trajectories in office.

In developing these historically grounded case narratives, we incorporate existing explanations that highlight the importance of underlying structural factors and changing economic conditions for shaping the prospects of the left in power (Campello and Zucco 2020). Our analysis, however, highlights how and why the populist and social democratic lefts navigated that volatility and structural constraints differently, given their very different conceptions of democratic governance. In short, our "political" approach takes into account the economic and structural underpinnings of political actors' strategic choices and behavior while also recognizing how the actors themselves have been shaped by their historical experiences and institutional environments. The development strategies and social and economic reforms adopted by different leftist governments in Latin America are surely deserving of scholarly attention (Flores-Macías 2012; Ellner 2021), but our focus here is on the political challenges, constraints, and contradictions encountered by leftist governments that pursue radical reforms of unequal societies in democratic settings.

Following the same analytical approach, chapter 4 develops a broader comparison with other regional cases—Argentina, Ecuador, and Uruguay—that also experienced political shifts to the left. Whereas Argentina's left turn fits uncomfortably within the existing binary subtypes of leftist governments and is often placed somewhere in the middle, Ecuador and Uruguay are additional examples of the populist and social democratic lefts, respectively. The comparative historical analysis of this larger set of cases enhances the overall evidentiary base of this book, and it provides further theoretical leverage to assess the generalizability of the patterns we identify and potential variation within them. The inclusion of the Uruguayan case, for example, provides insight into the types of party characteristics and party-movement ties that may allow the social democratic left to avoid some of the pitfalls experienced in Brazil and Chile.

Chapter 5 provides a comparative and quantitative analysis of polarization dynamics across multiple dimensions in our seven cases. We use Varieties of Democracy (V-Dem) expert survey data to track changes in social and political polarization over time across the region.[3] We then marshal evidence from public opinion surveys by the Latin American Public Opinion Project (LAPOP) to assess the left-right ideological structuring of mass publics over time in the region. Although measures of aggregate public opinion indicate only a modest increase in ideological polarization during the left turn and its aftermath, statistical techniques demonstrate that citizens located near the left and right ideological poles are more actively engaged in political affairs—a finding that helps explain why democratic contestation may assume more polarizing dynamics than aggregate public opinion alone might suggest. We then examine polarization dynamics in partisan and electoral arenas in our seven cases to explain how systemic polarization is influenced by changes in the relative strength of left, right, and center parties.

Finally, the conclusion summarizes the findings of this book and lays out tentative conclusions about the scenarios going forward. Given that polarization appears to be highly prevalent in other regions beyond Latin America, this chapter explores the general conditions under which polarization might be linked to democratic erosion or backsliding, as well as the obverse: the conditions under which polarization might bring about democratic advances. This study makes clear that political polarization is a virtually inevitable—and perhaps a necessary—by-product of efforts by underprivileged groups to enhance their social status and life opportunities in societies marked by profound and deeply entrenched inequalities, as well as the efforts of privileged actors to defend existing social hierarchies. Our central concern is explaining how this polarization emerges and how the dynamic interaction among contending actors realigns democratic contestation and reshapes democratic institutions.

This book is also motivated by the conviction that, by uncovering underlying factors behind the strategic decisions and behaviors of different lefts that contributed to their political defeats, we may be able to draw valuable lessons regarding the political conditions that have led to the relative successes and shortcomings of leftist governments in Latin America over the past two decades. We hope this book can contribute to vigorous discussion of the pitfalls that lie ahead for the democratic left—whether in power or in opposition—and the opportunities for lasting reform in rapidly changing societies marked by profound inequalities and the durable legacies of historical patterns of political exclusion.

CHAPTER ONE

The Left Turn, Democracy, and Dynamics of Polarization

Latin America's left turn in the early twenty-first century was unprecedented in its scope and duration. This chapter places that left turn and its polarizing dynamics in a broader historical perspective. It compares the formative experiences of the populist and social democratic lefts that played leading roles in the left turn, as well as the radically different institutional contexts in which they rose to power. These formative experiences and institutional contexts weighed heavily on the different conceptions of democracy—or democratic imaginaries—that guided the left in power, and they were associated with very different political vulnerabilities and patterns of polarization over time. This polarization had important historical precedents in the region, but it marked a sharp departure from the era of political and economic convergence associated with the "dual transitions" to democracy and neoliberal orthodoxy in the 1980s and 1990s. The new polarization in Latin America occurred along both economic and cultural axes of political contestation, and it possessed both elite and mass-level political dynamics. This chapter thus provides conceptual and theoretical building blocks for the comparative historical analysis of different left turns in the chapters that follow.

The Left Turn in Historical Perspective

Latin America's social and political landscapes were thoroughly transformed by the democratic transitions and the neoliberal economic restructuring of the 1980s and 1990s. At the time, there was little reason to suspect that a major political shift to the left would follow in the wake of these dual transitions as the twenty-first century got underway. Historically, elected governments of the left were few and far between in a region where many countries lacked a major party of the left, and election contests were generally dominated by elite-based conservative parties or ideologically ill-defined populist parties. With the notable exception of Chile's democratic socialist experiment under Salvador Allende in the early 1970s, the most radical redistributive reforms in the region were implemented by nonelected governments (Albertus 2015), such as the revolutionary socialist regimes in Cuba and Nicaragua and the leftist military regime of Juan Velasco Alvarado in Peru (1968–1975). Although moderate center-left parties like Democratic Action (AD) in Venezuela and the National Liberation Party (PLN) in Costa Rica were able to complete multiple terms in office, democratic leftist governments across much of the region were short-lived, as conservative forces routinely resorted to military coups to restore forms of political domination and social control that democracy threatened to undermine. Military interventions against Jacobo Árbenz in Guatemala (1954), João Goulart in Brazil (1964), and Allende in Chile (1973) testified to the fragility of democratic leftist rule in the region.

The early twenty-first-century left turn, therefore, was unprecedented in the number of countries it involved and the duration of leftist rule. Beginning with Venezuela in 1998, the left turn produced thirty presidential election victories in eleven different countries between 1998 and 2015, including an impressive number of reelections in nine of those countries (table 1.1).

Given its historical significance, this political shift to the left generated a copious literature examining its origins and causes, the different types of leftist parties, movements, and leaders included within it, and the social, political, and economic changes it produced (Cameron and Hershberg 2010; Weyland et al. 2010; Levitsky and Roberts 2011; Flores-Macías 2012; Queirolo 2013; Anria 2018; Balán and Montambeault 2020). Although the left turn had elements of a routine democratic alternation in office driven by retrospective anti-incumbent economic voting (Murillo et al. 2010; Arnold and Samuels 2011; Murillo and Visconti 2017), a historical perspective suggests that more deeply rooted political realignments were also underway. The left turn began during a period of region-wide economic hardship associated with the international financial turmoil of the late 1990s, but most countries joined the political trend during the period of relative

TABLE 1.1 **Presidential elections and reelections of left and center-left candidates in Latin America, 1998–2015, in chronological order**

Country	Initial presidential election	Presidential and ruling party reelections
Venezuela	Hugo Chávez (1998)	Hugo Chávez (2000, 2006, 2012); Nicolás Maduro (2013)
Chile	Ricardo Lagos (2000)	Michelle Bachelet (2006, 2013 non-successive)
Brazil	Lula da Silva (2002)	Lula da Silva (2006); Dilma Rousseff (2010, 2014)
Argentina	Néstor Kirchner (2003)	Cristina Fernández de Kirchner (2007, 2011)
Uruguay	Tabaré Vázquez (2004)	José Mujica (2009); Tabaré Vázquez (2014)
Bolivia	Evo Morales (2005)	Evo Morales (2009, 2014)
Ecuador	Rafael Correa (2006)	Rafael Correa (2009, 2013)
Nicaragua	Daniel Ortega (2006)	Daniel Ortega (2011)
Paraguay	Fernando Lugo (2008)	—
El Salvador	Mauricio Funes (2009)	Salvador Sánchez Cerén (2014)
Costa Rica	Luis Guillermo Solís (2014)	—

economic prosperity spawned by rising commodity prices after 2003. Retrospective economic voting, therefore, cannot readily account for the full range of cases; nor can it explain why, in countries with multiparty systems that included multiple centrist and right-of-center alternatives, retrospective anti-incumbent voting resulted in such a large number of victories for the left (in contrast, for example, to the anti-incumbent voting patterns of the 1980s). Likewise, the post-2003 "commodity boom" cannot explain the origins of the left turn, although it undoubtedly helped to extend it by allowing leftist parties to reap political rewards—that is, reelection—from positive economic performance, including steady growth, declining poverty levels, and reduced inequalities (López-Calva and Lustig 2010; Huber and Stephens 2012; Cornia 2014). Not surprisingly, the demise of the left turn coincided with the end of the commodity boom in 2014–2015 and the onset of a new period of economic stagnation.

More fundamentally, however—beyond these short-term contextual factors—the left turn posed a basic challenge to the neoliberal Washington Consensus of the late twentieth century. It reflected the politicization of extreme inequalities in contexts of increasingly institutionalized democratic competition and the restructuring of that competition along a left-right axis across the region following the crisis-induced process of market liberalization (Roberts 2014). This restructuring occurred in a number of countries where the left-right axis historically played a minimal role in dividing the electorate, and in countries with fragmented multiparty systems where anti-incumbent voting and alternation in office did not require, and were not in the past synonymous with, a political shift to the left. Indeed, in eight of the eleven countries, the party or movement leading the left turn elected a president for the first time—an indicator of the novelty of the process. The basic realignment of partisan and electoral competition along a left-right axis also emerged in several countries that did not join the initial left turn before 2015 but subsequently elected a leftist president in its aftermath, including Mexico (2018), Peru (2021), Honduras (2021), and Colombia (2022). This is also evident in Chile, where a new, more movement-based leftist alternative captured the presidency in 2021 after overtaking the mainstream Socialist Party, which had elected presidents three times during the left turn. Some might add Guatemala's Bernardo Arévalo (2024) to the list; doing so would signify that sixteen of the eighteen Latin American countries with competitive regimes—all but Panama and the Dominican Republic—have elected a leftist or center-left president since the turn of the century.

Nevertheless, as a dominant regional trend, Latin America's initial left turn experienced a turbulent demise starting in 2015 with the election of conservative leader Mauricio Macri in Argentina, setting the stage for new and more intense forms of political polarization in much of the region. The political science field has yet to produce a comparative, systematic account of this demise and its aftereffects—a primary motivation for this study. Reversals of the left turn came in a variety of forms and with no clear-cut common underlying cause: The left was removed by routine electoral alternations of power in Argentina (2015), Chile (2017), Uruguay (2019), and El Salvador (2019); through presidential impeachments by hostile legislatures in Paraguay (2012, an early case) and Brazil (2016); through an internal schism in Ecuador (2017); and by a thinly veiled military coup following a contested electoral outcome and right-wing protests in Bolivia (2019).[1] Costa Rica's center-left government shifted in a conservative direction in its second term after 2018, whereas leftist presidents in Venezuela and Nicaragua held onto power through increasingly authoritarian measures.

As a project of "deepening" democracy, therefore—which we discuss later in this chapter—the left turn seemingly reached a dead end during the second decade of the twenty-first century. In so doing, it allowed conservative forces—sometimes with questionable democratic vocations—to reclaim their customary hold on the reins of state power across most of Latin America (Borges et al. 2024). The conservative backlash produced a series of right-wing electoral victories, but their often fleeting character—conservative leaders governed for a single term or less before turning power back over to the left in Argentina, Bolivia, Chile, Brazil, and Uruguay—suggests that the region had returned to fairly routine anti-incumbent voting patterns rather than a generalizable region-wide shift toward the left or the right (Luna and Rovira Kaltwasser 2021; Lupu et al. 2021).

In comparison to the past, however, this renewed pattern of anti-incumbent voting and alternation in office plays out on a political field restructured along a left-right competitive axis in the wake of free-market reforms in highly unequal societies. This restructuring transformed historical patterns of political representation, strengthening parties or movements of the left in much of the region, but it took distinct forms and spread at different speeds across different national contexts. It also occurred in countries where established parties of the left, center, and right were often gravely weakened, and new alternatives remained far from institutionalized in contexts of deepening political polarization and widespread social mobilization.

Recent electoral victories by the left magnify the importance of examining the shortcomings of the initial 1998–2015 left turn to see what lessons can be learned from its limitations and failures. As we explain, both populist and social democratic lefts pledged to "deepen democracy" by making it more inclusive, participatory, and responsive to citizens' needs. Although tangible achievements were often made, each type of left was ultimately susceptible to a particular set of vulnerabilities and shortcomings, leaving the region prone to ongoing cycles of political conflict and polarization. These cycles generate the central questions that motivate this book: How did the populist and social democratic lefts understand democracy, and how did these understandings shape their major vulnerabilities in power? To what extent did these limitations constrain, distort, or block their efforts to deepen democracy, and how did they influence—or accelerate—the end of the left turn? Finally, what legacies did their trajectories in power generate for post–left turn political orders, particularly their dynamics of polarization and the quality and stability of democratic governance in Latin America?

This book addresses these questions by examining different types of left turns and their often polarizing legacies. It shows that the course of the left turn in different national settings was neither preordained nor inevitable, even if it was heavily conditioned by political factors traceable to the formative experiences of the dominant leftist party and its antecedent movements in each country, as well as the institutional contexts in which they eventually rose to power. These formative political and institutional contexts are not readily captured in the binary subtypes that scholars used to categorize different Latin American lefts during the heyday of the left turn, such as right versus wrong (Castañeda 2006), populist versus social democratic (Lanzaro 2014), or moderate versus radical (Ellner 2014) or contestatory (Weyland et al. 2010). As we explain, we follow Lanzaro's (2014) lead in making a primary distinction between populist and social democratic trajectories within the left turn, but we are wary of essentializing the parties or movements that shaped these trajectories. "The left" in each country was politically heterogeneous, often with competing populist, social democratic, radical democratic, and revolutionary currents, and the balance of power between the currents was heavily conditioned by the political opportunities and constraints they encountered in critical institutional settings.

Ultimately, the distinctions between populist and social democratic lefts influenced the timing of acute political polarization more than its presence, as polarization occurred earlier in the populist cases and later in most of the social democratic cases, despite explicit efforts in the latter to avoid polarizing left turns. Since important previous research (Handlin 2017) has highlighted the intrinsic polarizing logic of the populist cases, the eventual rise of polarizing dynamics in social democratic cases like Brazil and Chile is a major theoretical and empirical puzzle that our analysis seeks to explain. Polarization in the social democratic cases is more surprising, and it was hardly an expected outcome at the beginning of the left turn. Within the social democratic camp, moreover, differences across cases—in comparing Uruguay to Brazil and Chile—are especially puzzling. Our analysis also shows that both populist and social democratic lefts were prone to "bad endings" characterized by political defeats and institutional decay or upheaval. The most successful case—Uruguay—appears in many respects to be a political outlier, albeit a highly instructive one for identifying constructive responses to the most common problems and challenges of the left in power.

But if the conventional subtypes offer limited explanatory leverage for differentiating outcomes, they do help identify the distinct political defects to which Latin America's "two lefts" were prone. As discussed in the pages that follow, these defects—what we call an "autocratic temptation" for the populist left and a "conformist temptation" for the social democratic left—derailed projects to deepen democracy and ultimately set the stage for similar outcomes of political defeat, upheaval, and polarized conflict.

We would not go so far as to claim that our comparative analysis illuminates a process of equifinality, whereby multiple pathways to the same outcome exist. Clearly, Venezuela's descent into single-party authoritarian rule and acute economic crisis had no parallel within the social democratic set of cases, or even within the broader populist-left camp. Nevertheless, our analysis does help to identify different paths toward political decay and polarization, with identifiable roots in the signature defects of the alternative lefts. These defects reflected the tensions between two very different conceptualizations of democracy that became crystallized within the region's "two lefts," each with a characteristic set of blind spots and political hazards. For the populist left—a "new left" spawned by the social and political backlash against democratic establishments that converged around neoliberal orthodoxy in the late twentieth century—an understanding of democracy as popular sovereignty produced a range of autocratic proclivities, including highly concentrated and personalistic authority that clashed with democracy's pluralist ethos. By contrast, the more established social democratic left parties, following traumatic experiences with military repression, helped to construct new democratic regimes in the 1980s and 1990s around a vision of safeguarding human rights, expanding social citizenship, and resolving political conflicts through an institutionalization of pluralist competition. Rather than crafting new and more radically democratic ways of "doing politics," however, these latter parties gradually internalized and conformed to the political logics of the flawed democracies they had pledged to transform. In so doing, they were remolded in the image of these flawed democracies and reproduced their basic logics: a technocratic logic in Chile's neoliberal showcase and a transactional, rent-seeking logic in Brazil's fragmented and patronage-based political order. In the end, these autocratic and conformist temptations were self-limiting for the left in power, producing alternate pathways to political defeat or upheaval and polarizing effects during the waning stages and the aftermath of the left turn. It is to this theoretical discussion that we now turn.

A Tale of Two Lefts: The Roots and Consequences of Alternative Democratic Imaginaries

Latin America's "two lefts," however defined and categorized, were never all-inclusive. Several leftist parties and governments were awkward fits in the binary subtypes given the prevalence of hybrid or idiosyncratic traits, particularly in Argentina, Paraguay, El Salvador, and Nicaragua. Even among the paradigmatic cases that largely defined the two dominant patterns—Venezuela, Bolivia, and Ecuador for the populist left, and Brazil, Chile, and Uruguay for the social democratic left—significant variation existed. Nevertheless, as explained in Levitsky and Roberts (2011a, 16–19), the parallels within these respective groupings were pronounced, reflecting similar formative experiences with authoritarianism, democratization, and market liberalization that indelibly marked—and sharply differentiated—the trajectories in power of the social democratic and populist lefts.

These formative experiences gave rise to alternative conceptions of democracy—or democratic imaginaries, so to speak—within Latin America's two lefts, with tensions and contradictions between them that crystallized over time. With deep historical roots in classical and modern democratic theory, these imaginaries embodied radically different beliefs about what democracy is, or should be, and divergent—though not necessarily irreconcilable—democratic vocations. Stripped to their essential core, one of these rival imaginaries—that of the populist left—conceived of democracy in terms of popular sovereignty; it understood democracy to entail substantive, mass-based political empowerment and increased equality in social and economic outcomes. The other imaginary, characteristic of the social democratic left, understood democracy to be a form of institutionalized pluralism, an order designed to process and regulate conflicts of interest between rival social and political actors, including claims for socioeconomic reform.

Democracy conceived as an expression of popular sovereignty—or power to "the people"—has deep roots in democratic theory, arguably tracing back to classical Greek philosophy. In its purest forms, this popular sovereignty is understood to be plebeian in character, majoritarian in scope, relatively unconstrained by institutional checks, and unmediated in its exercise of power. Democracy, therefore, becomes an exercise in popular self-determination and self-rule—a plebiscitary form of majoritarianism that directly empowers (*kratos*) the common people (*demos*) (Espejo 2011; C. de la Torre 2015; Vergara 2020). Exercising popular sovereignty in a Greek city-state, however—typically by means of a popular assembly—is very different from doing so in a complex modern nation-state with expansive territory and a diverse array of societal interests and preferences. This scale shift and increasing social heterogeneity were integral to Laclau's (2005) influential conception of populism. For Laclau, populism is a way of structuring and aligning the political field by constituting "the people" as a political subject; it condenses social complexity along a binary divide, or an "antagonistic frontier," between a power elite and a heterogeneous "people" who aspire to be sovereign. Following this logic, Latin America's populist left conceives of democracy as a redemptive invocation of popular sovereignty—that is, an invocation of the constituent power of an expansive political community arrayed in opposition to a power elite that has chronically neglected or betrayed "the people." The assertion of such constitutive power is often associated with a refounding of the political order and its institutional coordinates.[2]

Alternatively, democracy as a form of institutionalized pluralism has more recent philosophical roots in the liberal tradition of Montesquieu and Madison, one that is wary of the unrestrained or unmediated empowerment of popular majorities (see Madison 1787). The liberal tradition emphasizes the separation of powers across different branches of government and institutional checks and balances against unwarranted concentrations of power. Democracy, therefore, disperses power across separate and mutually restraining institutions that are ultimately accountable to distinct constituencies. Above all, it provides a set of rules and procedures to process and mediate conflicts of interest among a plurality of actors by institutionalizing the competition among them. It also enshrines a wide range of civil rights and liberties to protect political minorities, ensure that their interests and preferences can be aired in the public sphere, and induce opposition groups—the "losers" of the previous cycle of democratic contestation—to stay in the game and compete for public office in future iterations of the democratic process (see Rustow 1970; Przeworski 1991). The reliance on a concept of the public sphere, moreover, suggests that, even in robustly diverse democracies, individual citizens have a duty to one another to deliberate "over issues of public concern and common interest" and, in doing so, place an active check against any antidemocratic power possessed by the state (Habermas 1991). Therefore, in a democracy conceived as institutionalized pluralism, political majorities—the winners in an electoral contest—are presumed to be transitory, fluid, and contingent. They are institutionally restrained in their pursuit of policy preferences and, crucially, in their constitutive authority to redesign the very rules and procedures of democratic contestation itself (Schmitter and Karl 1991). The losers, in turn, expect to have a reasonable opportunity to dispute power, win future elections, and remove incumbents peacefully by electoral means.

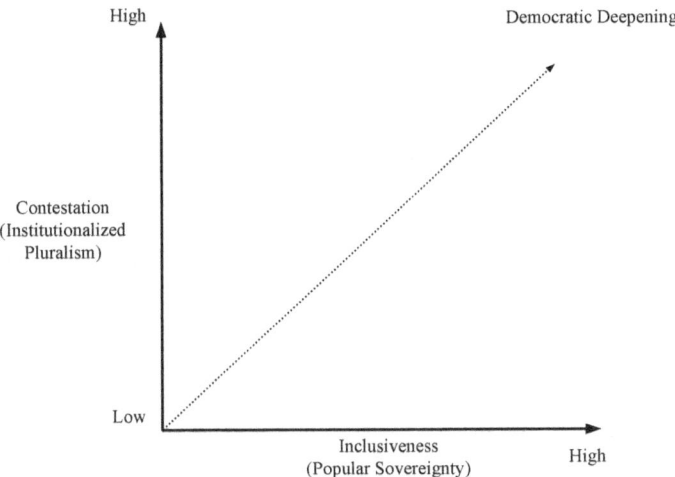

FIGURE 1.1. Mapping the left's democratic imaginaries onto Dahl's two dimensions of polyarchy.

These alternative democratic imaginaries correspond, in general terms, to Dahl's (1971, 6–7) classic two-dimensional conceptualization of polyarchy (a term Dahl preferred over democracy), with institutionalized pluralism mapping onto his vertical axis of public contestation, and popular sovereignty arrayed along his horizontal axis of participation or inclusiveness.[3] As Dahl (1971, 4) recognized, these two dimensions "vary somewhat independently." The extent to which they vary independently or even come into conflict with each other — or, alternatively, interact synergistically to mutually reinforce each other — lies at the heart of the left's democratic dilemma in Latin America. One can surely imagine a highly inclusive, radical democratic order that empowers popular majorities and reduces inequalities in participation and policy responsiveness while still respecting opposition rights and institutional checks and balances (Mouffe 2018). Indeed, that synergy is integral to the concept of "deepening" democracy, whereby civil rights and liberties enable forms of grassroots mobilization that empower popular majorities in a wide range of democratic institutional settings — and that empowerment in turn supports greater participation, institutional accountability, and the effective realization of civil rights and liberties. Such conceptualizations seek to reconcile the two axes in figure 1.1, adapted from Dahl, and they are commonly found within both populist and social democratic lefts in Latin America (Roberts 1998;

Van Cott 2008; Cameron and Sharpe 2012). Variants of them are also found in work on the historical extension of citizenship rights from civic to political and social spheres (Marshall 1950), as well as work on formal democratic rights as a foundation for the participation and collective empowerment of working and lower classes in pursuit of redistributive reforms and other social citizenship claims (Huber et al. 1997).

However, in practice, "deepening democracy" has proved an elusive goal.[4] Rather than synergistic reinforcement, tensions and trade-offs between the two core dimensions of democracy are routinely encountered in historical and contemporary cases. Institutionalized competition often serves to fragment popular constituencies or subordinate them to elite actors with ample political and economic resources at their disposal. When popular majorities *are* politically constituted, their empowerment may assume unbridled or even autocratic forms that clash with minority political rights and/or institutional checks and balances. In other words, just as these two dimensions can theoretically be part of a virtuous cycle that makes possible projects of democratic deepening, they can also work at cross-purposes to each other. Progress on one dimension may come at the expense of progress on the other and produce highly destabilizing side effects (Anria 2016; Rhodes-Purdy and Rosenblatt 2023).

Given these potential trade-offs, a primary line of demarcation between Latin America's two lefts lay in which of the dimensions they ultimately prioritized (see fig. 1.1). The prioritization of one over the other nearly always entailed a political battle within the left, as rival social democratic and populist or radical left political currents existed within each country. As Handlin (2017) suggests, the populist left during the 1990s and early 2000s was more likely to ascend in contexts of state crises and mass discontent with established representative institutions, but we reach back farther in time—to the authoritarian experiences and democratic transitions of the 1970s and 1980s—to trace the conditions that empowered social democratic currents within the left. We also stress the importance of electoral competition and the institutional presence of established centrist and conservative parties in shaping the prospects for different types of left in power.

Our analysis suggests that the alternative democratic imaginaries of populist and social democratic lefts were more than a simple strategic choice or ideological preference. They were also, in part, the product of generational cohort effects that emerged from the exposure of left-wing activists and movements to very different types of political experiences, learning processes, and competitive dynamics across the two sets of cases (Hite 2000). Although the parties—or antecedent movements—that constituted the social democratic left in Chile, Brazil, and Uruguay had different origins and birth dates, all were seared by the experience of violent repression under bureaucratic authoritarian military regimes during the 1970s (O'Donnell 1973). All incorporated activist networks and revolutionary currents that were forced to operate clandestinely to survive systematic repression, and many of these cadres came to see liberal democracy and the civil liberties it provided—whatever its limitations in practice—as a popular victory over reactionary foes (Pribble 2013; Van Dyck 2014; Pérez Bentancur et al. 2019).

Wary of strategic overreach, and knowing firsthand the dangers of unmitigated political confrontation, dominant factions in the major leftist parties in these countries came to embrace democracy as institutionalized pluralism for its conflict-mediating properties, and they made it an institutional precondition for the pursuit of other, more substantive programmatic goals (Garretón 1987; Hite 2000). They supported democratic transitions in the 1980s and helped integrate popular constituencies into the new democratic orders, even when they were critical of liberal democracy's shortcomings and ideologically committed to more radical projects of deepening democracy (Roberts 1998). Indeed, new democratic regimes not only offered protection from military repression but also provided ample opportunities for leftist parties to articulate demands in the public sphere, pursue public office, obtain governing experience in legislatures and subnational governments, and consolidate and expand their bases of support. Competing in countries where more conservative political actors had managed the 1980s debt crisis and imposed neoliberal reforms, a democratic left could aspire to national office by channeling dissent from market orthodoxy and articulating claims for greater equity and social inclusion following economic stabilization in the 1990s.

Formative experiences for the populist left in Venezuela, Bolivia, and Ecuador were markedly different and far more conducive to a conceptualization of democracy as popular sovereignty. These Andean countries did not experience bureaucratic authoritarian rule in the 1960s and 1970s, and leftist parties did not live through the trauma of prolonged and systematic military repression. Democratic regimes in the 1980s and 1990s were saddled with severe economic crises, and traditional center-left or labor-based parties assumed responsibility for the implementation of unpopular austerity and neoliberal structural adjustment measures.

As national party systems converged around neoliberal platforms, dissent from market orthodoxy was channeled into mass social protest, and elected presidents were impeached (Venezuela) or forced out of office (Bolivia and Ecuador) following popular uprisings in all three countries (Silva 2009). These systemic crises severely weakened and discredited mainstream political parties (Cyr 2017) while fostering the rise of new and more radical populist-left alternatives that not only challenged traditional parties but also explicitly rejected the democratic orders controlled by establishment elites.

Consequently, the presidential elections that brought populist-left alternatives to power in Venezuela, Ecuador, and Bolivia were not simply routine alternations in office within the parameters of established democratic regimes. They were, more fundamentally, "constituent moments" (Frank 2010) in a series of quasi-insurrectionary episodes that culminated in a rupture and/or refounding of the constitutional order in all three countries. Upholding their campaign pledges, Hugo Chávez, Rafael Correa, and Evo Morales moved immediately to convoke constitutional assemblies, and they employed popular referenda to approve new constitutions and "refound" their national democratic regimes. Chávez and Correa sidestepped discredited legislative and judicial bodies along the way — a far cry from the agenda of institutionalized leftist parties in the social democratic cases that worked exclusively within established regime institutions. In Jason Frank's (2017, 631) terms, the populist left enacted "populism's defining claim" to "transcend the authorized but corrupted institutions of popular representation through a purifying appeal to unmediated popular voice." This was, in short, an appeal to democracy conceived as popular sovereignty, plebeian in nature, and exercised through plebiscitary acclamation.

The populist left, therefore, not only ascended to power with a different democratic imaginary than the social democratic left; it did so in very different institutional contexts. In both sets of cases, conditions surrounding the lefts' access to power reinforced early formative traits and generated durable legacies that shaped their trajectories in public office. For example, insurrectional sequences had severely weakened democratic regimes and pushed party systems to the verge of collapse in Venezuela, Ecuador, and Bolivia. As such, populist-left leaders with commanding majority support could invoke plebiscitary mandates to sweep aside the institutional detritus of the old order and fill the political void with their own movement networks and emerging party organizations. The demise of traditional parties thus created asymmetries of power that enabled populist-left leaders to found new constitutional orders that concentrated authority in their own hands and weakened mechanisms of horizontal accountability associated with institutional checks and balances (Corrales 2018; Selçuk 2024; Weyland 2024). By contrast, Chile's Socialist Party (PSCh), Brazil's Workers Party (PT), and Uruguay's Broad Front (FA) came to power via routine alternations in public office; their access to power was not premised on doing away with the existing political order. Chile, Uruguay, and Brazil elected presidents after 2000 in contexts where democratic regimes were intact, institutional checks and balances were operative, and opposition political parties remained electorally competitive and well represented in congress. Indeed, in both Chile and Brazil, leftist parties lacked a legislative majority and could govern only at the head of broad multiparty coalitions that made them dependent on centrist or even, in the Brazilian case, conservative allies.[5] These competitive dynamics and institutional constraints clearly tempered the parties' more radical impulses, forced them to compromise and share power, and ultimately weakened their linkages to organized popular constituencies.[6]

In short, different formative experiences spawned national lefts inclined toward very different democratic imaginaries, which were then reinforced and reproduced by the institutional contexts under which leftist parties accessed power during Latin America's left turn. But how did these distinct developmental trajectories condition the kinds of political vulnerabilities and limitations to which they were prone? Our comparative analysis suggests that the two types of left had corresponding defects and vulnerabilities that contributed to their respective political defeats.[7] The social democratic left, which initially entered "the system" with hopes of transforming it and crafting a new way of "doing politics," found ample opportunities over an extended period of time to access public office within new democratic regimes by adhering to their rules, internalizing their norms and practices, and adapting to their institutional constraints. Rather than transforming the system, however, this "conformist temptation" allowed the system to transform the left instead and remold it in the image of the established order.[8] Having learned Brazil's transactional mode of clientelistic, rent-seeking coalition politics all too well, the PT became ensnared in a web of corruption scandals that ultimately left the party susceptible to opportunistic betrayals by its coalition partners and a furious right-wing backlash. Meanwhile, Chile's PSCh was transformed over time into a pillar of a technocratic neoliberal establishment that has become increasingly detached from Chilean society, allowing the party to be outflanked on the left by iterative cycles of mass social protest against economic inequalities and the political order that reproduced them. Both the PT and the PSCh allowed their roots in organized popular constituencies to wither as they contested and exercised power at the national level, thoroughly undermining their prospects of leading a radical democratic transformation.

The counterpart for the populist left, the "autocratic temptation," had a different political logic but equally deleterious—or even more severe—political consequences. Given its majoritarian electoral support and the steep decline of traditional parties, the populist left was able to fill a political vacuum, gain hegemonic control over a wide range of governing institutions, and exercise constitutive powers by plebiscitary means. Not surprisingly, it used those powers to erect new regime institutions that served its own interests and gave rise to several authoritarian distortions, such as the concentration of power in the executive branch, the weakening of horizontal checks and balances, and placing opposition and minority political rights in jeopardy (Corrales 2018). The autocratic temptation to concentrate state power in the hands of a dominant party or political movement highlighted the classic tension in democratic theory between majority power and minority rights discussed earlier. It also demonstrated the porous and slippery boundaries between forms of popular hegemony that are participatory, empowering, and consensual in nature and patterns of political domination that are more coercive and autocratic in practice. Autocratic tendencies were reinforced by the reliance on charismatic figures to unify disparate social groups, part of the process of condensing social complexity that is integral to any construction of "the people" as a populist subject (see Weyland 2001; Urbinati 2017, 578–583).

The concentration of power in the hands of a dominant party and its charismatic leader generated difficulties with political succession as well. This concentration made it extremely hard for new leaders to emerge and carry forward the transformations begun by the "founding" leader, and it made the logic of continued reelections particularly troubling. At the same time, the autocratic temptation became a flash point for political opposition in Venezuela, Ecuador, and Bolivia, as it raised the stakes of democratic competition and threatened the core democratic rights of opposition actors, who sometimes countered with responses that also transgressed democratic norms (Gamboa 2022). As such, the autocratic temptation was intrinsically polarizing. It also clashed with the grassroots, participatory logic of the left's radical democratic projects, causing atrophy of the two-way communication channels between leaders in office and their supporters and weakening linkages between the populist left and their organized social bases. Over time, this contributed to the demobilization of allied social groups (Bolivia), a weakening of the feedback mechanisms needed to safeguard against poor policy choices (Venezuela), and internal conflicts within the left itself (Ecuador).

Different formative experiences, then, combined with different institutional contexts to shape leftist governments that were susceptible to specific types of political failings. To be sure, these path-dependent trajectories were not ironclad. As we show in chapter 4, for example, for all its similarities to the PT in Brazil and the PSCh in Chile, the Broad Front in Uruguay stayed closer to its organized popular constituencies and arguably avoided the worst pitfalls of the conformist temptation. Likewise, autocratic tendencies in the populist-left cases did not culminate in the same types of performance failures or political endpoints. Venezuela's economic debacle under Maduro was a far cry from Bolivia, which achieved not only sustained economic growth but also a significant reduction in inequality under Morales and the Movement Toward Socialism (MAS). And while the autocratic temptation contributed to the downfall of populist-left governments in Bolivia and Ecuador, and eventually to the division of the MAS in Bolivia, it led Venezuela's populist left to entrench itself in power through increasingly authoritarian means—as it did in Nicaragua under Daniel Ortega.

Our comparative analysis demonstrates that the polarized and tumultuous endings of the left turn were not a simple function of performance failures or exogenous factors like global economic crises and the end of the commodity boom. Deeper political failings were at work as well. Those failings constrained the left's ability to deepen democracy, and they helped usher in its recent political defeats. They also set the stage for the kinds of polarized politics prevalent in the region today.

The New Polarization in Latin American Politics

Polarization is hardly a novel phenomenon in Latin American politics. Even in the nineteenth century, when political arenas were closed to nonelite actors, polarized conflicts between liberal and conservative factions of ruling oligarchies culminated in repeated cycles of civil warfare in

Colombia, Uruguay, and Honduras. Polarization intensified across much of the region in the middle of the twentieth century with the onset of mass politics and the rise of populist or leftist parties that mobilized labor unions, peasant associations, and other "popular sectors" around reformist platforms that challenged the dominance of traditional elites (Collier and Collier 1991; C. de la Torre 2010; Conniff 2012). Following the Cuban Revolution in 1959 and the youth rebellion of the 1960s, polarization reached new heights as Latin America became a battleground in the Cold War rivalry between the United States and the Soviet Union. With state-led models of capitalist development encountering major bottlenecks, socialist alternatives—both democratic and revolutionary—emerged as serious rivals, and armed insurgent movements contested incumbent regimes across much of the region (Wickham-Crowley 1993; Marchesi 2018).

The highly polarizing ideological conflicts of the 1960s culminated in a wave of military coups and authoritarian repression that crushed populist and leftist labor unions, social movements, and political parties in much of the region by the middle of the 1970s (O'Donnell 1973; Collier 1979; Winn 1986; Drake 1996). In essence, military rulers, business elites, and their technocratic allies sought to impose depolarization on society and insulate policymaking processes from societal pressures by closing political space, eliminating democratic contestation, and forcibly demobilizing working- and lower-class constituencies (Remmer 1980; Constable and Valenzuela 1993; Drake 1996).

Although democratic contestation was tentatively restored as regime transitions spread across Latin America starting in the late 1970s, the region did not return to the status quo ante. Polarization was often kept in check by the legacies—both organizational and ideational—of the severe repression suffered by leftist parties and their social bases under authoritarian rule, which included widespread disappearances, imprisonment, torture, and exile of leaders and activists. The dismantling of party organizations and the dramatic weakening of labor unions left these actors chastened and on the political defensive, anxious to restore a modicum of democratic protection for political rights and civil liberties, even if that required watering down or placing a hold on ideological commitments to radical social and economic change. Indeed, moderation and self-restraint were embedded in the very logic of democratic transitions, which often required the negotiation of political pacts between rival elites who supported and opposed military regimes. Democratization, therefore, unfolded under conditions of heightened political uncertainty. It was an institutional compromise that protected the interests of military and economic elites by narrowing the range of actors and issues subjected to democratic contestation and limiting the popular mobilization associated with that contestation (O'Donnell and Schmitter 1986, 40–41; Oxhorn 1995). Transitions to democracy in this period, therefore, were often quite conservative in nature, as pact making implied that broader agendas for redistributive reforms would be put on hold.

Furthermore, democratization in the 1980s occurred in the midst of severe economic crises that further narrowed the range of policy debate and reinforced the decline of labor and leftist political movements (Oxhorn 2011). As the debt crisis spread across the region in the 1980s, statist development models collapsed in a maelstrom of hyperinflationary spirals, foreign exchange bottlenecks, capital flight, and severe recessions. These crises gave leverage to international banks and creditor governments to push for aggressive market reforms. The rescheduling of debts to foreign banks and the International Monetary Fund was conditional on the adoption of stringent austerity measures and neoliberal structural adjustment programs that sharply curtailed the developmental and social welfare roles of state institutions. Tariffs were slashed, state enterprises and public services were privatized, wages were cut, labor and consumer markets were liberalized, currencies were devalued, and social programs and public employment were streamlined.

In a context of acute financial and global market constraints, even center-left and labor-based parties that were historical champions of state-led development opted to impose neoliberal "shock treatments" when they gained access to public office (Stokes 2001; Roberts 2014). By the early 1990s—with socialism extinguished in the Soviet bloc, and Latin American revolutionary movements facing defeat or negotiating their entry into democratic regimes (Castañeda 1993)—the so-called Washington Consensus (Williamson 1990) for neoliberal reform reigned supreme across the region, and democratic governments turned economic policymaking over to internationally trained free-market economists and technocrats. For a time, at least, neoliberal technocracy removed a wide range of social and economic outcomes from the sphere of democratic deliberation by relegating them to the marketplace, thus narrowing the grounds for polarized democratic contestation.

In the larger historical context, then, the 1990s appeared to be a singular period of political depolarization in Latin America—a period in which the "dual transitions" of the 1980s had seemingly left democracy and

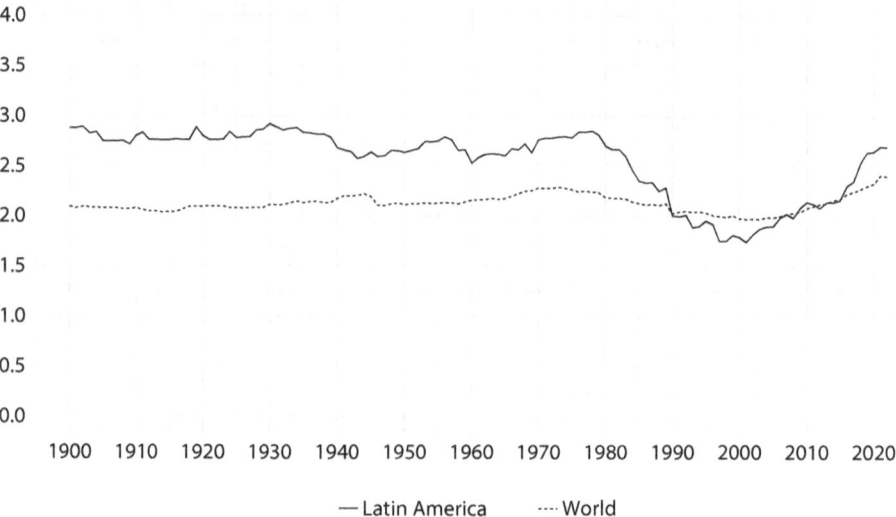

FIGURE 1.2. Political polarization, 1900–2022. V-Dem (Coppedge et al. 2024).

neoliberalism as "the only games in town." The convergence on both the regime type and the development model suggested a process of ideological moderation that was widely seen as conducive to democratic consolidation (Mainwaring and Pérez-Liñán 2014). This depolarization is readily apparent in the expert-coded survey data of the Varieties of Democracy (V-Dem) project, which provides a longitudinal measure of political polarization across the world since 1900 (fig. 1.2). The question on which this measure is based asks to what extent society is split into antagonistic political camps and political differences affect social relationships beyond political discussions. Levels of polarization are scored from 0 (supporters of opposing political camps generally interact in a friendly manner) to 4 (supporters of opposing political camps generally interact in a hostile manner).

Figure 1.2 shows that polarization has been historically high in Latin America, consistently scoring higher than world averages until 1990, when the dual transitions toward democracy and market liberalism dropped the region (temporarily) below the global average. The figure also shows that the historical anomaly is not today's polarization, which scores very close to Latin America's historical norms, but rather the depolarization of the 1980s and 1990s. The region reached an all-time low polarization score of 1.75 (out of 4) in 1997, the year before the left turn got underway in Venezuela. The graph then shows a sharp and sustained increase in polarization starting in the early 2000s, however, as the Washington Consensus began to erode and was increasingly challenged from below. This contestation often began in society, at the mass level, with the mobilization of social protest movements before the rise of polarized, elite-level contestation in the electoral arena (Silva 2009; Roberts 2014). On average, by the early 2020s, Latin American countries appeared to be far more polarized than they were in the 1980s and 1990s, approaching the levels of polarization seen in the highly contentious decades of the 1960s and 1970s.

In short, the elite-level political convergence around neoliberalism in the 1990s proved to be short-lived. Indeed, it did not extend far beyond the technocratic circles that implemented and managed the model, and it was surely not hegemonic within society at large. Within the general public, neoliberal reforms—which pushed public policies well to the promarket right—were often highly divisive and polarizing, as seen in the frequency of protests and mass riots in response to the adoption of austerity measures (Walton and Seddon 1994). The political convergence around neoliberalism was thus heavily dependent on the insulation of technocratic policymaking circles from societal pressures and democratic contestation—an insulation made possible in the short term by the weakening and fragmentation of labor and popular constituencies wrought by decades of military repression, economic crisis, and market-based structural adjustment. Rather than robust liberal democracy, this often gave rise to "delegative" forms of democracy—that is, polyarchies with powerful presidents unconstrained by either institutional checks and balances or the vertical accountability provided by well-organized societal actors in between elections (O'Donnell 1994). Depolarization was predicated, in part, on maintaining forms of democratic rule that were highly exclusionary of organized popular constituencies.

Although structural adjustment policies succeeded in defeating hyperinflation, once stabilization had been achieved across the region by the mid-1990s, it was only a matter of time before social mobilization and institutionalized democratic competition in contexts of acute economic inequalities would repoliticize the social deficits of the neoliberal model. This repoliticization was the hallmark of Latin America's second historical phase of mass political incorporation at the turn of the century (Roberts 2014; Silva and Rossi 2018), a successor to the initial labor-based forms of populist incorporation in the middle of the twentieth century. The region's left turn—preceded, in some cases, by widespread social protest

(Silva 2009; Arce and Bellinger 2007)—was the most visible manifestation of this new incorporation process. As this book shows, left turns varied considerably in their polarizing effects, at least in the short term; whereas social democratic left parties governed strictly within the confines of existing democratic regimes and proposed relatively moderate reforms of neoliberal models, populist lefts posed frontal challenges to both regime institutions and neoliberal orthodoxy. Over time, however, both types of left turn unleashed polarizing dynamics that would reshape democratic politics by the second decade of the new century.

Across the region, the strengthening of leftist alternatives expanded the range of democratic debate over the proper balance between states and markets and the reach of social citizenship rights. And while organized labor remained a weakened actor in most of the region, new patterns of mobilization by indigenous movements, unemployed and informal-sector workers, community activists, pensioners, environmentalists, and women's organizations heightened political contestation over neoliberal orthodoxy and the limitations of democratic regimes (Yashar 2005; Garay 2007; Ondetti 2008; Blofield 2012; Rosaldo 2016; Hummel 2017). Social mobilization placed pressure on governments—left, right, and center—to support higher wages, more inclusive pension systems, and targeted poverty-relief programs, including conditional cash transfers to low-income families. As the decade-long commodity boom got underway in the early 2000s, creating new jobs and alleviating government fiscal and debt constraints, favorable conditions allowed Latin American states to make a dent in the region's notorious economic inequalities (López-Calva and Lustig 2010). As table 1.2 shows, the Gini index of income inequality fell across most of the region between 2000 and 2016, by which time the commodity boom had ended and the left turn was in retreat. The decline was especially pronounced in the seven South American countries analyzed in this volume that experienced extended left turns, compared to other Latin American countries where leftist parties spent little or no time at the head of government. Bolivia and Argentina experienced the most dramatic declines in their Gini scores—in the Bolivian case, reflecting a major expansion of the indigenous urban middle class—whereas Uruguay was able to achieve a significant reduction in income inequality even though it started from a more equitable baseline.

Challenges to inequality were hardly limited to the economic sphere. Diverse social groups also pressed claims on cultural issues related to gender, sexuality, and multiculturalism that took aim at deeply entrenched

TABLE 1.2 **Changes in the Gini index of inequality in Latin America, 2000–2016**

	Initial Gini index (early 2000s)	*2016 Gini index*	*Change in Gini index*
Argentina	54.4	39.2	−15.2
Bolivia	64.3	45.3	−20.0
Brazil	63.9	51.1	−12.8
Chile	56.4	45.3	−11.1
Ecuador	55.9	44.5	−11.4
Uruguay	44.7	39.1	−5.6
Venezuela	46.8	37.8	−9.0
Average of Seven Left-Turn Cases	55.2	43.2	−12.2
Latin American countries without a leftist government (average)	54.0	49.7	−4.3

Source: ECLAC (2015, 68; 2016, 26).
Note: The countries without a leftist government for most of this period included Mexico, Guatemala, Honduras, Costa Rica, Panama, Dominican Republic, Colombia, and Peru. The cases of Paraguay, Nicaragua, and El Salvador are not included in the calculations, as they experienced shorter or later left turns or had different dynamics than the cases analyzed in this volume.

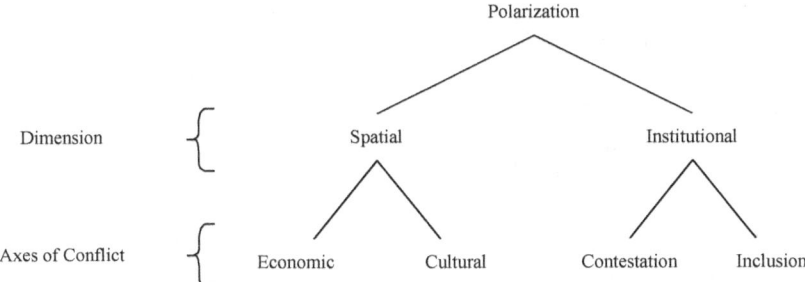

FIGURE 1.3. Polarization: spatial and institutional dimensions.

social hierarchies, often triggering countermobilizations by religious and conservative defenders of the traditional social order in the region. The Latin American experience thus makes clear the multilayered and multidimensional character of polarization processes (fig. 1.3). On the ideological or "spatial" plane, polarization signifies that rival political actors are far apart in their core political beliefs, values, and policy preferences. Simply put, it is a process of spatial distancing among major political contenders along either economic or cultural axes of contestation. Regarding the institutional plane, it is important to recognize that polarization also extends to basic conflicts over the institutional rules and procedures for democratic contestation and the breadth of inclusion (as depicted in figure 1.1). It arises when rival actors operate under divergent democratic imaginaries, with sharp disagreements over whether to prioritize contestation or inclusion—or when some actors are willing to transgress (or perceived to transgress) democratic norms and procedures in pursuit of their political agendas.

Although Sartori (1976) and Schedler (2023) have made compelling arguments for the centrality of institutional conflict in polarization processes, the spatial dimension has generally been stressed in prior research. Haggard and Kaufman (2021, 14), for example, define polarization as "the process through which political elites and publics become increasingly divided over public policy, ideology and ultimately partisan attachments." Likewise, Handlin (2017, 278) defines party-system polarization as "the degree of ideological differentiation between component parties in a party system, understood in terms of both distance and intensity." Conventionally, the left-right axis of political contestation differentiates actors according to their positions on economic issues; it locates those who support free markets and private property on the right pole and those who advocate more statist and redistributive platforms on the left pole. Although cultural issues related to religious and moral values, sexuality and gender rights, law-and-order issues, and racial, ethnic, and multicultural identities sometimes map onto this left-right axis (Martínez-Gallardo et al. 2023), they need not do so; indeed, they are at least potentially orthogonal or crosscutting, making it useful to conceptualize ideological contestation in two-dimensional space, as depicted in figure 1.4. The figure locates multicultural challenges to the social hierarchy on the upper pole of the vertical axis and defense of the traditional social order (including religiosity and moral traditionalism, exclusionary ethno-nationalism, and strict law-and-order appeals) on the lower pole.

Political contestation of neoliberalism takes place on the horizontal economic axis. Neoliberal orthodoxy positioned the Latin American right near the far-right pole in figure 1.4, while the Washington Consensus of the 1990s pulled other major actors to right-of-center positions that severely compressed the range of macroeconomic policy debate. The strengthening of leftist alternatives at the turn of the century eroded this consensus and expanded the space for policy contestation around issues like labor rights and collective bargaining, taxation policies, and the social welfare roles of states related to the provision of health care, education, and social security. It should be recognized, however, that even this space was com-

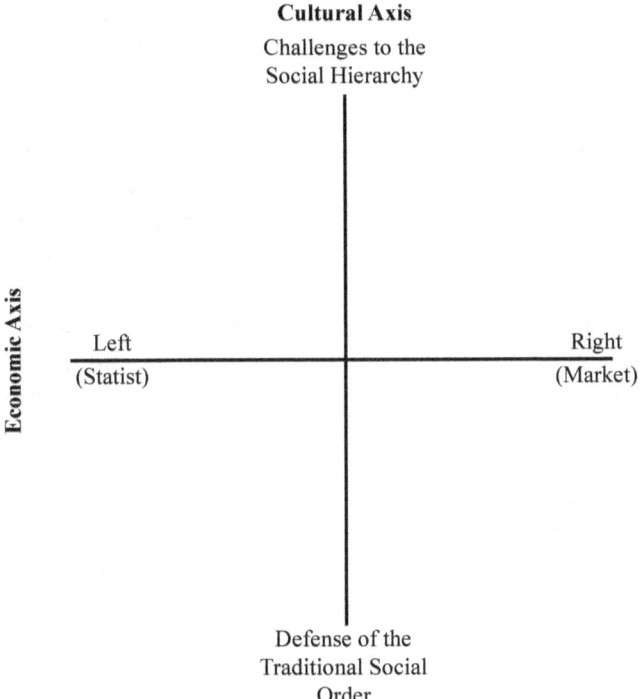

FIGURE 1.4. Axes of political contestation.

pressed, relative to the 1960s and 1970s, by the collapse of socialism as an alternative model of economic development. Despite Hugo Chávez's pledge to build "socialism for the twenty-first century," Latin America's populist or "Bolivarian" lefts generally experimented with statist varieties of capitalism—that is, capitalist alternatives to neoliberalism—rather than socialist alternatives to capitalism itself.

Nonetheless, polarization and policy contestation on the economic axis clearly intensified following the Washington Consensus of the 1990s, and they were reinforced by polarization on the cultural axis as well. Social movements and, in some cases, leftist parties have pushed to expand women's rights (including the right to abortion), LGBTQ+ rights, and the rights of historically marginalized racial and ethnic groups, moving toward the upper pole in figure 1.4 (Paschel 2016; Blofield et al. 2017; C. F. Anderson 2020; Corrales 2021). In response, this politicization of social hierarchies and inequalities other than class has triggered two interrelated phenomena. On the one hand, competitive pressures pushed some mainstream right-wing parties to gradually moderate their programs and try to win over centrist voters—a process that in some cases, such as Chile, opened political space for new far-right options (Rovira Kaltwasser 2019). On the other hand, the politicization of social inequalities beyond class has triggered a countermobilization near the lower pole of the cultural axis by conservative defenders of religious identities, moral traditionalism, and gendered or racialized social hierarchies (Mayka and Smith 2021). As in Europe, this countermobilization has increasingly been associated with the rise of a new, more radical right with populist tendencies centered largely on cultural identities (Ignazi 1992; Zanotti and Roberts 2021).

Arguably, the growing salience of cultural issues in the process of polarization reflects challenges confronted by political actors on both the left and right sides of the spectrum. For the left, the long-term decline in the political and organizational weight of labor unions, the collapse of socialism as an alternative model of society, and the constraints on reducing inequalities in highly globalized market economies may strengthen incentives to try to mobilize support within activist networks politicizing non-class-based forms of social inequality. For the right, cultural appeals to religious identities, moral traditionalism, anti-immigrant or anti-minority-group sentiments, and, increasingly, punitive law-and-order platforms may help attract support beyond what parties are able to obtain on the basis of their economic platforms alone. Indeed, these cultural appeals provide a potential response to the well-known "conservative dilemma" (Ziblatt 2017, 33–37)—that is, the challenge of attracting mass support when a party's "core constituencies" are drawn from elite sectors of society (Gibson 1996, 7).[9] That conservative dilemma is especially acute in Latin America, given the region's extreme inequalities, which reduce the relative size of middle and upper classes and swell the ranks of the underprivileged. It is compounded by the erosion of traditional patron-clientelist linkages between conservative parties and lower-class constituencies (Van Dyck and Montero 2015) and by the limited appeal of neoliberal orthodoxy in unequal societies where citizens expect states to address social needs—expectations that were surely raised by the social and political mobilizations associated with the left turn (Garay 2016).

Beyond the ideological plane, it is vital to recognize that polarization is not simply a matter of spatial distancing in policy or programmatic positions. Polarization often assumes powerful "affective" characteristics when rival social or political camps develop strong emotional ties to their "in-group" and express mutual distrust and animosity toward a different "out-group" (Mason 2016; McCoy and Somer 2018). In contexts where party systems are widely discredited or in crisis, polarization can also take the more inchoate form of mass opposition to the entire political establishment (Meléndez 2022; Kessler and Murillo forthcoming), which Luna (2024) characterizes as "disjointed" polarization. According to Schedler (2023), polarization has an essential institutional dimension, whereby parties diverge in their adherence to democratic norms and procedures, or distrust the willingness of their rivals to abide by the established rules of the game. As a set of conflict-regulating institutions, democracy is designed to process differences—even polarized ones—over ideological and programmatic preferences. Conflict over the *rules* for processing these differences, however, can exacerbate polarization by raising the stakes of democratic competition.

Polarization around institutions is especially likely where parties or movements claim exclusive or unilateral constitutive powers—that is, the authority to refound institutions and/or rewrite the rules of the game, without obtaining the consent or collaboration of other actors to do so. That is especially the case where opposition actors are too weak or lacking in institutional leverage to serve as a moderating or countervailing force, or where they employ extrainstitutional strategies of opposition—such as protests, strikes, and potential military interventions—that pose serious threats to incumbents (Gamboa 2022). Likewise, polarization results when incumbents try to tilt the democratic playing field to their advantage by concentrating powers, handicapping rivals, and undermining institutional checks and balances. Democracy's conflict-regulating mechanisms rest heavily on the iterative nature of democratic contestation, which lengthens actors' time horizons and lowers the stakes of contestation by giving parties that lose elections incentives to remain in the democratic game and compete again in future iterations. Constitutive conflicts over basic institutions and rules undermine this intertemporal character of democratic contestation, as they raise the specter of increasing or cumulative returns to the power of incumbency (Przeworski 1991, 25). By threatening to "lock in" temporary advantages or victories, they raise the stakes of any given electoral contest or policy choice. As such, they exert polarizing effects that are quite distinct from, and potentially independent of, spatial polarization attributable to ideological differences. This understanding of institutionally grounded polarization takes us back to the two different democratic imaginaries we outlined earlier, as polarization is rooted in the tension between the rules for democratic contestation, on the vertical axis of figure 1.1, and the terms of social inclusion or popular empowerment, on the horizontal axis. Polarization can occur along either or both of these dimensions, as shown in figure 1.3.

The Latin American experience also makes it clear that polarization can be driven by conflict dynamics at both the elite (supply-side) and the mass (demand-side) levels. From the top down, political elites may find it electorally and politically advantageous—in both intra- and interparty competition—to foster polarization as a way to claim "ownership" of an issue position, differentiate themselves from political rivals, and mobilize supporters against perceived adversaries. They can politicize an issue that was previously neglected by mainstream parties, stake out a more radical stance on an issue under debate, or challenge institutional arrangements for processing conflicts. In so doing, they expand the programmatic space for democratic contestation and reconfigure the issue agenda. They might also engage in discursive polarization, adopting more abusive, intolerant, or vituperative language to demonize opponents and discredit them as legitimate contenders in the democratic arena. Such tactics invariably foster affective polarization, whereby rival political camps not only disagree with each other on the issues but also harbor intense mutual animosities or contempt and distrust of those on the other side of the divide. This is sometimes recognized as a form of "negative partisanship," whereby hostility toward an out-group party is more powerful than political identification with any favored party (Webster and Abramowitz 2017; Samuels and Zucco 2018). Negative partisanship is hardly a new phenomenon in Latin America, as seen, for example, in the intense historical animosity toward Peronism in some sectors of Argentine society or hostility toward the populist American Popular Revolutionary Alliance (APRA) party in Peru.

Polarization at the elite level does not necessarily mean that public opinion itself is sharply divided; many democratic citizens, after all, do not have coherent or well-defined ideological identities or programmatic preferences (Achen and Bartels 2017). Elite polarization can, however, induce voters to "sort" themselves into socially distinct and ideologically defined partisan camps that are reinforced by affective attachments and negative partisanship (Levendusky 2009). Indeed, polarization may also have deep roots in society and reflect dynamic interactions between civil society actors and parties (Tarrow 2021, 22). It can be driven by mass-level or bottom-up dynamics—on either the political left or the right—when interest groups, civil society networks, and/or social movements politicize issues that mainstream parties have largely neglected or declined to make a focal point of democratic competition. As Tarrow (2022, 10) argues, social protest and other forms of "contentious politics" are typically employed by citizens "who lack regular access to representative institutions" and "act in the name of new or unaccepted claims."

Civic activism, therefore, may encourage established parties to adopt more radical issue positions closer to the poles in figure 1.4, and it sometimes spawns new types of movement-based parties that outflank established parties on one or another programmatic axis (Anria 2018). These dynamics will be seen in our case studies, as mass social protest against neoliberalism was an antecedent to the rise of Latin America's populist lefts at the turn of the century in Venezuela, Bolivia, Ecuador, and, to a partial extent, Argentina. Similarly, mass right-wing protests in Brazil that culminated in the impeachment of President Dilma Rousseff, of the PT, in 2016 helped set the stage for the electoral rise of the far-right populist Jair Bolsonaro in 2018. More recently, in Chile, social protest erupted on the left flank and challenged the political establishment at large, unsettling the party system, strengthening movement-based alternatives, and spawning efforts—ultimately unsuccessful—to draft a new constitution that would allow the country to break with the institutional legacies of former military dictator Augusto Pinochet.

Understanding polarization, therefore, requires an examination of political dynamics at both elite and mass levels of analysis, in both institutional and noninstitutional arenas of political contestation. Processes of polarization—and depolarization—are heavily conditioned by the reciprocal interaction of social and political actors at these different levels of analysis.

Conclusion

Polarization has deep historical roots in Latin America, but it has ebbed and flowed over time, intensifying in the 1960s and 1970s, moderating in the 1980s and 1990s, and then deepening again after the turn of the century. The left turn coincided with the onset of this most recent stage of polarization. However, the populist and social democratic lefts experienced quite different polarization dynamics, conditioned by their distinct formative experiences and institutional settings, and the alternative democratic imaginaries these fostered. The chapters that follow explore the origins and evolution of the two lefts in power, and they explain why their political logics made them vulnerable to specific types of polarization dynamics. The comparative case studies show how polarization occurred along both economic and cultural axes of democratic contestation, involving both elite and mass-level political dynamics. They also demonstrate that polarization cannot be reduced to ideological distancing, as it often involves basic conflicts over political institutions and the democratic rules of the game.

CHAPTER TWO

The Social Democratic Left and the Conformist Temptation

The Brazilian Workers' Party (PT) and the Socialist Party of Chile (PSCh) were well-established parties when their leaders were elected to presidential office in the early 2000s. This was in contrast to the newer, populist lefts that we analyze in chapter 3. The difference between them was not simply one of chronological age, however; we are not suggesting that aging or life cycle effects make older, established parties different from new ones or that those qualities necessarily exert moderating effects. Rather, the differences between the "two lefts" were largely those of historical contexts and formative experiences. Both the PT and the PSCh had been seared by military repression during periods of authoritarian rule in the 1970s and 1980s, and both parties evolved considerably—in their organizational forms, ideologies, and political strategies—following years of struggle against military dictatorship and active participation in national projects to reconstruct democratic institutions in the 1980s and 1990s. These experiences weighed heavily on the democratic imaginaries of both parties as they embraced the political rights and freedoms offered by liberal democracy and gradually—if grudgingly—adapted their goals for radical social and economic change to the institutional constraints of new democratic regimes.

In both parties, revolutionary Marxist currents were progressively sidelined, and linkages to social movements and organized popular constituencies atrophied as party organizations won elections, gained access to public office, and became increasingly professionalized pillars of national democratic establishments. Both parties found political success playing by the rules of their respective democratic regimes, but neither came anywhere close to capturing a governing majority on their own; they could wield power at the national level only in collaboration with other actors. Consequently, in an effort to ensure governability and avoid polarization, both governed through broad multiparty coalitions with more centrist or conservative parties that placed constraints on the left's transformative agenda. Indeed, both parties internalized much of the logic, and the defects, of their respective democratic orders, and in so doing, they largely reproduced them: a technocratic logic of managing the military regime's neoliberal legacy in Chile and a transactional rent-seeking logic of interparty coalitional dealmaking and brokerage politics in Brazil. Ultimately, these defects—products of what we call the "conformist temptation"—thwarted efforts to deepen democracy and empower popular majorities, and both parties fell prey to social uprisings that politicized their respective failings. If the conformist temptation left the PT vulnerable to a far-right populist backlash after a series of devastating corruption scandals and the impeachment of President Dilma Rousseff, in Chile it left the PSCh vulnerable to electoral defeat by the right, a social backlash on the left flank against the entire post-Pinochet democratic establishment, and the eventual rise of a far-right alternative staunchly committed to the defense of Pinochet's legacies.

In the pages that follow, we trace the roots of the conformist temptation by providing a detailed analysis of the formative and historical experiences that shaped the political profile of the social democratic lefts in Brazil and Chile. These experiences produced lasting legacies that conditioned how the PT and PSCh would compete in the democratic arena and govern once they accessed power. We also document the institutional contexts in which both parties ascended to power, which reinforced these earlier traits and shaped governing opportunities and constraints. Finally, we examine the political defects associated with the conformist temptation in each country and how they contributed to the rise of mass protest movements on the right or left flanks, the political defeat of the social democratic left, and deepening patterns of political polarization.

Our analysis makes clear that political parties can change over time. Although their founding organizational traits tend to endure (Panebianco 1988) and condition how they change (Hunter 2010), they are not locked into a genetic imprint that makes them impervious to external or internal pressures for change. Nevertheless, major changes are unlikely in the absence of severe challenges or perturbations, and they are invariably contested by internal factions beholden to the status quo. This internal pluralism is actually conducive to organizational change, however, as it allows dissident factions to become champions of reform when the opportunity arises. That was surely the case in the PT and the PSCh, as both parties contained internal factions or currents drawn to the different democratic imaginaries of institutionalized pluralism and popular sovereignty. Intraparty competition between these factions was integral to any process of party change, and the outcome of such competition was hardly preordained. In both countries, however, the political logic of conservative democratic transitions proved highly advantageous in this intraparty competition to the more moderate, social democratic factions embracing institutionalized pluralism. Simply put, the moderate factions were better positioned to build broad coalitions, be tolerated by the right, win elections, and mobilize the leadership and organizational resources attached to public office.

Even in the absence of predetermination, then, there was a cumulative or path-dependent logic to the consolidation of internal authority by these social democratic factions and to the moderating trajectories of organizational change they charted. This path-dependent logic was only reinforced by the progressive detachment and demobilization of the organized social bases that were integral to any alternative radical democratic imaginary, much less one centered on popular sovereignty. The logic of path dependency essentially pulled up the drawbridge and foreclosed, or at least impeded, any return to a political project of mass mobilization intended to empower popular majorities under the leadership of the PT or the PSCh. Where such mobilization *did* occur—through repeated cycles of mass social protest in Chile—they were not led by the PSCh but instead outflanked it on the left and largely eschewed partisan leadership altogether.

Formative Processes, Historical Experiences, and Political Learning

The experience of military dictatorship and severe political repression played a formative role in the leftist projects in both countries. In Brazil, they were central features of the political context in which the PT was born, as the party was founded in 1980 through a convergence of diverse labor unions, social movements, and small leftist parties that protested the country's military dictatorship in the late 1970s. In Chile, military dictatorship and political repression after 1973 transformed a party with a long record of democratic participation and a recent experience of anchoring the more radical wing of Salvador Allende's democratic socialist government in the early 1970s. In many respects, the PSCh offers a microcosm of the twists and turns of the Latin American left over the better part of the past century.

The Development of the Chilean Socialist Party

The PSCh was founded in 1933 during Latin America's turbulent transition to mass politics, when Chile's historically oligarchic republic was in the process of being refounded as a new mass democracy. The party was born highly fractionalized,[1] as it was an eclectic meeting ground for diverse socialist and populist-left currents that did not fit within Chile's orthodox, Moscow-aligned Communist Party (PCCh) (Jobet 1987; Drake 1978). With close ties to a strong, militant labor movement anchored in Chile's mining camps and emerging industrial sectors (DeShazo 1983; Bergquist 1986), the PSCh and the PCCh constituted the most electorally formidable left in Latin America for much of the twentieth century. The two parties participated in a series of "popular front" coalition governments led by the centrist Radical Party in the late 1930s and early 1940s, but these alliances splintered the PSCh and weakened it electorally in the post–World War II period. The party reunified in the late 1950s and forged a new electoral alliance with the PCCh that supported Socialist leader Salvador Allende in a series of presidential campaigns in 1958, 1964, and 1970 (Rosenblatt 2018, 79). During this period, however, the PSCh also redefined itself ideologically as a more orthodox Marxist-Leninist party, clearly reflecting the influence of the Cuban Revolution and Latin America's youthful groundswell of revolutionary activism in the 1960s (Marchesi 2018). Paradoxically, then, although Allende and his Popular Unity (UP) coalition of Socialist, Communist, and Christian left parties became synonymous in Latin America with the *vía pacífica*, or the "peaceful road" to socialism, his own party cast doubt on the electoral process and openly identified with the region's armed insurgent movements.

The PSCh thus anchored the more radical current within Allende's UP government (1970–1973) following his election to the presidency. Although the party remained highly fractionalized internally, its leadership rejected compromise with opposition forces and denied the possibility of a democratic transition to socialism, believing that a break in the constitutional order was inevitable on the road to socialism (Faúndez 1988). Allende, however, with staunch support from the Communist Party, embraced a legal and electoral path to power and was committed to socialist reforms—including land redistribution and the nationalization of banks and major industries—within the strictures of constitutional democracy.

During his government, therefore, the UP coalition was deeply divided over Allende's willingness to compromise on socialist reforms in order to dampen intense class conflict, reduce ideological polarization, and safeguard the democratic regime. The more radical wings of the PSCh and the Christian left, along with the militant Movement of the Revolutionary Left (MIR) outside the UP coalition, challenged any accommodation with the opposition that entailed watering down socialist reforms. They believed it was necessary to "advance without compromise," anticipating an eventual breakdown of the democratic order and the onset of a revolutionary situation. As such, the radical left adopted an instrumental approach that valued liberal democracy as a means to accumulate forces for radical change, but not as an end in itself, with its own intrinsic value. Because the radical left conceived of formal representative democracy as a bourgeois creation—a form of class rule that protected elite interests—it privileged building grassroots "popular power" as an alternative. The radical left, therefore, focused on organizing labor, peasant unions, and community councils as the building blocks of a new, more participatory socialist order (Winn 1986; Schlotterbeck 2018), while believing that the *vía pacífica* was likely to culminate in armed conflict and revolutionary struggle. With social mobilization and protest occurring on both the left and right flanks—one side advocating revolution, and the other a military takeover—class conflict and ideological polarization escaped the confines of Chile's democratic institutions, derailing Allende's democratic road to socialism (Valenzuela 1978).

The military coup of September 1973 did not merely topple Allende; it crushed the parties, unions, and other organized social bases painstakingly built up by the Chilean left over four decades of democratic participation. Along with the Communist Party and the MIR, the PSCh was severely targeted and repressed by the military and secret police, the Directorate for National Intelligence (DINA) led by Gen. Manuel Contreras (Esberg 2018, 15). The party organization inside Chile was dispersed and forced underground by the imprisonment, forced disappearance, or exile of successive leadership cohorts (Constable and Valenzuela 1993; Policzer 2009). In response to this devastating defeat, many prominent socialist intellectuals (initially in exile) engaged in a vigorous self-reflection and self-criticism of the party's radicalization process under Allende. This critical perspective, which came to be known as the "socialist renovation," deepened existing lines of conflict within the already-fractionalized party, producing a major split within the exiled party diaspora in 1979 (Muñoz Tamayo 2016, 9). Proponents of the renovation process believed the party's radicalization had contributed to the polarization of the political arena and narrowed Allende's base of support.[2] By failing to recognize the essential character of a broad social and political base for any program of radical change, the argument went, the party's radicalization had set the stage for Allende's political defeat and contributed, at least indirectly, to the breakdown of democracy (Viera-Gallo 1976–1977).[3]

Combined with the party's traumatic experience of repression under military rule, a long process of critical self-reflection encouraged the PSCh to question its Leninist positions and redefine its political goals and strategic orientation (Rosenblatt 2018, 88). It especially encouraged party leaders to revalue liberal democracy as the guarantor of political rights and liberties and as an institutional framework to regulate conflict among bitter political adversaries—the essence of democracy conceived as institutionalized pluralism. Critical self-reflection also led party leaders to support broad-based social and political alliances as the foundation for any transformative project. These planks were at the heart of the party's ideological renovation under the Pinochet regime, essentially redefining its socialist objectives in terms of an open-ended process of "deepening" democracy (Garretón 1987; Roberts 1998). In practice, this meant the construction of a new, center-left alliance between the newly reunified PSCh and the Christian Democratic Party (PDC) to confront the military dictatorship and lead Chile's democratic transition at the end of the 1980s.

This renovation process also led the PSCh to break with its historical ally, the PCCh, which had radicalized and taken up arms against the dictatorship, playing a central role in a quasi-insurrectionary protest movement that sought to overthrow Pinochet between 1983 and 1986. Although PSCh activists were highly involved in the protest movement as well, the party leadership associated with the renovation process did not believe that social pressure alone could topple a dictator backed by such formidable and cohesive support from military institutions and economic elites. Indeed, the leadership feared that mass protest, especially when it turned violent, would exacerbate the country's polarization and further entrench Pinochet in power. The leaders opted, instead, for a "political" exodus from the dictatorship, within the institutional parameters established by the regime itself to extend Pinochet's rule—namely, a popular referendum that allowed an opposition coalition led by Socialists and Christian Democrats to contest the dictator where he was weakest, at the ballot box. This option channeled Chile's social mobilization into more formal and institutionalized electoral arenas while deactivating many of the grassroots networks, especially among shantytown youth, that were at the core of the anti-Pinochet protest movement (Oxhorn 1995).

Self-reflection on the Allende experience and its aftermath thus generated important lessons for the PSCh that heavily conditioned the party's role in Chile's regime transition. It taught Socialist leaders about the risks of mobilizing civil society to push governments into faster and more far-reaching reforms than are politically feasible in highly unequal and institutionally unfavorable contexts. Arguably, it encouraged them to demobilize their social bases in the transition and post-transition periods and redirect their energies toward electoral activities (Oxhorn 1995; Luna 2016). It also taught leaders on the left a broader, sobering lesson on the politics of Latin America: the perils that "scaring the right" might have for democratic stability, or even organizational survival (Hoffman and Centeno 2003). In short, political learning not only transformed the PSCh's democratic imaginary but also prompted a reformulation of its policy preferences and strategic orientation—at the same time that crisis and reform in the Soviet bloc were challenging ideological orthodoxy on the left. This transformation encouraged PSCh leaders fighting for a transition to democracy to embrace a pragmatic, depolarizing, "small steps" approach to political change and redistributive reform—a hallmark of the party in the years to come (Pribble 2013, 122).

The Founding of the Workers' Party in Brazil

In contrast to the PSCh, which was formed during the region's transition to mass politics early in the twentieth century, the Brazilian PT emerged much later under the military dictatorship that ruled Brazil between 1964 and 1985. The PT was founded in 1980, incorporating a number of pre-existing radical left parties and militant organizations into its ranks. In its origins, the PT was a classic movement-based party, as it was founded by movement activists in the aftermath of a massive strike wave that fought for workers' rights and challenged the military dictatorship in the late 1970s (Keck 1992). The militant unionism (*novo sindicalismo*) that spawned the party was a radical social movement autonomous from Brazil's traditional, state-controlled labor unions, which dominated the scene until the late 1970s—an enduring institutional legacy of the conservative corporatist and populist rule of strongman Getúlio Vargas between 1930–1945 and 1951–1954. When the military regime purged union leaders and tightened state controls over union representation following the 1964 coup, rank-and-file workers began to create independent factory councils in the 1970s that pushed for higher wages, collective bargaining rights, and recognition of independent unions. As French (2009) notes, under the leadership of Luiz Inácio Lula da Silva, a skilled metalworker and union organizer with only a sixth-grade education (Bourne 2008), trade unions in the industrial belt surrounding São Paulo would try to "extend [their] fight for recognition and power into the realm of mass electoral politics" as Brazil embarked on a protracted transition back to democracy in the early 1980s (French 2009, 165).

Early works on the PT stress the party's distinctiveness in the Brazilian political arena (Meneguello 1989; Keck 1992; see also Amaral and Power 2016, 149). Keck (1992, 239), for instance, argues that during its first decade, the PT represented an organizational "anomaly" in Brazilian politics because of its strong connections with social movements, its radical political proposals and socialist platform, and its participatory and pluralistic organizational model. This model was envisioned in the late 1970s by would-be PT founders (Souza 1988). Their vision was a decentralized organization characterized by bottom-up leadership and decision-making structures—called "basismo" for its emphasis on community or base-level grassroots participation (Guidry 2003, 91). This organizational model would be a break from the vertical patterns of elitism and patron clientelism that long characterized Brazilian parties, not to mention traditional Leninist models of party vanguardism and centralized, hierarchical authority (or "democratic centralism") on the left. For PT founders, then, efforts to reestablish and then deepen Brazilian democracy at the national level would be "prefigured" in the organizational model of the movement-based party itself.[4] The hallmarks of this model were the party's "base nuclei" (*núcleos de base*), small local groups "organized by neighborhood, job category, workplace, or social movement" (Keck 1992, 104) that served to forge strong links with preexisting social movements and created opportunities for bottom-up participation. Over time, however, base nuclei declined in importance, at least partially in response to electoral imperatives—a key early step in transitioning from a movement-based party to a more conventional and professionalized party organization (Ribeiro 2014, 101).[5]

The party itself embraced a democratic socialist platform in its formative stage and sought to maintain strong linkages with organized labor (Barros 2022). Even in its formative stage, however, the PT was "not just another labor party" (Guidry 2003). Rather, it also incorporated a wide array of social movement activists, rural and urban revolutionary groups, and radical intellectuals who were forced to operate clandestinely as a result of political repression. Lula himself had been imprisoned for a month for leading a wildcat strike that was ruled illegal under Brazil's highly restrictive labor code. In that repressive context, the PT became a "place of convergence" for various forces from the left, including politicians linked to the Brazilian Democratic Movement (MDB), university students, middle-class professionals, Afro-Brazilian grassroots networks, the Landless Workers' Movement (MST), community organizations, and Catholic lay organizations (French and Fortes 2005; Mische 2009; Wolford 2010; Amaral and Power 2016; Trejo and Bizzarro 2015; Paschel 2016; Tarlau 2019).[6] Despite their ideological and strategic differences, these disparate activists agreed that a transition to formal democracy, however "shallow" or imperfect it might be, should serve as a bedrock for the pursuit of economic redistribution, social inclusion, and basic citizenship rights. The broad constellation of movements that formed the PT—forming a broader coalition with a wide range of autonomous prodemocracy movements (Alvarez 1990; Avritzer 2002)—thus called for liberalizing political reforms that would enable the possibility for deepening democracy down the road (Kadivar et al. 2020, 1329).

In short, as Van Dyck (2016, 134) argues, the PT developed under "adverse circumstances" of political repression, with no access to state resources or mass media. Exposure to adverse conditions created strong incentives for party founders to invest in "the slow, labor-intensive, and non-vote maximizing work" of developing a robust party organization with territorial branches capable of incorporating a wide network of committed activists (Van Dyck 2016, 134). Adversity and political exclusion also put a premium on grassroots participation in civil society as an organizational strategy. This process of party development was consistent with the argument of Levitsky et al. (2016, 3) that "robust parties emerge not from stable democratic competition, but rather from *extraordinary conflict*—periods of intense polarization accompanied by large-scale popular mobilization and, in many cases, violence or repression."

The PT's movement origins and pivotal role in opposition to the military regime thus set the party on a distinctive path that shaped its democratic vocation (Barros 2022). Brazil experienced a slow, incremental, and negotiated transition to democracy whose terms were largely "imposed" by the military (Karl 1990). Although the PT did not join in the elite political pact making (Hagopian 1990, 162), it played an important role in the construction of a new democratic order and sought to "promote a more democratic and egalitarian political culture in Brazil" (Hunter 1995, 432). Union activists linked the absence of representation on the shop floor to the lack of democracy in the national government (Seidman 1994), and starting with the strike waves of the late 1970s (French 2020, 247–263), the movement currents that spawned the PT kept strong social pressure on the military to accept a democratic opening. After fifteen years of a military-imposed two-party system with highly restrictive forms of electoral contestation, the dictatorship began to legalize new political parties in 1979. It allowed multiparty competition in national legislative elections in 1982, as well as the direct election of mayors and state governors. The fledgling PT took advantage of this electoral opening to propose a list of candidates, earning 3.55 percent of the vote and electing eight representatives to the 479-seat Chamber of Deputies. Although the PT's electoral appeal was initially quite limited (Keck 1992, 143), its presence in civil society was more formidable (Avritzer 2002; Barros 2020, 77), and the party played a prominent role in the Diretas Já (Direct Elections Now) protest movement in 1983–1984. This movement demanded direct presidential elections rather than the military's carefully scripted plan for indirect elections through an electoral college composed of national senators, federal deputies, and state representatives.

Although the Diretas Já campaign failed to sway the military, leaving Brazil to transition to civilian leadership by means of indirect presidential elections in 1985, the movement clearly positioned the PT as a proponent of democratization and a leading advocate for its progressive deepening following the regime transition. It also was the party's first real experience with *frentista* coalitional politics—a key instance of political learning (Power 2022, 164). Seeing democracy as a popular victory over a military dictatorship helped to solidify the party's commitment to institutional politics and electoral participation—a process that was not without sharp conflicts, especially between radical and moderate internal factions and also within each faction, several of which contained more revolutionary Leninist and Trotskyist currents (Ribeiro 2008, 200) that advocated for the development of different party organizational models (Barros 2022, 93–118). As we discuss in the next section, conflicts intensified as the party pursued public office and obtained governing experience in legislatures and subnational governments, but the generational cohort effects that emerged from the exposure to authoritarian rule and the struggle to restore democracy proved to be resilient.

Democratization and Roads to Power

The PT and the PSCh were both central players in their respective democratic transitions, even as the transitions left behind important institutional legacies of authoritarian rule. Despite these legacies and the presence of radical currents in both parties that once advocated revolutionary alternatives, the PT and the PSCh treated democratization as a popular conquest over reactionary forces that had sought to destroy their activist networks. In restoring basic civil and political rights, regime transitions provided shelter from persecution and allowed leftist parties to resume practicing politics in the open and aboveground. They also opened new channels of representation at both local and national levels that allowed party leaders to pursue public office, influence policy choices, and reach out to broader constituencies beyond their core networks of committed activists. Both parties brought their more radical currents into the fold by recasting socialist objectives in terms of popular empowerment and the deepening of democracy to make it more inclusive, participatory, and responsive to popular needs. As Hunter (2011, 308) states with respect to the PT, "While it called for socialism, the PT's endorsement of democracy was unequivocal."

The starting points for attempts to deepen democracy were quite different for the two parties, however. The PT entered Brazil's gradually opening democratic arena as a small, newly founded party with a radical reputation, limited electoral appeal, and no significant political allies—but an unusually strong organizational presence in a vibrant civil society and diverse social movements (Barros 2022). From this modest beginning, the PT sought to expand its democratic influence from the bottom up and from the institutional margins of the democratic order to its central core. The PSCh, by contrast, was a historical party with broader electoral appeal and, through its newfound alliance with the centrist Christian Democrats, access to the commanding heights of state power from the day Pinochet stepped down on March 11, 1990. In the PSCh, the process of ideological and strategic moderation, along with progressive detachment from and demobilization of militant grassroots activists, was well underway when regime change occurred; indeed, they were arguably a prerequisite for the regime change. In the PT, these internal transformative processes would occur later, very gradually, as the party broadened its electoral base, expanded its influence in formal institutional arenas, and began to contest political power at the national level.

The PT's Road to Power

The PT entered electoral politics shortly after its founding, as the political liberalization associated with the 1982 mayoral, gubernatorial, and national assembly elections organized by the military (Keck 1992, 143) provided ample opportunities for the party to extend its organizational reach, campaign for public office, acquire governing experience at local and/or national levels, and ultimately influence public policy. Electoral participation, along with the broader restoration of civil liberties and political rights in early 1985, also meant a major reevaluation of the founding principles of the party (Barros 2022). This process involved significant ideological sparring among competing factions over questions of ideology and political praxis (Partido dos Trabalhadores 1998). In the PT's founding phase, for example, the idea of "participation" was linked to a radical transformative goal—the creation of "popular power" as a necessary step toward the construction of socialism. For this to materialize, party leaders had envisioned the creation of "popular councils" that would delegate decision-making power to social movements (Bezerra 2019, 6–7). The creation of these councils remained largely aspirational, however, making them a major issue of internal dispute in the 1980s.

The champions of this approach were the more radical, "vanguardist" leftist factions of the party that embraced a democratic imaginary of popular sovereignty. However, the collective struggle for democratization in the 1980s—including the party's role in mass popular mobilization for direct presidential elections and its participation in the 1987–1988 Constituent Assembly—strengthened the more moderate internal factions grouped under an umbrella current called Majority Camp (Campo Majoritário).[7] This demonstrated that the party was "comfortable working within Brazilian state institutions" (Barros 2022, 128). In 1986, having elected sixteen deputies to the national assembly, which was charged with drafting a new constitution, the PT had a voice in constructing the institutional design and social rights enshrined in the new democratic order. Indeed, party representatives were active in channeling societal input, presenting popular amendments to the draft constitution, negotiating and writing different provisions, and building coalitions—especially with the leftist wing of the Brazilian Democratic Movement (PMDB)—to try to advance the PT's progressive goals. Even though the PT voted against the final constitutional text (Barros 2022, 137–138), its participation and experiences in coalitional politics strengthened a democratic imaginary of institutionalized pluralism within the party. As Majority Camp became dominant, it advocated for the "adoption of more flexible electoral strategies, especially with regard to the concept of democracy and participation, and the prioritization of parliamentary activity as a method of action" (Santos et al. 2020, 10). Although the different political currents within the PT largely converged on a redefinition of the party's socialist objectives in terms of more open-ended visions of "democratic deepening," vigorous debates existed regarding the different institutional channels and strategies to attain it (Bezerra 2019, 9).

Winning elections was vital for implementing these visions. Although the PT performed better in the 1985 mayoral elections, particularly in state capitals, and in the 1986 legislative elections, a major electoral breakthrough for the party occurred only in 1988 (French and Fortes 2005, 19). The party gained control of thirty-one municipalities, including major state capitals and rural districts where the MST had been active (Keck 1992, 157). Subnational governing experience allowed PT leaders to experiment with new institutional innovations to promote citizen involvement, such as participatory budgeting, which were introduced in PT-governed cities, including São Paulo, Belo Horizonte, Belém, Recife, and Porto Alegre (Baiocchi 2003; Wampler 2007; Avritzer 2009; Goldfrank 2011). This promotion of participation was in line with the party's emphasis on *basismo* discussed earlier, and it was mostly associated with the party's more radical, non-hegemonic factions (Santos et al. 2020, 25; Bezerra 2019, 20). Regardless of which internal faction promoted these participatory channels more or less intensely, or how effective the channels were, a commitment to honest government and grassroots participation would become the trademarks of the "PT way of governing" (*o modo petista de governar*) in the 1990s. These principles defined the party's distinctive goals of mass empowerment and inclusion as it struggled to gain national power. This effort to engage civil society and community-based activist networks in the policymaking process sought not only to "reverse priorities" but also to translate these efforts into policies that favored workers, the urban and rural poor, and other subordinate social actors (Bittar 1992, 210). The expression "PT way of governing" was pervasive in the 1990s, but it was more than just a phrase.

It was both an effort to consolidate and "brand" the party as fundamentally different from establishment parties and an attempt to create new, nonclientelistic ways of "doing politics" in a country where traditional elites notoriously relied on patronage and rent seeking to co-opt support and demobilize the poor. These ideas were deeply embedded in the party's ethos and a distinctive marker of its political reputation (Abers 2000; Baiocchi 2003).[8] And because these ideas produced electoral rewards, they became a cornerstone of the party's strategy to gain national-level power (Bezerra 2019, 9).

In general, however, successful governing experiences at the subnational level in the 1990s led the PT to focus increasingly on institutional and electoral strategies, as opposed to strengthening social mobilization (Lacerda 2002, 63) or boosting unbridled "popular power." The party concentrated its efforts on strengthening its electoral base from the local to the national level by expanding its foothold in subnational governments and in Brazil's national Congress (Ribeiro 2014, 88). While the party was undergoing a major internal evaluation of its ideological profile and relationship to democracy (Barros 2022, 170–175), its electoralist orientation prompted the PT to gradually "moderate its discourse, platform and political practices, in terms of public administration and/or its attitude toward other actors, such as in the political alliances it formed" (Ribeiro 2014, 89). Growing pragmatism in office (Couto 1995; Samuels 2004) led to a progressive demobilization of the party's organized social bases, especially as the PT became electorally competitive at the national level and expanded its institutional presence, making a return to a project of mass mobilization increasingly difficult. Competitive pressures also forced a major shift in the party's approach to alliance making. Initially restricted to like-minded leftist parties (Hunter and Power 2005, 129), that approach allowed the PT to consolidate its brand as an internally cohesive leftist party in opposition (Hunter 2010), and it even strengthened links between the party and its bases (Baiocchi and Checa 2007, 42). However, a growing commitment to working with other political forces in a landscape of a fragmented party system had strong demobilizing effects. Although it signaled moderation to voters and was highly successful electorally, it also revealed the limits that the party would encounter at the national level—or the formidable capacity of "the system" to incorporate the PT while at the same time subverting its radical agenda.

At the national legislative branch, the PT developed a distinctive antineoliberal orientation. PT representatives gradually moderated their views, however, from advocating socialism and radical change to a pragmatic but progressive platform aimed at reforming capitalism to protect the interests of the underprivileged. Experience in the legislative opposition helped not only to strengthen the party's position in representative institutions but also to consolidate Lula—who served as a federal deputy between 1987 and 1991 as well as a member of the Constituent Assembly—as a prominent political figure with national aspirations. During those years of political learning, moreover, he gained crucial "experience in logrolling and legislative compromise" (Power 2022, 165). These experiences in legislative coalitional politics allowed the party, with Lula at the helm, to project itself onto the national political arena as a viable alternative to the status quo (Secco 2011). That shift in reputation would become crucial for the party's success in the 2002 presidential victory—when Lula was elected on his fourth try.

A first failed attempt occurred in 1989, Brazil's first direct presidential election under the new democratic order. In a highly fragmented presidential race, Lula surprisingly advanced to the presidential runoff against right-wing candidate Fernando Collor but fell just short of capturing the presidency. This was in a context of economic crisis and high social mobilization, and Lula used his "politics of cunning" learned during his formative union years (French 2020), which deepened during his years on the congressional floor, to "assemble a much more inclusive coalition in the runoff than would have been possible in the mid-1980s" (Power 2022, 165). Although he led the polls in the early 1990s—during a period of economic stagnation, high unemployment, and hyperinflation, along with a corruption scandal that led to Collor's impeachment and resignation—the following two presidential campaigns in 1994 and 1998 were both unsuccessful against Fernando Henrique Cardoso of the Brazilian Social Democratic Party (PSDB). In spite of those losses, Lula "emerged as the recognized voice of opposition to the Cardoso government" and its general course of neoliberal reform (French 2020, 8). Cardoso's presidencies, however, generated real improvements in the standard of living of vulnerable sectors of society; even before he was elected president, his 1994 Plano Real currency stabilization dramatically curbed the hyperinflation that hit the poor disproportionally, and it generated an economic recovery in the middle of the decade. Cardoso capitalized on this stabilization to build a powerful electoral coalition and win the presidency in 1994 and 1998—against Lula's opposition to the Plano Real (Guidry 2003, 97–98).

Cardoso's victories not only prompted significant introspection within the party (Barros 2022, 195–190) but also led the PT to further moderate its positions in response to these defeats. The party began to back away from its commitment to socialist transformation and adopted a broader approach to alliance making—first to include other parties unambiguously on the left and then, starting in the late 1990s, with centrist and even conservative actors (Power 2022, 166). This recalibration was both a response to electoral losses and a reflection of deeper economic and societal changes that had driven unions and social movements into retreat. It also revealed how, by the end of the 1990s, the party's bottom-up participatory élan had been weakened and "gradually displaced by a reverential delegation of personal authority to Lula" (Power 2022, 162; also see Keck 2022, 154). By 2002, on Lula's fourth try, the PT was "stronger in the institutional field but weaker in its organic base" (French and Fortes 2005, 27). A new economic downturn in Cardoso's second term helped make Lula the front-runner in the 2002 presidential race. Attempts by conservatives to instill fear among potential Lula voters, in a context of capital flight in anticipation of a PT victory (Campello 2015), led Lula to release "Letter to the Brazilian People" (da Silva 2002), which signaled to the public and to domestic and international markets the PT's commitment to work within the constraints of the existing economic model (Samuels 2004, 1004). This could be seen as a part of a vote-maximizing strategy, as Hunter (2010) argues and French (2020, 8) questions, or as a tactical concession required to calm the markets, ensure governance, and reconcile the different democratic imaginaries in an effort to deepen democracy. Either way, running on a platform that avoided socialism and the confrontational rhetoric of his earlier campaigns, Lula won 46.4 percent of the first-round vote and reached 61.3 percent of the valid votes in the runoff election against José Serra of Cardoso's PSDB. The challenges of deepening democracy under major institutional and market constraints would soon surface.

Coalition Politics and the Socialist Party's Road to Power in Chile

Deepening democracy would pose challenges in Chile as well, as Pinochet's legacies were formidable, and the regime transition was a tenuously negotiated compromise (see Weyland 2014, chap. 6). The democratic opening began in 1987 as the protest movement against Pinochet tapered off and the dictatorship, under the terms of its 1980 constitution, began preparations for a 1988 plebiscite designed to extend Pinochet's rule for another eight years. In an effort to try to legitimize the plebiscite, the regime liberalized authoritarian controls over the media, civil society, and party activities, and exiled leftists cautiously reentered the country, encouraging a major reconfiguration of Chile's fractured socialist camp. The process of socialist renovation had splintered the party in exile, while the bulk of its internal organization, save for some high-profile leadership networks, had remained wedded to more orthodox positions, including support for the Communist Party's strategy of "popular rebellion" against the dictatorship. The democratic opening in advance of the plebiscite strongly reinforced the weight of the party's renovated currents, however, which included the PSCh's highest-profile leader, Ricardo Lagos. To circumvent the dictatorship's proscription of the PSCh—and to broaden their appeal to moderate and independent centrists and leftists—Lagos and his supporters formed a new "instrumental party," the Party for Democracy (PPD), which facilitated Socialist participation in the opposition coalition that challenged Pinochet in the plebiscite. The Socialist-PPD bloc joined the Christian Democrats (PDC) in spearheading a sixteen-party coalition (known as the Concertación de Partidos por el No) to defeat Pinochet, by a vote of 56 percent to 44 percent, in the October 1988 plebiscite.

Following Pinochet's defeat, the dictatorship negotiated a limited package of constitutional reforms with the democratic opposition, setting the stage for national elections in December 1989. The Concertación elected PDC leader Patricio Aylwin as president in Chile's first competitive national election since 1970, ushering the country back to democratic rule in early 1990. The PSCh regained its legal status and reunified its varied factions in late 1989, under the leadership of its renovated currents, while maintaining a close alliance and a "dual militancy" arrangement with the PPD within the larger Concertación coalition. The Socialist-PPD bloc placed six of its members in Aylwin's initial cabinet, and it elected sixteen deputies to the 120-member lower house of congress, along with seven other Socialists elected through various coalitional arrangements. The definitive victory of the renovated current within the PSCh, and the party's strategic partnership with its offshoot, the PPD—a top-heavy party with a pronounced technocratic bent and minimal grassroots organization—ratified the increasing professionalization of the Socialist bloc and the diminished role of organized popular constituencies in the internal life of the party.

Despite the package of constitutional reforms, the military regime was able to impose explicit measures to limit popular sovereignty and tie the hands of new democratic rulers. Indeed, it bequeathed a constitutional framework that was "both formally democratic and intensely elitist," with "interlocking rules" that placed "filters and barriers between the people and the state," blocked majority rule, and discouraged parties from mobilizing popular constituencies for policy reforms (Rhodes-Purdy and Rosenblatt 2023). These interlocking rules included a bloc of unelected right-wing senators, an electoral system that overrepresented conservative parties, supermajority requirements for legislation in key areas of public policy, and a powerful and conservative constitutional court that subordinated social citizenship claims to the rights of private property. This institutional engineering prevented the Concertación from governing with a congressional majority, despite consistently winning a majority of the vote (Siavelis 2000), and it allowed conservative forces to wield a legislative veto to block major political and economic reforms. Any effort to deepen democracy thus encountered serious institutional constraints, including "wall after wall of undemocratic veto players" in a system designed "to preserve the balance of power that had been structured under military rule, where economic elites were protected against incursions by democracy and redistributive demands" (Rhodes-Purdy and Rosenblatt 2023, 245). Fearing that any effort to mobilize mass support to overcome these barriers would be highly polarizing and potentially destabilizing for the democratic transition, the PSCh and the Concertación agreed to operate within their constraints. They negotiated compromises with the right on modest policy reforms and eschewed popular mobilization while adopting a more technocratic approach to policymaking in office.

These strategic choices were also conditioned by the market revolution that Pinochet's University of Chicago–trained technocrats had overseen in Chile—Latin America's, and the world's, first grand experiment in neoliberal restructuring (Foxley 1983; Silva 1996). Thoroughly reversing Allende's reforms, the "Chicago Boys" had privatized hundreds of state-owned enterprises; returned land to private owners; liberalized trade; eliminated price controls and subsidies; slashed social programs, public employment, and real wages; liberalized labor markets; and privatized education, health-care, and pension systems. Business elites and right-wing parties—overwhelmingly pro-Pinochet—were ardent defenders of the neoliberal model, especially as the Chilean economy recovered from the early 1980s debt crisis and resumed rapid growth behind new agricultural and commodity export sectors over the latter half of the decade. The leaders of the Concertación knew that business elites' tolerance of a democratic transition was conditional on a continuation of the economic model.

Indeed, by the time the Concertación took office in 1990, the PSCh and PDC had relaxed their initial staunch opposition to the neoliberal model and signaled their intent to keep the core of it intact. The coalition pledged to respect private property, maintain fiscal and monetary discipline, and continue privatization and trade liberalization policies. Still critical of neoliberalism's highly unequal distribution of riches, the coalition promised a more inclusionary "growth with equity" strategy (Weyland 1997). Social policy initiatives, however, largely adhered to neoliberal prescriptions, including targeted poverty-relief programs and credits to help students access the privatized higher education system, and they were largely implemented in a top-down manner with little input from below (Huber and Stephens 2012, 160–162; Garay 2016, chap. 7). Because unions had been decimated by military repression, economic restructuring, and labor-market flexibilization under Pinochet—the rate of unionization plunged from 32 percent of the workforce in 1973 to 9.9 percent in 1983 (Roberts 1998, 152)—the PSCh advocated reforms to the labor code to strengthen workers' bargaining rights, but conservatives in Congress blocked any significant reform. Likewise, business elites and their conservative allies in Congress were strenuously opposed to higher taxes and forced the Concertación to negotiate a very modest tax reform in support of its social programs (Fairfield 2015).

Not surprisingly, organized labor became critical of the limited scope of reforms under the Concertación administrations (Ahumada 2023, chap. 2), and leadership of the national labor confederation passed into the hands of dissident Socialist and eventually Communist union officials. Chile's union movement, however, was a shadow of its former self and had little capacity to mobilize pressure on the government from below. Likewise, the community-based activist networks that had been central to the protest movement against Pinochet largely demobilized during the democratic transition and the period of economic recovery (Oxhorn 1995). The economic growth spurt that began in the mid-1980s continued in the 1990s under the Christian Democratic leadership of Aylwin and his successor, Eduardo Frei Ruiz-Tagle, with annual growth rates exceeding 6 percent over a fifteen-year period. Sustained growth increased employment, helped raise real wages, and fueled the Concertación's targeted poverty-relief programs, allowing the democratic government to sharply reduce poverty levels over the course of the 1990s without implementing the kinds of major redistributive reforms that would have altered the prevailing distribution of income—and provoked elite opposition. The policy-making process was thus dominated by elite-level negotiations and technocratic management, as the Concertación did little to experiment with the kinds of participatory innovations that the PT adopted in Brazil. Indeed, in an effort to stabilize the new democratic order and alleviate the fears of conservative business and political elites of a return to the Allende era, the Concertación discouraged social mobilization outside formal institutional channels (Hipsher 1996; see also Delamaza 2010). As a junior partner in a coalition government at the helm of Latin America's neoliberal showcase, the PSCh was not about to rock the boat.

Ultimately, the PSCh, like the PT, was well positioned to reap electoral rewards and capitalize politically on its growing moderation and institutional participation. In both countries, new democratic regimes stabilized over the course of the 1990s and enjoyed broad-based support after extended periods of authoritarian rule. Regime transitions, combined with the collapse of communism in the Soviet bloc, thoroughly marginalized revolutionary currents within the left in both countries (Castañeda 1993). With the end of the Cold War, the collapse of state-led development during the Latin American debt crisis of the 1980s, and the ensuing process of neoliberal structural adjustment and market-based globalization across the region, socialism itself was largely extinguished as a viable development alternative, even if it remained a badge of political identity and dissent from neoliberal orthodoxy. Because neoliberal reforms had been implemented by more conservative actors in Brazil and Chile, however, the PT and the PSCh could both channel part of this dissent within democratic institutions and broaden their electoral appeal by promising moderate redistributive reforms and committing themselves to established rules of the democratic game.

This strategy, intrinsically social democratic in nature, fell well short of the radical transformative projects that both parties had aspired to during their respective struggles against authoritarian rule. It had the advantage, however, of mitigating the perceived threat of a leftist takeover in countries where conservative political actors and military institutions were still important players, and where powerful business elites and financial markets were capable of punishing any leftist government that strayed too far from established neoliberal models. As we will explain, this moderate strategy was powerfully reinforced by the institutional contexts in which the PT and the PSCh ascended to power after the turn of the century, which placed severe constraints on their modes of governance and sharply narrowed their range of policy choices.

Institutional Contexts and Trajectories in Power: Explaining the Conformist Temptation

Having amply demonstrated their democratic vocations and moderated their respective platforms, the PT and the PSCh ascended to power in the early years of the twenty-first century through highly institutionalized alternations in office within established democratic regimes. The PSCh captured the presidency with Ricardo Lagos in 2000 by means of a leftward shift in the balance of power within the ruling Concertación coalition. The PT, by contrast, elected Lula to the presidency in 2002 in his fourth campaign as an opposition candidate, as Cardoso departed the political scene and his PSDB lost ground to the PT. Neither country faced the levels of mass social protest or systemic crises that caused party systems to implode in countries like Venezuela and Bolivia, opening the door for populist-left "outsiders" to challenge the political establishment.

Indeed, the PT and PSCh continued to compete against other established parties, and neither party commanded an electoral or legislative majority on its own. Both parties had to rely on broad, multiparty coalitions to win elections, access executive office, and pass legislation. The PSCh and PT thus forged pacts with centrist parties or even, in the Brazilian case, with conservative parties that were willing to cut a deal. These political alliances were vital for governance, but they placed major constraints on the transformative agendas of the PT and the PSCh by ensuring that reforms would have to be negotiated with nonleftist coalition partners. The resulting compromises reinforced the moderating tendencies in both parties and ensured that elite bargaining, rather than social mobilization, would define the terms and content of reformist initiatives. This distanced both parties from organized popular constituencies, contributing to their process of mainstreaming within the larger political system. Democratic institutions thus incorporated leftist parties and provided opportunities for them to thrive in the electoral arena—but, in the process, transformed them into pillars of political establishments they had once sought to eclipse. Following multiple terms in office, the eventual demise of the PT and the PSCh followed very different scripts, but both could be traced to the party's conformance to the logic of their respective postauthoritarian political orders and to their internalization of a mode of "doing politics."

The Rise and Fall (and Comeback) of Brazil's PT

After being in opposition for over two decades while also growing at the subnational level, the PT won the presidency in 2002 and placed a politically atypical presidential candidate—a former union leader, Lula—in national office.[9] On the face of it, Lula's capture of the presidency meant something potentially deeper than any routine alternation of power in a country with marked social hierarchies. As Perry Anderson (2019, 53) notes, "The symbolism of a former shoeshine-boy and street-vendor achieving supreme power in the most unequal major society on earth speaks for itself." Although other Brazilian presidents had been of comparatively humble origins, what set Lula apart is that he remained "culturally a worker from a poor rural family, raised in the industrial belt round São Paulo" (P. Anderson 2019, 53). His government was the first to represent and empower the working class and the poor and was greeted with huge enthusiasm by subordinate social actors across the board. It was seen as a collective triumph of a generation of leaders that not only helped to put an end to the military regime but also formed a mass party capable of bringing a worker, one "of them" to power.

By the time the PT arrived in office in its fourth attempt, however, it was a far more moderate, bureaucratic, and professionalized party than it was in the 1980s, even though others still regarded the party as more radical (P. Anderson 2019, 113). Decades of opposition in Congress had created strong incentives for party representatives and leaders to moderate their views, from openly advocating socialism to taking a pragmatic but progressive position toward greater equity and social inclusion. In combination, subnational experiences of public administration and national legislative opposition helped to switch the party's internal balance of power in favor of the more moderate internal factions (Ribeiro 2014), which prioritized an electoral-institutional rather than a social mobilization strategy. Those factions came to accept and adapt to institutional constraints and existing ways of doing politics, steering the party in that direction (Hunter 2010).

The type of political learning acquired during those executive and legislative experiences, and the hard realities of power, including the strong influence of Brazilian domestic capital, also encouraged broad alliance making across the ideological spectrum. In the 2002 presidential campaign, running on a platform that avoided confrontational rhetoric and sought to calm the markets, the PT allied with the small right-wing Liberal Party (PL). The PL provided José Alencar, a man with close ties to Brazil's business community, as Lula's vice presidential candidate (Hunter 2007, 463). And instead of articulating a clear alternative to the dominant market orthodoxy, Lula signaled his acceptance of the constraints of the economic model. That strategy ended up yielding electoral majorities to capture the presidency in the second round, but it helped to atrophy the linkages with the party's social movement bases, deeply undermining the prospects of leading processes of radical transformation and "deepening" democracy down the road. By the time Lula captured the presidency, decision-making within the party had become more centralized, and the party leadership had also become increasingly distanced from the social movements out of which the party had emerged. Indeed, the social mobilization capacity of these movements themselves had sharply declined (P. Anderson 2019, 69; also 105).

The PT took office in 2003, not only embracing democracy as institutionalized pluralism and accepting its limitations—a by-product of its formative experience—but also via routine turnover. This meant that its access to power was not premised on doing away with the existing political order, as in the cases of the populist left. It also meant that the party embraced gradualism, or a weak form of "reformism" (Singer 2019). The PT ascended to power facing an extremely fragmented and undisciplined party system and broader state institutions riddled with patronage and rent seeking, and it was unable to escape these institutional strictures.[10] Indeed, seen in a regional comparative perspective, the country was an outlier, with an exceptionally large number of parties in Congress.[11] The presence of a multitude of parties without party discipline made governing without a majority extremely difficult. Similar to what had happened at the local level, the PT governed nationally from a weak legislative position, as it never held more than a fifth of seats in Congress, and was forced to rely on its leadership of an ideologically heterogeneous and fractious governing coalition (Hunter 2010, 147; Pereira et al. 2016; Taylor 2020, 241).[12]

The PT's inability to secure a stable legislative majority and full control of core state institutions made the party highly dependent on centrist and even conservative allies to ensure governability and design and implement coherent reform policies (Gómez Bruera 2013)—a dynamic that pulled the party further away from its organized social bases, tempered their most radical energies, and weakened their mobilizational capacity. It also created strong incentives for the party to buy support the "traditional way" (P. Anderson 2019, 113; see also French 2020, 239). Having learned and internalized Brazil's transactional model of elite-level brokerage politics all too well, the PT became caught in a web of corruption scandals early in Lula's presidency, starting with the 2004–2005 Mensalão vote-buying scandal.[13] This scandal involved monthly payments to members of Congress to support the PT's agenda and was arguably born of political necessity, as a way to increase legislative capacity to pass at least some of the party's reform agenda.[14] In the long run, however, it left the party vulnerable to opportunistic betrayals and a furious right-wing social and political backlash. Dias et al. (2021, 76) identify the political context surrounding this scandal as key in the development of an emerging field of grassroots right-wing activism, in a country where political parties of the right were organizationally weak, fragmented, and opportunistic.

To a significant degree, Lula's policies and those of his handpicked successor, Dilma Rousseff, contributed to reducing historical inequalities and expanding social inclusion (Hagopian 2016, 127).[15] While Lula's presidencies (2003–2010) largely respected the economic model of Cardoso (1995–2003) and even intensified it (Hunter and Power 2005, 131), major innovations took place in the realm of social policy (Huber and Stephens 2012, 190–192; Garay 2016, 153–161). The results were impressive achievements in terms of substantive social citizenship rights, including social policy expansion in areas like nutrition, housing, and education; steady growth in the real minimum wage; the reduction of poverty and inequality; and significant improvements in the standard of living of the poor.[16] During Lula's two terms, land reform efforts—which had been increasing since the 1990s alongside the MST's increasing power (Wolford 2010)—expanded further, although the reformers' achievements have been widely criticized (see Ondetti 2008). Under Rousseff, land reform then declined quite substantially (Sauer and Mészáros 2017). Signature policy innovations like the Bolsa Família (family allowance) program were widely criticized on the left for lacking a participatory design and having limited effects (Lavinas 2013, 28). Nevertheless, the PT reinforced an existing safety net, expanded policies that reached excluded populations, and created broadly inclusive and highly visible benefits (Garay 2016, 123). These policies enjoyed wide popular support and politically rewarded Lula—more than the PT—in electoral returns (Hunter and Power 2007; Samuels and Zucco 2018, 35–42).[17]

Despite these efforts to build a more inclusive democracy and a more robust safety net while facing strong institutional constraints, the party has a share of responsibility in explaining its own downfall. As noted, the party had deep roots in radical social movements committed to new ways of "doing politics," but in the process of winning elections, calming financial markets, and building supportive governing coalitions, it had become largely detached from the social movements it once championed. Sustained formal democracy, economic stability, and advances in social inclusion provided the foundation for a shift toward a more participatory democracy—a shift that started before the PT came to power in 2003 but that the party intensified (Baiocchi 2003)—and new forms of cooperative state–civil society relations (Rich 2019; Wolford and French 2016). But the PT encountered significant challenges translating successful local-level participatory experiences into the national political arena (Goldfrank 2011b) and sustaining grassroots linkages (Handlin and Collier 2011, 149–151). And while those participatory experiences opened policy access to previously excluded groups, the results in terms of inclusion of those groups and their demands were mixed at best (Mayka 2019, 261–263). During the PT administrations, Brazil became a more inclusive and participatory democracy than ever before (Hagopian 2016, 124) and made enormous strides in implementing egalitarian policies (Sader 2013). However, in the process of winning elections and exercising power, the PT grew increasingly professionalized, distanced from social movements, and deeply immersed in the normal give-and-take of Brazilian politics. To a large extent, the party was remolded in the image of the very institutions it had once pledged to transform.

The PT paid a high price for accommodating (and arguably profiting from) the "old order" while failing to translate its ideological commitments to social and political change into a resilient transformative strategy—a fatal blow to the party's reputation as an agent of radical change. The beginning of the end can be traced to the social protests that broke out against Dilma Rousseff in June 2013—a cycle of protests that came to be known as the 2013 June Journeys. Initially, Rousseff's government—like that of the Socialist Michelle Bachelet in Chile—faced challenges from the left, with opposition movements emerging from outside the PT. The protests included social actors that were seen as "natural" social bases for the PT, which expressed grievances related primarily to the quality of public services like transportation. Small leftist parties were also broadly represented in the protests (Winters and Weitz-Shapiro 2014). As the protest cycle developed, claims were broadened to include improvements in other unmet demands, including urban infrastructure, health care, education, police violence, LGBTQ+ and women's rights, corruption, taxation, and more. As Alonso and Mische (2017) show, part of this protest can be explained by the inability of the PT to ensure continued responsiveness in a context of rising expectations (see also Bradlow and Gold 2025). For example, improvements in inequality reduction under Lula and Rousseff and the expansion of higher education generated expectations for continued improvements. Meanwhile, new generations of progressive actors came to "see the PT government as the status quo," so when transportation fares increased and the economy contracted, fear of losing the recent gains turned into frustration and anger at the PT (Alonso and Mische 2017, 147). Support for the PT declined dramatically, and as McKenna (2020, 614) documents, "between 2012 and 2016, the PT lost 60% (374) of its mayorships" and a significant portion of congressional seats.

As protests continued, however, those on the left became less visible, and protest turned into a more elite and middle-class conservative movement. This new wave of protest challenged the PT from the right flank, pushing back against the party's inclusionary gains. These gains included advances in the realm of domestic workers' rights, which increased costs for middle-class families; affirmative action policies in universities, which reduced advantages for their children; and the socioeconomic rise of Afro-Brazilians, which enabled greater participation in traditionally white social spaces (Porto 2023). Right-wing activism was hardly new in Brazil, but the organizations that had been organizing during Lula's two terms as president swelled in size, and a strikingly heterogeneous set of actors united in a common cause against the PT and deployed an impressive mobilizational capacity (Dias et al. 2021, 75). From then on, mobilized actors on the right became "well positioned to take advantage of these general feelings of dissatisfaction" and launched an anti-PT crusade (Dias et al. 2021, 78).

Although Rousseff's popularity declined, she was reelected president in 2014 by a thin margin. But the PT (along with top politicians and officials of all parties) became engulfed in a second massive corruption scandal called the Petrolão.[18] This system-wide scandal was related to money laundering on public-sector contracts and involved prominent PT leaders, revealing that the PT had made extensive use of kickbacks from Brazil's state oil giant Petrobras to get Rousseff elected. This led to several arrests of prominent PT leaders, including sitting senators. The scandal involved other parties as well, but in the end, it generated the large-scale rejection of the PT as the leading ruling party, including a dramatic drop in partisan self-identification and major setbacks in subnational elections (Mainwaring et al. 2018, 195; see also Hagopian 2016, 126).[19] This political backlash culminated in massive pro-impeachment demonstrations, where social protests helped to cement "anti" partisan identities and rabid hostility toward the PT (Samuels and Zucco 2018; see also Borges and Vidigal 2018).[20] Defections and a loss of support from allies further weakened the PT. All this, in turn, unfolded within a changing international environment, following the decline in commodity prices in 2013 and a rise in interest rates, which constrained Rousseff's space to maneuver. A deep recession beginning in late 2014—combined with austerity measures that clashed with the PT's reputation and campaign platform—aggravated the severity of the challenges. This not only isolated Rousseff but also accelerated the PT's downfall, creating in turn "new opportunities for previously peripheral right-wing civil society organizations to seize on outrage at revelations from anti-corruption prosecutions to articulate a range of socio-cultural grievances" (Bradlow and Gold 2024, 16).[21]

The PT left the presidency not through a routine alternation in power but following the highly politicized impeachment of Rousseff on charges of fiscal improprieties, which the PT denounced as a legislative coup d'état (Barros 2022, 344).[22] Rousseff was impeached when key PMDB allies, Vice President Michel Temer and the leader of the Chamber of Deputies, Eduardo Cunha—both directly implicated in major corruption scandals—turned on the president when she and PT legislators refused to shield them from investigations (De Micheli et al. 2022, 18–19). While adversaries, including former allies, clearly did not play nice, and worsening economic conditions played a devastating role in Rousseff's demise, the long-term effects of the conformist temptation had left the PT with weak political defenses, embroiled in a corrosive corruption scandal, and vulnerable to reactionary backlashes "from below" in a context of intensified anti-PT sentiments (McKenna 2020, 614–616; Bradlow and Gold, 2025, 12–15).[23]

The impeachment process allowed Rousseff's vice president, Temer, an ally of Brazil's traditional ruling class, to assume power until the 2018 election of Jair Bolsonaro in a context of compounding crises and deepening polarization (Hunter and Power 2019; Nicolau 2020). A retired military officer and an apologist for the military regime that ruled Brazil between 1964 and 1985, Bolsonaro was a radical proponent of a strict law-and-order discourse. He filled his government with military ministers, and with staunch support from evangelical networks (Smith 2019), he advocated a culturally conservative and antirights agenda "in the name of the family" (de Souza Santos 2023). This agenda included opposition to abortion, LGBTQ+ rights, and sex education in schools (Rennó 2023), as well as hostility toward environmental measures and indigenous rights that limited the expansion of agro-export activities and cattle ranching in the Amazon region. Altogether, Bolsonaro threatened to charter Brazil along an increasingly exclusionary and authoritarian path (Power and Rodrigues-Silveira 2018, 264–265). Nevertheless, Brazil's democratic courts and institutions, its robust state bureaucracies, and its active civil society pushed back to preserve the democratic core (Rich et al. 2024) and, at times, mobilized to defend previous inclusionary gains (Anria et al. 2024).

Ultimately, however, the price of conformism and participation in "the politics of patronage" was too high for the PT (French 2020, 239), even if some programmatic moderation was unavoidable to build a governing coalition in Brazil's fragmented democratic institutions. Weakened and largely demobilized after fourteen years of PT rule, the party's organized social bases could offer only limited countermobilization to defend a president of its own ranks from a highly politicized impeachment process—something unthinkable in earlier phases of the party's development—or to resist conservative and reactionary forces seeking to reclaim their customary hold on the reins of state power. As Samuels and Zucco (2018, 3) note, "Brazil's way of doing politics had changed the party more than the PT had changed Brazil's way of doing politics." Following Rousseff's impeachment and during Bolsonaro's presidency, moreover, the PT found it difficult to reconnect with its historic grassroots bases. The party became increasingly personalized, relying heavily on Lula's venerable aura and continued popularity, and moving steadily in an electoral-professional direction. Meanwhile, social and political mobilization on the right flank fundamentally altered the anti-PT side of the country's major divide (Smith 2019; Mayka and Smith 2021). Over time, that mobilization led to the demise and displacement of the centrist PSDB by conservative forces, and to the displacement of traditional conservative parties by the more autocratic far-right alternative of Bolsonaro—trend lines that pulled the parameters of Brazilian politics further to the right.

Lula himself was blocked from running for president again in 2018—while he was leading in the polls—when he was convicted and sent to prison on politically contested money-laundering charges (Morais 2024). The narrative of a politically motivated prosecution of Brazil's most popular leader offered a convenient scapegoat for a party facing significant challenges. Following his release from prison the following year, after the Supreme Court nullified his conviction, Lula reentered the political fray, climbing a steep hill to restore the PT's political credibility in the eyes of Brazilians and reconnect with its organized social bases. The former president staged an impressive electoral comeback, defeating Bolsonaro in a highly polarized second-round election by a razor-thin margin in October 2022. Bolsonaro refused to concede defeat and made baseless allegations of electoral fraud, and according to Brazilian federal police allegations, he conspired with top aides and military officials to organize an *autogolpe* (presidential coup) to block the transfer of power (Nicas 2024). The coup attempt culminated in a violent storming of the presidential palace, the national Congress, and the Supreme Court by Bolsonaro supporters following Lula's inauguration in January 2023, which was put down by militarized police forces and the Brazilian army. Bolsonaro was subsequently disqualified from running for office again until 2030 by Brazil's Superior Electoral Court for making false claims about electoral fraud, then convicted and sentenced to twenty-seven years in prison for plotting a coup.

The PT and anti-PT polarization will surely continue to be a prominent feature of Brazilian politics in the years to come. Even after Lula's return to the presidency in early 2023, Bolsonaro's supporters maintained a formidable opposition bloc in Congress and laid the groundwork to challenge an aging Lula or his PT successor in the next round of elections, with or without Bolsonaro himself. While the PT is a much more moderate force than it was at its founding, and less deeply rooted in organized popular constituencies, it remains more socially grounded than its competitors, and it is the primary political actor committed to redistributive reforms and more inclusionary democracy. The party's commitment to pursuing such reforms within the parameters of democracy's conflict-regulating institutions has been amply demonstrated, and its tendency toward compromise has only intensified during Lula's third term (Singer 2024). Nevertheless, a patently autocratic and socially conservative right led by Bolsonaro and his social and political allies remains a major driving force for polarization on the anti-PT side of the central political divide—even if affective polarization can be found among followers on both sides of that divide (Samuels and Belarmino 2024).

The Rise and Eclipse of Chile's PSCh

After a decade of centrist, Christian Democratic leadership, Chile's center-left coalition elected Socialist presidents Ricardo Lagos in 2000 and Michelle

Bachelet in 2006 and 2013 (the latter following one term out of office). The PSCh-PPD bloc within the Concertación strengthened electorally over the course of the 1990s, approaching parity with the Christian Democrats in legislative elections. Lagos—who had risen to prominence for his bold defiance of Pinochet as an opposition leader under the dictatorship, then served as a high-profile cabinet minister during the presidencies of Aylwin and Frei—easily defeated the Christian Democratic candidate in the Concertación's 1999 primary election, winning more than 70 percent of the vote. In the presidential race, Lagos narrowly prevailed with 51.3 percent of the second-round vote, defeating the candidate of the conservative coalition, Joaquín Lavín of the staunchly pro-Pinochet Independent Democratic Union (UDI).

Despite this leftward shift in coalition leadership, policy continuity combined with technocratic, incremental reforms were the hallmarks of the Lagos administration (Rhodes-Purdy and Rosenblatt 2023). Given the structural power of private capital in Chile's liberalized, export-driven economy, and business elites' close ties to conservative parties that were overrepresented in Congress (Fairfield 2015), any effort to break with neoliberal orthodoxy was sure to encounter fierce political and financial market resistance. It would also bump up against a wall of institutional barriers erected by the military regime to safeguard neoliberalism from popular majorities under democracy. Pinochet's reformed constitution—what Weyland (2014, 221) called "the legal scaffolding" for the post-1990 democratic regime—was designed "to entrench the primacy of the market," relegate the state to subsidiary roles, and insulate policymakers from societal pressures (Heiss 2021, 35). Indeed, it contained "extreme protective measures designed to limit the exercise of popular sovereignty" (Rhodes-Purdy 2017, 201), ranging from malapportioned representation to burdensome supermajority requirements and judicial vetoes exercised by a powerful and conservative Constitutional Tribunal. The balance of power in Congress alone precluded any radical change of course; when Lagos took office, the PSCh-PPD bloc held only 27 of 120 seats in the lower house of Congress elected in 1997, and six out of forty-eight senators. Unelected senators gave conservatives a majority in the upper house, and while Christian Democratic and small-party allies within the Concertación provided Lagos with a legislative majority in the Chamber of Deputies, it was certainly not one inclined toward radical change. These multilayered, interlocking, and countermajoritarian institutional constraints ensured that societal demands for economic and social reform would be filtered through extensive elite-level political bargaining among governing and opposition parties, along with their technocratic networks with expertise in specific policy spheres. The consensual approach to policy-making that resulted earned Chile the moniker of *la democracia de los acuerdos*, or "the democracy of agreements."

A decade of democratic governance had demonstrated that the Concertación could significantly reduce poverty levels by managing economic growth and making modest efforts to distribute its benefits downward, and Lagos had no intention of departing from that model. Lagos made his priorities explicit, stating, "The first question is to have order in your economic and fiscal policies; second, to have growth, and then after you have growth ... we are going to discuss how to distribute the outcome of that growth, and not the other way around" (*Commanding Heights: Ricardo Lagos on PBS* 2002). As such, Lagos reassured business elites of policy continuity by selecting market-friendly technocrats to head the major economic ministries, and he continued "an informally institutionalized pattern" of government-business negotiations on economic policies (Fairfield 2015, 69)—an incorporation of elite societal actors into Chile's "democracy of agreements." His government also adhered to strict fiscal and monetary discipline as the economy rebounded from a mild recession induced by the Asian financial crisis of the late 1990s. Under Lagos, Chile adopted many policies favorable to private business interests, negotiating a series of free-trade agreements with international partners, reducing already-low tariff rates, easing regulatory burdens on the private sector, relaxing short-term capital and exchange controls, shoring up the independence of the Central Bank, and encouraging private investment in infrastructure and state-owned mining projects. The government produced large fiscal and foreign trade surpluses that generated savings for a "rainy day" economic stabilization fund, which Bachelet would eventually use to cushion the impact of the 2008–2009 global financial crisis.

Within the constraints of Chile's neoliberal model, the Lagos government tried to address social needs through a range of programs that were highly technocratic in their design and implementation and would not require large tax hikes or structural changes in the economy to deliver (Garay 2016, chap. 7). In response to the Citizens Council convoked to help formulate policies to strengthen civil society, Lagos issued a presidential directive for government ministries to develop specific goals for the incorporation of civic participation in their programs (Delamaza 2009, 2019). This and other related initiatives had little concrete effect on citizen engagement, however, and they clashed with the overarching technocratic orientation of government policymaking. As Pribble (2013, 48–50, 75–78) notes, social programs were designed through a top-down process that allowed the austere Finance Ministry to serve as a check on the various social ministries, and the programs generally provided individualized benefits that were not designed to elicit collective action or social mobilization from below. To the contrary, technocratic policymaking sought to insulate social programs from civil society actors, associating the latter with "populist" patterns of mobilization that protect vested interests, magnify societal demands, undermine program efficiency, and heighten the risks of political polarization and elite conservative backlash. As Rhodes-Purdy (2017, 195) argues, the Allende experience had left behind an "intense fear of popular mobilization and political engagement" that first developed on the right but "later spread to a renovated left" that accompanied Lagos to power.

Following a technocratic logic, then, the Lagos government launched a new family assistance and counseling program that provided modest cash benefits for Chileans living in extreme poverty, and it invested in targeted housing, education, and infrastructure programs in low-income communities. It also expanded credits to help students and their families pay tuition fees in the highly privatized education system. Most ambitiously, Lagos initiated a new public health-care plan with universal coverage for a wide range of medical needs, ensuring that low-income citizens without private health insurance would have access to basic medical care (see Delamaza 2009; Pribble 2013; Garay 2016).

To help fund the health-care and family assistance programs, Lagos induced Congress to enact a modest 1-percentage-point increase in the value-added tax, and a small hike in the corporate tax rate was offset by a cut in personal income taxes (Fairfield 2015, 83–87). Lagos also introduced reforms to shorten the legal workweek to forty-five hours, create unemployment insurance for formal-sector workers, legalize divorce, and, shortly before he left office, eliminate the notorious institution of unelected senators left behind by Pinochet. Business and conservative opposition in Congress, however, blocked other efforts to raise tax revenues, narrowed the scope of major social reforms, and forced the government to water down a labor reform bill that might have strengthened unions and enhanced their collective bargaining rights (Haagh 2002, 105–106).

With Chile enjoying the fruits of the post-2003 commodity boom, Lagos left office a popular president, having demonstrated that the PSCh could govern responsibly and introduce pragmatic social reforms while maintaining political and economic stability. He was succeeded by Michelle Bachelet of the PSCh, who had served Lagos as both minister of health and minister of defense. Bachelet was the daughter of an air force general who had served under Allende and died in prison, following torture, under Pinochet; Bachelet herself had been held in a detention facility and exiled by the dictatorship. She earned 53.5 percent of the vote to defeat Lavín in the January 2006 second-round election, becoming South America's first elected female president.

Bachelet took office with a commitment to extend the social reforms initiated by Lagos and expand access to public provision of social services. In particular, she created a basic public pension system for low-income Chileans, including women and informal-sector workers whose work-life experiences left them outside or inadequately covered by the private pension system established under Pinochet (Pribble 2013, 78–82). She also expanded coverage under Lagos's public health-care plan, provided financial support for low-income families to purchase homes, made kindergarten mandatory, and created new preschool and day-care programs for young children. In response to concerns that Chile's "social technocracy" discouraged popular participation in the democratic arena, Bachelet also pledged to open new channels for civic engagement (Weeks and Borzutzky 2012).[24] These plans were quickly overtaken by events on the ground, however—namely, the onset of the first of three major cycles of social protest, each one larger and more diverse than the last. Together, these protest cycles frontally challenged and eventually eclipsed Chile's vaunted "democracy of agreements," exposing the elite-level character of its transpartisan consensus, its failure to engage or incorporate mass constituencies, and its ultimate dependence on the institutional vetoes and countermajoritarian principles of a constitutional order bequeathed by a military dictator (Heiss 2021, 38).

The protest cycles of 2006, 2011–2012, and 2019 politicized the social fault lines of Chile's neoliberal model—its deeply entrenched inequalities and exclusionary properties—as well as its technocratic mode of governance under mainstream political parties. Successive waves of protest were directed primarily at the social pillars of the neoliberal model: the privatized systems for education, pensions, and health care, along with its liberalized labor markets, environmental effects, and the steep cost of public services like transportation. With each wave, the protest movements became more "systemic" in their willingness to confront the political establishment in its entirety, as they incorporated a plethora of distinct material grievances into a wholesale attack on the detachment of Chile's party elites, the dearth of opportunities for popular participation, and the technocratic, consensus-seeking political logic of the post-1990 democratic settlement. Far from channeling this social mobilization, the PSCh became a target of it, along with the rest of a party system that was clearly outflanked to the left by emerging grassroots activist networks.

After a decade and a half of relative social quiescence following the regime transition, the protest cycle began in earnest in April 2006, shortly after Bachelet's inauguration. Rebelling against a heavily privatized and market-based education system that the Organisation for Economic Cooperation and Development (2004, 254–255) said "was consciously class-structured" and "highly stratified" in its access to quality education, high school students went on strike and conducted sit-ins that paralyzed hundreds of schools (Donoso 2013). This so-called *pingüino* (penguin) rebellion—named for the color scheme of the students' school uniforms—was soon followed by protests by public transportation users and subcontracted mining workers (Somma 2012, 305). The student rebellion was put on hold when Bachelet created an expert advisory commission to engage in dialogue with student and teacher representatives (Weeks and Borzutsky 2012). The proposal for education reforms that came out of the dialogue, however, was heavily watered down by the time it worked its way through Congress in 2009, and the final package left the basic structure of the privatized education system intact (Pribble 2013, 104–105). This party-brokered, elite-level compromise on education reform was widely interpreted as a betrayal by the student movement (Bidegain Ponte 2015, 252–255), and it served as a prelude to the massive social uprisings looming on the horizon.

Indeed, while Chile remained, for the time being, electorally stable—and widely regarded internationally as having one of the strongest and most institutionalized party systems in Latin America (Mainwaring 2018)—evidence was mounting of citizen detachment and disengagement from formal representative institutions, political parties in particular (Heiss 2021, 34). Voter registration and turnout steadily declined during the first two decades of democratic rule, especially among youth, and public opinion surveys showed Chileans ranking at or near the bottom of Latin American countries for party identification, interest in politics, and participation in election campaigns and local-level politics (Luna et al. 2010, 135, 143, 170; UN Development Programme 2015, 34). As Luna and Altman (2011) argue, Chile's parties were stable but top-heavy and uprooted, with weak ties to societal actors, shallow grassroots organizations, and diminishing legitimacy as representatives of societal interests in the democratic arena.

Although Bachelet's personal appeal and deft management of the 2008–2009 global financial crisis allowed her to finish her term with approval ratings higher than 80 percent, she was constitutionally barred from running for reelection. Amid splinters and defections within the PSCh and the Christian Democratic Party (PDC), Bachelet was unable to transfer her popularity to the Concertación's candidate for the 2009–2010 presidential race, former president Eduardo Frei Ruiz-Tagle, of the PDC. Frei was defeated by the candidate of the conservative coalition, the wealthy businessman Sebastián Piñera, allowing the Chilean right to capture the presidency by democratic means for the first time in over half a century.

Piñera's honeymoon proved short-lived. Disillusioned with the government's tepid response to the *pingüino* rebellion, and dismayed by the return of even more orthodox neoliberal governance under Piñera, college students spearheaded a massive uprising in 2011–2012 that took aim at the highly privatized education system. Protesting the high costs of student debt, the quality gap between public and private schools, and the prevalence of for-profit education providers, student occupations forced hundreds of universities and secondary schools to close. The protest movement received widespread support from professors, teachers' unions, and the national labor confederation, culminating in more than nine hundred demonstrations across the country on a national day of protest in August 2011 (Guzman-Concha 2012, 410). With environmental, labor rights, women's rights, and Mapuche indigenous rights activists mobilizing as well, the 2011–2012 protest cycle expressed a multifaceted critique of Chile's neoliberal model, entrenched social and economic inequalities, and a transpartisan political establishment wary of rocking the boat (Donoso and Bülow 2017).

Leading activist networks clearly outflanked the party system, including the PSCh, on the left programmatically, as they articulated demands for structural reforms—such as free universal public education and an end to for-profit schools—that went well beyond anything attempted by the Concertación in office. This outflanking was also evident in the organizational realm, as political leadership of student and labor organizations had moved progressively leftward over the course of the democratic period. Political activism among youth was increasingly channeled outside, then ultimately against, the party establishment; whereas Christian Democratic and Socialist student activists led the majority of university federations in the powerful Confederation of Chilean Students (CONFECH) in the 1990s, they were progressively displaced by Communist activists and, eventually, independent left "social collectives" as the protest movements got underway (Bidegain Ponte 2015, 235). In 2012, the Socialist leadership of the central labor confederation, the United Workers Central (CUT), also passed to a Communist slate headed by a leader of the teachers' union with close ties to the student protest movement. Simply put, political linkages between the PSCh and activist networks in civil society had progressively withered over the course of two decades in power, as the party became highly professionalized and technocratic in its approach to governance, and unwilling to entertain the fundamental reforms of the neoliberal order that social actors were demanding.

Although Bachelet returned to office after the 2013–2014 elections with a new coalition—the New Majority (Nueva Mayoría), which incorporated the previously excluded Communist Party—and pursued a reform agenda that introduced free university education for low-income students, Chile's crisis of representation only intensified (Castiglioni and Kaltwasser 2016; Luna 2016; Piñeiro Rodríguez and Rosenblatt 2020). A series of corruption scandals, including one that involved Bachelet's son and daughter-in-law, undermined the credibility of established parties across the ideological spectrum, reinforcing steep secular declines in partisan identification and voter turnout, especially among youth. Bachelet was able to replace Pinochet's much-criticized and highly disproportional binomial electoral system with a new system of proportional representation, but in a context of widespread antipathy for mainstream parties, this reform predictably reinforced preexisting tendencies toward party-system fragmentation. Student and other movement activists founded a new, more radical leftist coalition known as the Broad Front (FA) to contest the November 2017 national elections, challenging the PSCh-led New Majority coalition as well as the Christian Democratic Party, which withdrew from the center-left coalition after thirty years together. A weakened and divided New Majority selected an independent journalist as its presidential candidate, who narrowly defeated the FA candidate in the first round of the elections to make it into the runoff, only to lose to the right-wing candidate Piñera in the second round of a close election in which less than half of registered voters bothered to participate.

The 2017 election effectively marked the end of Chile's once-interrupted, Socialist-led left turn. The conservative Piñera's second term in office, however, was even more tumultuous than his first. Within two years, Piñera's presidency and the entire post-1990 democratic order were challenged by a third, and even more massive, social uprising. On October 17, 2019, the *Financial Times* published an interview with Piñera in which he lauded Chile's stability in a turbulent Latin America. "Look at Latin America," he stated. "Chile looks like an oasis because we have stable democracy, the economy is growing, we are creating jobs, we are improving salaries and we are keeping macroeconomic balance" (Stott and Mander 2019). The following day, a hike in metro fares sparked protests that started whimsically with high school students hopping over metro turnstiles but swelled into the broadest and most contentious cycle of protest yet, as workers, pensioners, women's and indigenous rights activists, and others joined students in open revolt (Somma et al. 2021). The mobilization placed over a million protesters on the streets of Santiago in a single day, and by the end of the year, it led to takeovers or attacks on over eighty metro stations as well as buses, banks, gas stations, supermarkets, and Santiago's landmark telecommunications tower. With Piñera proclaiming, "We are at war," the government declared a state of emergency, deployed military troops in a futile effort to restore order, and resorted to heavy-handed police repression. The protest cycle left a toll of thirty-one deaths, some seven thousand arrests, and over thirteen thousand people injured, including more than 350 who suffered eye damage from police shotgun pellets (Amnesty International 2020).

In an effort to quell the uprising, Congress reached an agreement with the Piñera government to do what was previously unthinkable—hold a referendum on the election of a constituent assembly to draft a new constitution, in replacement of the one left behind by Pinochet. The 1980 constitution had been modified on a number of occasions since the democratic transition got underway (Fuentes 2015), but the political impasse created by the protest movement opened the door to a much more far-reaching "refounding" or reconstitution of Chile's democratic regime itself. Although the COVID-19 pandemic put the referendum and the protest movement on hold, the referendum was finally held on October 25, 2020. A resounding 78 percent of voters supported writing a new constitution, and 79 percent voted for a directly elected constituent assembly rather than a body half comprising sitting members of Congress. Elections for the 155-member constituent assembly were subsequently held in May 2021, under rules that ensured gender parity in the assembly and reserved seventeen seats for representatives of indigenous communities. A broad coalition of right-wing parties that had opposed a constituent assembly participated in the assembly elections and elected the single largest bloc of delegates, although it fell short of the one-third of seats required to veto constitutional reforms. The second-largest bloc of delegates was elected by a leftist coalition led by the FA and the Communist Party, followed by a list of independent candidates drawn largely from civil society networks—clearly demonstrating that Chile's massive protest movement was not fully channeled by any party organization, new or old. There was, in short, no Chilean equivalent of Bolivia's movement-based MAS party. The PSCh-led successor to the center-left Concertación and Nueva Mayoría coalitions placed the fourth-largest bloc of delegates in the assembly.

The eclipse of the old order was ratified in national legislative and presidential elections in late 2021. The presidential race was notable for its bilateral outflanking of traditional parties on both the left and the right—in short, a process of left-right electoral polarization within an overarching context of antisystem polarization (see Luna 2024). On the right, the mainstream party coalition was overtaken by far-right candidate José Antonio Kast of the Republican Party, an ardent supporter of Pinochet's legacy noted for his hard-line law-and-order positions on immigration, crime, and social protest; his support for orthodox free-market economics; and his opposition to abortion, same-sex marriage, and indigenous multiculturalism. On the left, the PSCh—once again in alliance with the centrist Christian Democrats—was overtaken by a new leftist front with movement origins that sponsored the candidacy of former student leader and FA deputy Gabriel Boric. Boric defeated Kast in the runoff election with 55.9 percent of the vote and proceeded to form a cabinet with a majority of female ministers and prominent leadership roles filled by veterans of the 2011–2012 student protest movement.

Chile, therefore, embarked upon a new left turn in the aftermath of the 2019 *estallido social* (social explosion)—but it did so under the leadership of a new generation of movement-spawned activists with a very different set of formative experiences from those that shaped the Socialist Party's left turn after 2000. It also did so in a context of regime-level institutional uncertainty that, in dramatic contrast to the institutional constraints of the earlier left turn, seemed to provide novel opportunities to exercise constitutive powers, expand social citizenship rights, and deepen democratic participation.

The exercise of constitutive powers, however, required that the activism and energy of Chile's social movements be channeled into the formal institutional arenas where any refounding of the democratic regime would occur. This proved inordinately difficult in a context of acute polarization and political gridlock. The elected constituent assembly—dominated by representatives of the political left and independent civil society networks—drafted a markedly progressive constitution that would have made Chile a plurinational state with new rights for Indigenous peoples, along with women, LGBTQ+ individuals, citizens with disabilities, and the environment. It was also designed to supplement the country's market economy with a much stronger set of social citizenship rights, including new rights to education, social security, housing, health care, and digital connectivity (Green Rioja et al. 2022; Piscopo and Siavelis 2023). Conservative and right-wing forces went on the offensive from the outset of the process, however, attacking the credibility of the assembly and proclaiming the new constitution to be a threat to Chile's national unity, public security, and economic vitality. The political winds shifted dramatically over the course of the debate, and in the September 2022 popular referendum organized to ratify the new constitution, a stunning 62 percent of Chileans voted to reject it.

In response to this defeat, Congress passed a law to initiate a second attempt at a constitutional rewrite, one that relied heavily on established parties and technical expertise rather than representatives of civil society (Piscopo and Siavelis 2023). A congressionally appointed commission of experts and lawyers wrote an initial draft based on constitutional guidelines established by Congress itself. This draft was then debated and modified by the Constitutional Council, elected from party lists and dominated by Kast's far-right Republican Party and its conservative allies. Remarkably, the centrist Christian Democratic Party that anchored Chile's democratic transition was unable to elect a single representative to the Constitutional Council. Not surprisingly, the new draft offered strong protections for private property and Chile's neoliberal model, clearly representing political continuity with Pinochet's institutional legacies. It, too, was rejected by more than 55 percent of voters in a popular referendum held in December 2023. Having gone full circle, the Chilean government abandoned its effort to refound the constitutional order, and it continued to operate under the charter whose origins lay in the military dictatorship.

Chile's constitutional stalemate was indicative of the political gridlock and polarization that fundamentally transformed its internationally acclaimed *democracia de los acuerdos*. Dynamics of polarization not only pit the left against the right in a context where centrist parties have dramatically weakened; they are also expressed in widespread societal rejection of parties and political elites system-wide (Luna 2024). Neither the Socialist Party nor the new leftist alternatives spawned by the protest movements have been able to devise a formula to break through the underlying political gridlock—one that is rooted in the ease of mobilizing "negative" popular majorities in opposition to constituted authority and the difficulty of mobilizing a "positive" democratic majority in support of any alternative within formal representative institutions. Although Boric's leftist government has been able to push through a moderate reform of the pension system, an increase in the minimum wage, and a plan to phase in a forty-hour work week, it backed away from its more ambitious structural reforms of economic and social institutions and found much of its progressive agenda overtaken by conservative politicization of immigration, crime, and security issues. Meanwhile, the process of electoral outflanking continued: In presidential primaries held in advance of new national elections in 2025, Jeannette Jara of the Communist Party, a former labor minister under Boric, soundly defeated the candidates of the PSCh and the FA to become the standard bearer of the left in a high-stakes contest against mainstream and far-right conservative forces.

Conclusion

Social democratic left turns led by the PT and the PSCh were heavily influenced by the parties' formative experiences with authoritarianism and redemocratization, as well as the institutional imperatives of building multiparty electoral and governing coalitions in contexts where ruling leftist parties were hardly majoritarian actors. These formative experiences and institutional contexts strengthened moderate currents within the left—those that accepted democracy as a form of institutionalized pluralism—at the expense of more radical currents attached to a democratic imaginary of popular sovereignty. Although both parties made efforts to couple redistributive social reforms with greater popular participation in the democratic arena, progress toward "deepening" democracy was modest, at best—though arguably more substantial in Brazil than Chile. Both parties were able to increase their power and influence by internalizing the logic of elite-level politics in their respective democratic orders: the transactional politics logic of patronage, brokerage, and rent seeking in

Brazil, and the technocratic logic of neoliberal continuity and elite-level bargaining in Chile.

Under this logic of political conformism, both the PT and the PSCh made explicit efforts to avoid highly polarizing strategies of political or economic transformation, and they marginalized or demobilized their internal currents that advocated such strategies. The parties adhered to the formal rules of the democratic regimes they inherited from military dictators, even when those rules were biased against them, and they made little or no effort to use state power as a platform to mobilize and empower mass constituencies. Doing so undoubtedly would have exacerbated the risks and uncertainties of political polarization at an earlier stage of their rule; given their countries' traumatic recent histories and formidable institutional constraints, the cautious and pragmatic course of action the social democratic parties adopted was arguably overdetermined.

Nevertheless, that pragmatic course of action came with its own costs, and it ultimately failed to prevent the eruption of powerful polarizing dynamics. Both parties became increasingly professionalized, top-heavy, and detached from their social bases over time. This detachment became a source of frustration for their popular constituencies, and it left both parties vulnerable to new forms of social protest against material grievances and the political establishments with which they had become synonymous. These protests emerged on the left in both countries; whereas in Chile they spawned movement-based alternatives to the left of the PSCh, in Brazil they exposed the weakness of the PT and opened the door for intense right-wing mobilization that capitalized on a system-wide corruption scandal to bring down the PT. Both countries, therefore, exited the left turn with new and more polarizing forms of sociopolitical mobilization — on the right flank of the party system in Brazil, and on the left flank and, eventually, the right flank in Chile.

As the next chapter shows, the dynamics of polarization were quite different in the populist left turns of Venezuela and Bolivia. Formative experiences and institutional contexts spawned a very different type of governing left in these countries — one beholden to the democratic imaginary of popular sovereignty and susceptible to the intrinsically polarizing political temptations of autocratic authority. It is to these cases that we now turn.

CHAPTER THREE

The Populist Left and the Autocratic Temptation

In contrast to the Brazilian PT and the Chilean PSCh analyzed in the previous chapter, neither Hugo Chávez's Fifth Republic Movement (MVR) in Venezuela nor the Movement Toward Socialism (MAS) in Bolivia was shaped in its formative phase by sustained military repression under bureaucratic authoritarian rule and the struggle to reconstruct democracy. Rather, both populist lefts were newly founded in the 1990s within formal democratic regimes that generally respected civil and political liberties. Although neither of these lefts was seared by traumatic experiences of state repression comparable to those in Brazil and Chile (or Uruguay, in chapter 4), their founding generational cohorts were exposed to deep experiences of social, political, and cultural marginalization under democratic institutions with collusive party systems that often excluded popular majorities from effective representation and political power. These experiences weighed heavily on the democratic imaginaries of both lefts as they organized to challenge mainstream parties, capture public office, and transform national democratic regimes.

These populist lefts were created differently, however. While the MAS was an organic, bottom-up expression of largely indigenous social movements (Van Cott 2005), Chávez's MVR—renamed the United Socialist Party of Venezuela (PSUV) in 2006—emerged in a more top-down manner under the direction of a charismatic leader while drawing support from preexisting grassroots and radical left movements (Fernandes 2010; Ciccariello-Maher 2013). In spite of these differences, both were explicitly committed to breaking down traditional social hierarchies and barriers to political participation. In addition, both lefts rose to power as mass rebellions against traditional parties, political and technocratic elites, and the neoliberal economic models they had imposed under democratic auspices. In both countries, traditional center-left and labor-based political parties had supported and implemented neoliberal reforms following the debt crisis of the 1980s, causing mainstream party systems to converge on market orthodoxy and channeling societal dissent into extrasystemic forms of social and, eventually, electoral protest (Roberts 2014).

The populist lefts in Bolivia and Venezuela, then, were forged by the social and political backlash against the mainstream parties and democratic regimes that imposed market reforms in the 1980s and 1990s. Both were elected on a platform of radical institutional change—including the convocation of constituent assemblies—and they came to power committed to openly confronting the establishment and asserting popular sovereignty, the centerpiece of their democratic imaginaries. In contrast to the social democratic cases analyzed in chapter 2, moreover, they captured governing majorities on their own and gained fuller control of core state institutions. Committed to fighting the establishment and not facing strong countervailing forces with institutional power once elected, the populist lefts in Bolivia and Venezuela enjoyed unparalleled opportunities for the plebiscitary exercise of majoritarian constitutive powers to refound governing institutions. And they did so in ways that concentrated power, causing the gradual erosion of checks and balances on presidential authority, the political marginalization and radicalization of opponents, the partial demobilization of social allies, and the weakening of societal and institutional feedback mechanisms to correct for policy mistakes.

Ultimately, these distortions—products of what we call the "autocratic temptation"—were self-limiting for the left in power. In contrast to the conformist logic described in chapter 2, the autocratic temptation itself was highly polarizing, even in contexts where economic policies and redistributive efforts were not especially radical, as in Bolivia. If the autocratic temptation culminated in a major political defeat for the left and democratic "careening" in Bolivia, in Venezuela it led to a progressive erosion of democratic norms, a drift toward authoritarian rule, and a major humanitarian crisis.

Our analysis makes clear that these leftist projects were neither doomed nor fully autocratic from the start. Indeed, we highlight that, even considering their different founding processes, both lefts contained contradictory internal currents that coexisted in tension with each other (Ellner 2008, 138–174). Some internal currents were independent of vertical authority and oriented toward political autonomy and pluralism, with a serious commitment to liberal representative democracy. Other currents were more skeptical of liberal democracy and inclined toward a democratic imaginary of mass empowerment and popular sovereignty, exercised through a more centralized political leadership. The notion of deepening democracy was arguably a way to reconcile these two democratic imaginaries, but conditions surrounding their access to national power and the nature of the oppositions they faced empowered the latter over the former. Both lefts invoked plebiscitary mandates to "refound" the existing political order and attempted to make democracy more participatory or "protagonistic" (Hawkins 2010b; Brown 2022). These ideas became integral to the construction of new constitutional orders in each country, and both lefts encouraged extensive grassroots participation in practice, at least in their early years in power (Handlin and Collier 2011, 148–150; Anria 2018, 200–201). Ultimately, however, both ruling parties assumed hegemonic forms that clashed with institutional checks and balances, sharply polarized the political arena, raised the stakes of political contestation, and produced destabilizing side effects.

In the pages that follow, we trace the roots of the autocratic temptation by providing a detailed analysis of the formative and historical experiences that shaped the political profile of the populist lefts in Bolivia and Venezuela. Unlike the social democratic cases discussed in chapter 2, the roads to power of these "new" lefts—the distance between their founding and their ascent to power—was much shorter and posed more direct challenges to existing regime institutions. We also document the institutional contexts in which both lefts accessed power, which reinforced these earlier traits and shaped governing opportunities and constraints. Finally, we examine the political defects associated with the autocratic temptation in each country, how they contributed to their political misfortunes, and the extent to which they paved the way for deepening patterns of political polarization.

Formative Processes and Historical Experiences

Hugo Chávez and the Origins of the Bolivarian Left in Venezuela

Although Latin America's "left turn" arguably began at the subnational level with the election of mayors from left-wing parties in major cities in the 1980s and 1990s (Baiocchi 2003; Goldfrank 2011a), it did not take hold at the national level until the election of Hugo Chávez as president of Venezuela in 1998. Chávez was a vintage populist-left outsider, and his election—in a country previously thought to have one of Latin America's most stable and institutionalized party systems (Coppedge 1994)—sent shock waves across the region. The diverse political currents that gradually congealed around Chávez's leadership—Chavismo, for short—were not only a rebellion against Venezuela's established parties and the post-1958 democratic regime they dominated but also a frontal assault on Latin America's neoliberal order and the transnational Washington Consensus that underpinned it (Williamson 1990). A redemptive invocation of popular sovereignty was at the core of this rebellion, and it is an essential starting point for understanding its internal contradictions and the autocratic temptations to which it fell prey.

Although its tentacles reached deep into Venezuelan history, Chavismo was unquestionably a "new" left, a product of the political and economic crises that befell Venezuela's oil-fueled statist development model (Karl 1987; Tinker Salas 2009) and its erratic (and very partial) transition to market liberalism in the late 1980s and 1990s. It was certainly not a left shaped by military repression under bureaucratic authoritarian rule and the struggle to reconstruct democracy. Having transitioned to democracy in 1958 after ten years of military dictatorship, Venezuela was one of only three Latin American countries—Costa Rica and Colombia were the others—not to experience authoritarian rule in the 1960s and 1970s. The democratic regime's founding pact, the Pacto de Puntofijo, was negotiated between the leading parties in opposition to the dictatorship of Marcos Pérez Jiménez in 1958. This pact established a basic consensus around regime institutions and economic policymaking that heavily influenced scholarly theorizing about regime transitions when other Latin American countries returned to democratic rule in the 1980s (O'Donnell and Schmitter 1986). The political pact helped to stabilize the new democratic regime under the leadership of two dominant parties, the left-leaning Democratic Action (AD) and the conservative COPEI (Independent Political Electoral Organization Committee), while inducing other key actors like the armed forces and the national business and labor confederations to accept the democratic process (Levine 1973). What came to be known as the Puntofijo system, however, largely excluded the country's radical left and its affiliated youth and social movements that sought deeper social reforms and more expansive opportunities for democratic participation (Karl 1987), and dissident leftist groups launched a series of guerrilla insurgencies over the course of the 1960s and 1970s.

Over time, the limitations of Venezuela's pacted, two-party democracy became increasingly hard to overlook (Coppedge 1994; Crisp 2000; Buxton 2001). In the 1960s and 1970s, the country's windfall oil rents induced AD and COPEI to converge around state-led development policies. With the debt crisis of the 1980s, however, Venezuela's oil boom went bust, putting fiscal austerity and neoliberal structural adjustment on the political agenda of a country unaccustomed to belt-tightening (Karl 1997). As inflationary pressures mounted and foreign currency reserves dwindled, Venezuela's political leadership postponed the day of reckoning, using price controls to mask the effects of inflation, avoid structural adjustment, and keep the economy growing. The day of reckoning finally came in February 1989, in classic bait-and-switch fashion, or what Stokes (2001) called "neoliberalism by surprise." Newly elected AD president Carlos Andrés Pérez—who had served a presidential term as a free-spending populist during the oil boom of the mid-1970s and campaigned on a platform promising to bring back prosperity—took office and, with foreign currency reserves virtually depleted, quickly imposed comprehensive neoliberal "shock treatment" (Buxton 2003). With the lifting of price controls, a steep hike in bus fares sparked protests that culminated in a five-day popular uprising—the so-called Caracazo—in Caracas and other major cities, when protesters took over the streets, and rioters looted thousands of stores. Pérez declared a state of emergency, suspended civil liberties, and sent in the military to restore order, with thousands of arrests resulting from military sweeps of low-income neighborhoods (López Maya 2005, 61–84). The riots and repression cost somewhere between 246 and 1,500 lives (Silva 2009, 204), and the president's credibility was irrevocably shattered. Indeed, the credibility of the democratic regime itself was increasingly at stake, as the economic crisis was transformed into a political crisis that revealed the limited capacity of the Puntofijo system to channel or respond to dissent.

At the time of this urban uprising, Hugo Chávez was a major in the Venezuelan army and a leader of a clandestine movement of military officers that he and several colleagues had founded as captains in 1982—the Revolutionary Bolivarian Army-200 (EBR-200). Following a modest upbringing as a mixed-race son of rural village schoolteachers in the western state of Barinas, Chávez had used a career in the military as a stepping stone to political activism. As a student in Venezuela's military academy in the 1970s, Chávez studied military and national history and acquired a devout identification with the Venezuelan and Latin American independence hero Simón Bolívar, as well as other nineteenth-century national figures. He also acquired personal exposure to the socially reformist, left-leaning populist military regimes of Omar Torrijos in Panama and Juan Velasco Alvarado in Peru, and he later declared his admiration for their brand of nationalistic civil-military activism (Blanco Muñoz 1998, 38–45; Chávez and Harnecker 2005, 24–28; López Maya 2003, 74–75).

After graduating from the academy in 1975 and entering active military service, Chávez was assigned to a counterinsurgency battalion but later professed to have sympathies for the guerrillas he was sent to combat. By 1977 he was already experimenting with the formation of a clandestine political cell within the army. After returning to the military academy as an instructor in 1980, Chávez founded the EBR-200 in 1982 as a political cell and study group (Blanco Muñoz 1998, 56–58), and he recruited students to join the clandestine Bolivarian movement. Through family and personal contacts, he also established ties to revolutionary networks that descended from Venezuela's 1960s guerrilla movements (Gott 2000, 39–42, 60–62). As Gott (2000, 31) states, therefore, "Hugo Chávez did not emerge from a vacuum," as he was "the heir to the revolutionary traditions of the Venezuelan left." These formative military and insurrectionary influences undoubtedly left an imprint on Chávez's revolutionary imaginary that was at odds with a liberal democratic notion of institutionalized pluralism.

The EBR-200 continued to organize within the military as Venezuela's political and economic crisis deepened over the course of the 1980s. Although Chávez was not among the troops ordered to quell the Caracazo uprising in February 1989, some of his comrades were, and the bloody repression was a turning point for the EBR-200. According to Chávez, "We had passed the point of no return, and we had to take up arms. We could not continue to defend a murderous regime," one that he characterized as a "false democracy that ended up being nothing more than a power-sharing pact between political parties" (Chávez and Harnecker 2005, 32). In an effort to forge a broader civil-military insurrectionary movement, Chávez and the EBR-200 intensified their outreach to radical leftist organizations like Radical Cause (LCR) and the Party of the Venezuelan Revolution (PRV), and the EBR-200 was rebaptized as the Revolutionary Bolivarian Movement-200 (MBR-200). Disagreements over the respective roles of civil and military forces, however, prevented the formation of a secure revolutionary alliance between the MBR-200 and these civilian leftist groups (López Maya 2003, 78–79).

Acting largely in isolation from civilian support networks, therefore, the MBR-200 launched a military coup against Carlos Andrés Pérez on

February 4, 1992. Insurgent forces gained control of several provincial cities, but the troops under Lt. Col. Chávez's command were unable to capture the presidential palace and other key sites in the capital, leading Chávez to surrender and face arrest. As fate would have it, authorities allowed Chávez to appear on television—wearing the red beret that became the symbol of his Bolivarian movement—to admit defeat and call on his forces to relinquish their struggle, "por ahora" (for now), as he put it. The failed coup landed Chávez in prison, but it also made him a symbol of rebellion against the established regime, the two-party system, and the neoliberal economic model supported by both major parties.

The following year, after weathering a second military coup attempt in November 1992, Pérez was impeached on corruption charges for misusing a presidential discretionary fund. The removal of Pérez, however, could not prevent the AD and COPEI from suffering the political costs of a deepening crisis. Although rising oil prices helped Venezuela's newly liberalized economy resume growth in the early 1990s, structural adjustment policies were associated with falling real wages, cutbacks in government social programs, and an increase in the percentage of the population living below the poverty line (República de Venezuela 1995). Simmering discontent led to over three thousand separate protest events between 1989 and 1993, as citizens expressed their contempt for a political establishment blamed for squandering the country's oil wealth (López Maya 2005, 90, 94). This contempt translated into unprecedented vote losses for AD and COPEI in the 1993 national elections; the two historical parties saw their presidential vote share slashed by more than half between 1988 and 1993, finishing second and third, respectively, with less than a quarter of the national vote apiece. The rising leftist movement party LCR finished right behind them in a four-way race won by former president Rafael Caldera, who had broken with the conservative COPEI and launched a new partisan vehicle while campaigning as a critic of Venezuela's neoliberal model.

Upon taking office, Caldera moved quickly in 1994 to pardon Chávez and other MBR-200 leaders imprisoned for their role in the 1992 coup attempt. Once out of prison and barred from reentering the military, Chávez traveled the country to build grassroots civic networks for his political movement, which—in contrast to LCR—rejected electoral participation. Fearing that participation in elections would trap his movement within a decaying system that served corrupt party elites rather than the popular will, Chávez insisted on an alternative—a national constitutional assembly—meant to break with the old order and refound the democratic regime. In the words of Chávez, "I don't think that we skipped a single city, town, encampment, Indian village, or neighborhood. We went from town to town with the flag of the constitutional assembly, building the organization, strengthening it. For example, we set up local and regional coordinators of the MBR 200. We went from being a clandestine military organization to a popular movement, though there was always a military presence; it was a civilian-military movement" (Chávez and Harnecker 2005, 42).

The strategy of electoral abstention, however, was not embraced by all sectors of the MBR-200, which became increasingly heterogeneous as it absorbed civilian activist networks into its ranks. One of Chávez's earliest military collaborators, Francisco Arias Cárdenas—who had commanded troops that captured Venezuela's second-largest city, Maracaibo, during the February 1992 coup—broke with the movement and was elected governor of the oil-rich province of Zulia on the ticket of LCR in 1995 subnational elections. Indeed, the possibility of using existing democratic institutions as a springboard to power led Chávez himself to reconsider his stance as the Caldera government progressively weakened and neither AD nor COPEI seemed poised for a comeback. Following a series of bankruptcies in the liberalized banking sector and a costly state bailout of the financial system, Caldera faced a politically lethal combination of recession, capital flight, and rising inflationary pressures. He ultimately acceded to a package of orthodox structural adjustment measures negotiated with the International Monetary Fund in 1996 (Weyland 2002, 225–226), despite having campaigned against them—in essence, introducing Venezuela's second major round of bait-and-switch neoliberal reform (Roberts 2014, 222–223).

With the political establishment gravely weakened, the doors were clearly open for outsider candidates in the 1998 presidential election. In this context, Chávez and the MBR-200 engaged in vigorous internal debates about the potentials and pitfalls of electoral participation. By April 1997, they had chosen a new course: Chávez would enter the presidential race, hoping that existing institutions would allow him to capture executive power by legal means, and then use that power to dismantle and refound Venezuela's democratic regime. This refounding was symbolically captured in the renaming of the MBR-200 in July 1997 as the Fifth Republic Movement (MVR), as the post-1958 Puntofijo system was recognized to be Venezuela's fourth historical republic. The demand for a constituent assembly and a clean break with the post-1958 constitutional order thus lay at the very heart of Chávez's political project. This project relied heavily on the redemptive imagery of taking power back from a corrupt *partidocracia* ("partyarchy") and reclaiming it for a sovereign people, as embodied in the charismatic populist figure of Hugo Chávez (Zúquete 2008).

The Rise of Bolivia's MAS

Born as a direct creation of a rural social movement in the Chapare region of Cochabamba Department, the Movement Toward Socialism (MAS) was founded in 1995. It followed a bottom-up logic of party genesis, making the MAS a paradigmatic example of a movement-based party—a hybrid fusion of movement and party networks, much like the Brazilian PT during its formative stage of development (Anria 2018). From the beginning, the MAS combined contentious social mobilization with participation in formal electoral politics, and its leaders conceived of it more as a "political instrument" or an electoral arm of a rural-based social movement than a traditional political party (Van Cott 2005, 103). It was created around the idea of achieving "self-representation" of coca growers and other rural social groups in formal institutional politics (García Linera et al. 2004; García Yapur et al. 2015).[1]

The history of the MAS, including its roots in the *cocalero* (coca growers) movement, has been widely documented (Van Cott 2005; Stefanoni and Do Alto 2006; Komadina and Geffroy 2007; Zuazo 2008; Madrid 2011, 2012, chap. 2). It began as a political instrument called the Assembly for the Sovereignty of the People (ASP) and evolved not only in the specific context of the *cocalero* unions in the Chapare region (Burgoa and Condori 2011, 20) but also as part of the more-than-decade-long low-intensity conflict there related to coca grower resistance to the US-sponsored "war on drugs" (Farthing and Ledebur 2004; Postero 2010, 22; Grisaffi 2019, 12–16).[2] This region was, as well, an area of significant migration from other locales, including mining centers and urban spaces, from the 1950s to the 1990s (Canessa 2014, 160). Overwhelmingly indigenous in origins, many of these internal migrants had brought with them a Trotskyist union-organizing (*sindicalismo*) background and a tradition of militant struggle and solidarity, and they played an important role in organizing the coca growers around the idea of forming their own party (Escóbar 2008). By the early 1990s, Chapare coca growers had become the most prominent actors within the Unified Confederation of Rural Laborers of Bolivia (CSUTCB), a national organization that represented highland "indigenous" and "peasant" groups and that, at least since the late

1970s, welded both political identities within the national union hierarchy. Formed in 1979 in opposition to state-sponsored unions, the autonomous and highland-dominated CSUTCB joined the Bolivian Workers' Central (COB) and together with an indigenous women's organization called "the Bartolinas" played a leading role in the country's restoration of democracy in 1982. It also participated in the founding congresses of the "political instrument" as a sponsoring movement.[3]

Although the MAS was born as a small, localized party viewed as an electoral arm for a specific and geographically concentrated rural union movement, it experienced vertiginous growth in a short period of time to become an instrument for a much broader fusion of movement and party networks across the country (Giusti-Rodríguez 2023). Taking advantage of new opportunity structures created by decentralization reforms in the mid-1990s (Kohl 2003), it grew territorially, organizationally, and sociologically at a dramatic speed to become a national political actor by building a web of connections with a wide array of social movements in rural and urban areas (Anria 2013; Giusti-Rodríguez 2023; Poertner 2024). As discussed in the next section, that it emerged so powerfully and quickly onto the national political scene has much to do with the circumstances of *cocaleros* in the early 2000s in Bolivia. Specifically, the MAS capitalized on the explosion of mass protests against neoliberal policies by creating a "master frame" of opposition to neoliberalism, which helped to unify different social actors against the political establishment and the neoliberal model and by providing representation in organized politics to a remarkably diverse set of urban and rural social movements. Although the MAS underwent significant internal transformations during its organizational expansion and pursuit of electoral majorities, it maintained "organic" and more "institutionalized" connections with the rural social movements that founded the party (Anria et al. 2021) and those that participated in anti-neoliberal protests along with the MAS in the early 2000s (Poertner 2024, 72–75).

The centrality of Evo Morales's leadership cannot be overstated. Himself a migrant to the Chapare, Morales started his political career as the secretary of sports for his local union in 1982 — the San Francisco Syndicate. He then climbed the union ladder and was elected executive secretary of the Federation of the Tropics in 1988 (Sivak 2010, 42), in the context of grassroots campaigns against coca eradication. *Cocalero* unionism was his political school; it largely shaped Morales's understanding of politics and democracy, with the latter seen as an extension of union democracy.[4] His leadership was distinctively bottom-up in its origins, but over time, Morales's visibility and personal appeal played a central role in transforming the MAS from a localized party into an electorally viable national party. According to Madrid (2008), part of this can be explained by Morales's adoption of an ethnically inclusive message that had broad appeal among peasants and Indigenous peoples while he was also seeking support from a wider constituency by blending class and ethnic identities.[5]

Unlike the social democratic left cases shaped by bureaucratic authoritarian regimes, the MAS was founded under a formally democratic regime with no legal restrictions on civil liberties but weak safeguards for upholding them. Its founding generational cohort of movement activists, however, was exposed to deep experiences of social, political, and cultural exclusion and seared by the experience of state repression (Oikonomakis 2019, 655) under a fairly restrictive democratic regime that systematically excluded Indigenous peoples and other stigmatized groups from political power (Gamarra 1997). This system, dubbed "pacted democracy," functioned between 1982 and 2003 through a mix of formal and informal power-sharing arrangements between the country's three major political parties. These three parties (Nationalist Revolutionary Movement, or MNR; Revolutionary Left Movement, or MIR; and Nationalist Democratic Action, or ADN) all converged around neoliberal economic and social policies in the 1980s and 1990s (Cyr 2017, 178). Market reforms, in fact, were imposed in Bolivia—as in Venezuela—by parties that had campaigned against neoliberal orthodoxy, dealigning the party system and eroding institutional channels for dissent (Roberts 2014, 274). Under Bolivia's "pacted democracy," the majority of the indigenous population, though formally recognized as citizens since at least the National Revolution of 1952 (Yashar 2005), remained politically marginalized and with little representation in organized politics (Van Cott 2000), whereas the country's traditional parties traded office among themselves and rotated in office. Slater and Simmons (2013) rightly called this "promiscuous powersharing."

The MAS was spawned and molded, then, by social movements engaged in the struggles against the limitations of an exclusionary democratic regime (Postero 2007), and it took advantage of the steep decline of the traditional parties and the established political class to develop its organization. Those largely indigenous movements had long-standing claims to recognition, inclusion, and representation, and starting in the 1970s and 1980s, they began to challenge prevailing notions of citizenship in which they were relegated to second- or even third-class citizenship rights within a political system dominated by white and mestizo minorities (Yashar 2005; Van Cott 2007).

The MAS was a product of these larger struggles, but it also emerged in the specific cultural context of the Chapare region, where coca unions have long functioned as quasi states (Healy 1991), and it came to embrace a democratic imaginary of popular sovereignty since its early days. According to Grisaffi (2019, 11), "for the Chapare coca growers," which sponsored the MAS and still today form its organizational core, "democracy really has nothing to do with what are often taken to be the core elements of the liberal system, including competitive elections, individual liberties, and the secret ballot."[6] In their unions, moreover, Chapare coca growers "pursue a form of direct participatory democracy in which all members of the community meet to debate, decide, and enact their laws" (Grisaffi 2019, 11). That the MAS was formed in the Chapare meant that in its genesis it was infused with collective decision-making traditions found in the coca growers' unions, which provided a framework for decision-making deeply embedded in a "culture of delegation and accountability" (Crabtree 2013, 284). A remarkable feature about the MAS as a party is that coca growers turned these ideas, understandings of democracy, and political practices into a national-level organization that ultimately captured the presidency and governed for fourteen years—attempting, in all this, to carry out a project of mass empowerment.

Several other left-wing ideological currents converged around the MAS, however. The most prominent of these included revolutionary nationalism, a current traceable back to Bolivia's 1952 National Revolution that blended *lo nacional* and *lo popular* in opposition to Bolivia's oligarchic elites and their foreign allies; Katarista Aymara nationalism, which evoked a more ethnically driven form of radicalism; and creole-developed *indigenismo* focused on resisting racism.[7] Despite their differences and distinct emphases on what a desirable society should look like, an understanding of democracy as entailing mass empowerment, inclusion, and equality of substantive outcomes was a unifying thread. Stefanoni and Do Alto (2006, 62) called this blending of ideas a plebeian form of "left-wing nationalism."

According to Molina (2007), the different ideological currents that preceded the MAS and shaped its political profile were highly skeptical of formal, procedural democracy and its institutions. The MAS's participation in the electoral arena, therefore, was largely a tactical shift—a "conversion [to democracy] without faith [in it]" that did not fundamentally alter the party's instrumental approach to democracy as a means to radical egalitarian change (Molina 2007, 107). A group of urban left-wing intellectuals known as the Grupo Comuna played an important role in articulating this vision, and although they were never *the* unified voice of the MAS, they generated a critique of Bolivian democracy and liberal institutions that was a reference point for the Bolivian left.[8] Álvaro García Linera, who would later become Bolivia's vice president under Evo Morales, was arguably the most influential figure in the group, proposing in his writings to replace Bolivia's formal representative democracy with a more participatory and egalitarian democracy—an idea he sustained over time.[9] As he commented in a personal interview in 2013, "If there is no equality, there is no democracy, and we value the more radical and 'deeper' dimensions of democracy higher than representative democracies that are decrepit and in absolute decline" (author's interview with Álvaro García Linera).

Nevertheless, the MAS embraced an electoral path to power rather than an insurrectionary path (Oikonomakis 2019, 656), and it took advantage of the spaces created by formal democracy to expand its base and grow electorally. Morales's leadership was key in the adoption of a pragmatic strategy. He skillfully weaved together the different ideological currents that converged around the MAS and, perhaps more fundamentally, embraced radical rhetoric with a pragmatic approach to politics—two features that would then become hallmarks of his presidencies (Mayorga 2020b). In political campaigns, he promised to "refound" Bolivia to make its state and democratic regime more participatory by allowing social movements—and other actors that had not participated in the first foundation of the country—to be the base of the MAS's national-popular political project (García Linera 2006). As we show in the following pages, this conception was not abandoned throughout Morales's tenure as president from 2006 to 2019, and Morales sustained this view even after his resignation (J. L. Anderson 2020).

Roads to Power

Neither the MVR in Venezuela nor the MAS in Bolivia had extensive experience with electoral politics before the landslide victories that ushered them into power at the national level in 1998 and 2005, respectively. The

MVR captured the presidency behind Chávez in its very first national election, a little over a year after the populist figure founded the party as an electoral vehicle for his insurgent movement, aiming to contest the Puntofijo system within its own electoral institutions. In Bolivia, the MAS had participated in municipal elections as well as two national legislative elections and one national presidential election before Morales's election as president. In neither country was the election of a leftist president a routine alternation in office; both Chávez and Morales were elected on platforms that promised to break with the established constitutional order, convoke a constituent assembly, and refound their respective democratic regimes. As such, both elections had the hallmarks of "constituent moments" whereby highly mobilized mass publics rebelled against established orders to claim constitutive powers and thoroughly reconfigure regime institutions (see Negri 1999; Frank 2010). They were, in short, exercises in popular sovereignty that translated mass social protest into novel forms of mass electoral protest and used the latter to access governing institutions for the purpose of reconstituting them from within.

The Election of Hugo Chávez and the Demise of the Puntofijo System

Chávez's landslide victory in the December 1998 presidential race was hardly a foregone conclusion when he threw his hat into the ring in April 1997. The failed 1992 coup and Chávez's dramatic television appearance assuming responsibility for it had thrust him into the popular imagination as a symbol of rebellion against the old order, and his fledgling MVR had inherited from the MBR-200 an expanding network of grassroots "Bolivarian circles," or local committees, along with municipal and regional coordinators across much of the country. Nevertheless, Chávez had long advocated electoral abstention, and he was a long shot for the presidency when he changed course and entered the race. Indeed, his support initially hovered in the single digits in public opinion surveys of electoral preferences. That would change dramatically over the next year, however, as Chávez and the MVR consolidated their turn to electoral politics and launched their campaign as outsiders unsullied by any connection to a discredited political establishment. Pledging to convoke a constituent assembly and oppose "savage neoliberalism," Chávez quickly established himself as the most viable left-wing antiestablishment candidate in the race. He also built a broad electoral coalition, the Patriotic Pole (PP), which included, among others, his MVR, the Movement Toward Socialism (MAS), the Venezuelan Communist Party (PCV), and the Fatherland for All (PPT), which had split from LCR and taken the bulk of the party's membership with it.

The campaign unfolded in a context of plunging oil prices and a deepening economic recession whose effects were compounded by the Caldera government's adoption of neoliberal austerity and structural adjustment policies. After fifteen years of recurring economic crises and mounting hardships, Venezuela's per capita gross domestic product had fallen by 20 percent, returning to the levels of the 1960s (Crisp 2000, 175). Real wages had experienced a 60 percent plunge, the worst in Latin America (International Labour Organization 1998, 43). The economic crisis not only undermined public support for an aging conservative president who had staked his political comeback on an unlikely critique of neoliberal orthodoxy; it also accelerated the demise of AD and COPEI, the partisan architects and cornerstones of the post-1958 democratic order, as their fate was tightly coupled to that of the regime they had created. Public opinion surveys found that only 6 percent of Venezuelans expressed confidence in political parties, compared to 91 percent who declared a lack of confidence (Luengo and Ponce 1996, 70).

In this context, AD's candidate for the 1998 election was unable to gain any traction, and COPEI opted to support the presidential campaign of an independent conservative mayor of a wealthy district in Caracas, former Miss Universe Irene Sáez. Sáez took the lead in early public opinion polls, but a surging Chávez closed the gap and then overtook her in the spring and summer of 1998 (Canache 2002, 84). In response, AD and COPEI separated presidential and legislative elections and moved forward the latter, hoping this would minimize Chávez's potential presidential coattails and deprive him of a legislative majority. The ploy helped ensure that Chávez would be a minority president—at least at the outset of his term—but the establishment had no institutional formula for blocking his ascent to executive office. With Sáez sinking in the polls, COPEI withdrew its support, while AD abandoned its own candidate and joined COPEI in backing the campaign of an independent conservative ex-governor, Henrique Salas Römer, in a last-ditch effort to derail Chávez. Hardly an antiestablishment figure, Salas Römer had close ties to COPEI and a track record of supporting political decentralization.

Unswayed by the erratic maneuverings of AD and COPEI, the electorate gave 56.2 percent of the presidential vote to Chávez, the candidate with the most impeccable antiestablishment credentials and the most strident critique of Venezuela's neoliberal model. Over the course of his campaign, Chávez reached well beyond his initial base of left-leaning, civil-military insurgents to mobilize support among a broad and diverse cross section of Venezuelan society disillusioned with politics as usual, including sectors of the middle class and even the business community along with the urban and rural poor (Canache 2002; Kronick et al. 2021). His discourse was anti-neoliberal but not explicitly socialist or anticapitalist, and it was antisystem and revolutionary but not antidemocratic (see Blanco Muñoz 1998). Indeed, it pledged to deepen democracy and establish popular sovereignty through a constitutional assembly, and it appealed to many voters with democratic commitments seeking a transformation of the Puntofijo system (Canache 2002; Kronick et al. 2021).

As such, Chávez campaigned for—and received—a democratic mandate to do what he had failed to achieve as an insurgent military conspirator: break apart the Puntofijo system and reconstitute Venezuela's political order. Upon taking office, he wasted no time in demonstrating how the constitutive powers of this new popular sovereignty would be exercised. Doing so, however, revealed the inherent tensions between Chavismo's autocratic origins, its centralized charismatic authority, and its newly mobilized base of diverse voters and grassroots activists with quite different understandings of deepening democracy.

The Vertiginous Road to Power of Evo Morales and the MAS

By the late 1990s, Bolivia's pacted democracy was exhausted, and the country experienced a generalized crisis of democratic representation (e.g., Drake and Hershberg 2006; Mainwaring et al. 2006). The "promiscuous powersharing" between the three traditional parties had enhanced elite coordination and technocratic policymaking, but it also made elites less accountable to voters, and it made politics highly exclusionary of organized popular constituencies (Slater and Simmons 2013).

Ultimately, the collusive nature of the system was its political weakness and carried the seeds of its own demise (Cyr 2017). As a result of the controlled policy space and neoliberal convergence, the left and right distinctions that initially separated the traditional parties lost their meaning and vote choice diminished (Centellas 2007, 183). Pacted democracy gradually eroded support for the traditional parties and created space for the emergence of new populist-left alternatives to represent sectors that were "affected by adjustment policies and unrepresented by the established parties" (Mayorga 2006, 154). The most prominent of these new parties was Conscience of the Fatherland (CONDEPA), which was formed in 1988 by the popular media figure Carlos Palenque (Archondo 1991). CONDEPA made major electoral inroads among indigenous Aymara and Quechua constituencies in cities such as La Paz and El Alto between 1989 and 1997 (Alenda 2003; Madrid 2010, 599).[10] Both cities are key for gaining electoral majorities in Bolivia (Arbona and Kohl 2004).

The collapse of CONDEPA after Palenque's 1997 sudden death created an opportunity for the MAS to become a national-level actor: It allowed the party to capitalize on the electoral inroads and symbolic and cultural strategies made by CONDEPA and, also, to expand its civic and party networks in the department of La Paz, and to a lesser extent in Oruro, Potosí, and Cochabamba. This would allow the MAS to extend its reach in cities and boost its electoral support among poor, urban, and mostly indigenous sectors—excluded majorities that had no firm allegiances to the country's traditional parties—and capture much of the "antisystem" vote.

By the early 2000s, the Assembly for the Sovereignty of the Peoples (ASP)—the MAS's antecedent electoral vehicle for Chapare coca growers—had taken over the United Left (IU), contested national elections under the IU label, and placed four representatives in Congress to represent the Chapare region, including Evo Morales.[11] From there, its representatives challenged US imperialism, its "war on drugs," and neoliberal policies while their social movement bases remained engaged in contentious politics—operating, as McAdam and Tarrow (2010) would put it, between "ballots and barricades." To a large extent, within the halls of Congress, *cocalero* representatives focused their legislative activity on resisting coca eradication campaigns. Seen as a "controversial" figure by the long-standing political elite, Evo Morales was expelled from Congress in January 2002 on charges of inciting violence against coca eradication forces.[12] A likely objective of the expulsion was to neutralize his growing popularity, but that move may have produced the opposite effect. Campaign managers claimed that Morales's expulsion helped to unite a wide array of hitherto fragmented *campesino* social movements and boosted popular support for the *cocalero* leader.[13]

In its vertiginous road to power, the MAS took advantage of the administrative decentralization reforms implemented between 1994 and 1995 and made significant gains in accessing municipal office (Zuazo 2008). Indeed, as Faguet (2013, 282) notes, "The advent of local government in Bolivia was crucial for the rise of the MAS." Although it did not develop a comparable experience to that of the PT by winning major cities or developing a sharply differentiated brand over a sustained period of time (as discussed in chapter 2), the MAS did fill municipal councils across the country—initially, or in the first few local elections, in alliance with established parties. This "served as a platform and training ground, allowing [local leaders] to ascend to departmental and national politics through successive elections" (Faguet 2013, 283). The MAS used those subnational experiences to establish a foothold, project an image of clean government responsive to citizens' needs, and continue developing its territorial organization from the local to the national level.[14] This organizational growth also included attempts to unite the Bolivian left behind its project—for example, by naming first José Antonio Quiroga and then Antonio Peredo as vice presidential candidates in 2002—although the party refused to form formal alliances with the traditional parties, which were seen as corrupt, inefficient, and linked to unpopular neoliberal policies.[15] This "antialliance" position was seen as an attempt to protect the MAS's antiestablishment stance, and it was modified only later on.[16]

A major turning point for the MAS was the 2002 national election, when it captured 27 percent of the vote and significant minorities in both legislative chambers, shaking up Bolivia's pacted democracy. To the surprise of many, Morales, who was seen as an "antisystem" candidate, nearly captured the presidency, and the MAS became the leading opposition party in Congress.[17] By then, it had capitalized on the explosion of mass social protests that emerged between April and September 2000 in response to government efforts to deepen the neoliberal model by privatizing municipal water services—the so-called water wars of Cochabamba.[18] The lack of democratic responsiveness of the traditional parties fatally weakened them electorally. And the heavy use of state repression intended to quell protests produced the obverse effect; it intensified social mobilization and state-society conflict, transforming at the same time Evo Morales and other indigenous leaders—such as the Aymara leader Felipe Quispe—into symbols of rebellion. The MAS swelled in size by harnessing much of the political energy behind those massive, largely indigenous anti-neoliberal protest movements and fostering "trust and a shared identity" (Poertner 2024, 92). And although it did not win the presidency in 2002, it gained a much stronger institutional position in Congress. At that point, the party switched from a focus on street mobilization to congressional opposition, but it never fully abandoned the former (Mayorga 2020, 59).[19]

Antigovernment protests intensified between 2003 and 2005, deepening the crisis of Bolivia's pacted democracy and ultimately leading to the resignation of two successive presidents: Sánchez de Lozada in 2003 and Carlos Mesa in 2005 (Silva 2009, 131–141). While the MAS as a party was not always *the* instigator of the protests, it used the popular uprisings to its advantage. It developed a "master frame" of opposition to neoliberalism and explicitly rejected the restricted democratic regime monopolized by establishment elites. In the process, the MAS expanded its reach in cities—such as La Paz and El Alto—by building a territorial party structure on top of preexisting networks from older parties and grafting onto densely organized civic networks (Anria 2013, 33–55). This expansion was also based on the ability of the party to aggregate interests together by finding common programmatic ground with a diverse array of social movements, including the *campesino* movements that in 2004 had formed a Unity Pact opposing neoliberalism and the traditional parties that managed it. In particular, the MAS embraced the bottom-up demands to convoke a constituent assembly to rewrite the country's constitution and establish the foundations for a plurinational state.[20] As Webber (2010) argues, by adopting the discourse and incorporating the demands of the most mobilized groups during these popular protests, Morales and the MAS ultimately were able to shift the prevailing balance of social forces to their advantage, winning the 2005 presidential election in a landslide and a record majority victory (53.7 percent of the valid votes) since Bolivia's democratization in the early 1980s. In 2006, it assumed national-level power with a mandate for radical change—an agenda of mass popular empowerment developed by the movements that sponsored the party and those others that helped to propel Morales to the presidency.

Institutional Contexts: Popular Sovereignty and the Autocratic Temptation

Although the Venezuelan MVR and the Bolivian MAS had different political origins and relationships to social movements, both parties came to power with democratic mandates to empower "the people" and refound their national constitutional orders. Moreover, they took control of the reins of state power in institutional contexts where democratic regimes were in crisis and mainstream party systems had been gravely weakened and thoroughly eclipsed by their rising populist-left challengers. Institutional constraints on the MVR and MAS, therefore, were relatively weak—especially in the Venezuelan case, where the MVR was able to sidestep or override various checks and balances through the majoritarian electoral appeal of Chávez. The widespread discontent and power asymmetry that structured the Venezuelan institutional context enabled the plebiscitary exercise of constitutive authority—that is, the reconstitution of regime institutions by means of plebiscitary appeals to popular majorities (see Corrales 2018, 118–129). The process of regime reconstitution unfolded by less unilateral means in Bolivia, through a negotiated compromise between the MAS and opposition parties that was subsequently ratified in a popular referendum.

These plebiscitary assertions of constitutive authority were expressions of popular sovereignty par excellence, but they were not without internal contradictions. The contradictions included the tensions between centralized, personalistic authority and more autonomous forms of social mobilization or grassroots, participatory self-governance. They also included the tensions between de facto single-party hegemony and the norms of political pluralism and opposition political rights that are integral to any liberal democratic order. The exercise of constitutive authority in a context of power asymmetry made Venezuela especially susceptible to autocratic temptations, but the MVR and the MAS both contained internal currents that promoted pluralistic visions of deepening democracy and more radically democratic forms of civic engagement and grassroots participation. The autocratic temptation was embedded in these basic contradictions and power asymmetries, but its ultimate resolution was not preordained; outcomes hinged on how these contradictions were managed by governing parties and their charismatic leaders, as well as the responses of their political opponents.

Venezuela: Institutional Change and the Contradictions of Chavismo in Power

Although Hugo Chávez ran for president on a pledge to convoke a constituent assembly and refound Venezuela's constitutional order, there was no clear institutional path for implementing that pledge within the parameters of the existing constitutional order. The Puntofijo-era 1961 constitution under which Chávez took office contained no provision for convening a constitutional assembly. And with the MVR and its allied parties claiming only around a third of the seats in both houses of Congress, there was little chance of securing a constitutional amendment to fully legalize such an assembly.

Nevertheless, Chávez made clear his intent to invoke the constitutive powers of the sovereign "people" by means of popular referenda to circumvent these institutional constraints (Lissidini 2012). Wary of challenging a popular president-elect, the Supreme Court recognized the legality of holding a referendum to gauge public opinion, and it declined to state whether a constitutional amendment was required to convene a constituent assembly (Brewer-Carías 2010, 52). Unimpeded, Chávez used his inaugural address on February 2, 1999—after taking his oath of office "upon this moribund constitution" (Braver 2016, 565)—to issue his first presidential decree ordering a consultative popular referendum on the election of a constituent assembly. Although voter turnout was low, a resounding 81.9 percent of voters supported a popularly elected constituent assembly in the April referendum. In short order, elections were held in July under a new regional first-past-the-post list formula that excluded incumbent officeholders—a clear rebuke of a fragmented and discredited political establishment. Chávez traveled to every state to promote his regional candidate lists, and the majoritarian electoral formula translated his candidates' 65.8 percent of the vote into a crushing majority of 123 out of 131 seats in the constituent assembly (Brewer-Carías 2010, 56; Braver 2016, 567). The assembly, therefore, was a highly partisan body, albeit one that reflected the diverse social and political base of Chavismo. As Velasco (2022, 31) states, it was "a coalition of nationalists, socialists, communists, trade unionists, feminists, human rights activists, civil society reformers, former guerrillas, and former military with wide-ranging views on how to transform Venezuela," ensuring that the new constitution "would reflect rather than resolve tensions between Chavismo's statist, top-down currents and its participatory, bottom-up ones." Diverse civil society organizations also had input in the drafting of the constitution, submitting over six hundred proposals, of which more than half were accepted by the assembly (Lissidini 2012, 166; García-Guadilla 2018, 65).

Against the bitter objections of the opposition-controlled Congress, the assembly declared Venezuela to be in a state of emergency and boldly claimed supraconstitutional powers to reorganize state institutions. Bowing to Chavismo's majoritarian support, the Supreme Court reversed an earlier ruling and upheld the assembly's assertion of constitutive powers. A new constitution was quickly drafted and ratified in yet another popular referendum with 71.8 percent of the vote in December 1999. To symbolize the break with the past, the new constitution formally renamed the Venezuelan state the Bolivarian Republic of Venezuela. More tangibly, the assembly dismissed both houses of the national congress as well as state legislative bodies, and legislative powers were assumed by a committee of the constituent assembly itself (see Brewer-Carías 2010, 57–60). As such, Chávez and the assembly bypassed and then disbanded the representative bodies with electoral mandates of their own that were bastions of the traditional party establishment and potential institutional checks on executive power. The assembly also appointed the Commission of Judicial Emergency to remove and replace members of the judicial branch, including the Supreme Court itself. New elections for all national, regional, and local officials were then scheduled under the auspices of the new constitution in 2000. This allowed Chávez to renew his presidential mandate with over 60 percent of the vote and reconstitute a national legislature in which the MVR and smaller pro-Chávez parties claimed 60 percent of the seats.

Consequently, although Chávez came to power in a country with one of Latin America's oldest democratic regimes and most institutionalized party systems, he encountered remarkably weak institutional constraints on his initial efforts to sidestep, dismantle, and reconstitute Venezuela's governing institutions. The crisis and delegitimation of the old order made institutional checks and balances largely inoperative in the face of Chávez's superior mobilizational capacity, as Chávez was able to use plebiscitary measures and majoritarian support to neutralize and subordinate the courts and sweep aside independent legislative bodies. With strong support in the military and the bulk of "the people" behind him, no countervailing forces existed to block his largely unilateral exercise of constitutive powers.

Ultimately, Chávez enacted popular sovereignty in ways that revealed its internal tensions and contradictions. He employed democratic mechanisms, like popular referenda and an elected constituent assembly, to transform governing institutions, but he did so in ways that skirted the law, concentrated power in the hands of the victors, and deprived political minorities of significant institutional influence. The new constitution strengthened executive powers by extending presidential terms, allowing presidential reelection, and granting presidents the authority to dissolve congress, control military promotions, and convoke popular referenda and constitutional assemblies. At the same time, it also called for new forms of popular participation and "protagonism" in the democratic arena and direct forms of popular accountability, including referenda and recall elections (López Maya 2011, 220; Lissidini 2012; García-Guadilla 2018, 65–66). As Velasco (2022, 31) suggests, Chávez employed political polarization as a weapon to mobilize popular support in his battle against established institutions and political elites—a weapon that served to justify a complete institutional overhaul and the relegation of traditional elites to the political sidelines. In classic populist terms, Chávez adopted a highly moralistic and Manichaean discourse that framed politics as an existential struggle between a heroic "people" and a nefarious elite, depicting the latter as a rancid or "squalid oligarchy" and the corrupt beneficiaries of Venezuela's "partyarchy" (see Zúquete 2008; Hawkins 2010a; Ostiguy 2022). The political animosity that drove polarization was mutual, however, as "public discourse grew more and more acerbic as Chávez took to referring to detractors, especially elites and Puntofijo stalwarts, as *escúalidos* (squalid), while they in turn drew on ever more hyperbolic and at times racist language to denounce Chávez and Chavistas as uneducated apes, puppets of Fidel Castro, and unfit to govern" (Velasco 2022, 33). Likewise, Teichman (2024, 180) finds that Chávez's polarized rhetoric intensified in response to the opposition's rejection of his initial economic policies—some of which were conciliatory in nature—and the vilification of his class, ethnic, and racial background.

Rather than moderating, polarization further intensified after Chávez completed the initial process of institutional transformation and consolidation of power, which dominated the government's political agenda during his first year and a half in office. Despite Chávez's staunch antineoliberal stands, economic policymaking was characterized by more continuity than change during this initial period (Buxton 2003; Corrales and Penfold 2011, 50–51), and while the new constitution called for a reinvigorated role for the state in the economy and a wide range of social citizenship rights, it was not socialist in content. Chávez's primary initiative to address social and economic needs during his first year in office, the Plan Bolívar, involved the mobilization of military personnel to support new public works projects and social services for the poor. He also successfully pushed the Organization of Petroleum Exporting Countries (OPEC) to tighten global oil supplies so as to raise market prices and boost export revenues. Although economic elites in general were wary of Chávez's ultimate intentions, some business owners—typically "outsiders" to the business elites that benefited from close ties to the traditional party establishment—supported the new government and reaped substantial rewards from their collaboration (Gates 2010; Ellner 2020a,

165–174). Business opposition hardened after late 2000, however, when the newly elected unicameral legislature dominated by the MVR granted Chávez "enabling powers" to rule by decree for one year on a wide range of policy issues. Chávez used these powers to pass a package of forty-nine decree laws in November 2001, including measures that allowed for the expropriation of unutilized farmland, increased royalties on oil production, and strengthened state controls over the oil industry and financial institutions (Hellinger 2018, 263–264).

As Chavismo consolidated its control over governing institutions and exercised unilateral decree powers, hard-line tendencies strengthened within the opposition and increasingly resorted to extrainstitutional strategies in a futile effort to bring down Chávez (Gamboa 2017, 2022; Ellner 2022). With AD and COPEI gravely weakened, civil society networks in the loosely organized opposition front known as the Democratic Coordinator took the lead in organizing resistance, including the peak business association Fedecámaras, the AD-aligned Confederation of Workers of Venezuela (CTV), and much of the private media (Jiménez 2021). Fedecámaras and CTV jointly called for a national strike in December 2001, and pro- and antigovernment forces began to organize mass demonstrations and counterdemonstrations in early 2002. Tensions peaked in early April when Chávez unilaterally appointed a new board of directors of Petroleum of Venezuela (PDVSA), the state-owned but largely independent oil company, in an effort to assert greater executive control over its revenues and management in pursuit of national goals. In response, opponents called for another national strike and organized a mass protest march on April 11 that culminated in violent clashes between pro- and anti-Chávez groups. Amid the chaos, Chávez was detained by military forces, and the military command called for the formation of a transitional government. The next day, Fedecámaras leader Pedro Carmona was installed as national president and immediately announced the suspension of the 1999 constitution, the national assembly, and other signature Chavista reforms. The coup triggered a rapid countermobilization by Chávez supporters, however, including junior military officers with troop commands and grassroots civilian "Bolivarian circles" that began to march toward the presidential palace from low-income districts across Caracas. By the morning of April 13, Chávez had made a triumphal return to the presidential palace, the coup attempt in shambles (Ellner 2022).

The aborted coup and Carmona's heavy-handed power grab, which had been welcomed by the US and much of the private media, reinforced political and strategic divisions between moderate and hard-line sectors of the opposition (Jiménez 2021; Ellner 2022). They damaged the opposition's claims to be principled defenders of liberal democracy in Venezuela while reinforcing fears within Chavismo that powerful elite actors both inside and out of the country posed an existential threat to the Bolivarian experiment. As such, they served to justify government efforts to limit the opposition's resources and institutional access (Gamboa 2017, 465–466). These polarizing dynamics were aggravated in December 2002 when the opposition front led by Fedecámaras and CTV called for a general strike and weaponized the oil industry to try to bring down Chávez. PDVSA executives and managers launched an industry-wide lockout, while much of the white-collar technical and managerial staff joined in by going on strike. After two months of conflict and severe economic losses, the lockout and strike fizzled out, and Chávez took the offensive in February 2003 by firing eighteen thousand PDVSA employees and asserting state control over the industry. In so doing, he subordinated PDVSA to the government's strategic political and economic goals just as the region-wide commodity boom was about to get underway.

Having failed to topple Chávez through a military coup, street protests, and an oil industry lockout, the opposition switched gears in 2004 to employ an institutional recourse for removing the president—a recall referendum, as provided for in the 1999 constitution. Despite a massive opposition campaign to gather signatures to initiate the recall process and turn out voters, however, Chávez remained unassailable in the electoral arena. He comfortably defeated the recall effort with 60 percent of the vote, at least partially revalidating—once again by plebiscitary means—a democratic mandate that had been tarnished by acute political conflict and hardball institutional tactics. With the onset of the commodity boom swelling Venezuela's state coffers with oil rents (Corrales and Penfold 2011, 54–61), and with Chavismo by far the best-organized political force at the grass roots, a demoralized opposition made little effort to contest municipal and state gubernatorial elections later in 2004. Claiming a lack of confidence in the political independence of electoral institutions and fears of voter fraud, the opposition boycotted legislative elections in 2005, giving the MVR and its allies complete control of the national assembly (Gamboa 2017, 467). Now openly declaring Venezuela to be on the path to socialism for the twenty-first century, Chávez won reelection as president in 2006 with 62.8 percent of the vote, the high point of his political and institutional powers. The following year, Chávez formed a new unified official party—the United Socialist Party of Venezuela (PSUV)—through a merger of his MVR with other smaller parties that supported his government.

This high point, in fact, provided an unusually transparent crystallization of the potential trade-offs and tensions between the democratic imaginary of institutionalized pluralism and that of popular sovereignty. In filling the political void created by the crisis of the old order, Chavismo was clearly susceptible to the autocratic temptation; it did not completely extinguish political space for other actors, but it reserved the key institutional levers for itself. This dynamic made it extremely difficult for opposition forces to challenge the dominance of the populist-left movement within the parameters of the new regime institutions. When opponents resorted to extrainstitutional strategies of resistance or employed hardball tactics that created doubts about their own commitment to democracy, these efforts typically backfired, ultimately reinforcing the autocratic tendencies within Chavismo itself (Gamboa 2022). Chávez controlled the executive and legislative branches of government after writing a new constitution and convoking new elections in 2000, and he gradually whittled away at the political independence of the judiciary (Brewer-Carías 2010), the national electoral commission, the state-owned oil company, the mass media (Corrales and Penfold 2011, 34–35), and the armed forces (Trinkunas 2011).

Nevertheless, Chávez repeatedly sought and received democratic mandates—conceived in terms of popular sovereignty—to legitimize or cloak such autocratic encroachments on institutionalized pluralism. He boasted an impressive string of electoral victories between 1998 and 2006, including three consecutive victories with increasing margins in presidential elections, two consecutive conquests of legislative majorities, a lopsided victory in constituent assembly elections, the defeat of a presidential recall, and victories in referenda to convene a constituent assembly and ratify a new constitution.

Moreover, Chavismo experimented with an ambitious—if somewhat fluid—array of participatory sites and channels at the national and subnational levels, extending beyond the narrow confines of electoral representation (Smilde and Hellinger 2011; Brown 2022; Hetland 2023). In addition to the widespread use of popular referenda as instruments of direct democracy, Chávez encouraged extensive grassroots, community-based organization and participation around a wide range of issues and concerns. Initially this involved the organization of Bolivarian circles as local study groups and activist nuclei, but grassroots Chavismo evolved and expanded over time—especially after 2003—to include local land use and water service committees, community radio and cultural groups, local election campaign networks, and neighborhood organizations formed around high-profile social "missions" designed to expand access to health care, subsidized food, education programs, and other basic services (see Fernandes 2010; García-Guadilla 2018). By 2006, Chávez was promoting the formation of participatory communal councils to oversee local public goods, infrastructure, and development projects, parallel to the more institutionalized (and elected) municipal governments of varied political persuasions. Over forty thousand communal councils were established in the years that followed, involving millions of Venezuelan citizens in grassroots discussions about local needs, spending priorities, and infrastructure projects (Goldfrank 2020, 145).

These initiatives were consistent with the constitution's emphasis on participatory or "protagonistic" democracy. As several studies have found (Handlin and Collier 2011, 155–157; Rhodes-Purdy 2017, 164–175), they were also instrumental in securing the regime's base of popular support, and the grassroots participation they fostered created Chavista organizational networks in low-income communities long neglected by the traditional parties. These participatory channels were authentic, though hardly unblemished; their dependence on state resources allowed clientelist tendencies to emerge, and while they were open to citizens not affiliated with Chavismo, participation was skewed toward regime loyalists (Hawkins 2010a; Rhodes-Purdy 2017, 158–154; García-Guadilla 2018). As Fernandes (2010, 239, 241) suggests, chronic tensions existed between grassroots demands for autonomous political expression and the more centralized and hierarchical "vanguardist logic" of national party leaders who sought to harness mass constituencies to broader regime goals. Nevertheless, cross-national surveys discovered "amazingly widespread" participation in Venezuela's community-based associational life under Chávez, with levels of mass participation that far surpassed those associated with the PT's vaunted participatory initiatives in Brazil (Handlin and Collier 2011, 150; see also Goldfrank 2020, 145).

Mass participation at the grass roots, however, did not prevent electoral challenges to Chavismo from developing over time. Neither did it provide adequate safeguards against the worst defects of the autocratic temptation, which became increasingly apparent after 2007 as the opposition regrouped and strengthened its capacity to contest Chávez in the electoral arena. These defects included hyperpolarization, the neutralization of electoral challenges to dominant party rule, and the erosion of democratic accountability and feedback mechanisms. The latter are especially important for encouraging policy adaptation, the timely identification of mistaken strategies or corrupt practices, and the adoption of corrective measures to avoid egregious failures. Their weakness in Venezuela would weigh heavily on the demise of Chavismo, as the windfall oil rents of the 2003–2013 period encouraged undisciplined—and ultimately unsustainable—state spending to subsidize infrastructure investment, social services, consumer goods imports, and an ambitious web of transnational alliances and institution building. In the absence of effective democratic oversight and accountability, the spending was riddled with inefficiencies and corruption, and the resulting economic imbalances fed inflationary pressures and capital flight that the government's price and currency controls were unable to contain. To the contrary, these policies spawned black market activities and spot shortages that bred political discontent but no effective political responses, given the erosion of accountability and feedback mechanisms both horizontally (to other independent institutions) and vertically (to the electorate at large).

Chávez's first, and only, electoral defeat occurred in late 2007, when he narrowly lost a popular referendum on a package of constitutional reforms that would have eliminated presidential term limits and introduced other measures that Chávez said were necessary for building socialism (López Maya 2011, 226–230). Although Chávez accepted this defeat, he sidestepped it by winning a more streamlined referendum in early 2009 that eliminated term limits, raising the prospect of his remaining in power indefinitely. In this context, a diverse coalition of traditional and new opposition parties—the Democratic Unity Roundtable (MUD)—was founded in 2008, for the purpose of challenging Chavismo in the electoral arena, where it was showing newfound vulnerabilities (Jiménez 2021; Hellinger 2018, 265–266). The MUD captured the mayoralty of Caracas and five state governorships (out of 22) in 2008, and it put up a formidable challenge to PSUV in the 2010 national assembly elections. The opposition coalition lost this legislative vote by only 48.2 percent to 47.2 percent, depriving PSUV of the supermajorities needed for unilateral decision-making. In response to the opposition's electoral gains in these institutional sites, however, Chavismo took action to weaken those sites by transferring powers from the mayor to a new appointed position in the Caracas municipality, and from the national assembly to the executive within the national government (Velasco 2022, 65).

A pattern was established, therefore, under which the erosion of Chavismo's hegemony and opposition electoral gains failed to produce more pluralistic politics or stronger institutional checks and balances. Instead, Chavismo resorted to increasingly autocratic measures to reproduce its institutional dominance and avoid sharing power. This pattern intensified after Chávez's death from cancer in 2013, following his final presidential reelection in 2012. The loss of the Bolivarian Revolution's undisputed leader laid bare another pitfall of the autocratic temptation—the challenge of political succession in contexts where leadership is highly centralized in the hands of a dominant figure and largely unaccountable to institutionalized mechanisms for the oversight and circulation of political elites. Potential rivals to Chávez within his movement had long since drifted away or been subordinated, leaving Chávez in a position to handpick his successor, Nicolás Maduro, vice president and former minister of foreign affairs. A former union official who had been a loyal Chavista since the early 1990s, Maduro had performed a variety of leadership roles within the MBR, MVR, and PSUV, but his charismatic appeal and commanding authority paled in comparison to Chávez (see Andrews-Lee 2021).

To compound the challenges of political succession, Maduro took office—and then narrowly defeated the MUD candidate in a new election to win a presidential mandate of his own—as Venezuela teetered on the cusp of an unprecedented economic crisis (Bull and Rosales 2020, 6–8; Rodríguez 2025). When the commodity boom went bust and oil prices plummeted by 70 percent between the middle of 2014 and early 2016, Venezuela entered a prolonged period of both economic recession and hyperinflation that was only compounded by US economic sanctions. According to CEPAL (2020), gross domestic product contracted by an estimated 63.4 percent between 2013 and 2019—and 71 percent, according to other estimates, between 2012 and 2020, which Rodríguez (2024, 1) described as "the equivalent of three Great Depressions." Meanwhile, the hyperinflationary spiral reached a staggering rate of over 130,000 percent in 2018 (CEPAL 2020, 1–2), the highest ever recorded in Latin America. Shortages of food and medicine combined with rising levels of criminal violence to produce a humanitarian crisis and a mass exodus from the country. An estimated 7.7 million Venezuelans have been displaced globally, producing "one of the largest international displacement crises in the world," with 6.5 million currently residing in Latin America and the Caribbean.[21]

As the economic downturn got underway, Maduro was forced to contend with a major cycle of opposition protests in 2014. This revival of mass protest strengthened hard-line currents within the opposition that believed Maduro and the PSUV would never recognize an electoral defeat and would have to be driven from office, by insurrectionary means if necessary. PSUV did, in fact, lose its legislative majority to the MUD in the December 2015 elections for the national assembly, but the ruling party used other institutional levers to neutralize the assembly, rather than allow the opposition to deploy it as an institutional check on executive power. Following a conflict over the seating of several assembly delegates, the Supreme Tribunal of Justice declared the assembly to be in contempt, nullified its decisions, and transferred legislative functions to the courts and the executive branch. Maduro then called for special elections—boycotted by much of the opposition—for a new constituent national assembly, which subsequently claimed supreme powers and assumed legislative responsibilities from the opposition-controlled national assembly in 2017. The latter proceeded to appoint an alternative supreme tribunal in exile as well as an alternative head of state, Juan Guaidó, who was recognized by the US and many of its allies. With the Maduro regime becoming increasingly militarized and repressive of opposition political activity, however, the possibility of an alternation in power by democratic means was largely foreclosed, affirming the regime's increasingly authoritarian character (Cameron 2018, 12; see also Rosales and Jiménez 2021). International organizations documented widespread violations of basic human rights and the excessive use of force in the policing of protests, drug trafficking, and crime prevention operations, ranging from arbitrary and unlawful detentions of political opponents to torture and extrajudicial executions (OHCHR 2018; Human Rights Watch 2022; Smilde et al. 2022).

While opposition parties have long been divided over political strategies to contest Chavismo (Jiménez 2021; Gamboa 2022), many of them coalesced around a single presidential candidate—Edmundo González Urrutia—in the 2024 national elections. Waves of mass mobilization and polls indicated the possibility of an opposition victory, but the integrity of the electoral process was deeply compromised from the beginning. In the lead-up to what seemed like a watershed election, the Maduro government manipulated the Supreme Tribunal of Justice, arrested prominent figures, and disqualified other leading opposition candidates, such as María Corina Machado (Corrales and Kronick 2025, 46). On election day, Maduro promptly declared victory amid broad domestic and international skepticism—with no published detailed vote results and facing challenges from the very few independent groups allowed to monitor the elections—and revealed once again that he would resort to autocratic measures to hold onto power. There is little doubt that Maduro lost the presidential election in a landslide but nevertheless managed to subvert its results with the backing of the military and the Supreme Tribunal of Justice (Corrales and Kronick 2025, 37). Despite growing regional isolation, he was sworn in as president for a third consecutive term, facing little domestic countermobilization.

Ultimately, then, the autocratic temptation led Chavismo down a perilous path that suppressed its internal democratic currents and culminated in extreme polarization, institutional gridlock, political violence, and authoritarian backsliding. Tragically, it also prevented governing institutions from receiving the types of societal feedback that might have encouraged midcourse policy corrections to avoid the human costs of a devastating economic crisis, a virtual collapse of the public health-care system, a crisis of public security, and the massive exodus of Venezuelans who left the country to escape its multiple crises. The Venezuelan case had the most devastating outcome within Latin America's left turn, clearly illustrating that the costs of the autocratic temptation may extend far beyond the violation of minority political rights.

The Rise, Fall, and Comeback of Bolivia's MAS

Molded by social movements organized around inclusion, the MAS took office embracing a democratic imaginary as mass empowerment. In its diagnosis, the prevailing democracy was not only shallow; representative institutions were seen as fundamentally corrupt and decrepit. In addition to receiving 54 percent of the vote in the first round of the 2005 election, the symbolism of a coca grower of indigenous background and humble origins achieving national-level power cannot be overstated. After almost five centuries of colonialism and white minority rule, Morales's rise to power represented something far deeper than any routine alternation in power. It was a break from the status quo like the country had not seen since the 1952 revolution (Hylton and Thomson 2007), which ultimately failed to live up to expectations. In addition, the MAS received a radicalized policy agenda from Bolivia's popular and indigenous movements and a mandate for profound institutional change. Its rise to power was, therefore, a "constituent moment" (Frank 2010) that reinforced the plebiscitarian orientation of Morales's leadership and gave impetus to the idea of doing away with the old order and creating a new one. While there were tensions and contradictory tendencies within the MAS—including conflicts between moderate positions and more radical currents—Morales was able to "glue" these together to attempt a project of mass empowerment.

The MAS gained office by a landslide—and in an institutional context where the traditional parties and the party system had imploded (Cyr 2017; Roberts 2014, 274–275). It rose to power, then, in a propitious context to "take it all" and with opportunities and a broad societal consensus to reshape the political arena. At the same time, it did not gain full control of Congress, as during Morales's first term (2006–2009) the political opposition controlled the Senate and served as a check on the power of the MAS.[22] This meant that when Morales convened the election of a Constituent Assembly in 2006—under the framework of existing laws, in contrast to Chávez in Venezuela—the MAS clearly lacked the supermajority in congress necessary to pass the new constitution drafted and approved by the Constituent Assembly. This text incorporated many of the proposals developed by the social movements that formed the Unity Pact (Zegada et al. 2011), and it emerged from a more pluralistic constituent assembly than that which produced the new constitution in Venezuela. Whereas Chávez's MVR had over 90 percent of constituent assembly seats, allowing it to unilaterally impose a new constitution, the MAS claimed only 54 percent of the assembly seats in Bolivia and had little choice but to negotiate and compromise with opposition actors on the content of the new constitution (Romero et al. 2009).

During this first term, and especially during the 2006–2007 constituent process, the MAS also encountered strong mobilized resistance from the guardians of the ancien régime, who were entrenched in Bolivia's most prosperous eastern departments—the so-called Half Moon (Media Luna) region. Threatened by indigenous mobilization, the rise of Morales, and the ongoing constituent process that threatened their status, this opposition from traditional political elites—backed by powerful agribusiness elites—demanded regional autonomy and even threatened secession (Eaton 2007). These traditional white and mestizo elites resented an empowered indigenous-led government and feared state capture of hydrocarbon rents and the implementation of a new land reform. To confront the MAS, these "conservative autonomy movements" (Eaton 2011) adopted mobilizational strategies and rhetorical frames commonly used by indigenous social movements (Centellas 2016).

Thinking that social mobilization tactics—and power centralization—would be essential to overcome resistance from the guardians of the old order,²³ Morales and the MAS intentionally confronted political elites in that region (see also Brown 2022). In the short run, this polarization pushed Bolivia to the brink of a civil war.²⁴ It also strengthened both government and opposition coalitions. But in an effort to restore peace, break the political impasse, and facilitate the approval of the new constitution, Morales sought a truce with economic elites by promising macroeconomic stability, a favorable investment environment, and decentralization reforms, as well as significant concessions in the realm of agrarian policy, so long as they refrained from political interference (Eaton 2016, 394). Eastern economic elites accepted the terms of the truce, resulting in congressional negotiations between the MAS and opposition lawmakers that led to the amendment of more than one hundred articles of the constitutional text (Garcés 2011), a "retreat from the agenda of redistributive structural reforms" (Crabtree et al. 2023, 155), and the deactivation of the conservative autonomy movement. Moreover, according to Hetland (2023), this tactical concession to elites—a key element of Morales's "passive revolution"—contributed to the gradual demobilization of the MAS's social allies.

The contrast to Venezuela—where the constituent assembly claimed supraconstitutional powers and dissolved the sitting legislature—was notable. In 2009, therefore, the MAS promulgated, with broad public support (61.43 percent of the vote), a new constitution that prioritized the construction of a more inclusive state and reflected elite compromises between the government and opposition forces (Centellas 2013). Bolivia moved from a period of sharp polarization between west and east to a period of relative political stability in which conflict normalized and became more institutionalized. By 2009, traditional elites "tolerated the MAS for pragmatic reasons" but "never embraced its project" (Farthing and Becker 2021, 66). This was especially the case as the MAS increased its popular support in every election and gained ample control over core state institutions. Thereafter, the opposition weakened and fractured and held no real countervailing power in Congress. Opposition forces did, however, gain control over key subnational districts, including municipalities and governorships, which served to check the MAS and disperse political power.

The Bolivian left turn was peculiar in several respects. Compared to other populist-left cases, including Venezuela and Ecuador, the MAS had stronger and deeper roots in social movements, and linkages with sponsoring and allied movements remained strong while in power. Its experience in power, moreover, ushered in a historically unprecedented "process of political and social integration that has brought excluded indigenous populations closer to the center of power" in ways that fundamentally altered the political power game (Crabtree 2020, 389). Groups that previously had little say over how the country was run—such as Indigenous peoples, peasants, informal-sector workers, and women—gained greater power and influence. Changes were especially evident in the new sociodemographic composition of the executive branch (Laruta 2008; Zegada et al. 2011), national and subnational legislative branches (Zegada and Komadina 2014; Justiniano 2022), and state bureaucracies (Soruco et al. 2014). Traditional hierarchies and barriers to political participation broke apart (e.g., Crabtree 2020, 380; see also Mayorga 2020a), systematic differences in participation across social categories withered (Stoyan 2014), and social relations changed as well (Molina 2020). This decade-long inclusionary project constituted an exceptional change in a society characterized by deep ethnic divisions and exclusion. It also enabled a shift in domestic power relations at the state and societal levels, thereby generating conditions conducive to a shift from a "formal" to a more "participatory" or "deeper" democracy. Additionally, the same movement actors that promoted greater participation also supported the party's redistributive efforts, acting as both pressure and support groups for the MAS and counterbalancing the power of business and elite opposition during the passage of important tax reforms (Fairfield 2015) and other redistributive measures (Niedzwiecki and Anria 2019).

Nevertheless, while the MAS had deep roots in social movements, its relationships with those movements were not without tensions. Having expanded access to the political arena and greater influence in the policymaking process did not mean that social movements gained control over the national agenda.[25] Rather, it meant that their interests, demands, and policy priorities became harder to ignore (Anria 2016, 104). This often forced the MAS to negotiate and reconcile competing political pressures from below, and it led to instances of collaboration as well as occasions of subordination to the MAS (Mayorga 2020b). This expanded access also created an intermediate party-society relationship, whereby societal actors had a significant measure of organizational and political autonomy but nonetheless remained organically connected to the MAS and its larger project (Mayorga 2011; Rivera 2019; Poertner 2024). Conflicts between social movements and the MAS—and clashes among rival social movements themselves—escalated after Morales's reelection in 2009, when the MAS became electorally dominant and gained full control of Congress. They intensified after 2011 with the TIPNIS crisis, a conflict over internal land colonization and roadbuilding across a national park recognized as an indigenous territory (Farthing 2018, 223). This dispute exposed the government's developmentalist policy agenda and revealed the sharp conflicts of interest that existed within the MAS's highland and lowlands indigenous bases (and more generally between its original core *cocalero* constituency and its more recent lowlands and urban-popular constituencies). Autonomous social mobilization from below forced the party leadership to negotiate and reach a compromise, and therefore served as a check on executive power when other independent branches of power were weak. This was a regularized pattern of societal accountability that influenced and constrained Morales's power from below and held the MAS accountable to organized constituencies (Anria 2018; Mayorga 2020b) — a pattern not seen in Venezuela.

But the TIPNIS conflict was a breakpoint in governing party-society relations. It led to the splintering of important movements, including some of the well-organized indigenous movements that had propelled the MAS to the presidency, into "loyalist" and "dissident" factions.[26] It also led to increased government attempts to narrow the space for the autonomy of civil society (Postero 2017). These efforts weakened the mobilizational capacity of Bolivia's social movements (Fabricant and Gustafson 2020, 107), and several of them "were left with a diminished capacity to pressure the government effectively" (Farthing and Becker 2021, 62). Although dissident movements at times aligned with opposition forces, opposition parties and candidates remained, at least until 2019, too fragmented and tied to the upper classes to pose electoral threats to the MAS. The different interests of dissident groups also often collided with each other, which hindered their coalition-building capacity.

Bolivia, however, was also a high performer in its economic management, in sharp contrast to Venezuela under Chavismo. Morales combined soaring rhetoric about nationalizations with moderate policies (Mayorga 2020b); he welcomed foreign investors in lucrative extractive sectors while increasing the taxes they paid, producing steady economic growth and low inflation (Molina 2019). While this was not the radical "nationalization" that parts of Morales's social movement base wanted, it generated an extraordinary increase in state revenues and enabled a substantial acceleration of public spending in infrastructure and social services without creating macroeconomic imbalances. High taxes on extractive industries in a context of booming international prices also helped to fund a wide range of social programs that helped to reduce poverty quite dramatically (from 63.5 percent in 2006 to 31.1 percent in 2019), redress gender and ethnic inequalities (Maclean 2023), and stimulate the creation of a new (largely) Aymara urban middle class (Shakow 2014; Villanueva Rance 2022). Finally, Morales and the MAS directed an economy that managed not only to register sustained growth—even after commodity prices dropped in 2014—but also to achieve a steep drop in the Gini index of income inequality (from 0.604 in 2006 to 0.430 in 2019), the sharpest decline in the Latin American region.[27]

It might be tempting to see Morales and the MAS as "victims of their own success" (Crabtree 2020, 389). In this type of reading, tangible improvements in a supportive environment for redistributive reforms generated expectations for continued improvements as well as new types of priorities and societal demands—for "improved education, better health provision, decent housing, and access to justice" (Crabtree 2020, 389). When conditions changed after commodity prices dropped and the economy slowed, fear of losing the recent inclusionary gains led to frustration with the government and multiplied societal demands by the largely urban, and growing, populations that the MAS helped to lift into the middle class, together with the traditional middle-class segments that the MAS helped to expand. These pressures not only intensified conflict within the MAS's governing coalition; they also gradually weakened its electoral bases of support and helped to unsettle Bolivia's political equilibrium. While the MAS won the presidential election of 2014 with ample majorities, it began to lose subnational-level elections even in its own strongholds, losing races in important cities and governorships in departments across Bolivia, and reversing a trend of sustained electoral dominance since Morales's election in 2006 (Mayorga 2019).

Changing economic conditions undoubtedly helped to usher in the demise of Bolivia's left turn, but the seeds of political decay were sown earlier on and conditioned how the left turn (temporarily) ended. The party's formative and historical experiences in opposition to an exclusionary political and economic system had created an inclination toward a conception of democracy as mass empowerment. As a governing party, it faced highly fragmented oppositions with little electoral and institutional capacity, especially after the MAS consolidated power after 2009.[28] Commanding overwhelming electoral support and control over core state institutions, it unsurprisingly fell prey to the pitfalls of the "autocratic temptation" and could not escape its damaging side effects. Although in the short run those proclivities were at least partially offset by societal forms of accountability and bottom-up influences, in the longer run they gave rise to authoritarian distortions and abuses of power. The political dynamics of executive aggrandizement and weak respect for institutional checks and balances on presidential authority that were present since early on (Levitsky and Loxton 2013) intensified over time (Lehoucq 2020; Sánchez-Sibony 2021; Cameron and Jaramillo 2022, 6–9). The manipulation of courts, themselves used at times as tools against critics, culminated in attempts to remove constraints on term limits imposed by the constitutional order that the MAS itself helped to create. It bears noting that assessments of media censorship, harassment of journalists, equality before the law, freedom of expression, and other basic rights and freedoms suggest mild but not drastic deterioration during the Morales presidencies (Anria and Cyr 2022). But sustained attempts to tilt the democratic playing field proved self-limiting for the MAS in power, producing polarizing effects and paving the way for its political demise. While the first backlash in 2007–2009, as described earlier, was at least partially an elite reaction to fears of radical redistributive reform and institutional change, the second backlash—emerging as the MAS became dominant—had broader societal bases. It represented a more diffuse yet broad-based response to a movement-based party that had gradually constructed a new form of popular hegemony. Fear of hegemonic authority helped to crystallize a broad right-wing opposition coalition, as outlined below.

Morales's personalistic and autocratic proclivities—what Brown (2022) refers to as "authoritarian centralization"—led to a gradual insulation of the MAS from its organized social bases. This also created strong difficulties with leadership succession, making it extremely hard for new leaders to emerge and carry out the transformations begun by the founding leader.[29] This became clear since at least 2014, when the MAS decided to avoid grooming a new party leader and claimed that Morales was, in effect, "indispensable" for the party's electoral success and for holding it together in an unstable regional and international context.[30] Ultimately, this miscalculation—an initiative that, Morales claims, came strictly "from below"—left Morales and the MAS vulnerable to opposition charges of antidemocratic behavior, creating space for a conservative backlash that mobilized heterogeneous groups concerned with the closing of political space and the risks of democratic backsliding.[31] These antidemocratic charges gained critical strength after Morales lost a referendum in 2016 to remove term limits. Despite the loss, Morales's first since he had won power, he insisted on reelection, claiming that he had a "human right" to run for office indefinitely—a clear challenge to conventional democratic norms and practices in presidential systems, and a challenge to historical precedents in the country. The country's highest court, dominated by Morales's allies, supported his reasoning in a controversial ruling the following year and abolished term limits. In essence, Morales had succumbed to the autocratic temptation—the illusion that a redemptive leader or political movement can not only speak and act on behalf of the entire people but also do so indefinitely, disregarding the "hard realities" of constitutionally established term limits.

Morales's democratic legitimacy was severely undermined from the moment he did not accept the results of the 2016 referendum, which helped to intensify elite-level polarization. Polarization, in turn, facilitated opposition unity and helped to revitalize opposition movements in different parts of the country, including former bastions of support for the MAS— such as El Alto and Potosí—and among economic elites in the departments of Santa Cruz, Beni, Pando, and Tarija (McNelly 2019; Rivera 2024). Opposition outrage quickly grew and brought together middle-class segments—such as students and professionals—with dissident groups that previously supported the MAS (Velasco Guachalla et al. 2021, 72). It catalyzed a civic movement dubbed "Respect the Vote," whose masterframe slogan first decried "Bolivia said no [to reelection]" and then, in the lead-up to the 2019 election, "Yes to democracy, no to dictatorship." In fact, the electoral campaign was a dispute between opponents with two starkly different notions of democracy that map neatly onto our explanatory framework (see fig. 1.1). While Carlos Mesa, a centrist opposition candidate backed by more conservative forces, campaigned on a notion of democracy conceived as institutionalized pluralism and pledged to restore procedural rules if elected (Lehoucq 2020, 134), Morales campaigned on democracy as popular sovereignty and promised to defend the inclusionary gains of his governments and to continue "deepening" democracy (Mayorga 2020, 18–22). Morales may well have won the disputed elections of 2019 with a sufficient number of votes to claim victory outright in the first round (Idrobo et al. 2022).[32] Critically, however, he lost the overwhelming majoritarian electoral support that his government had reproduced for almost fourteen years.[33] By 2019, Morales's electoral decline was real, especially in urban areas and among urban middle classes and the youth, and it left him vulnerable to opposition charges of electoral manipulation.

While his signature policies remained widely popular and Morales's leading opponent did not compete for votes based on promises to undo the MAS' policy legacies, dismissing electoral democracy as merely formal proved perilous and politically irresponsible. Morales's willingness to alter constitutional term limits raised the stakes of democratic contestation and made it increasingly intense and conflictual. This not only sharply polarized politics at the elite level; it also helped to strengthen opposition movements, which mobilized prior to the election but especially in response to irregularities (and possible fraud) in the vote count itself, adding a mass dimension to the ongoing polarization process. Starting in La Paz, protest movements swelled in former bastions of support for the MAS, like Potosí, as well as in traditional bastions of political opposition, especially in Santa Cruz. In turn, social mobilization radicalized the opposition. It eclipsed political moderates and gave the upper hand to minority segments of Bolivian society that always derided—even if at times tolerating—the MAS and whose privilege and social status were threatened by MAS governments (Molina 2020). This opposition was closely tied to landowning elites and prominent advocates of neoliberal reforms; it pressed for Morales's resignation and pushed postelection protests far to the right by using fiery rhetoric, calling for violence, and pleading to restore Christianity and to bring the Bible "back in." Indeed, protests demonstrated to right-wing political movements that they could effectively mobilize large numbers of people. In so doing, they contributed to fueling *antimasista* feelings, denying the MAS (and its supporters) democratic legitimacy.

Morales's refusal to pass the torch—a by-product of the autocratic temptation—thus paved the way for the rise of new right-wing contenders with transparent antidemocratic tendencies—as seen, for example, in their explicit racism and commitments to restore old social and political hierarchies (Walters 2019; Molina 2021). That refusal not only strengthened and radicalized opposition coalitions; it also weakened the MAS's bases of support and encouraged important former social allies, such as the powerful Bolivian Workers' Central (COB), to join the postelection protests and move into opposition (McNelly 2019; Brown 2022, 177; Rivera 2024). Segments of the party's social bases took to the streets in the 2019 postelection protests in support of Morales (Díaz-Cuellar 2019, 8) but offered weak countermobilization to defend "their" government (Stefanoni 2020; Brown 2022, 178). A defiant Morales held out for three weeks. However, on November 10, the government's defeat in the streets was followed by a rank-and-file police mutiny and pressure from the army chief, which ultimately became the death knell for Morales. With critical support from the military, this conservative backlash ousted Morales, forcing him to flee to Mexico two days later. This paved the way for an interim right-wing presidency led by Jeanine Áñez, a little-known, far-right Evangelical and Senate vice president with close ties to Bolivia's traditional elites. The violent reclamation of power by the old elites and conservative forces was facilitated, at least in part, by the fragmentation and lack of mobilization among Morales's social allies—a consequence of his autocratic tendencies.

Rather than leading a caretaker government, Áñez attempted to establish a political order that maintained the scaffolding of democracy while trying to limit democratic competition—for example, by finding ways to restrict the participation of the MAS, by placing criminal charges against (and jailing) its leaders, and by framing its supporters as "terrorists" and "seditious." She also moved swiftly to undo Morales's legacy. But she failed to achieve her goals and could not consolidate a strong coalitional base (Velasco Guachalla et al. 2021). Attempts to roll back the clock set the country down a perilous path of social conflict, and in response, the president resorted to violent repression against pro-MAS protesters, leading to multiple deaths in at least two protest sites (Senkata and Sacaba). A report issued by the Inter-American Commission on Human Rights declared the killings at each site a massacre.[34] Predictably, Áñez's attempts to roll back inclusion and suppress protest helped to remobilize the actors who had been empowered by the MAS; even if many had ceased to support the party, they organized roadblocks and protests against a government that was openly racist, anti-indigenous, and violent—and in defense of indigenous symbols like the Wiphala flag (Mamani 2020).

The adversity that followed Morales's forced resignation posed an existential threat for the MAS and much of its social base, as the interim government attempted not only to roll back previous gains but also to marginalize the party and its organized social bases from the political arena. The magnitude of the threat was such that, in the short run, it created incentives for unity, and it facilitated a strategic realignment between the party and its core social movement allies—including those that had moved into opposition. This alignment was key for the MAS to stage an impressive electoral comeback in 2020, despite Morales being in exile, having limited access to public resources, and with MAS leaders and supporters facing violent— even deadly—repression (Bjork-James 2024).[35] Violent repression not only fostered unity but also raised the costs of exiting the MAS. It also induced a "return to the origins" type of dynamic—an attempt by its organized social bases to reclaim control over the "political instrument" (Mayorga 2022).

Scarred by violent repression, the MAS managed to overcome the backlash and largely contain the extent of the conservative rollback (Crabtree et al. 2023, 161) through a combination of coordinated social mobilization and legislative activity (Resmini and Silva 2024). It was difficult for a minoritarian and illegitimate government to effectively roll back a more than decade-long and historically unprecedented inclusionary project that had created a "new normal" in the country. When the MAS returned to power in 2020, it did so under new leadership—a product of an agreement, albeit fraught with tensions, between Morales and the Unity Pact.[36]

At the time of this writing, however, the party remains in an uncertain and precarious position. On the one hand, the MAS's impressive comeback in 2020 signaled at least a partial solution to the tense political impasse in the country (Alberti 2021). And yet, while the arrival of Luis Arce of the MAS to the presidency and the more plural composition of Congress also signaled the possibility of a reequilibration of the democratic regime—a chance to institutionalize the alternation in power, deepen inclusion, and strengthen institutionalized pluralism (Anria and Cyr 2022)—a deep economic contraction and leadership disputes between Arce and Morales made that possibility particularly challenging.

Ahead of the 2025 elections, the MAS split into three rival camps that fragmented the once-dominant party into electoral factions (Molina 2023). At the heart of the dispute was a power struggle between Morales and Arce over control of the party and the presidential nomination. These political divisions also had a grassroots dimension (Rodríguez García 2024), as social movements and labor unions were divided between supporters of the rival leaders (Arigho-Stiles 2024).[37] The official MAS candidate, Eduardo del Castillo, captured only 3 percent in the first round—barely enough to preserve legal status—while the other factions, one aligned with Morales and the other with Andrónico Rodríguez, ran uncoordinated campaigns that split the vote. Although the roots of the MAS's current predicament are clear—they go back to the autocratic temptation, which continues to have debilitating effects—its consequences are unmistakable. That temptation hindered the party from "routinizing" charisma and renewing leadership, undermining cohesion.[38] While the loss of cohesion may have opened the door for power alternation, opposition to the MAS remains fragmented, elite-driven, and poorly connected with organized popular constituencies

(Exeni Rodríguez 2024). Much of the opposition has found it hard to reclaim democratic credentials after providing support for Áñez's violent interim government. Only time will tell whether the MAS's demise marks the end of an era or merely a reconfiguration of a movement whose social base remains deeply rooted in Bolivia's popular sectors.

In short, the Bolivian left turn reconfigured the parameters of the country's politics. It produced a major restructuring of its party system along a MAS versus anti-MAS cleavage with left-right underpinnings. However, this restructuring did not generate cohesive political blocs on either side of the binary divide. Although segments of the MAS side of the divide may yet unite in the future—drawing on Bolivia's long tradition of popular politics and echoing the comparative experience of Peronism, which historically prioritized unity in the face of adversity—the 2025 elections revealed how internal leadership disputes eroded that capacity. The once-dominant party's fragmentation has now produced its worst electoral defeat, raising questions about whether its social base can reconstitute out of the wreckage or whether the MAS has entered a terminal decline akin to the historic unraveling of the MNR. Meanwhile, Morales's continued support, despite exclusion from organized politics,[39] can reignite a difficult—if not impossible—game in Bolivian politics, along the lines of O'Donnell's (1973, 167–201) classic depiction of Argentina's historical efforts to ban Peronism from the democratic arena. This could create a deeply polarizing path. As of October 2025, Bolivia thus enters a new, uncertain chapter—one in which power alternation may help to re-equilibrate its democracy but also test the capacity of its political actors to transcend the polarized legacies of the left turn.

Conclusion

Populist-left governments in Venezuela and Bolivia were products of social and political backlashes against established party systems, political elites, and the neoliberal economic orders imposed by these elites during the era of the Washington Consensus. The new populist or movement-based parties spawned by these backlashes arose explicitly in opposition to established yet deeply flawed democratic regimes, and they sought—and received—democratic mandates to refound their national political orders and empower mass constituencies. The crises of established representative institutions and mass mobilization against them allowed MVR and the MAS to claim constitutive powers to redesign governing institutions as expressions of popular sovereignty, exercised largely (Venezuela) or partially (Bolivia) by plebiscitary means.

This democratic imaginary of popular sovereignty was conducive to a wide array of new social programs and participatory experiments aimed at making democracy "deeper" and more inclusive. It was integral to the mass mobilizations that ushered Hugo Chávez and Evo Morales into power and sustained them over time. In practice, however, this imaginary was also susceptible to the autocratic temptation, given the demise of traditional political actors and the crushing popular majorities that mobilized behind Chávez and Morales. In such contexts, popular sovereignty was too often conceived in terms that were socially heterogeneous but politically unitary, embodying or reifying it in the figure of a single dominant leader, party, or movement. Such unitary conceptions of popular sovereignty proved difficult to reconcile with the rights of political minorities, institutional checks and balances, and the basic norms and procedures of institutionalized pluralism. They also proved intrinsically polarizing, as their antipluralist logic and their tendency to concentrate power and entrench it over time—effectively blocking any prospect of political alternation—transformed political contestation into high-stakes existential conflicts.

These polarizing effects were especially acute in Venezuela, where Chávez's exercise of constitutive powers was unrestrained and highly unilateral. In the Venezuelan case, the autocratic temptation and the conflicts it unleashed culminated in the suppression of Chavismo's internal democratic currents and a steady descent into full-fledged authoritarianism and economic collapse. Notably, however, polarization also occurred in Bolivia, where the MAS's exercise of constitutive and governing powers was more institutionally constrained and less unilateral, and where social and economic policies were decidedly moderate and highly effective in comparative terms. In both countries, polarizing dynamics were driven not only by autocratic temptations on the left but also by autocratic reactions on the right that were quick to abandon democratic arenas that escaped their control and deploy antidemocratic power resources at their disposal. The Bolivian case, in particular, suggests that novel challenges to traditional social hierarchies are bound to elicit polarized responses, no matter the breadth and democratic legitimacy of the challenging forces.

CHAPTER FOUR

Comparative Perspectives

Argentina, Ecuador, and Uruguay

As the preceding chapters make clear, even similar cases that are routinely placed in the same category may vary in significant ways along one or another dimension of comparative analysis. A broader regional perspective may thus help illuminate the full range of variation that exists within as well as across the modal patterns of social democratic and populist-left trajectories. More important, perhaps, a broader comparative perspective may provide valuable analytical leverage and novel theoretical insights for explaining patterns of variation across cases. This chapter, therefore, provides short comparative analyses of three additional cases, one typically associated with the populist-left path (Ecuador), another with the social democratic path (Uruguay), and a third which manifests markedly hybrid traits (Argentina), such that it does not fit neatly into one or the other modal pattern.

As shown in this chapter, the populist-left pattern under Rafael Correa in Ecuador provides additional leverage for understanding the pitfalls of the autocratic temptation, in particular the challenges of leadership succession and democratic accountability in the absence of effective party development and organic linkages to organized popular constituencies. The Uruguayan case under the Broad Front (FA), by contrast, suggests that strong organic linkages to labor and grassroots constituencies may help social democratic experiments minimize the perils of excessive conformism. Finally, the case of left Peronism in Argentina sheds light on certain hybrid features that may help guard against the worst excesses of both the autocratic and conformist temptations, even if they do not preclude the emergence of significant performance failures and polarization dynamics.

Correa and Left Populism in Ecuador

Although the descriptive labels varied, scholars from a range of different theoretical and political perspectives placed Ecuador under Rafael Correa in the same general category as Venezuela and Bolivia within the left turn, for understandable reasons (Levitsky and Loxton 2013; Weyland 2013; Handlin 2017; Ellner 2020b, 6). Correa was a close political ally of Hugo Chávez and Evo Morales, aligning Ecuador with Venezuela and Bolivia in regional and international affairs. Like Chávez and Morales, Correa was elected president as an antiestablishment figure and a staunch critic of neoliberalism. His election occurred in the context of a severe crisis of representation, in a country where mainstream parties had converged around variants of the neoliberal model and the last three elected presidents had all been forced out of office during periods of mass social protest (Silva 2009; Roberts 2014, 152–163). Also, like Chávez and Morales, Correa had campaigned for office on a platform of convening a constituent assembly and refounding the national democratic regime. In all three countries, therefore, the redemptive populist pledge to empower the people—that is, to invoke popular sovereignty—was enacted through an assertion of constitutive powers to thoroughly overhaul governing institutions. Like the new populist left in Venezuela and Bolivia, that in Ecuador erupted as the primary political expression of a popular backlash against established democratic institutions—in the name of a deeper, more authentic, and more inclusive or participatory mode of democratic governance.

A distinctive feature of the Ecuadorian case, however, was the Correa regime's marked detachment from organized mass constituencies in both civic and partisan arenas—a detachment that undermined the prospects for any kind of radical democratic trajectory while reinforcing the regime's susceptibility to autocratic temptations (Sánchez and Pachano 2020). Ecuador after 1990 boasted the earliest and most sustained pattern of indigenous social and political mobilization in modern Latin America, leading to the formation of an indigenous political party, Pachakutik, as the political instrument of the powerful national indigenous confederation CONAIE (Confederation of Indigenous Nationalities of Ecuador) (Sawyer 2004; Yashar 2005; Van Cott 2005; Marc 2008; Lucero 2008; Madrid 2012). Pachakutik, however, was less successful than the Bolivian MAS in building a broad, multiethnic base of support (Madrid 2008), and it generally supported independent presidential candidates with broad appeal rather than a leader from within its own ranks. The series of mass protests that helped bring down elected presidents in 1997, 2000, and 2005, therefore, did not spawn a unifying partisan vehicle comparable to the MAS in Bolivia, which effectively channeled much of the popular mobilization associated with Bolivia's "water wars" and "gas war" in the early 2000s (Anria 2018). As such, Correa—like Morales—was elected following a series of mass uprisings that toppled his immediate predecessors, but he did not lead a mass party with roots in social movements like Morales's MAS. His party, Proud and Sovereign Homeland Alliance (AP), developed into a formidable electoral vehicle for his self-proclaimed Citizens' Revolution, but it was, as Conaghan (2022, 200) states, an "unrooted party" with minimal ties to organized societal interests, and it did little to vertically integrate Ecuadorian citizens into the democratic order.[1]

The AP was founded by Correa in April 2006 as an electoral vehicle for his presidential campaign, a mere six months before the first round of the election. The fledgling party helped Correa coordinate the informal network of political activists and academics that supported his candidacy. An economist with a PhD from the University of Illinois, Correa had served a short-lived stint as an outspoken, left-leaning minister of economy and finance in 2005 before falling out of favor for his criticisms of free-trade accords and international financial institutions, his efforts to redirect oil export revenues from debt service to social programs, and his cultivation of economic ties to Hugo Chávez's Venezuela (Kozloff 2009, 52–53). These stands helped brand Correa as a political maverick and a trenchant critic of both neoliberal orthodoxy and Ecuador's political establishment. They also positioned him to launch an independent, "outsider" campaign for the presidency the following year, essentially claiming to be the electoral expression of Ecuador's myriad anti-neoliberal protest movements. Correa's independence was accentuated by his decision to run for president without an accompanying slate of AP congressional candidates—a decision that also reflected his pledge to convene a constituent assembly and refound Ecuador's democratic regime, rather than pursue reforms within the confines of inherited institutions (Hernández and Buendía 2011, 132–133). Unbeholden to any organized interests, Correa framed his candidacy as a direct, unmediated appeal to "the people," or the citizenry at large—the essence of his Citizens' Revolution.

Paradoxically, Correa portrayed a nefarious *partidocracia* (partyarchy) as the principal nemesis of "the people" (Hernández and Buendía 2011,

132–133), even though Ecuador's party system—unlike that in Venezuela during the Puntofijo era—was notoriously weak, fragmented, and volatile. Following Ecuador's transition to democracy in 1978–1979 at the onset of Latin America's "third wave," candidates from seven different parties captured the presidency in the seven election contests that preceded the rise of Correa. In the context of the region-wide debt crisis and chronic inflationary pressures after the early 1980s, presidents from all the major parties adopted elements of orthodox neoliberal austerity and structural adjustment policies, even though most of them had campaigned for office as critics of neoliberalism.

The first in a series of indigenous and popular uprisings erupted in 1990, taking aim at these structural adjustment policies along with myriad inequalities and political elites at large. Mass protest cycles culminated in the removal of the last three presidents elected before Correa: the flamboyant populist figure Abdalá Bucaram in 1997, Jamil Mahuad of the centrist Popular Democracy party in 2000, and the populist leader Lucio Gutiérrez in 2005 (Marc 2008; Silva 2009; C. de la Torre 2010). The latter had led a group of junior military officers who sided with indigenous protesters and launched a short-lived military coup that toppled Mahuad in 2000, in the midst of a financial crisis that led to a massive bailout of private banks and a dollarization of the economy. Gutiérrez was subsequently elected president in 2002 with the support of CONAIE, and he proceeded to name four cabinet ministers and eight subsecretaries from Pachakutik. In office, however, Gutiérrez signed a letter of intent with the International Monetary Fund and aligned with conservative parties to adopt neoliberal policies—an about-face that created divisions within the indigenous movement and brought about a rupture of his alliance with Pachakutik. Although Pachakutik's brush with power left the indigenous movement weakened, divided, and demobilized (Wolff 2007), social actors continued to pressure the government; Gutiérrez himself was driven from office in 2005 by a largely urban uprising, triggered by a combination of policy dissent and disgust with political corruption and a court-packing scheme. The demise of Gutiérrez helped set the stage for Correa's outsider candidacy against the establishment writ large in 2006; as Conaghan (2011, 261) states, "Correa's rapid ascent took place in the political vacuum created by Ecuador's crumbling party system."

In contrast to Chávez and Morales, however, Correa did not capture the presidency with a resounding first-round electoral majority or a significant bloc of congressional support. In a crowded field of thirteen candidates, he finished second in the first round of the election with 22.8 percent of the vote, lagging conservative banana tycoon Álvaro Noboa, Ecuador's wealthiest citizen—a billionaire who cultivated a populist touch by pledging social programs and distributing handouts to his followers at campaign rallies. Little known to the broader public before the start of the campaign, Correa rose to contention through aggressive television, radio, and internet advertising and colorful, charismatic campaign rallies across the country. To highlight his antiestablishment message, Correa not only called for a constituent assembly but also parodied the *partidocracia*, accusing it of rampant corruption, incompetence, and selling out the country to foreign interests. He brandished a belt at campaign rallies, and in a play on his name—*correa* can be used for "belt" in Spanish—he promised to give the establishment a whipping. His redemptive populist and nationalist messaging pledged to restore Ecuador's national honor and uphold the dignity of its people, while his ability to speak the indigenous Kichwa language sent a message of inclusiveness to the broader population. After besting other left-leaning candidates to make it into the second-round runoff, Correa challenged Noboa by pledging a wide range of social programs to benefit popular sectors, including initiatives to expand employment, housing, health care, family assistance, and subsidies for small businesses, gasoline, and electricity (C. de la Torre 2010, 179–185; Conaghan 2011, 268–270). This platform earned Correa the endorsement of Pachakutik and other small centrist or leftist parties and civic groups, including leading women's and environmental organizations (Corrales 2018, 175–178; Riofrancos 2020). Despite Noboa's efforts to discredit Correa by invoking the specter of Chavismo, Correa prevailed in the second round with 56.7 percent of the vote.

Neither the tenuous nature of Correa's organizational base nor his party's absence from Congress blunted his ambitious agenda. To the contrary, he was emboldened by taking office amid a groundswell of popular support that far surpassed that of established parties and political institutions. In Latinobarómetro's (2006) regional survey, a mere 6 percent of Ecuadorians expressed confidence in the Congress, compared to 93.3 percent who said they had little or no confidence in the institution and 91.7 percent who had little or no confidence in political parties. Confidence in the judiciary—15 percent—was not much higher, with 83.6 percent of survey respondents expressing little or no confidence (Latinobarómetro 2006). By contrast, Correa was basking in a public approval rating of 74 percent after taking office in early 2007 (Latinobarómetro 2007)—a key element of the "informal powers" the president was able to exercise (Polga-Hecimovich 2020, 31–33). Given the delegitimation of established institutions, Correa went on the political offensive; rather than moderating his course to assuage elite opposition in Congress and the business community, he mobilized his public support to pressure and transform governing institutions. In the process, he tilted the balance of institutional power decisively to his advantage.

Convening a constitutional assembly was the centerpiece of Correa's strategy—one that was highly popular but also intrinsically polarizing, as it was fraught with potential conflict between the executive, legislative, and judicial branches of government. Under Ecuador's prevailing 1998 constitution, Congress was intended to take the lead in a process of constitutional reform, and no provisions were made for the convening of a new constitutional assembly (República de Ecuador 1998). Nevertheless, Correa's first act as president after taking the oath of office on January 15, 2007, was to issue a decree calling for a popular referendum on the election of a constitutional assembly. The decree was clearly designed to circumvent an opposition-controlled Congress through an appeal to the sovereign "people," and Correa used the president's bully pulpit and street protests against Congress by his followers to pressure legislative and judicial bodies to bend to his will. Ecuador's Electoral Tribunal ruled that a referendum would need to be approved by Congress, which it initially did with the understanding that a constitutional assembly would not displace or dissolve the elected Congress itself. Congress subsequently withdrew its approval, however, when Correa modified the guidelines for the constitutional assembly to augment its powers, including the power to dissolve Congress. When a majority of the seven-seat Electoral Tribunal approved the new referendum guidelines, Congress voted to remove the Tribunal's president and three of its other members; the Tribunal retaliated by ordering the removal of fifty-seven of the one hundred members of Congress for intervening in the electoral process. Correa backed the tribunal, and alternate congressional deputies were sworn into office, creating a compliant majority in the legislative body that supported Correa's call for a referendum. When Ecuador's Constitutional Court attempted to reinstate the congressional deputies who had been removed, the new Congress voted to sack the judges on the court ("Ecuador's Congress Sacks Judges" 2007; Corrales 2018, 178–179). In the midst of this institutional tug-of-war, Correa proceeded to hold the referendum on April 15, 2007, receiving landslide support from 81.7 percent of voters to elect a constitutional assembly.

In short, the informal powers associated with Correa's overwhelming popular support—in a broader political context of institutional crisis and delegitimation—made it possible to exercise constitutive authority and reconfigure governing institutions. Correa did so in a manner that combined mass mobilization with plebiscitary appeals and an autocratic circumvention, and eventual capture, of countervailing institutions. He effectively neutralized the horizontal checks and balances of both legislative and judicial institutions, ultimately transforming his position of institutional weakness into one of formidable, and largely uncontested, institutional strength. Elections were held for the Constitutional Assembly on September 30, 2007, giving Correa's AP a solid majority of 80 seats in the 130-seat assembly, and de facto control over the content of the new constitution. This allowed Correa to proceed in a more unilateral fashion than Morales and the MAS in Bolivia. Asserting plenipotentiary powers, the assembly suspended the sitting Congress and assumed legislative functions while drafting a new constitution. The new constitution called for a vigorous state role in both economic and social development, ratifying Correa's decisive break with the neoliberal economic model of his predecessors. It also established formal executive powers that were among the most expansive of any constitution in the world, as well as a greater number of enumerated citizenship rights than any other world constitution (Elkins et al. 2016). The constitution was approved in yet another popular referendum in September 2008 with the support of 64 percent of voters.

Correa's exercise of constitutive powers to refound Ecuador's democratic regime provided a paradigmatic example of the democratic imaginary for enacting popular sovereignty. It also laid bare the inherent tensions embedded in such assertions of popular sovereignty—in particular, the tensions between formal institutions, the rule of law, and the popular will; the tensions between majority rule and minority political rights; and the tensions between autocratic concentrations of decision-making authority and radical democratic forms of civic participation and deliberation. These latter tensions were evident from the outset of the process, but they increased their salience and crystallized over time, especially when Correa's technocratic pursuit of state-led development centered on natural resource extraction clashed with the environmental and indigenous movements that initially supported his push for a new constitution (Riofrancos 2020).

Building off the electoral alliances Correa had forged with civic groups during his campaign for the presidency—and, arguably, reinforcing the political fragmentation of opposition forces—civil society organizations were encouraged to sponsor candidates for the Constitutional Assembly and submit proposals to its working groups. As Corrales (2018, 179) states, "Nine political parties, 104 political movements, and 23 citizens' movements participated" in the assembly elections, placing over three thousand candidates on nearly five hundred different national and provincial lists. Once installed, the assembly formed ten thematic working groups, which traveled across the country to meet with civic groups and solicit feedback and proposals. The Carter Center (2008, 12) reported that the assembly received seventy thousand citizens and processed 1,632 proposals from civic groups. The first article of the new constitution affirmed the principle of popular sovereignty, as well as that of participatory democracy, stating that "Sovereignty lies with the people, whose will is the basis of all authority, and it is exercised through public bodies using direct participatory forms of government" ("Constitution of the Republic of Ecuador" 2008).

The civil society–based impetus for "deeper" or more radical forms of grassroots democratic participation, however, clashed with the autocratic tendencies inherent to Correa's personalistic and charismatic brand of authority. Correa's leadership made it possible to stitch together the disparate strands of Ecuador's popular movements behind a shared, majoritarian electoral project. In so doing, it overcame—at least temporarily—the fissiparous tendencies that had long plagued the civic networks that coalesced to protest neoliberalism and bring down unpopular governments but failed to cohere behind a common political project in the more institutionalized partisan and electoral arenas of democratic contestation. Correa's top-down charismatic mode of articulating and constructing "the people," however, allowed little space for autonomous expressions of the popular will, even those emerging from within his diverse coalition.

This tension was apparent during the deliberations of the Constitutional Assembly, when a clash between Correa and the assembly's president Alberto Acosta led to the latter's resignation from his leadership post and his turn toward political opposition. Acosta, a founding member of AP and a leader of the environmental organization Ecological Action, had received more votes for the assembly than any other delegate. Under his leadership, Ecuador's assembly welcomed input from civil society groups and advanced landmark provisions affording constitutional recognition to the rights of nature. Acosta's inclusive and deliberative style of leadership, however—at one point, he proposed a "popular consultation" on whether to allow open-pit metallic mining (Riofrancos 2020, 53)—strained the patience of Correa, who set a strict timetable for writing and approving the new constitution. Correa criticized Acosta for being "too democratic," and following the latter's exodus, the president asserted hierarchical control over the writing of the final draft of the constitution with a small circle of advisers (Corrales 2018, 182–185). Thereafter, civil society groups increasingly distanced themselves from Correa, and the final draft of the constitution—while affirming new rights for women, indigenous communities, and the environment—fell short of the expectations of many of the activist groups that initially participated in the process. Indigenous and environmental organizations, in particular, chafed at the watering down of constitutional guarantees for the prior consultation of communities affected by major new extractive projects, such as oil, gas, and mining. Rather than requirements for consultation and community consent, which would have given indigenous communities veto power over extractive activities in their territories, the assembly and the Correa administration settled on a much weaker form of consultation as information sharing, which ultimately ensured that the state would have the final say over the development of new projects (Riofrancos 2020, chap. 3; see also Eisenstadt and West 2019).

Indeed, Ecuador's "constituent moment" (Frank 2010) exposed the internal contradictions and the highly contingent character of the broad, left-leaning social and political coalition that congealed around Correa in 2006–2007. Diverse leftist currents converged in their opposition to neoliberal forms of extractivism that generated windfall profits for private investors, often foreign multinational corporations, while leaving behind environmental destruction and limited resources to help communities ameliorate the threats to local land, water resources, and community livelihoods. But with Correa coming to power at the height of Latin America's post-2003 commodity boom (A. de la Torre et al. 2020), the left sharply divided between indigenous and environmental movement currents that rejected any development model rooted in extractivism, and the more technocratic "resource nationalist" currents associated with Correa that sought to capture export commodity rents through a state-led model of extractive development (Riofrancos 2020). Correa and his allies thus doubled down on extractivism while hiking the taxes and royalties paid by foreign investors and redirecting the rents toward myriad forms of social spending and infrastructure investment. As stated by Conaghan (2011, 276), "Public investment as a percentage of GDP more than doubled from 2006 to 2009, growing from 5% to 14%" as Correa plowed resources into roadbuilding, housing projects, school construction, public health and education initiatives, targeted antipoverty and social assistance programs, and support for small businesses.

This state-led model of extractive development was the centerpiece of Correa's version of twenty-first-century socialism, and it generated substantial political dividends, despite the fissures within the left. Under the terms of the new constitution, new elections were scheduled in 2009, with Correa unshackled to run for reelection. Correa won comfortably with 52 percent of the vote, by far the largest vote haul of any presidential candidate in Ecuador's fragmented party system since the return to democracy in 1978–1979. Although the AP did not capture a majority of the seats in the Congress, its 47.6 percent of seats was also the largest obtained by any party during the democratic period. Both of these figures increased in the 2013 elections, when Correa received 57.2 percent of the presidential vote, and AP captured a formidable 73 percent of legislative seats.

This deepening electoral hegemony, however, came with a cost—namely, a reinforcement of the autocratic tendencies embedded within Correa's brand of personalistic and charismatic rule. From the outset, Correa ruled through an unusual hybrid blend of populist appeal and technocratic governance (C. de la Torre 2020), reflecting in part his own academic background and that of many of his closest advisers. Like Chávez in Venezuela, Correa had a ubiquitous presence in the mass media, traveling weekly with cabinet members for meetings in local communities broadcast over national radio and television outlets (Burbano de Lara 2020). His administration prioritized direct contact between citizens and the executive branch, while clashing repeatedly with organized interests in civil society that were independent of state control and averse to technocratic management. Under Correa, the state sometimes co-opted local groups or their leaders to help implement specific programs, and it also created parallel unions and civic groups to weaken, divide, or counterbalance more autonomous forms of association (Conaghan 2022, 206–210). But these state-directed groups were quite weak, and Correa rejected corporatist modes of interest representation that might have provided societal actors with institutionalized channels of access to policymaking arenas. Indeed, he saw organized intermediaries as narrow and self-serving interest groups that ignored the broader public interest and interfered with state technocrats' ability to define and pursue it. As such, he passed legislation to weaken unions and limit collective bargaining, and his government bypassed CONAIE by delivering public goods and services directly to local communities (Silva 2017, 105).

Furthermore, Correa routinely lambasted "infantile" environmental and indigenous activists who opposed his extractive development model, as well as elite interests hostile to his "citizens revolution" (C. de la Torre 2020, 95–96). He also introduced a maze of new regulations that placed restrictions on independent media and civil society organizations, including decree laws that strengthened the ability of the state to extend or withhold legal recognition of civic associations and even order their dissolution (Conaghan 2015; Martínez Novo 2020; Mantúfar 2020). Critics accused Correa of criminalizing protest, leaving "over 200 peasant-indigenous activists" facing "accusations of terrorism for resisting mineral resource extraction" (C. de la Torre 2020, 99; Mantúfar 2020, 78–81). As Selçuk (2024) suggests, Correa's brand of populist leadership was inclusionary for some Ecuadorian citizens but exclusionary for others, accentuating its polarizing tendencies.

As Mantúfar (2020) suggests, restrictions on the media and civil society served to undermine vertical or societal forms of democratic accountability under Correa, at the same time that hyperpresidentialism and single-party hegemony weakened the horizontal or institutional forms of accountability afforded by legislative and judicial checks and balances. Not surprisingly, Bermeo (2016, 12) highlighted Ecuador under Correa in her influential analysis of "executive aggrandizement" as a pathway toward democratic backsliding. By weakening the ability of other actors to oversee and monitor executive actions, this diminished accountability created novel forms of institutional impunity that enabled corruption and rent seeking, as they magnified presidential discretion to rule by decree and exercise unilateral control over the contracting of public works, state spending, and the operation of public enterprises (Mantúfar 2020). This lack of oversight and accountability was especially problematic in the context of the commodity boom, when Ecuador experienced the largest increase in state fiscal revenues and state expenditures in all of South America (A. de la Torre et al. 2020, 185). It fostered an institutionalization of corruption that subjected the Correa administration to renewed political criticism, while also insulating government technocrats from the kind of feedback mechanisms that might have encouraged more efficient and farsighted management of the country's temporary commodity windfall.

Ultimately, Ecuador avoided the type of economic calamity that befell Venezuela at the end of the commodity boom in 2013–2014, as well as a descent into a hardened form of authoritarian rule such as that of the Maduro regime in Venezuela. Political opposition to Correa was highly fragmented—indeed, it was split between leftist and rightist currents—and conservative forces did not radicalize or mobilize societal resistance to the extent seen in Venezuela and Bolivia. Nevertheless, the left turn began a tumultuous unraveling during Correa's third and final term in office after 2013, and it eventually imploded as a result of its internal contradictions. Correa was forced to make a series of difficult economic adjustments as export revenues plunged and the fiscal deficit surged (A. de la Torre et al. 2020, 192–205). Accustomed to governing in a period of economic prosperity and fiscal profligacy, the transition to renewed austerity, belt-tightening, and debt servicing proved divisive and disheartening for the populist regime. The AP suffered a series of high-profile defeats in the 2014 municipal elections for mayor, indicating a renewed strengthening of opposition political forces, and social protest activities increased among environmental and indigenous rights groups. By 2016, public opinion surveys for the first time indicated that more Ecuadorian citizens disapproved than approved of Correa's leadership (Latinobarómetro 2016). In this context, despite having passed a constitutional amendment allowing for indefinite reelection, Correa opted not to run for a fourth consecutive term in office. Correa and the AP designated former vice president (2007–2013) Lenín Moreno to be his successor in the 2017 election contest. Moreno came in first in the initial round of the election, but he finished just shy of the 40 percent of the vote needed to claim a first-round victory. In the second round of the election, Moreno edged out conservative former banker Guillermo Lasso with 51.2 percent of the vote to claim the presidency. The AP retained a congressional majority, but lost over a quarter of its seats and saw its share of the vote dip below 38 percent.

Moreno, however, quickly proved far more than a caretaker preserving the presidency in anticipation of Correa's return in 2021—indicating, once again, the challenges of leadership succession in the populist-left cases. Reading the shifting political winds, Moreno broke with Correa after taking office and criticized his government's corruption, economic mismanagement, and autocratic tendencies (Wolff 2018). Despite this break and Moreno's steering of the economy in a more orthodox conservative direction, the bulk of the AP sided with the new president in control of the reins of state power and resources (Conaghan 2022, 216–217). Moreno adopted several measures to strengthen accountability institutions and curtail corruption, and he called for a referendum in February 2017 that limited officeholders to one reelection and barred anyone convicted of corruption from holding public office. Moreno's campaign against corruption led to the prosecution of several of Correa's former cabinet ministers and a former vice president (C. de la Torre 2020, 106–107), and it put Correa himself—now in self-exile in Belgium—on the run. Correa's arrest was ordered by a judge in July 2018 in connection with an attempted kidnapping of a political opponent, and in 2020, the former president was tried in absentia and sentenced to eight years in prison on bribery charges for accepting kickbacks on government contracts for his political campaigns. This conviction prevented Correa from returning to Ecuador and running for office in 2021.

Correa's exodus and Moreno's conservative shift did little to stabilize Ecuadorian politics, however. Moreno's popularity plummeted over the course of his term in office, and a major new outbreak of indigenous-led social protest spearheaded by CONAIE in October 2019 forced him to temporarily relocate the seat of government from Quito, shortly before the devastating onset of the COVID-19 pandemic. AP all but collapsed in the 2021 national elections, losing all seventy-four of its seats in Congress after Correa and his supporters abandoned the party to form a new political movement, Citizens' Revolution Movement (CR), and then a new electoral front, Union for Hope (UNES). UNES elected the largest block of deputies to the national assembly in 2021, winning 49 out of 137 seats, while its presidential candidate, Andrés Arauz, an economist and former cabinet minister under Correa, received the largest percentage of votes (32.7 percent) in the first round of the presidential election. With the left divided between UNES and a newly strengthened Pachakutik, however, conservative leader Guillermo Lasso narrowly edged Pachakutik candidate Yaku Pérez to make it into the second round of the election. Lasso then defeated Arauz in the runoff, when many of Pachakutik's first-round voters opted to abstain or vote for the staunch neoliberal Lasso rather than support the candidate of Correismo (see Moncagatta et al. 2023).

Yet another major indigenous uprising led by CONAIE in June 2022 placed Lasso on the political defensive, however, clearly signaling a revival of the social protest cycles against neoliberal austerity and extractivism that so profoundly shaped Ecuadorian politics before Correa's ascendance in 2006. With Lasso buffeted by corruption charges and a steep rise in criminal violence related to drug trafficking, the national assembly launched an investigation and impeachment hearings in March of 2023. As formal impeachment proceedings got underway in May, Lasso abruptly invoked a constitutional provision that allowed him to dissolve the national assembly, govern by decree, and schedule new elections within six months. Lasso declined to run for another term in office, leading to a wide-open presidential race that was marred by the assassination of one of the eight candidates, who had run on an anticorruption platform. As in 2021, Correa's chosen candidate, Luisa González, came out on top during the first round of the presidential election but lost in the runoff to a conservative member of the business elite, Daniel Noboa, a son of the billionaire banana tycoon and five-time presidential candidate Álvaro Noboa. Upon taking presidential office, Noboa was quickly faced with an armed uprising by drug-trafficking cartels and responded by militarizing domestic security policies and declaring a state of exception that placed restrictions on civil rights and liberties.

In short, Correa's populist interregnum undoubtedly left its mark on Ecuadorian politics, but it failed to build a sustainable democratic majority around an alternative to neoliberalism, much less ground it in deeper and more inclusive forms of civic engagement and popular participation. Instead, it left behind a legacy of a divided left and political instability, with a ruling conservative elite confronting highly mobilized popular movements and a deteriorating security situation that opened the door for a more militarized state response. Rather than spawning a deeper and more radical form of democracy, Correa's Citizens' Revolution and its aftermath, it appears, took Ecuador full circle.

Uruguay's Broad Front

Uruguay under the Broad Front (FA) is a case of a left turn that largely followed the social democratic modal pattern. It shares many similarities with the experiences of the social democratic left in Brazil and Chile, including its formative experiences and repression under military rule, but also important differences in terms of the institutional context in which it rose to power. Compared to the PT and the PSCh, the three consecutive FA presidencies of Tabaré Vázquez (2005–2010), José "Pepe" Mujica (2010–2015), and Vázquez again (2015–2020) had a much stronger position in Congress, with a partisan majority in both houses of Congress across all three administrations. This meant that the FA could pursue its reformist agenda and devise formulas to address social needs without an intransigent legislative opposition wielding veto power or the need to engage in broad multiparty coalition building with centrist or conservative parties. This strong position in Congress also meant that, to pass legislation, the FA did not need to cut deals with conservative parties or mobilize its organized social bases to put pressure on Congress.

What also set apart the FA from its counterparts in the social democratic camp was the same feature that distinguished Bolivia's MAS from its counterparts in the populist-left camp: It managed to cultivate and preserve strong organic ties with unions and social movements, which in turn retained autonomous mobilization capacity (e.g., Doglio et al. 2004; Pérez Bentancur et al. 2019; Anria et al. 2021; Anria and Bogliaccini 2022). These connections were critical and two-sided in nature; they helped the party expand social and political inclusion, although at times they also posed constraints on the political leadership and its social agenda. But in general, seen in comparative perspective, these societal linkages helped the FA limit professionalization around party and technocratic elites as well as the worst excesses of the conformist temptation—from systematic corruption, as occurred in Brazil, to the kinds of mass discontent, social protest, and political outflanking that the Chilean PSCh eventually encountered. After fifteen years in power, the FA was narrowly defeated electorally by conservative forces in 2019. Similar to Argentina, this produced a routine alternation in office after multiple terms, while keeping the FA as the main opposition contender. In 2020, the FA had a strong performance in subnational elections, demonstrating continued electoral strength and a capacity to compete for the presidency. It then reclaimed the presidency in 2024 after five years under the conservative administration of Luis Lacalle Pou.

Although the FA was founded in 1971, its formative experience goes back further in time. It was the result of, on the one hand, the unification of the labor movement that began in the 1960s, and on the other hand, a decade-long effort by Uruguay's Marxist and non-Marxist leftist groups to build a broad electoral coalition to break the historic political domination of the Blanco and Colorado parties (see Caetano et al. 2021, 71–94). This strategy of developing alliances between different leftist parties, splinter groups from the traditional Blanco and Colorado parties, and different class and cultural interest groups yielded several different electoral "fronts" in the early 1960s, with varying levels of electoral success (Giorgi 2011).

Parallel to this unification and strengthening of an electoral left, after the mid-1960s—much like Argentina, Brazil, and, more tentatively, Chile—Uruguay experienced the rise of a Marxist insurgent movement committed to revolutionary change. Inspired by the Cuban Revolution, a well-organized urban guerrilla movement—the Tupamaros—sought to precipitate a social revolution by carrying out a series of high-impact operations. In 1967, the government of Jorge Pacheco Areco (1967–1972) of the Colorado Party responded to this ideological and strategic radicalization with violent repression by security forces. This ushered in a period of escalating state violence and the eventual establishment of a bureaucratic authoritarian military regime in 1973, which was committed to the destruction not only of the Tupamaros insurgency but also of civilian leftist networks. It was, as Gillespie (1985, 99) says, "the first military dictatorship the country had known."

Upon its founding in advance of the 1971 elections, therefore, the FA faced the adverse conditions of political repression. The shared trauma of repression provided incentives to unite many groups on the left, each with different histories, organizational identities, and grassroots followings, under a single "front" (Aguirre Bayley 2000; Lanzaro 2004). It also drove efforts to develop a political alternative that "transcended political violence," implicating both government repression and guerrilla activity (Caetano et al. 2021, 95). The idea of forming such a front had deep roots in the history of the Uruguayan left (Alonso 2021, 201). Much like the PT, the FA became a place of convergence for various forces from the left, including Communists, Socialists, Christian Democrats, the labor movement, the student movement, and community organizations.[2] The FA was born, then, as a coalition of previously existing parties, political factions, and social movements drawn to the different democratic imaginaries of institutionalized pluralism and popular sovereignty (Giorgi 2011). This convergence and unification process on the left was a major challenge, but the "harsh times that the country was suffering" eventually resulted in "an agreement on a few major ideological and programmatic issues" and a consensus on a unified presidential candidacy (Rosenblatt 2018, 186; see also Lanzaro 2004; Yaffé 2005).

The FA first ran for office in the 1971 presidential election—amid deepening polarization—with a "clearly leftist platform" (Rosenblatt 2018, 185), which emphasized the need to respect liberties, rights, and freedoms, as well as the importance of democracy and pluralism (Caetano, Marchesi, Markarian 2021, 96). In that election, it received close to 20 percent of the vote (Lanzaro 2011). Much of its early organizational development, however, was conditioned by the country's bureaucratic authoritarian regime between 1973 and 1985. The military, as Van Dyck (2021, 163) puts it, "severely curtailed left opponents' freedom of speech, press, and association. It incarcerated more political prisoners, in per capita terms, than any other bureaucratic authoritarian regime. It exiled thousands of opponents and disappeared dozens more." It even imprisoned the FA's leader and first presidential candidate, General Líber Seregni, sending powerful shockwaves throughout the organization. Much like the PT, in clandestine opposition the FA developed a strong and cohesive organization with territorial branches. It also developed a network of independent Base Committees capable of incorporating committed activists (Pérez Bentancur et al. 2019), and several internal factions came to recognize the need to broaden the scope of alliance building (Caetano et al. 2021, 105). Although the party was not founded directly by social movements as their electoral vehicle—as was the case with the PT, described in chapter 2—it developed strong linkages to organized labor, the highly mobilized student movement, and community-based activist networks (Luna 2007). These societal connections were critical for the party in developing a robust organizational infrastructure and activist base during the military-authoritarian period, enabling it to survive political repression and retain a stable core of grassroots support.

This resilience became evident in 1983, when Uruguay began its redemocratization process and the FA reemerged as a relevant actor in the country's "pacted" transition (Karl 1990, 13–14). Akin to what happened in Brazil and Chile, the party's early formative experience in opposition to a military regime deeply shaped its democratic vocation down the road. The harsh authoritarian regime and escalating levels of violence had "inflicted a traumatic experience on its activists and leaders," who experienced repression and suffered the costs (Rosenblatt 2018, 186). This collective experience of trauma infused the party with a common purpose "that transcended the left's factional divisions" (Van Dyck 2021, 164). Despite their ideological and strategic differences, and despite their differential exposure to repression (Rosenblatt 2018, 188), the broad constellation of groups and political factions that shaped the FA came to agree that a transition to democracy should serve as a base for the pursuit of economic redistribution, social inclusion, and basic citizenship rights. By the beginning of the negotiations for regime transition, even significant segments of former Tupamaros had abandoned armed struggle and opted for a peaceful electoral route, inching along with the idea of becoming part of the FA. As Caetano et al. (2021, 118) note, by the early 1980s the trauma of repression had fundamentally transformed the Uruguayan left: "The experiences of imprisonment and exile in different parts of the world had led to an appreciation of other political experiences, such as European social democracy or Latin American national-popular movements ... or to critically reassess the perception of the socialist bloc. Likewise, the suffering caused by state terrorism and dictatorships led to a renewed appreciation of the democratic question and basic political and civil rights, which had been relativized in the 1960s."

Uruguay experienced a transition to democracy whose terms were less unilaterally imposed by the military than those in Brazil and Chile. After receiving a crushing defeat in a constitutional referendum held in 1980, the same year that Pinochet won his in Chile, the military had no choice but to accept a regime transition (Lissidini 2001; Cason 2000, 87). Facing a wave of destabilizing protests and strikes in which core social allies of the FA, such as the PIT-CNT (the national labor confederation), played a leading role, the military junta invited the FA to join the negotiations of the so-called Naval Club Pact. This inclusion was conceived as a way out of the dilemma of wanting to hand back power to civilians while preventing a Blanco victory in the elections promised for 1984 (Gillespie 1985, 103). It entailed a rehabilitation of the left, albeit a "partial rehabilitation," as the Communist Party and groups linked to the Tupamaros guerrilla movement remained excluded (Rial 1985, 85).

The political logic of the regime transition thus strengthened the more moderate, social democratic currents within the FA that embraced institutionalized pluralism as an essential foundation for diverse popular struggles aimed at deepening democracy. The FA joined in the elite pact making and opted for a strategy of "mobilization *and negotiation*" along with the Colorados and the clerical Civic Union (Gillespie 1985, 104, emphasis in original). The Blancos, by contrast, followed a more confrontational strategy and opted out of the negotiations. In March 1984, the military government released General Líber Seregni, the leader of the FA who had spent nine years in prison. Although Seregni—along with the leaders of the main national parties—was banned from voting or running for office, he accepted the military's terms, and "his first speech was moderate in tone, committing the Left to a peaceful electoral road" (Gillespie 1985, 103; see also Rial 1985, 85). While dissident groups existed within the FA and there were "significant discrepancies" regarding the desired form of democracy, the more radical factions advocating a purely mobilizational strategy remained marginal (Caetano et al. 2021, 115–116).

Behind this strategy of seeking a broad consensus were electoral considerations and a commitment to institutionalized pluralism. The Blanco Party was hemorrhaging voters because of its uncompromising approach and its proposed free-market economic policies. At the same time, support for the FA remained stable when compared to 1971, as polls showed (Gillespie 1985, 105). The FA attempted to capitalize on the Blanco Party's loss of support, especially among low-income voters. It took advantage of its legalization to propose a unified list of candidates, earning 21.3 percent of the vote in the 1984 general election under the registration label of the Christian Democratic Party (Rial 1985, 103).[3] Although it did not win any major posts, the party continued to play a major role in the construction of a new democratic order, placing pluralism and human rights at the center of its platform. The FA fought hard, for example, along with civil society organizations, to repeal a law that granted amnesty from possible prosecution to members of the military and the police who had committed crimes against humanity. Known as the Law on the Expiration of the Punitive Claims of the State (Ley de Caducidad), it was the product of an agreement between the traditional parties in the immediate aftermath of the democratic transition. The FA also participated continuously with workers and human rights movements in an annual "march of silence" to remember the lives of those disappeared during the authoritarian regime (Rosenblatt 2018, 189–190).

A major electoral breakthrough occurred in 1989 when the FA won the municipal election in Montevideo—Uruguay's capital city. This was the first time that a party other than the Blanco and Colorado parties won a major executive election, and it was a significant blow to Uruguay's historical two-party system. Thereafter, the FA made steady electoral growth at the local and national levels, achieving governing experience at the subnational level and experience in legislative opposition in the national Congress. Local experiences in public administration, especially governing Montevideo for successive terms, encouraged a focus on electoral and institutional activity, which was supplemented with grassroots activism and periodic mobilization campaigns around popular referenda to block the adoption of specific neoliberal reforms. The experiences of the FA mayors (Tabaré Vázquez and Mariano Arana) governing Montevideo also encouraged a process of ideological and programmatic moderation to focus on concrete problem-solving tasks, which—in contrast to the parallel processes of moderation experienced by the PT in Brazil and the PSCh in Chile—did not necessarily distance the party from its union and social movement bases.

As Luna (2014, 246) argues, these experiences helped to *strengthen* the linkages between the FA and popular movements by developing a "close to the people administration" with tangible results in Uruguay's capital.

An important factor helping to preserve and strengthen party-society ties—and boost lower-class support—was a municipal decentralization process propelled by the FA in Montevideo. Following campaign promises, the FA implemented decentralizing reforms that placed "strong faith in the participation and transformative power of civil society" (Álvarez-Rivadulla 2017, 120). This process enabled local activist networks to engage in public deliberations and in social welfare provision.[4] Although the results of this process were uneven in terms of their impact on governmental decisions, some scholars identified positive effects on political participation (Canel 2014). Most agree that decentralization reforms brought the city government "closer to citizens" (Álvarez-Rivadulla 2017, 121) while "increasing the party's electoral dominance in the historical constituencies of both traditional parties" (Luna 2014, 247). Local experiences of decentralization demonstrated the party's commitment to institution building and to preserving feedback channels with its grassroots social bases. As Rosenblatt (2018) argues, moreover, those experiences enabled the party to strengthen organizationally by raising the "exit" costs for party leaders and activists.

While governing experiences at the municipal level induced moderation, experience in legislative opposition encouraged the party to consolidate its brand and distinctiveness in a different institutional arena—the Congress. As in the case of the PT, the FA's role in legislative opposition allowed it to develop a strategy to differentiate itself from Uruguay's dominant parties, the Blancos and Colorados. These parties had dominated Uruguayan politics for nearly two centuries, and since the late 1980s and early 1990s, they had been committed to dismantling the import substitution industrialization (ISI) model and implementing neoliberal reforms. In that context of dominant party ideological convergence, the FA gradually abandoned its more radical Marxist and anti-imperialist rhetoric while developing a consistent anti-neoliberal orientation (Lanzaro 2004). Party representatives from different factions at times managed to function as a veto coalition against the advance of market-friendly legislation (Luna 2014, 239–242).

The FA defended the interests of ISI beneficiaries, including organized labor, and expanded its reach to new constituencies, such as the informal sector and the non-unionized poor (Yaffé 2005, 95; see also Luna 2014, 252). This opposition role allowed representatives in Congress "to mount aggressive resistance to proposed [market-oriented] legislation" initiated by the dominant parties while preserving party discipline (Pribble 2013,

130). At the same time, the party relied on the use of mechanisms of direct democracy, particularly popular referenda, to strengthen its coalitional power, mobilize popular constituencies, and challenge important market reforms, including pension reforms and the privatization of state-owned industries (Altman 2002). As social discontent with the dominant parties and their economic policies grew in the late 1990s, the then-three-party alignment began to shift toward a two-block alignment, with the country's two traditional parties forming a conservative block against a rising leftist challenger (Roberts 2014, 232).

Engaging in institutional arenas following Uruguay's pacted transition to democracy induced moderation and foreclosed attempts to carry out a project of extrasystemic mass mobilization. But as the FA moved toward the center while pursuing national-level power, its successful experiences at the subnational level and legislative opposition to neoliberalism allowed the party to defend its historical commitments. Those experiences also enabled the party to expand its bases of support without alienating its more radical internal currents and its network of independent grassroots activists (Pérez Bentancur et al. 2019). As Sells (2022, 279) notes, moreover, the FA continuously deepened its inclusivity. Since the late 1980s, its "structure as a coalition was particularly useful for absorbing new actors from outside its original founding group," and this became vital for the party's growth in the 1990s and early 2000s. In 1989, for example, it incorporated far-left groups, including the Popular Participation Movement (MPP), a faction organized by ex-Tupamaro guerrillas, and the Party for the Victory of the People (PVP), an anarchist faction. Starting in the mid-1990s, the FA also incorporated splinter groups from the traditional parties and a wide array of new sectors. This growing inclusivity helped to broaden the party's reach as well as its internal heterogeneity, thereby "expanding the range of ideological space that the Frente occupied" (Sells 2022, 280).[5]

Tensions between factions promoting the two democratic imaginaries (see fig. 1.1) increased as the party pursued national office and as the Cold War drew to a close, sparking heated debates about the relationship between democracy, authoritarianism, and the left (Caetano et al. 2021, 119–130). But unlike the PT, the FA did not develop a dominant coalition that could control the party from the top down, and party structures remained important in managing internal conflict and leadership disputes (Caetano et al. 2003). This meant that issues related to programmatic orientation, party strategy, and the scope of electoral alliance making remained intensely debated and, at times, challenged by the more radical factions and allied civil society groups. At times, those challenges remained disruptive. And yet, the FA leadership, like that of the PT in Brazil, progressively sidelined radicalized groups that were reluctant to participate in elections and formal institutions (Yaffé 2005; Luna 2014, 243).[6] While the FA built broad alliances (Luna 2014, 242–245), it did so only with leftist factions and splinter groups from both traditional parties that were integrated into its coalitional structure and committed to deepening democracy within established regime institutions.

By 1999, the FA had become Uruguay's largest party. With a victory looking increasingly likely since 1994, when the FA almost won the presidency, Colorado and Blanco leaders proposed a constitutional reform that, among other things, introduced a presidential runoff formula for the two highest vote getters in the first round (Cason 2002, 97). The reform, approved in 1996, created strong incentives for the traditional parties to unite against the FA in the runoffs. The reform worked as designed in 1999, when Vázquez won a plurality in the first round with over 40 percent of the vote but lost in the runoff to Colorado leader Jorge Batlle. But the reform proved only a temporary roadblock for the FA to access power via institutional means, as the Blanco and Colorado parties were experiencing significant declines in support (Buquet and Chasquetti 2005) in a context of rising economic and political discontent (Luna and Filgueira 2009).

Popular discontent intensified in the early 2000s, as Uruguay faced an economic and social crisis parallel to (and in part caused by) that of neighboring Argentina (Panizza 2014). However, social mobilization remained comparatively contained relative to the more explosive protest patterns seen in Argentina, Bolivia, and Ecuador at the turn of the century. The FA and its social allies—such as the PIT-CNT, Uruguay's chief trade union federation—showed a commitment to electoral mobilization and to channeling discontent through existing institutional arenas. This was evident in 2002, for example, when in the heat of the crisis, the FA supported Colorado leader and incumbent president Jorge Batlle, "at a time when it could have forced his removal by promoting street riots like those seen in Argentina" (Luna 2014, 244). Facing a deepening recession and rising unemployment, support for the Blanco and Colorado parties and the neoliberal policies they adopted plummeted. They were defeated for the first time in 2004, with the creation of an electoral alliance between the FA and two smaller leftist groups. This alliance enabled the reincorporation of groups that had abandoned the FA in the early 1990s, as well as the incorporation of new splinter groups from the traditional parties, taking Tabaré Vázquez to the presidency (Yaffé 2005, 105).

The triumph of Vázquez in 2004 ended the historic monopoly of the Blanco and Colorado parties (Caetano et al. 2021, 133). It also brought the FA to power in Uruguay, following the election of Lagos in Chile and Lula in Brazil. Unlike the PT and the Chilean PSCh, however, the FA assumed power as a majoritarian party, winning 51.7 percent of the first-round presidential vote and securing a majority of seats in both houses of Congress. This institutional leverage, unseen in the country since the 1958 election, made it possible for the FA to legislate and implement its program—so long as it remained cohesive—without having to cut deals and compromise with other centrist or conservative parties, an advantage never enjoyed by the PT and PSCh. At the same time, the FA, in contrast to the Socialists in Chile, retained strong organic ties to the PIT-CNT and other organized popular constituencies (Doglio et al. 2004; Anria et al. 2021). It also retained over three hundred active grassroots Base Committees with institutionalized voice in the party organization, making the FA a party "with intense activism from voluntary grassroots members" (Pérez Bentancur et al. 2019, 2–3). Although these organizational linkages and activist networks did not prevent the FA from moderating programmatically over time, they arguably constrained such moderation (Álvarez-Rivadulla 2017, 113–120), kept the party leadership more accountable to its social bases, and precluded mass social or electoral mobilization to the left of the FA, as eventually occurred in Chile (Yaffé 2013, 74).

Indeed, the FA is a major outlier to the dominant international trends, recognized since the classic study by Michels ([1911] 1962) and subsequently documented in numerous other works (Kirchheimer 1966; Panebianco 1988; Katz and Mair 1995; Dalton and Wattenberg 2000; Hunter 2010), whereby mass-based party organizations evolve toward increasing levels of organizational hierarchy, bureaucratization, and professionalization, accompanied by a withering of their local grassroots activist networks outside short-term electoral cycles. As stated by Pérez Bentancur et al. (2019, 7), the FA is a "deviant case," as the party retains "large numbers of engaged activists who are not a cadre of bureaucrats nor a part of a structure to deliver clientelistic goods." As such, the "crucial difference" between the FA and other parties "is the significant and permanent presence of activists throughout the territory who have an active role in the party organization and in the party's decision-making bodies" (Pérez Bentancur et al. 2019, 15). This permanent grassroots activism helped reproduce the FA's organizational ties to labor and popular movements and restrain the autonomy of office-seeking party elites. In so doing, it prevented major policy switches and moderated the conformist temptations that eventually took their toll on the PT and the Chilean Socialists.

Vázquez and the FA captured the presidency during the early stages of the commodity boom that helped Uruguay recover from the most severe recession in the country's modern history—a contraction of over 20 percent between 1999 and 2002 (ECLAC 2004, 56). In contrast to neighboring Argentina, the turn-of-the-century economic crisis did not spawn destabilizing mass protests; instead, it weakened the incumbent Colorado Party within the two-party conservative bloc that had promoted neoliberal reforms, while channeling dissent into the electoral arena toward the steadily rising FA. With commodity exports generating robust growth and ample state resources, Vázquez avoided a radical break with the inherited economic model, as he maintained fiscal and monetary discipline, contained inflationary pressures, and encouraged foreign and domestic private investment. At the same time, he adopted a series of pragmatic reforms aimed at redistributing income, strengthening the social safety net, and enhancing the bargaining power of organized labor. Indeed, Pribble and Huber (2011, 119) assert that Uruguay moved further in a social democratic direction under the FA than other countries within Latin America's left turn (see also Lanzaro 2014).

Reflecting the FA's organic linkages to the PIT-CNT, social policy reforms under Vázquez included a sharp increase in the minimum wage, which had declined precipitously since the 1970s (Bogliaccini 2024). Vázquez also issued a decree to reestablish Uruguay's Salary Councils, a form of sectoral neo-corporatist tripartite bargaining that had been abandoned during the neoliberal reforms of the 1990s. As Etchemendy (2019, 1434–1438) demonstrates, Uruguay joined Argentina as the two countries within Latin America's left turn with the most centralized wage bargaining institutions, the broadest collective bargaining coverage, and by far the highest rates of labor union density, at over 30 percent. In Uruguay, this represented a return to a centrally coordinated wage model with deep roots in the ISI period. Under Vázquez, over four hundred new grassroots unions were established and union membership nearly doubled (Lanzaro 2011, 368–369; Rodríguez et al. 2016). This strengthening of labor's collective voice helped Uruguay achieve a 65 percent increase in real wages during the FA's first ten years in office (Etchemendy 2019, 1434–1438). As Bogliaccini (2024, 38–44) further demonstrates, wage recentralization helped to reduce the gap between minimum and average wages, differentiating the Uruguayan experience from that in Chile, which remained under a decentralized bargaining scheme.

Beyond this support for workers, social and economic reforms under the FA aimed to broaden the coverage of various social welfare programs, in particular by extending their reach to the urban and rural poor outside the formal sectors of the workforce (Doglio et al. 2004). Vázquez launched new programs in nutrition, housing, and employment, along with a conditional cash-transfer program targeted at families living in extreme poverty—a stepping stone to an expanded, more universalistic family assistance program (Rossel et al. 2014). Notably, rather than relying on technocratic program management, he incorporated the FA's grassroots territorial networks to implement these social programs, "enrolling (often unpaid) volunteers to do everything from neighborhood visits, to survey design, to the distribution of information" (Pribble 2013, 85). Under Vázquez, the FA also introduced major reforms to Uruguay's health-care system "following an extensive process of consultation with organized interest groups and party militants" (Pribble 2013, 62). The reforms increased funding for the public health-care system and sharply reduced the disparities in services between private- and public-sector providers, in the process expanding coverage to achieve virtual universalism in health-care services. Vázquez paid for these ambitious social programs in part by introducing a progressive income tax as a supplement to Uruguay's traditional, regressive value-added consumption tax (Lanzaro 2011, 359–360). Both the income tax and the health-care reforms were adopted over the opposition of the traditional Blanco and Colorado parties, relying on the FA's legislative majority to implement key elements of the party's platform.

Active participation by the FA's grassroots Base Committees and union allies shaped the party's platform, while placing constraints on Vázquez and other party leaders in government positions. In the area of education policy, Vázquez was able to increase public spending and strengthen the representation of teachers' unions on administrative bodies, but union opposition blocked deeper structural reforms aimed at enhancing educational quality (see Pribble 2013, 113–116). In other areas, grassroots activism within the FA challenged moderating and technocratic tendencies within the party leadership, for example by blocking Vázquez's efforts to negotiate a free-trade accord with the US (Pérez Bentancur et al. 2020, 133–136) and advancing legislation to decriminalize abortion (which

Vásquez ultimately vetoed). The FA's organizational rules that institutionalized grassroots participation in local, regional, and national party governing bodies proved highly resistant to leadership efforts to professionalize the party, and meaningful participation bred a sense of efficacy that helped reproduce activism over time (Pérez Bentancur et al. 2020, 116–119), albeit at levels below their peak before the capture of national executive office. Cross-national surveys provided persuasive evidence that levels of grassroots activism within the FA were substantially higher than those found within the leftist governing parties in Brazil and Chile to which the FA was often compared. As reported by Handlin and Collier (2011), FA adherents boasted higher levels of partisan identification, meeting attendance, party campaign work, and union participation than their leftist counterparts in Chile and Brazil.

With Vázquez basking in high approval levels but prohibited from immediate reelection under the Uruguayan constitution, the FA nominated former Tupamaros leader José "Pepe" Mujica as its presidential candidate in 2009. Mujica, who spent fourteen years in prison under the military dictatorship and was revered for his austere lifestyle and common touch, swept to victory with 49.3 percent of the first-round vote and 54.6 percent in the runoff. Under Mujica, Uruguay maintained a healthy rate of economic growth during a period of international financial turmoil, and his government continued to devote public resources to strengthening the social safety net. By the end of Mujica's term in office, the percentage of the population living below the poverty line had fallen to 4.4 percent, down from 18.8 in 2005 (ECLAC 2007, 74; ECLAC 2016, 24), while the Gini index of inequality had fallen from 0.455 in 2005 to 0.381 in 2014 (*Estimación de la Pobreza* 2018, 45), the lowest level in Latin America. Mujica's FA government also advanced a series of liberalizing social reforms, including the decriminalization of abortion (which, as noted above, Vázquez had vetoed) and the legalization of gay marriage and cannabis, the latter under a state-regulated system of production, distribution, and sale (Tremlett 2014; Queirolo et al. 2019).

Although these social reforms sparked opposition from the traditional parties and conservative sectors of Uruguayan society, the FA was able to win a third consecutive term in office, returning Tabaré Vázquez to the presidency with 49.5 percent of the first-round vote and 56.5 percent of the second-round vote in the 2014 national elections. With the end of the commodity boom and a slowdown in economic growth between 2015 and 2019, however, Vázquez's second term proved rockier than his first (Anria and Bogliaccini 2022, 427). Rising concerns over crime and security weakened the FA government, as did a series of scandals related to the education credentials and alleged misuse of public funds by Vice President Raúl Fernando Sendic (Bogliaccini and Queirolo 2017). As Latin America's political winds shifted in a more conservative direction, political attrition after three terms in office for the FA allowed its conservative rivals to recapture the presidency in the 2019 general elections. FA candidate Daniel Martínez, the former mayor of Montevideo, won a plurality of the first-round vote, but the FA's vote share fell to 40.5 percent. Conservative forces coalesced behind Blanco Party candidate Luis Lacalle Pou to win a narrow second-round victory with 50.8 percent of the vote, against the 49.2 percent Martínez garnered. The FA also lost its majority in both houses of Congress but still claimed forty-two of ninety-nine seats in the lower house and thirteen of thirty seats in the Senate.

Uruguay's left turn thus came to an end with the 2019 elections, but this routine alternation in office left the FA in a relatively strong position as the primary opposition party to the new conservative government. Indeed, the FA won the mayorship of Montevideo in 2020, one year after losing the presidency. In contrast to the PT in Brazil and the PSCh in Chile, the FA's presidential defeat in 2019 did not come on the heels of mass social protest on the left or the right, chronic corruption scandals, or the ascendance of a populist radical right figure to political prominence. Arguably, the FA avoided the worst pitfalls of the conformist temptation that plagued its counterparts in Chile and Brazil; it sustained high levels of grassroots activism within the party organization, strong ties to labor and popular movements, a relatively cohesive party organization, and a programmatic commitment to progressive and redistributive social reforms, even as it backed away from its historic commitment to socialist transformation. The FA's mode of governance was less technocratic than that of the Socialists in Chile, and far less distorted by the requisites of multiparty coalition building that plagued the PT in Brazil. Ultimately, Uruguay exited the left turn with its party system relatively intact and with lower levels of political polarization than Chile and Brazil.

A LAPOP AmericasBarometer survey in 2021 provided ample evidence of some of the consequences of these distinct trajectories. In response to a question regarding the protection of citizens' basic rights by their national political system, 57 percent of Uruguayans said their rights were well protected, the highest percentage in Latin America (LAPOP 2023). Chileans ranked the lowest, with only 20 percent of citizens saying their rights were well protected; Brazil scored only a few points higher than Chile, at 24 percent.

Despite its electoral defeat in 2019, the FA maintained unity by drawing on its strong societal roots in Uruguay's popular sectors (Pérez Bentancur 2023). It retained the capacity to channel social discontent against the center-right government of Luis Lacalle Pou (2020–2024) and his Multicolor Coalition, which comprised the Blanco and Colorado parties, along with several smaller right-wing parties. The FA's continued ability to represent popular constituencies and channel social discontent—particularly among formal-sector workers—likely helped to prevent a movement-based outflanking on the left, as seen in Chile and discussed in chapter 2.

Although there remains significant ideological distance between the country's major partisan blocs, there is no polarized conflict in the post–left turn period over the basic rules of democratic contestation, and relatively little over the terms of social inclusion. A limited process of right-wing radicalization emerged in the run-up to the 2019 elections, echoing broader regional dynamics seen in the Southern Cone, where right-wing sectors have a recent history of military support and an emphasis on public security and social conservatism. The leading figure on the far right—Guido Manini Ríos, an army general under former president Tabaré Vázquez—captured 11.46 percent of the vote in the 2019 presidential elections, and his Open Cabildo party secured a handful of seats in Congress. However, Manini Ríos's vote fell to 2.6 percent in the 2024 presidential elections, leaving the far-right electorally marginal in Uruguay, without a major outflanking on the right comparable to that of neighboring countries.

Indeed, the traditional Blanco and Colorado parties still serve as crucial anchors of Uruguay's party system on the right, competing with the FA on the left within South America's most highly institutionalized party system, where the major players remain socially rooted (Piñeiro and Rosenblatt 2020). This two-block dynamic was readily apparent in the 2024 presidential election, which pitted the governing Multicolor Coalition (rebranded as the Republican Coalition) against the FA and revealed a sharp decline in support for Open Cabildo as a far-right alternative, with the party losing most of its recently gained seats in Congress (Canzani 2024). The FA reclaimed the presidency behind the candidacy of former history teacher Yamandú Orsi in a runoff after five years under a conservative administration, this time without its historical leaders—Vázquez and Mujica—at the helm. The victory demonstrated the FA's internal vitality and—unlike many other leftist parties in the region—its capacity for leadership renewal (Pérez Bentancur et al. 2022). It also demonstrated the particular ability of the Uruguayan party system to avoid outflanking on both the left and the right, given the continued dominance of the mainstream parties that anchored the party system following the return to democracy.

Left Peronism in Argentina

Argentina is a case of a left turn with markedly hybrid features and many contradictory tendencies. It was propelled by a mass rebellion, but one that ultimately empowered an established party and did not translate into a full-scale antisystemic backlash in the electoral arena. It is also a case that escaped the worst excesses of the conformist and autocratic temptations, and yet the left culminated its experience in office politically weakened, divided, and defeated by a right-wing party. On the one hand, the center-left Peronist presidencies of Néstor Kirchner (2003–2007) and his wife Cristina Fernández de Kirchner (2007–2015) attained higher degrees of policy radicalism than the social democratic cases discussed in chapter 2 (Etchemendy and Garay 2011, 300–302), and they also empowered a broad segment of the popular sectors (Rossi 2017; Schipani 2019, 151–169). This helped to prevent large-scale outflanking on the left and explosive social mobilization, as occurred in Chile — although it did not preclude the eventual rise of a far-right alternative in the figure of Javier Milei.

On the other hand, autocratic temptations were present within the governing coalition from the onset of the left turn. This was especially evident in Kirchner and Fernández's antagonistic dichotomization of the political field, which reflected their populist tendencies and those of their historical party. But the autocratic temptations were constrained, at least initially and partially, by historical legacies and institutional impediments, and the Kirchners made no effort to rewrite the constitution or refound the democratic regime like left-wing presidents in Bolivia, Ecuador, and Venezuela. Yet those temptations did rear their head and intensified over time in response to deteriorating economic conditions and opposition strategies. Following a tumultuous episode of severe institutional instability in 2001–2002, Argentina enjoyed a period of relative political calm under Peronist rule between 2003 and 2008. It then moved to a period of deepening polarization between Peronist and anti-Peronist coalitions, one that had the long-term effects of dividing the former and unifying the latter. This polarization set the stage for Peronism's division and political weakening. Torn apart by internal conflict over rival presidential candidacies, left Peronism was defeated electorally by conservative forces in 2015. This produced a routine alternation in office after multiple terms for Peronism's electoral vehicle, the Justicialist Party (PJ), and Peronism remained the main contender ready to dispute the presidency from the moment it lost it.

Argentina's PJ governments are often treated as occupying a middle ground within the broader left turn, and Argentina's left turn is often seen as a case that does not fit neatly in either of the standard binary categories (Weyland et al. 2010; Etchemendy and Garay 2011, 284). We argue that these intermediate tendencies reflect the complex, hybrid conditions associated with the party's formative and historical experiences and its return to power in the midst of Argentina's 2001–2002 financial and political crisis. Levitsky and Roberts (2011a, 13) classify the interim Peronist presidency of Eduardo Duhalde (2002–2003) and those of Néstor Kirchner (2003–2007) and Cristina Fernández de Kirchner (2007–2015) as leftwing governments led by a populist machine—an established party born in the 1940s with historical ties to organized labor, significant stakes in the post-1983 democratic regime, control over key subnational districts, and a nationwide territorial presence. In contrast to the "new" lefts discussed in chapter 3, the PJ experienced state and parastate political violence in the aftermath of its founding, especially after Juan Perón's ouster and exile in 1955 and a lengthy proscription between 1955 and 1972—a period when Peronism split into rival ideological factions and subgroups (Feinmann 2010). Violence against Peronism, especially its more radical leftist currents, intensified in the early to mid-1970s. This was after Perón returned to Argentina and was reelected in 1973, but especially after he died a year later and the presidency passed to his widow and vice president, María Estela (Isabel) Martínez de Perón. During the 1973–1976 period, the use of right-wing parastate organizations such as the Argentine Anticommunist Alliance (AAA) to combat leftist insurgent factions (both Peronist and non-Peronist), and the state-sponsored ouster of Peronist governors with links to leftist currents, helped set the stage for a military coup and the violent repression that followed (Servetto 2010). Violence against Peronism intensified even further between 1976 and 1983, a period dubbed "El Proceso," with the severe political repression that characterized military rule (Jackisch 1997). During this so-called Dirty War, Peronist politicians, union leaders, youth leaders, and militants were jailed, tortured, and disappeared, which decimated radical wings of the Peronist movement, such as the insurgent Montoneros and the Revolutionary Peronist Movement (MRP).

This exposure to authoritarian rule produced lasting legacies. The period of violence that preceded the 1976 military coup and the violent repression of the 1976–1983 dictatorship generated a "society wide reevaluation of civil liberties, electoral competition, and party activity" (McGuire 1997, 152), much as it did for social democratic currents on the left in Brazil, Chile, and Uruguay. Yet, even after seven years of harsh military repression, Peronism "continued to portray itself as the party of nationalism, intransigence, and populism" (McGuire 1997, 184), traits that were deeply rooted in the autocratic leadership of Perón himself during his career in politics. It took the emergence of democratic rule in 1983, the party's first-ever electoral defeat that same year, and the onset of high-profile trials of former military rulers for human rights violations to encourage a process of internal renewal dubbed "La Renovación" (McGuire 1997, 189–190; Levitsky 2003, 108–109). This included not only a revalorization of electoral goals and the integration of Peronist subgroups into party and electoral politics (Levitsky 2003, 49–50), but also a major rethinking of the party's views on democracy. In the 1980s, many party and union leaders who had lived under bureaucratic authoritarianism came to see democracy as something worth preserving—as a goal in and of itself. They never forgot the lessons of political repression, as they had suffered the costs. The PJ even joined forces with the then-governing, rival Radical Civic Union (UCR) in 1987, when democracy was under attack by a military rebellion, and party leaders signaled a commitment to preserving democratic institutions. This renewal process and strategic behavior in sustaining democratic rule helped strengthen social democratic currents within Peronism, which gained preponderance within the party during the 1980s (Levitsky 2003, 115).

With the return of democratic rule in 1983, Peronism's historical linkages to unions weakened, and its social bases shifted (Martuccelli and Svampa 1997). It transitioned "from a de facto labor party into a predominantly patronage-based party" (Levitsky 2003, 107). Such change was possible with the institutionalization of elections, which allowed PJ leaders to access office at the subnational level, encouraged them to build territorial structures and support networks, and gave them a stake in the system. Although the PJ did not gain the presidency in 1983, it obtained ample governing experience in legislatures and subnational governments. Beginning in 1989, after winning the presidency under the leadership of provincial boss Carlos Menem, the PJ shifted programmatically to the right and adopted neoliberal policies "by surprise," that is, after campaigning on a starkly different platform (Stokes 2001). This policy shift, adopted in response to a severe hyperinflationary crisis, strengthened promarket liberal internal currents vis-à-vis the party's more left-leaning social democratic currents, breaking abruptly with Peronism's historical statist and redistributive programmatic stands. At the same time, these bait-and-switch tactics diluted the Peronist party brand (Lupu 2016) and enabled a broader party-system dealignment (Roberts 2014). Although Menem's exercise of power had "delegative" features—for example, he governed making extensive use of emergency decrees and with scant checks from institutions of horizontal accountability—in the end, he accepted (reluctantly) the "hard facts" of constitutional term limits, along with broader constraints of formal democracy. And in spite of a severe new economic crisis that began in the mid-1990s—a crisis that brought about historically high levels of unemployment and poverty and shrank the country's robust middle class—Argentina remained democratic during Menem's two terms in office. In 1999, however, Peronism was defeated at the polls, and for the first time in its history, the party prepared to leave office by institutionalized means. What followed was a peaceful transfer of power to Fernando de la Rúa, who led a coalition called the Alliance for Jobs, Justice, and Education, which included his centrist UCR and the center-left Front for a Country in Solidarity (FREPASO). Key leaders of FREPASO were drawn from a Peronist splinter that had abandoned the PJ following Menem's turn to the right.

The De la Rúa government (1999–2001) failed to deliver on both the political and economic fronts, and especially on the latter (Levitsky and Murillo 2003, 154). He had defeated Menem while pledging to keep the convertibility law intact—a highly successful policy introduced by Menem and his economy minister Domingo Cavallo in 1991 that had pegged the Argentine peso to the dollar on a one-to-one rate by law and brought hyperinflation down nearly to zero. Although convertibility was highly popular, it led to an overvalued peso that weakened Argentina's export competitiveness. It also imposed serious constraints on what governments could do in the face of an economic downturn, as it restricted monetary and exchange-rate policy. Unable to get rid of convertibility and facing a sustained economic downturn and pressure from the International Monetary Fund, De la Rúa imposed austerity measures, which only deepened the recession. While his coalition suffered a major loss in the October

2001 midterm elections, the real challenge to his government unfolded two months later, when mass social protest erupted, paralyzing the country and bringing down his government in December (Silva 2009, 88–98). Following De la Rúa's resignation, Argentina defaulted on most of its national debt, and in a chaotic period of less than a month, the country had five different presidents.

Peronism came back to power at the national level at the beginning of 2002, propelled by a massive popular rebellion against the entire establishment. But even though Peronism returned to power in the aftermath of mass protests with antisystem properties, the *que se vayan todos* (throw everyone out) sentiments that shaped the 2001–2002 protests did not give rise to a full-scale antiestablishment outsider dynamic, as they did in Venezuela and Ecuador, or even to the rise of new movement-based alternatives, as they did in Bolivia. Rather, it was Eduardo Duhalde, a PJ senator, former governor of Buenos Aires and vice president to Menem, and a politician deeply embedded in the powerful Buenos Aires PJ machine, who was selected by Congress to lead an interim presidency. In contrast to the De la Rúa presidency, Duhalde managed an economic recovery after repealing the convertibility law, attaining a modicum of social peace. But protests continued, and the murder of two protesters in 2002 was the death knell of his interim presidency, prompting an early call for elections that would take place in a context of intensifying popular frustrations and mass mobilizations.

In the presidential election of 2003, as Levitsky and Murillo (2003, 159) claim, "notwithstanding widespread anger at the political elite, establishment candidates carried the day." This showed the electoral resilience of Peronism and the weakness and fragmentation of its partisan opponents, given the political damage suffered by its historic rival, the UCR. The contrast to Bolivia, Ecuador, and Venezuela was notable in this realm. While representative institutions were in crisis in all four cases, Peronism rose to power in a context of a *partial* party-system collapse, where only the non-Peronist parties had collapsed. Although the PJ was also divided and unable to agree on a unified presidential candidacy, it was not eclipsed by new extrasystemic or antisystemic electoral challengers such as the Venezuelan MVR or the Bolivian MAS, despite the strength of protest movements in the streets.

The mobilization of unemployed workers, for example, was critical in the 2001–2002 protest cycle. The movement had emerged in the mid-1990s — a context of severe unemployment, poverty, and indigence following the implementation of neoliberal policies and the convertibility plan (Svampa and Pereyra 2003; Wolff 2007, 6; Longa 2019, 34–35). It encompassed a wide range of organizations—often dubbed the *piqueteros* (street picketers)— that pressed the De la Rúa and Duhalde governments for greater state assistance (Garay 2007) and eventually helped to bring down their governments. But the movement did not produce its own electoral vehicle capable of translating protest energy into institutional arenas. That was largely intentional. Wary of electoral politics, in the lead-up to the 2003 election, major portions of the mobilized social actors rejected electoral paths to power or alliances with existing parties, privileging the barricades over the ballots (McAdam and Tarrow 2010). Although the mobilized actors had a strikingly diverse range of political and tactical positions, this was arguably more of a *destituyente* (or "destituent") than a "constituent" moment—a period of generalized rage against the establishment that did not produce a unifying demand to rewrite the constitution and refound the political order as in Bolivia or Venezuela, even though several establishment politicians and segments of the protest movement did talk about the need for a constitutional reform.

In the end, lacking sufficient support from different *piquetero* organizations for a more radical break with the old order, it was Peronism—as noted, a party deeply embedded in the system—that channeled some of the energy of the protest movement and translated it into electoral mobilization. Once restored to power in 2002, it began a process of popular-sector "reincorporation" within the parameters of existing institutions, rather than a constitutional refounding (Rossi 2017). Subsequently, in the 2003 presidential election, three different Peronist candidates captured a majority of the first-round votes.[7]

Nevertheless, major social movements were often viscerally wary of political parties. Inspired by Marxist "autonomist" currents that were skeptical of formal representative democracy, they sought to "prefigure" alternative forms of more radical, grassroots participatory democracy. Seeking to "change the world without taking power" (à la Holloway 2019), these movement activists remained at arm's length and opposed creating a party or engaging in electoral activity (Massetti et al. 2010; Longa 2017).[8] Most did not back Kirchner and his newly created (but pro-Peronist) electoral front, the Front for Victory (FPV). Moreover, different Peronist union factions supported rival candidates, including Menem and Adolfo Rodríguez Saá running on other Peronist lists. Duhalde's support was ultimately crucial for Kirchner's victory. Like Chávez, in his early days in office, Kirchner was politically isolated; he also lacked support from organized mass constituencies with high mobilizational capacity, such as labor unions or social movements (e.g., Etchemendy and Garay 2011, 299). Unlike Chávez (and Morales), however, Kirchner had relatively weak electoral legitimacy. He came to national power by capturing only a small percentage of the vote—22 percent—and did not have the whole PJ party behind him. Indeed, he initially "faced opposition within his own PJ and a more consistent challenge of centrist parties in important districts" (Etchemendy and Garay 2011, 302; see also Schipani 2019, 151).

The presidency of Néstor Kirchner was thus fraught with contradictions, paradoxes, and ambiguities from the beginning. In his inaugural speech, for example, Kirchner used the language of mass popular empowerment and sovereignty. He also established a connection between his presidency and the violent political struggles of the 1970s, claiming that he belonged to a "decimated generation" marked by "painful absences," and noting that "[Peronism] returned [to power] without rancor but with memory—memory not only of the errors and horrors made by others, but also memory of our own mistakes." In the speech, in short, there was a revindication of the party militancy of the 1970s, but at the same time an *autocrítica* (self-criticism) of the more revolutionary currents of 1970s Peronism—a recognition, perhaps, that Peronist insurgent currents had gone too far, contributed to the disunity of Peronism and the polarization of Argentine society, and even paved the way for the 1976 military coup. Both Kirchner and Cristina Fernández had initiated their political activism in the 1970s and incorporated some of the language and ways of understanding politics of the so-called national left, which was highly skeptical of liberal democracy, institutionalized pluralism, and individual rights (Perochena 2022, 148). But they also sought to rethink the role of Peronism in history, and they embraced human rights and electoral democracy as fundamental to their political project.[9]

Although Kirchner used the language of mass empowerment and had an "agonistic" understanding of democracy centered on the importance of struggle (Wenman 2013), he did not invoke the constitutive powers of "the people" as did his counterparts in Venezuela, Bolivia, and Ecuador. The institutional context did not favor the plebiscitary use of constitutive powers. Not only did Kirchner lack control over the PJ—in contrast to populist-left leaders like Chávez, Morales, and Correa who dominated or wielded more centralized control over their own parties—but also the PJ had an established foothold in many subnational governments, including governorships and municipal governments. According to Levitsky and Murillo (2003, 161), this was an important reason behind the failure of antiestablishment outsiders to win at the national level to begin with. It also meant that, once in power, Kirchner had to deal politically with the influence of prominent Peronist figures who wielded control over powerful subnational party machines, and who thus had a major stake in system maintenance. For example, Duhalde's influence over the Buenos Aires party machine gave him "a potential veto power over government policy" (Levitsky and Murillo 2003, 165). The design of Argentina's fiscal federalism was also a constraint. It usually means that presidents need to negotiate legislation with governors, and the negotiations often revolve around the distribution of fiscal resources (Bonvecchi and Lodola 2011). Although presidents usually have significant resources to discipline governors, governors cannot be easily ignored. And while the PJ gained solid control over Congress and did not need to build broad multiparty coalitions, this institutional feature meant that intraparty negotiations and coordination created legislative dynamics that served as checks and balances. These checks were stronger than in the populist cases discussed in chapter 3, at least before Kirchner gained control over the PJ (Cherny 2014). Thereafter, Peronist governors, including those in Buenos Aires Province, fell in line with Kirchner and offered only weak countervailing power (Gervasoni 2011).

Instead of calling a constitutional assembly, therefore, Kirchner sought to build a strong coalitional base by securing support from Peronist governors and mayors—hardly antiestablishment actors—with control over territorial structures and little reason to support any effort to refound the democratic regime or exercise new constitutive powers by a sovereign people. He also sought to mobilize social movements and have them on his side as social pillars, and to strengthen an alliance with labor unions, including Argentina's General Confederation of Labor (CGT), which by then was divided into "official" Peronist and dissident factions. The reactivation of collective bargaining, greater union control over the union-run health system, and an economic policy that promoted industrialization helped solidify that alliance (e.g., Etchemendy 2011; Svampa 2013, 14; Schipani 2019, 152–153). Although movements, especially those of poor and unemployed workers (but also several human rights movements), were highly skeptical of state institutions and formal democracy, a series of audacious measures in the realm of human rights and foreign policy helped to signal anti-neoliberalism and a commitment to left politics (Sarlo

2011). These measures attracted support from highly mobilized social movements (Boyanovsky Bazán 2010) and ensured a degree of governability in the wake of the *que se vayan todos* uprising. But those measures also helped to wither away the more radicalized demands and contain social protest, which remained high well into Kirchner's presidency (Schipani 2019, 146). Targeted social policies, expanded at the behest of social movements (Garay 2016, 198–210) and in some cases administered by them, also helped Kirchner build a strong basis of support to compete against and thus weaken the influence of rivals within Peronism, including Duhalde and his allied mayors in greater Buenos Aires (Rossi 2017, 197). Building bottom-up support from movements of the unemployed was key for gaining control over the fractious PJ (Ostiguy and Schneider 2018; Schipani 2019, 162–163).

As Longa (2019, 52, 56–59) shows, some leaders of prominent social movement organizations that were "brought in" and attracted by Kirchner's political project, such as Emilio Pérsico of the MDT Evita (Movement of Unemployed Workers Evita), had been members of the Montoneros who were exiled during much of the 1970s.[10] They also remained strongly linked to the more revolutionary currents of Peronism during the country's transition to democracy in the early 1980s — currents that were highly skeptical of formal democracy and institutionalized pluralism. Similar visions were held by other prominent leaders with mass followings, such as Víctor De Gennaro and Fernando "Chino" Navarro (Boyanovsky Bazán 2010). This meant that, as social movements moved from the streets closer to institutionalized arenas, and even populated bureaucracies at the national and subnational levels (Etchemendy and Garay 2011; Perelmiter 2016; Rossi 2017), the two democratic imaginaries would coexist within the Peronist governing coalition — often in tension with each other. Such tensions also coexisted within major social movements that supported the government. In fact, their new proximity to state institutions and the "normalization" of institutional politics that took place under Kirchner helped trigger a process of introspection.[11] Movements like the MDT Evita, on the one hand, praised the militancy and confrontational (*movimientista*) nature of the left-wing Peronist Youth (JP) in the 1970s and, on the other hand, came to embrace, value, and respect the democratic rules of the game that took so much work and so many sacrifices to build.[12]

Although Néstor Kirchner backed away from invoking constitutive powers, he was willing to challenge the status quo in programmatic terms — far more than the PT in Brazil and the PSCh in Chile. Indeed, both Kirchner and Cristina Fernández "mobilized the organizations of the unemployed in support of their administration and against the economic establishment" (Etchemendy and Garay 2011, 301). Their willingness to challenge the status quo was immensely popular; it also helped Kirchner and Fernández mitigate the worst excesses of the conformist temptation and prevent the reemergence of destabilizing contentious politics such as that of the 2001–2002 protest cycle or something like the iterative cycles of student and mass protest in Chile. Commanding a high-performing economy between 2003 and 2010, they delivered tangible benefits to their expanding social base, preserved strong connections to organized popular constituencies, and used their rising popularity to seize greater control and consolidate dominance over Peronism. To do this, according to Andrews-Lee (2021, 184–185), Kirchner and Fernández recurrently employed the tactics of charismatic leadership: Evoking the Peronist legacy, they both launched audacious policies followed by portraying themselves as the champions of "the people" and defenders of their supporters against powerful, ill-intentioned enemies—the "antipeople." In so doing, these leaders "reanimated the cleavage Perón had emphasized between the privileged and the poor," between the "haves" and "have-nots" (Andrews-Lee 2021, 185). From the beginning, Kirchner and Fernández relied heavily on such symbolic constructions to ground their political project (Iraola 2011).

This was in essence a way of structuring and aligning political space following Laclau's (2005) classic conceptualization of populism—an antagonistic, binary division of the political field that was hardly novel in Argentina. As Perochena (2022) further demonstrates, Kirchner and Fernández, but especially the latter, relied heavily on the use of history to establish clear identity boundaries, create a distinctive Kirchnerist political identity, and polarize the political field. In presidential speeches, for example, Fernández recurrently found her core political adversaries, the roots of Argentina's historical "wrongs," in historical events, and she traced their long-term influence on present-day events and political alignments. The stronger the enemies of "the people" were, Perochena (2022, 30) further claims, the stronger the efforts to boost the Kirchnerist identity. This identity was framed using a bellicose metaphor, and Fernández portrayed herself as leading a "cultural battle" that was seen as necessary to deepen the "model of social and political inclusion" under her government. It was also an attempt to develop a new democratic imaginary. In speeches, for example, she emphasized that "we [Kirchnernists] are democratic." But, similar to Perón back in his day, she had an ambiguous relationship with the liberal tradition and a deeply majoritarian and "agonistic" view of democracy (Perochena 2022, 46, 148). This ambiguity was consistent; indeed, it was a hallmark of both Kirchner's and Fernández's presidencies.

Opposition strategies contributed to the radicalization of the government, especially after 2008 with the so-called farmers' rebellion—a series of protests, lockouts, and road blockades organized by rural producer's associations that was triggered by the government's attempt to raise taxes on soybean exports at the height of the commodity boom (Etchemendy and Garay 2011). Although the tax measure was defeated in a fairly dramatic twist of events in the Argentine Senate, it was a turning point that deepened political polarization. If Kirchner had been only "partially populist," Kirchnerism under Fernández made a "full-fledged populist turn" (Svampa 2013, 14). Cristina had won the 2007 presidential election by significant margins—45 percent to the 23 percent received by her main rival, Elisa Carrió, of the centrist Civic Coalition (CC)—thanks to a large extent on the positive legacies of Kirchner's presidency, the strength of Peronist territorial machines, and the weakness and division of the opposition (Levitsky and Murillo 2008). She also, like Kirchner, had built a "transversal" coalition which included non-Peronist forces—the so-called Kirchnerist radicals (*radicales K*) and other center-left parties. Once in office, Fernández had a majority of seats in both legislative chambers (Levitsky and Murillo 2008, 24). Peronist governors cooperated with her and backed most of the PJ's legislative initiatives. But the conflict with rural producers encouraged several Peronist legislators and members of the "transversal" coalition to align with agricultural interests in opposition to the government. Her popularity and electoral support declined sharply, and Peronism experienced a painful loss in the 2009 legislative election, including in key districts such as Buenos Aires Province. By then, the "transversal" coalition had broken apart and would not be reassembled. As Fernández's legislative support weakened, she intentionally sharpened the binary divide between "us" and "them." While the latter was a moving and expanding target (Perochena 2022, 27), it was portrayed as a threat—both real and latent—to her government and to democracy more generally. Fernández was explicit about this in her 2019 autobiography, *Sinceramente*, where she interpreted the conflict with rural producers, and several that followed, as one involving the forces of good, the people, against the forces of evil, the corrupt elites (Fernández de Kirchner 2019).

But Cristina Fernández thrived in adversity. As her FPV's electoral fortunes declined, rather than moderating, conflict intensified. Indeed, it became virtually existential even while it stayed largely within the institutional boundaries—in contrast to Venezuela, for example. As Perochena (2022, 30) suggests, in moments of electoral weakening, Fernández employed political polarization as a weapon to mobilize popular support in her battles against real and perceived enemies. After picking a fight with associations of rural producers in 2008, the following year she confronted the mass media with a new media law, which deepened the polarizing logic, and then challenged the judiciary, which was seen as an obstacle to the implementation of the new media law and as an "antidemocratic" branch more generally (Perochena 2022, 34). While animosity between government and the opposition was clearly mutual, this increased polarization strengthened the governing coalition but did not foster parallel unity among the opposition—at least in the short run. And indeed, after suffering a major loss in the 2009 midterm elections, Kirchner's sudden death in October 2010 helped to revitalize charismatic linkages and gave Fernández a major boost in popularity (Ollier 2015). Facing adversity, including sustained social protest by both unemployed workers' movements and—increasingly distant—union allies, the Fernández government expanded social policy, which included new and highly popular social policy innovations, including a universal child allowance program (Garay 2016, 212–217). She also signed into law a bill legalizing same-sex marriage, an advance in rights for LGBTQ+ people attained by social mobilization from below, but with clear support from the Fernández government (Díez 2015). Economic growth resumed in 2010, and Fernández was reelected in a landslide in 2011, having faced a fragmented opposition (Calvo and Murillo 2012, 155–157).

Having received 54 percent of the vote was emboldening, and it strengthened internal Peronist currents that, while being political minorities, held a deeply majoritarian understanding of democracy and wielded influence in the government. For Svampa (2013, 15), for example, this overwhelming electoral support intensified Fernández's "hegemonic temptation" and gave rise to a "governmental belief" that "only Peronism can articulate popular-sector interests." Other existential conflicts emerged in Fernández's second term, and they intensified when the impact of the economic downfall that started in 2012 was felt. Cristina pushed for the nationalization of YPF, the country's largest energy firm, and for a judicial reform. The growing separation between her government, unions, and the PJ created organizational space for the expansion of a youth organization—La Cámpora—which gained increasing influence within the government (Natanson 2012) and provided mobilizational support to carry out these bold initiatives (Russo 2013). But worsening economic conditions, including high inflation and a looming balance-of-payments crisis, served as a reality check and severely constrained the government's ability to deliver on its platform. They also distanced the government from former allies, like labor unions, deepened its autocratic proclivities, and set the stage for its division and eventual political defeat (Svampa 2013, 15).

Taken together, Kirchner's and Fernández's polarizing approach weakened political institutions (Andrews-Lee 2021, 189), but this needs to be qualified. Although both presidents, but especially Fernández, sought to concentrate power and establish a hegemonic project (Gamallo 2014; Pucciarelli and Castellani 2019), one "based on controlled social participation under state tutelage and the figure of a leader" (Svampa 2013, 16), Kirchnerism did not alter the rules of the game or tilt the playing field against opposition forces in highly skewed ways. Unlike the populist cases discussed in chapter 3, neither Kirchner nor Fernández attempted to "deepen" democracy via a constitutional refounding or the creation of formal new participatory initiatives to expand political inclusion and mass participation. But social citizenship rights expanded dramatically under their presidencies, and social organizations were granted new forms of access to government agencies and influence over social policies.

Unlike the populist cases, moreover, Kirchnerism did not attempt indefinite reelections and accepted, if grudgingly, the "hard facts" of constitutional term limits. But the increased polarization was a weakness. It not only brought Kirchnerism into conflict with opponents, but also made it clash with its social allies. As corruption issues emerged (Figueroa 2021), tensions between internal currents within the FPV governing coalition intensified. Anticorruption protests developed in Buenos Aires in 2012 and 2013 and expressed concerns about authoritarian and illiberal tendencies; tellingly, protesters, mostly middle-class segments, developed a frame in defense of "the republic." The defection of Sergio Massa, a prominent government official under Néstor Kirchner and then cabinet chief under Fernández between 2008 and 2009, revealed those tensions and dynamics. Massa left the FPV pledging to defend democracy against executive aggrandizement, claiming that it was necessary to "stop Cristina" and prevent an "eternal Cristina," alluding to ongoing discussions within the FPV to alter term limits. This revealed, in turn, the remarkable internal heterogeneity of left Peronism—the coexistence of internal currents promoting the two different democratic imaginaries (see fig. 1.1) that checked and restrained each other and, in this case, helped to prevent some of the excesses of the autocratic temptation. Massa formed a new party, the Renewal Front (FR), and attracted the support of several FPV mayors and legislators, winning heavily in the 2013 midterm legislative election (Gilbert 2013). Disagreement around the presidential candidacy of Daniel Scioli as the FPV nominee in 2015 added fuel to the fire. Seen by the more radical leftist wings of Kirchnerism as an imposition from above, this nomination created further division. In contrast, conservative opposition forces formed an effective national coalition, Cambiemos (Let's Change), which united the right-wing Republican Proposal (PRO) of Mauricio Macri with the UCR and the Civic Coalition Ari. Although in the 2015 election Macri placed second in the first-round vote, by uniting the disparate opposition parties, he secured 51.34 percent in the second round, winning the presidency and forcing left Peronism out of power via routine electoral alternation. Although left Peronism—a consistent hybrid that had features of both the social democratic and the populist patterns—culminated multiple terms in office weakened and politically divided, it remained a weighty actor in opposition and the main contender to a new conservative government.

Macri's victory was deeply symbolic. For the first time since the country's democratic transition in 1983, a right-wing political party gained power via democratic elections (Vommaro 2023). It also signaled the return to power of non-Peronist forces after a thirteen-year hiatus of consecutive left Peronist presidencies. Although Cambiemos envisioned "Argentina without Peronism," Macri's presidency proved a short-lived right turn (Anria and Vommaro 2020). Unable to muster political support to carry out a "gradualist" program of market reform (Vommaro and Gené 2023), Macri ended his four years in government with a dire economic record in the midst of a region-wide slowdown that began with the end of the commodity boom. Unable to consolidate a viable economic growth model and forced to resort to new International Monetary Fund lending, Macri ran for reelection in 2019 but was defeated by a revived coalition of Kirchnerist and non-Kirchnerist Peronist forces called Frente de Todos (Everyone's Front). This fractious alliance sought to unite all sectors of Peronism, from Kirchnerist to moderates and social democrats, and was led by former adversaries turned allies: Alberto Fernández as the presidential candidate and Cristina Fernández de Kirchner as the vice presidential candidate. The coalition enjoyed support from most labor unions, including the General Labor Confederation (CGT) and the Argentine Workers'

Central Union (CTA), as well as social movements representing unemployed workers.

Nevertheless, this coalition was fraught with internal tension between Alberto Fernández and Cristina Fernández (unrelated) from the very outset. The Peronist government was forced to confront the COVID-19 pandemic at a time when it was heavily constrained by foreign debt, contracted by Macri, and unable to contain spiraling inflationary pressures. These political and economic challenges paved the way for Peronism's dramatic electoral defeat. Its experience in office culminated in 2023, with the ruling coalition, by then called Unión por la Patria (Union for the Homeland), not only weakened and politically divided but virtually crushed via a far-right outflanking by a flamboyant, self-proclaimed "anarcho-capitalist" outsider, Javier Milei (Stefanoni 2021).

Milei, an economic libertarian and culturally conservative figure (Kestler 2022; Hora 2024; Murillo and Oliveros 2024), campaigned with a chainsaw as a symbol of his pledge to slash public spending—and as a symbol of a larger crusade against Peronism and the left more generally (Semán 2023). He won Argentina's second-round presidential election against the Peronist candidate and Economy Minister Sergio Massa by a wide margin, drawing significant support not only from "disenchanted" voters but also from young male voters aligned with his conservative and free-market preferences and opposed to social change (Calvo et al. 2024). This electorate was not merely defined by opposition to Peronism, but by its active support for Milei's program and his "anarcho-capitalist" vision for the future (Balsa 2024).[13] His victory, in short, signaled a sharp rightward shift in Argentine politics (Murillo and Oliveros 2024, 170–174).

Milei quickly forged a governing coalition with more mainstream conservative actors from Macri's party (and from the UCR). He embarked on a platform that called for yet another cycle of harsh neoliberal austerity measures and orthodox structural adjustment policies reminiscent of the 1990s, with these partisan allies playing an important role in their implementation. He also vowed to suppress social protest movements opposing his free-market reforms and to wage a "culture war" against progressive forces associated with, but not confined to, the legacy of Peronist governments (Saferstein and Goldentul 2022). Milei's vice presidential nominee, Victoria Villarruel, was the daughter of an army general and a political activist known primarily for her defense of the military against charges of human rights violations during the Dirty War of the 1970s. As such, in the aftermath of Argentina's left turn, the historical cleavage between

Peronism and anti-Peronism became even more sharply polarized. New far-right actors assumed the political leadership of the anti-Peronist bloc, absorbing much of its energies and leading to the displacement not only of the centrist UCR—the historical bastion of anti-Peronism—but also of the mainstream conservative PRO by Milei's more radical alternative. As Adamovsky (2024) observes, this new political force, called Liberty Advances (LLA), has merged anti-Peronism with right-wing authoritarian tendencies.

Milei's leadership style has markedly authoritarian features. In fact, applying Levitsky and Ziblatt's (2018, 23–24) indicators of authoritarian behavior raises significant red flags. Milei is the first president in Argentina's recent democratic era who openly refuses to affirm his support for democracy. He has expressed disdain for Congress and its representatives, whom he refers to as "cockroaches." He has labeled his rivals "enemies," "criminals," and even "subhuman," calling them "orcs" and delinquents. Milei appears indifferent to acts of political violence and, in some cases, actively encourages it—for instance, by ranting against rival governors, artists, and anyone who opposes him. Furthermore, he seems prepared to curtail civil liberties, as demonstrated by his threats of violence against protesters and his insults directed at journalists (see also Casullo 2024). Whether he will steer the country down an authoritarian path remains to be seen, but his rise to power and early policy measures have undoubtedly shifted the parameters of Argentine politics much further to the right and taken the country down an uncertain and potentially perilous path.

Conclusion

This chapter developed a broader comparative perspective on the political trajectories and polarization dynamics associated with populist and social democratic left turns. The case of Ecuador under Correa sheds additional light on the pitfalls of the autocratic temptation under the populist left, demonstrating how it can generate internal contradictions and leadership succession crises that undermine a leftist project even when its opponents are too politically weak and divided to defeat it on their own. The Argentine case suggests that hybrid tendencies may offer partial correctives to the limitations and defects of the social democratic and populist-left trajectories, but they provide no guarantees against bitter political defeats and steadily rising polarization. Finally, the Uruguayan case helps to identify how strong party-society linkages and grassroots participatory channels within a governing party can enhance the political resiliency of a social democratic trajectory—and, perhaps, help to contain highly polarizing social and political conflicts.

Our comparative case studies in the last three chapters have amply demonstrated the prevalence of polarization dynamics in national political orders in contemporary Latin America. The chapter that follows examines these polarization dynamics across multiple dimensions and different levels of analysis in all seven of our cases, incorporating data from expert surveys as well as public opinion surveys. The analysis addresses the puzzle of why partisan and electoral competition is often highly polarized even in countries where public opinion itself does not suggest heightened levels of polarization.

CHAPTER FIVE

Latin America's "New" Polarization
A Multidimensional Approach

In this volume, we have analyzed the origins and trajectories in power of seven left turns in Latin America, tracing their impact on the dynamics of political polarization. In Bolivia, Ecuador, and Venezuela, the left turn itself had a polarizing logic, as the populist left that came to power in these countries had roots in popular rebellions against established party systems and neoliberal orthodoxy. Populist leaders intentionally polarized the political arena from the outset to discredit established elites and justify their pursuit of radical projects of institutional transformation, including the drafting of new constitutions and the "refounding" of regime institutions. Plebiscitary assertions of popular sovereignty and constitutive authority inevitably clashed with elite interests embedded in, or shielded by, established institutions, and they intensified polarization over time. By contrast, having learned (or perhaps overlearned) from past experiences of democratic breakdowns and military repression in the 1960s and 1970s, the social democratic left in Brazil, Chile, and Uruguay embraced pragmatism and gradualism—a "small steps," moderate approach to redistributive reform and democratic deepening that was designed to minimize opposition, maintain economic stability, and contain polarizing dynamics. Argentina was somewhere in the middle.

And yet, despite their different strategic orientations and approaches to politics, most leftist governments (Uruguay being an exception) ended their experiences in power with dramatic defeats—that is, with the left weakened, discredited, and divided. In most cases, moreover, the left turn culminated in increased levels of social and political polarization between left and right, or between reformist and conservative forces—with the latter often explicitly committed to rolling back the social, economic, and political reforms adopted by leftist governments.

As we have seen, however, polarization is hardly new in the region. Indeed, Latin American politics have almost always been polarized. Depolarization and programmatic convergence in the 1980s and 1990s were the exception, when parties on the left, right, and center played within the rules of liberal democracy and embraced—or, at least, resigned themselves to—the neoliberal policies of the technocratic Washington Consensus (Williamson 1990). This period of centrist-to-conservative public policy tendencies and relative political tranquility was an anomaly in the broader arc of Latin American history. But things changed quite dramatically in the early decades of the twenty-first century, as centrifugal tendencies have reappeared and come to dominate the scene.

Although contemporary forms of polarization represent a sea change in the regional political landscape against the benchmark of the 1980s and 1990s, polarization has taken different forms in distinct national settings. In some contexts, such as Venezuela, it appears to be toxic and to have "pernicious" effects (e.g., McCoy and Somer 2019; McCoy 2023) that are causally linked to democratic "backsliding" (e.g., Levitsky and Ziblatt 2018; Haggard and Kaufman 2021). In others (e.g., Uruguay), moderate polarization that is institutionally channeled may have helped to reinvigorate democratic regimes. In other words, polarization in itself is neither unnatural nor pernicious, and it is not always, as we will discuss here, the product of elite (mis)behavior. It is a key reason political parties and social coalitions are formed (Levitsky et al. 2016), giving shape and structure to the inchoate "feckless pluralism" noted by Carothers (2002). Indeed, polarization can be a primary reason for the very rise of democracy itself, as a set of conflict-regulating institutions uniquely designed to process and mitigate conflicts of interests or values (Rustow 1970).

This chapter tackles the general question of why and how the common pattern of deepening polarization across our seven primary cases has played out differently across national settings. Prominent scholarly arguments suggest that increased citizen disappointment and frustration with democracy's unfulfilled promises are linked to polarizing elite strategies (Murillo 2021; Luna and Medel 2023). Polarization, in those accounts, is typically seen as a function of elite behavior—a "supply side" issue, where generalized social discontent and anger provide an opportunity for elites to polarize politics from the top down, helping to produce volatile cycles of social protest and anti-incumbency waves in elections (Murillo et al. 2010).

Although this is a plausible interpretation, it is also likely that the growing polarization of Latin American politics has roots in societal conflicts, and that elite strategizing is at least partially—if not heavily—conditioned by bottom-up mobilization and countermobilization dynamics on the "demand side." Polarizing elites who are unable to tap into popular sentiments or grievances and appeal to a broad constituency are likely to be marginal actors in a competitive democratic context; it is, therefore, always important to ask what attracts voters to polarizing elites rather than moderates when the latter are also available options on the supply side, as they typically are (at least in first-round elections) in Latin America's multiparty systems.

Polarization, in other words, may not be solely a supply- or a demand-side phenomenon in its origins and persistence—it may well have elements of both. We suggest, therefore, that it might be best understood as an interactive or reciprocal process that involves both political elites and masses—including political leaders, party organizations, social movements, activist networks, and the general public. As such, it invites us to rethink the relationship between political activism, social mobilization, and party-system development. This chapter, then, digs beneath the surface of elite politics and asks: How polarized is Latin America in the wake of the left turn? Where does polarization originate, and how does it become activated? To what extent is it elite or mass based, and what is the relationship between these two levels of analysis? And finally, to what extent are the dynamics observed in our seven cases country specific, and to what extent are they a part of a broader regional pattern?

The Multiple Faces of Latin America's New Polarization

As we discussed in chapter 1, polarization is a notoriously challenging concept to grasp empirically. There are not only different forms of polarization, including spatial (the ideological or programmatic distance between major political contenders), affective (the mutual dislike and distrust between rival camps), and institutional (confrontation among rivals over the basic rules of the political game); there are also different levels of analysis for identifying polarizing agents and processes. At its most basic level, polarization can have both elite (top-down) and mass-level (bottom-up) dimensions. To complicate things further, these two levels may or may not be aligned, as we explain.

Tracking Polarization Through Expert Surveys

One first approximation to grasping comparative levels of polarization in the region is through expert surveys. Here we use two indicators from the Varieties of Democracy (V-Dem) dataset. Based on national expert codings, they measure aggregate trend lines in political and social polarization:

Political polarization—This indicator, introduced in chapter 1 (see fig. 1.2), measures the extent to which society is split into antagonistic political camps, and political differences affect social relationships beyond political discussions. This indicator is scored from 0 (supporters of opposing political camps generally interact in a friendly manner) to 4 (supporters of opposing political camps generally interact in a hostile manner).

Polarization of society—This indicator measures the extent to which differences in opinions on all key political issues result in major clashes of views, scored from 0 (no clashes of views) to 4 (major clashes of view). Data for this indicator has been available only since 2000.

An advantage of the V-Dem dataset is that it covers a broader period than the existing public opinion surveys, allowing for longitudinal as well as cross-national comparisons. As we showed in chapter 1 (see fig. 1.2), the first indicator of political polarization has been historically high in Latin America, consistently scoring above the world average with the exception of the 1990s and early 2000s, when political challenges to the Washington Consensus and the onset of the left turn drove Latin America's scores back above the world average and approached the region's historical levels of polarization.

Figure 5.1 shows the 1980–2020 political polarization trend lines in our seven countries, along with the regional average. The figure provides evidence of the different polarization dynamics experienced in our populist-left and social democratic cases, following the sharp decline in polarization across the region in the 1980s. In the populist-left cases, polarization scores start to increase—during the 1990s in Ecuador and Venezuela, and in the early 2000s in Bolivia and the hybrid case of Argentina—before the election of leftist presidents, with social protest against neoliberal orthodoxy serving as a prelude to mass electoral protest. Leftist electoral victories then led to steep hikes in political polarization scores, well above regional averages, reflecting the polarizing character of the left turn itself in these four cases. Dynamics were quite different in the social democratic cases,

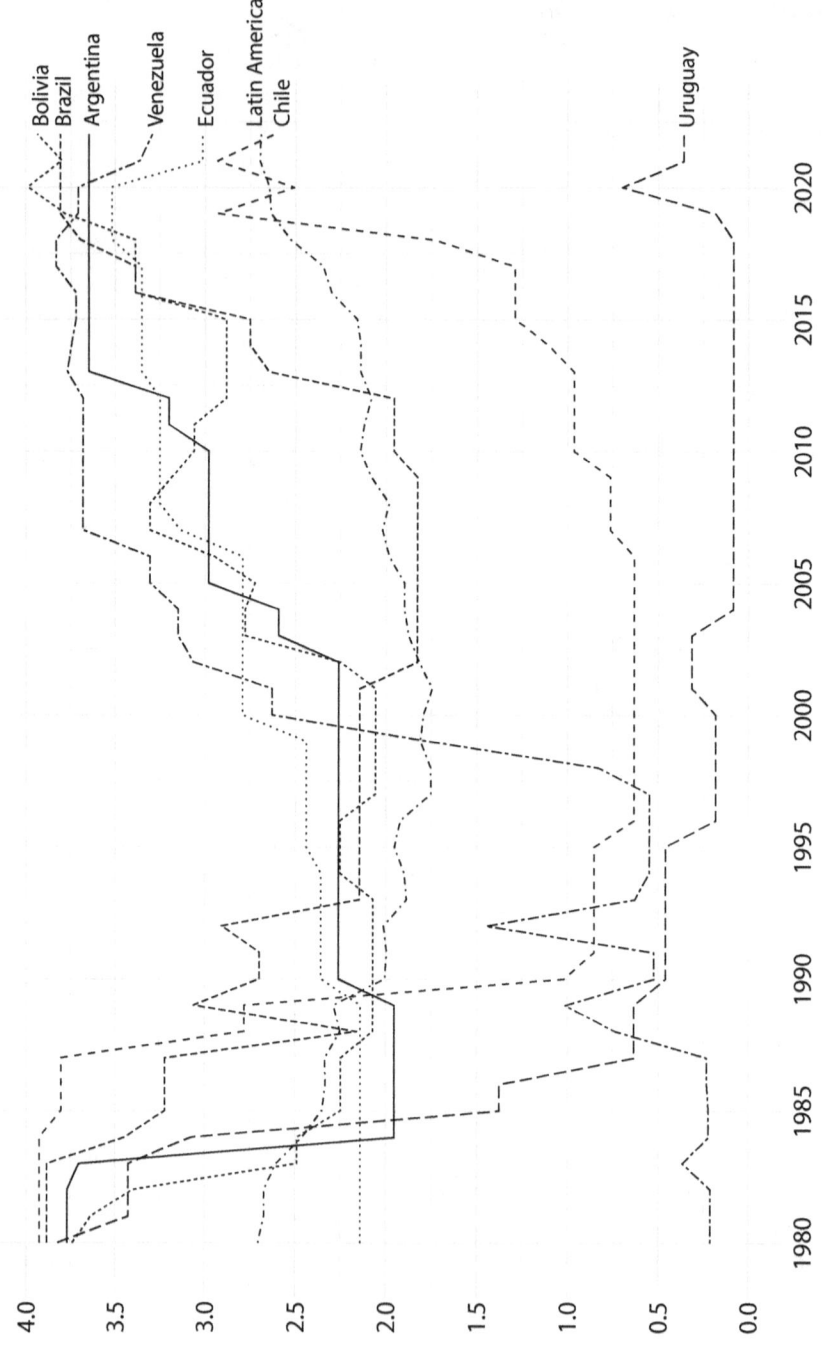

FIGURE 5.1. Political polarization, 1980–2020. V-Dem (Coppedge et al. 2024).

however. In Brazil, Uruguay, and Chile, polarization scores were flat or trending downward in the decade before the left turn, and they remained flat under the first leftist president, at levels well below the regional mean. This reflected the absence of mass protest movements before the left turn in these countries, the channeling of redistributive claims into established parties and regime institutions, and the relatively moderate, nonpolarizing logic of highly institutionalized left turns. That would change, however, starting with the second leftist presidents in Chile (Bachelet) and Brazil (Rousseff), as social mobilization and protest picked up—from the left in Chile and from the right in Brazil—and polarization scores began a steep rise. Only Uruguay remained well below the regional average.

The graph also shows that there was an overall increase in political polarization as a part of the left turn and its aftermath. All countries are more polarized now than at the beginning of their left turn, including countries that intentionally tried to contain polarizing dynamics and accommodate broader sectors of the political spectrum, such as Brazil and Chile.

As seen in figure 5.2, our second V-Dem indicator, polarization of society, shows a consistent pattern of increasing polarization between 2000 and 2020, although scores declined toward the end of this period in several countries. Every country experienced increasing societal polarization during the left turn, although, as with political polarization, the process began earlier, at the onset of the left turn, in the populist-left cases, whereas the onset was delayed in the social democratic cases. Brazil experienced the steepest overall increase on this polarization measure—an increase that started in 2012 during the presidency of Dilma Rousseff (2011–2016) and escalated after the June 2013 protests erupted. In short, whether or not governing parties pushed forth a polarizing political or policy agenda during the left turn, the end result was deepening polarization. Uruguay and Ecuador (following Correa's exodus from power) are the only two cases in 2022 with scores lower than the regional average (indicating that they are less polarized than their regional counterparts), but only Uruguay stayed consistently less polarized than the regional average over the entire period. What is striking is that Chile and Brazil started out less polarized than the regional average, but unlike Uruguay, they experienced highly polarizing sequences during the later stages and the aftermath of their left turns.

Figure 5.3 includes graphs for our two indicators—political polarization and polarization of society—for individual cases and reveals an interesting pattern. In most cases, except for Ecuador, societal polarization is

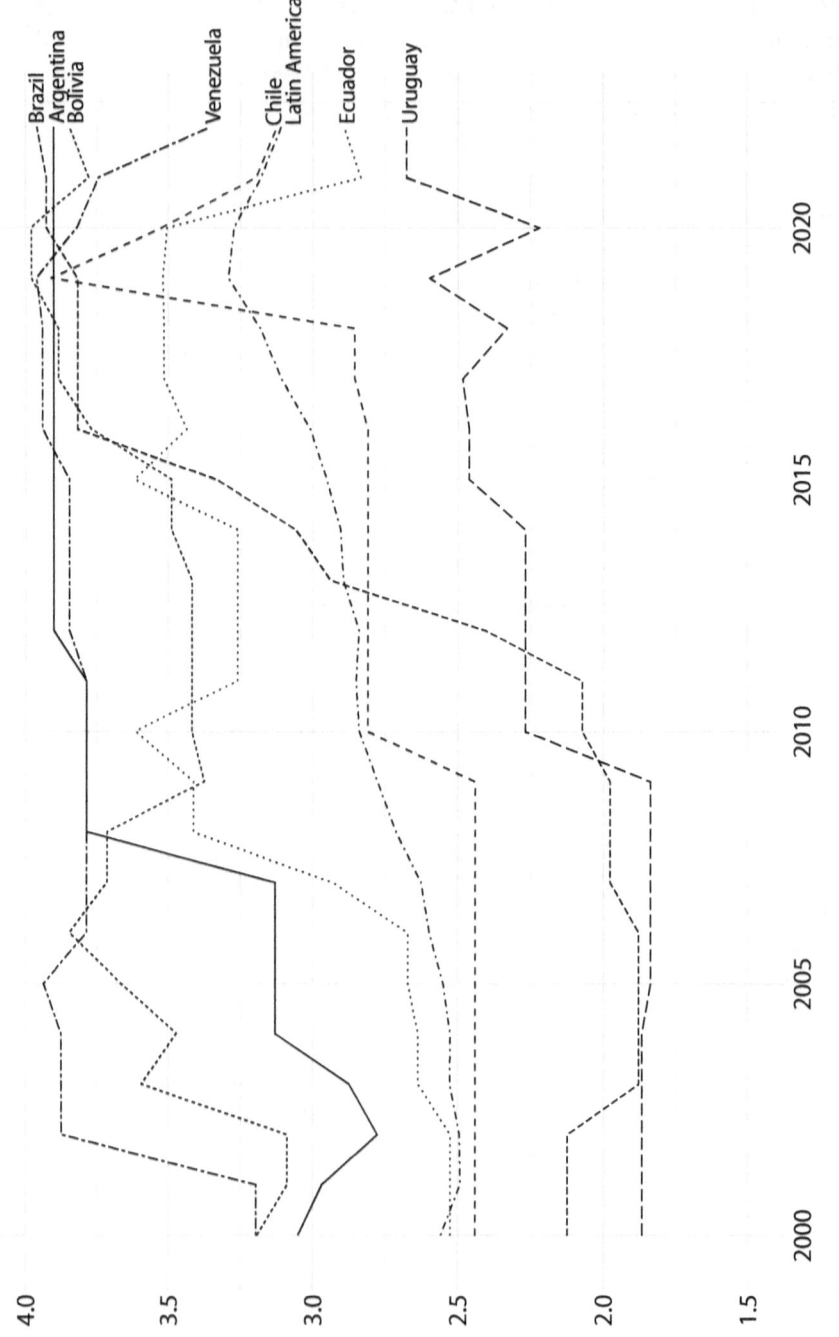

FIGURE 5.2. Polarization of society, 2000–2022. V-Dem (Coppedge et al. 2024). The original V-Dem scale for this variable runs from 0 (high polarization) to 4 (no social polarization). We inverted the scale so that higher numbers indicate greater societal polarization.

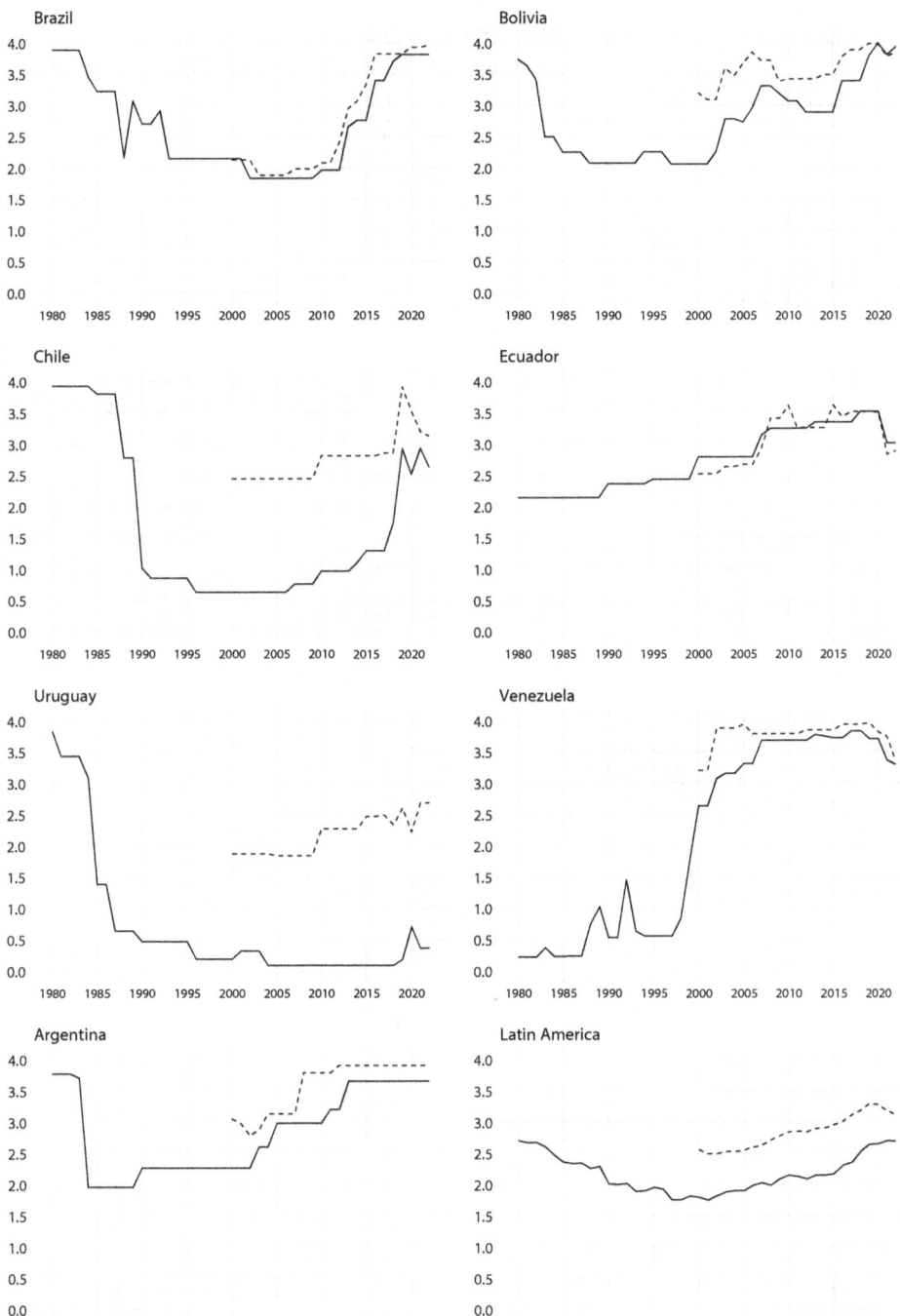

FIGURE 5.3. Political polarization (1980–2020) and social polarization (2000–2020). V-Dem (Coppedge et al. 2024).

consistently higher than political polarization.[1] Increases in societal polarization scores, moreover, appear to anticipate or precede increases in political polarization. This suggests that issues in society or at the mass level often make their way into the public sphere, serving at times as an antecedent to elite polarization in the political sphere.[2] An example might help to illustrate the point. Severe social polarization emerged in Brazil as the left turn ran its course, especially as corruption scandals and an economic slowdown weakened support for the PT. As Margaret Keck (2022, 154) notes, upper-class segments of Brazilian society "always derided—even sometimes expressed hatred for—both Lula and the PT. But until 2013, supporters and opponents could still be friends." Spontaneous social protests that started on the left flank of the PT in June of that year as an expression of dissatisfaction within the left were then captured by rival right-wing groups and broke that fragile equilibrium (e.g., Winters and Weitz-Shapiro 2014; Alonso and Mische 2017). An emerging field of grassroots right-wing activism working through Evangelical churches and social media helped to deepen latent anti-PT sentiments; large-scale social mobilization then set the stage for elite defections from the PT's legislative coalition, the impeachment of Dilma Rousseff, and the PT's demise in 2016 (Smith 2019; Mayka and Smith 2021). Mass social protest on the right thus migrated into—and sharply polarized—the electoral arena. It opened the door and served as a prelude to the rise of a far-right militaristic alternative, like that of Jair Bolsonaro in 2018 (Dias et al. 2021)—previously an obscure figure on the fringes of the Brazilian legislature.[3]

These V-Dem data should be interpreted with some caution, however, for methodological and substantive reasons. Several scholars have discussed the methodological challenges of relying on retrospective expert assessments, including, among others, issues of coder subjectivity and intercoder reliability.[4] In general, even though V-Dem has developed innovative methodologies and modeling strategies to mitigate those challenges, it could be added that country-expert assessments tend to reproduce the existing wisdom around cases and are therefore not particularly novel or revealing. The substantive limitations merit further discussion. The V-Dem indicator political polarization taps into "affective" notions of polarization—the emotional distance between groups in rival political camps and their mutual animosity. The indicator polarization of society, in turn, captures some degree of divergence or disagreement over what expert coders consider central political themes. This indicator aligns more closely with the "spatial" or ideological notion of polarization we have discussed in chapter 1. Systematic disagreements and differences of opinion can provide the basis for axes of conflict that, under certain circumstances, may become politicized and translate into programmatic differentiation—and even into polarized politics. But consistent disagreements among citizens and collective actors, even if they are over "heated" issues, can also be seen as ordinary politics in democratic contexts with some degree of pluralism (Schedler 2023, 345–346).

Both indicators shed light on aspects of citizens' experiences with polarization, and both anchor understandings of polarization around some type of conflict in the public sphere. However, the issues or domains of conflict and the actors that generate centrifugal effects in the electoral arena and the political process more generally remain outside their angle of vision. In other words, these two metrics provide some useful information on how experts evaluate general trend lines, but aggregate polarization scores tell us little about who is polarizing and what is being polarized. They don't tell us whether polarization is associated with a demise of the center, the growth of the left or the right, or a combination of these different dynamic "pull" forces. We conduct such an analysis in the following pages.

Polarization Dynamics and Public Opinion

Another, more direct way to assess polarization at the mass level is with time-series data on changes in the general ideological self-identification of survey respondents. Latinobarómetro measures the overall distribution of self-placements on a left-right ideological continuum—a measure of ideological distancing that is available for all Latin American countries since 1995. The scale runs from left to right and includes a "don't know, won't say" response option in the questionnaire. Using Latinobarómetro data, figure 5.4 maps the aggregate trend lines in ideological self-identification from 1995 to 2023—that is, from the height of the Washington Consensus through the left turn and into the aftermath period.[5]

As the graph shows, a plurality of Latin Americans consistently position themselves in the center. That plurality is relatively stable over time; even with some fluctuation, a little over a third of respondents consistently self-identify as centrists. Right-wing self-identification shows greater variation; it dipped and arguably shifted toward the center as the left turn reached its apex in the first decade of the twenty-first century, then rose again after 2011 as the conservative backlash against the left turn gathered

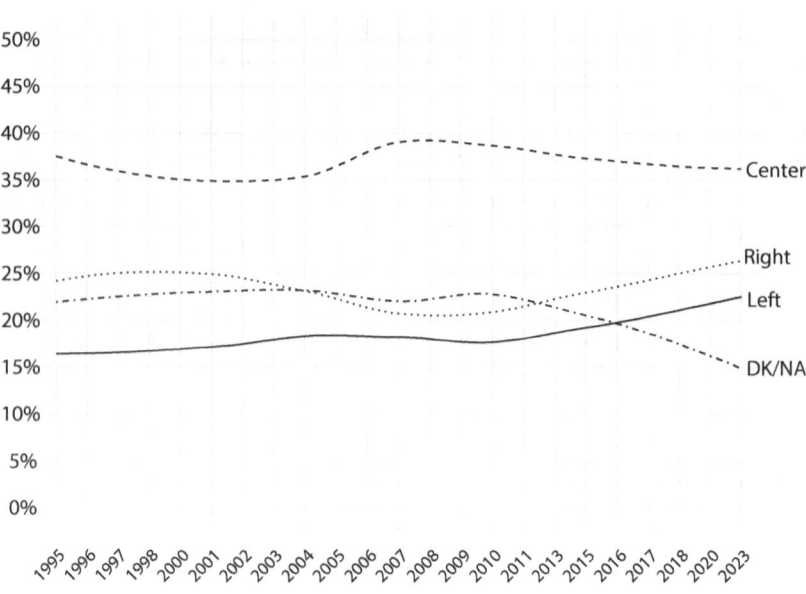

FIGURE 5.4. Left-right self-placement, 1995–2023. Latinobarómetro. DK = "don't know/won't say."

steam. While the right troughed in 2011 and then increased again, the left experienced a gradual and mostly sustained growth throughout the period. Both ideological "poles" reached their high point in 2023, the final year of the time series, with a little over a quarter of survey respondents identifying with the right, and a little under a quarter identifying with the left. This bilateral shift of survey respondents toward the two ideological poles provides evidence of some polarization in public opinion over time, although the aggregate shift is relatively modest. Notably, in aggregate terms, most of the increase near the poles has not come at the expense of the center; instead, it reflects a sizable decline in the proportion of Latin Americans who respond "don't know, won't say" over the past decade.

These trends in the data suggest that public opinion has become more ideologically structured along a left-right axis than it was at the turn of the century—a point also raised by Lupu et al. (2021). The trends do not, however, indicate a high level of polarization in public opinion. Instead, the distribution of public opinion suggests the possibility of developing party systems with a tripartite, or left-center-right structure. This would approximate the type of "three-thirds" alignment for which Chile was historically famous, even if the left and right "thirds" appear somewhat smaller than the center in the aggregate distribution of ideological identities.

This tripartite distribution of ideological identities stands in stark contrast to the trend toward increased polarization in the electoral arena seen in a number of countries, however. Although a plurality of Latin Americans claim to be in or around the center, it is important to note that this is a plurality and not a majority. Taken together, the left and the right poles attract more citizens than the center, creating the potential for centrifugal competitive dynamics, and they often appear to be stronger than the center in the electoral arena. Centrist or centripetal dynamics are hardly the norm in contemporary Latin American politics. There might be ample political space in the center, but this space is often heterogeneous or inchoate in its political organization, and too weak to spawn centrist competitive dynamics. In short, using Sartori's (1976, 135) classic parlance, the center may not be "physically occupied" by one or more parties with electoral weight, allowing centrifugal pressures to dominate. As we will discuss, what we are seeing might be best described as the "decentering" of political space.

This decentering presents a real puzzle: Latin Americans do not appear to hold extreme partisan or ideological views, yet most are not voting for centrist options in the electoral arena. Across the region, the clustering of votes around the centrist "median voter" has weakened in electoral campaigns. The political centers have dissipated almost everywhere, and in some cases, established parties have been outflanked and displaced to the margins by protest movements on the left and/or the right, strengthening centrifugal drives and leading to highly polarized, high-stakes electoral contests. Take the examples of Boric versus Kast in Chile, Bolsonaro versus Lula in Brazil, Milei versus Massa in Argentina, and more.

From the aggregate patterns in public opinion illustrated in figure 5.4, it appears that polarization in the region at the mass level remains modest, while more severe polarization, if it occurs, takes place only among political elites as a function of electoral calculations and competition (Murillo 2022). Aggregates of public opinion, however, weigh all survey respondents equally, glossing over substantial differences in political interest, engagement, and preference intensities—subjects that we address here. Moreover, surveys conducted at a particular moment in time may not capture how underlying social cleavages create conflict dynamics that remain latent until they are politically activated by elite political entrepreneurs, civic activist networks, or protest movements. A focus on a particular moment in time may thus lack the historical perspective needed to explain polarization dynamics; Latin America has almost always been polarized, with the brief exception of the Washington Consensus period of the 1980s and 1990s (see fig. 1.2).[6] And even if polarization is attributable to elite strategic behavior, history has taught us painful lessons: It can quickly become pervasive and polarize society as well.[7]

Mapping distributional patterns of self-identification yields valuable insights into the structuration of the ideological spectrum in public opinion, but it tells us little about the sources of polarizing conflict and the social actors who wage it. It is possible that present-day polarization is not simply elite driven—or only a function of elite-level competition. There might also be a bottom-up, grassroots component that conditions what elites do in the electoral arena and forces contentious issues onto the political agenda that elites might otherwise prefer to avoid. Given the preoccupation of sociologists with activist networks and social movements, it is not surprising that—studying other national settings, such as the United States—influential sociologists and social movement scholars have noted the possibility of misalignments between activist networks and mass publics (McAdam and Kloos 2014; Tarrow 2021). Something similar might be at work in Latin America, as a focus on aggregate trends in ideological self-reporting may simply not be capturing widespread ideological distance that exists within civil society and activist networks. Aggregated individual attitudes may tell us something about the potential bases of collective conflict, but they provide precious little information about the actors who might wield political influence and their degree of embeddedness in civic networks that are better able to translate numbers and grievances into an effective political mobilization strategy. Ideological radicals—and actors embedded in deep social networks—are often able to mobilize and sometimes wield outsized influence on the political process; as research in the United States shows (Hacker and Pierson 2015; Skocpol and Williamson 2016; Blum 2020; Kalmoe and Mason 2022), they can create centrifugal pressures that help to decenter and sharply divide the electoral arena, even where aggregate public opinion does not appear to be highly polarized. If they do not create polarization, they can help sustain or intensify it. One way to address this potential misalignment between mass publics and activist networks is by looking at the relationship between ideological self-placement and different indicators of political interest, participation, and engagement, to which we now turn.

Public Opinion: Numbers Versus Intensities

In the aggregate, public opinion surveys do not capture widespread ideological polarization on the left-right axis (see fig. 5.4). As others have shown, however, they do consistently capture a generalized and deeply seated sense of frustration with political elites and democracy's "unfulfilled promises"—a sense of frustration that has recently triggered episodes of explosive social mobilization in several countries (Luna and Medel 2023; Kessler and Vommaro 2024; Coronel and Donoso 2024). This takes place in a context where mainstream political parties are almost everywhere weakened, if not collapsed—Uruguay being a notable exception—and economies are in disarray. It also happens in a context of generalized political attrition that led to a strong anti-incumbency electoral wave across the region following the end of the commodity boom in 2014 (Campello and Zucco 2020; Murillo 2021). Partisan attachments are weak across the region, while negative partisanship—staunch opposition to the "other side"—and antipartisan sentiments in general are very strong in many countries (Meléndez 2022). Politics appear to be increasingly high stakes, as voters are left to choose between stark contrasts—polarizing choices between right and left alternatives such as Bolsonaro versus Lula, Kast versus Boric, Milei versus Massa, and more.

Yet, when asked in public opinion surveys, over one-third of respondents typically self-identify as centrist, while roughly one-quarter self-identify with the right, and another quarter with the left. What aggregate public opinion surveys do not reveal at first glance is that when it comes to shaping the political arena, citizens are not necessarily weighted equally; they may have differential impacts on politics. It is intense and active political minorities, especially those embedded within deep activist networks, who often have disproportionate influence in different spheres or stages of the political process—in political discourse, electoral campaigns, voting behavior, party building, grassroots social mobilization, and more (Wasow 2020; Gillion 2020; Han et al. 2021; Tarrow 2022). Small numbers of highly engaged activists are typically well positioned to shape the political arena by translating their preferences, passions, frustration, anger, and grievances into political mobilization strategies (e.g., McAdam et al. 1996). In general, they are better able to mobilize politically and have a voice and influence in the political process than the average citizen—the "median voters" or other individuals who are either disengaged or pay less attention to political affairs. The mobilization of few but active individuals can also stimulate the participation of those who are otherwise less engaged. In short, citizens whose participation is more intense and socially embedded can have magnifying effects. As such, they are more likely to play a prominent role in shaping polarization dynamics.

Using LAPOP's AmericasBarometer (2018–2019) survey data for six countries that experienced a left turn—Argentina, Brazil, Bolivia, Chile, Ecuador, and Uruguay—we constructed an index of political participation.[8] The index includes responses to questions on participation in community meetings, a demonstration or protest march, meetings of political parties, and voting in the previous election. We constructed the index by summing its four dichotomous dummy items of having participated or not, resulting in values from 0 to 4, where higher values indicate higher levels of participation.[9] To gain more insight into differential levels of engagement, we also constructed a media attention index, which aims to capture the extent to which respondents pay attention to politics and seek out media information to contextualize the happenings in their daily lives by relying on either traditional outlets or new forms of social media. The index is calculated as the mean response on four different items, including access to political information via social media (e.g., Facebook, Twitter, WhatsApp), or mainstream news media such as television, radio, newspapers, and the internet.[10] We also examined respondents' interest in politics and individual perceptions regarding their understanding of political issues. Response options for the political interest variable are coded on a four-point scale, and for understanding politics on a seven-point scale, with higher values indicating greater interest in politics and understanding of political issues. We thus test whether citizens closer to the left and right poles are more likely to be interested in politics and to believe they have a good grasp on political issues. That feeling of having a strong understanding of political affairs imbues individuals with some sense of political efficacy—a perception of political influence or control that can be a major driver of political participation (Rhodes-Purdy 2017).

In the analysis here, we first regress ideological self-placement on the participation index to see whether intensity of participation varies across ideological self-positioning. Additionally, we regress ideological self-placement on the media attention index and on the interest in politics and political understanding variables. We treat the "left-right" self-positioning scale as a nominal variable and use linear regression models to estimate the relationships with the "center" (coded 4–7 on the ten-point scale) as a reference category. We control for gender, age, and education to increase the efficiency of the estimates. We model the relationships with and without controls.[11]

Table 5.1 presents the results. We find that the intensity of participation does vary significantly across ideological positioning. As expected, it is lower in the center of the ideological space, while citizens near the left and right poles are more likely to participate in politics than centrists (columns 1-2). In addition, the relationships between ideological self-positioning and media attention, interest in political affairs, and understanding of political issues appear to be robust. These results reinforce the findings on the participation index. Citizens who are closer to the ideological poles are more likely to consume political information through either traditional or nontraditional sources (columns 3-4) and to be interested in political affairs (columns 5-6). These citizens also tend to think that they have a deeper understanding of politics than those located in the center (columns 7-8), and they are more likely to become active politically. Following the presumed logic of numbers versus intensities, committed and highly motivated citizens near the ideological poles, while small in numbers, may carry more weight in shaping the political process and polarization dynamics. They are loud and active minorities. They are more likely than the larger pool of self-identified centrists to translate their small numbers into political resources—and, arguably, their preferences and demands into viable electoral options.

Figure 5.5 provides the clearest illustration. The vertical axis shows the proportion of individuals who reported high levels of participation (values 3 and 4 on the participation index). The horizontal axis shows the ideological left-right scale. The figure shows that individuals who express centrist positions on the left-right scale tend to participate less than those who are closer to the left and right poles. This pattern suggests that although the center may be a large and diverse political space, it is likely that a significant portion of disengaged respondents claim to be centrist in the ideological space simply as a default position. Centrist citizens are hardly irrelevant in democratic politics (Fowler et al. 2023)—they can, of course, vote—and they need not be indifferent or uninformed. But a center filled with large numbers of politically disengaged and inattentive citizens hardly provides an anchorage for strong centrist parties in the Latin American context. Indeed, it may allow centrifugal pressures to predominate in the electoral arena.

Figure 5.6 reinforces the point; it shows the disparities between the participation (U-shaped) and ideological self-placement (inverted U-shaped)

TABLE 5.1 **Ideological self-placement and political engagement**

	DEPENDENT VARIABLE							
	Participation index		Media attention index		Interest in politics		Understand political issues	
	(1)	(2)	(3)	(4)	(5)	(6)	(7)	(8)
Left	0.244***	0.257***	0.051**	0.104***	0.219***	0.265***	0.113*	0.173***
	(0.025)	(0.024)	(0.022)	(0.020)	(0.030)	(0.029)	(0.047)	(0.046)
Right	0.213***	0.205***	0.018	0.136***	0.183***	0.254***	0.380***	0.444***
	(0.025)	(0.025)	(0.022)	(0.020)	(0.031)	(0.030)	(0.048)	(0.047)
Male		−0.004		0.074***		0.229***		0.437***
		(0.018)		(0.015)		(0.022)		(0.035)
Age		0.012***		−0.009***		0.001		0.012***
		(0.001)		(0.0005)		(0.001)		(0.001)
Years of education		0.038***		0.060***		0.069***		0.104***
		(0.002)		(0.002)		(0.003)		(0.004)
Constant	1.323***	0.412***	2.517***	2.179***	2.089***	1.164***	4.118***	2.270***
	(0.012)	(0.042)	(0.011)	(0.034)	(0.014)	(0.050)	(0.023)	(0.079)
Observations	9,345	9,288	9,460	9,398	8,668	8,621	9,308	9,249
R^2	0.014	0.073	0.001	0.164	0.008	0.088	0.007	0.079

Source: Authors' calculations from LAPOP AmericasBarometer, 2018–2019.
Note: Linear regression models with robust standard errors in parentheses.
*$p < 0.05$. **$p < 0.01$. ***$p < 0.001$.

LATIN AMERICA'S "NEW" POLARIZATION 191

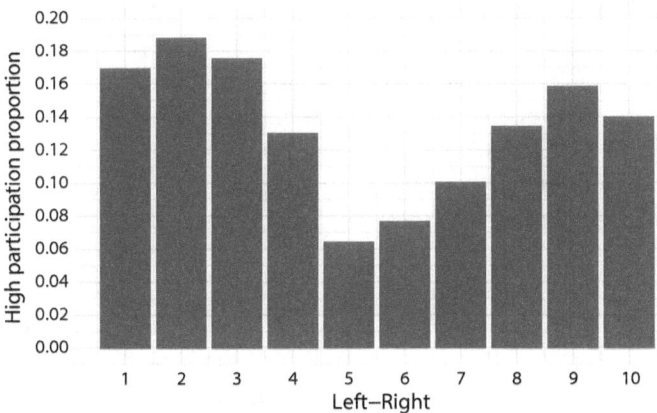

FIGURE 5.5. Relationship between participation and left-right self-placement (six countries). Authors' calculations from LAPOP AmericasBarometer, 2018–2019.

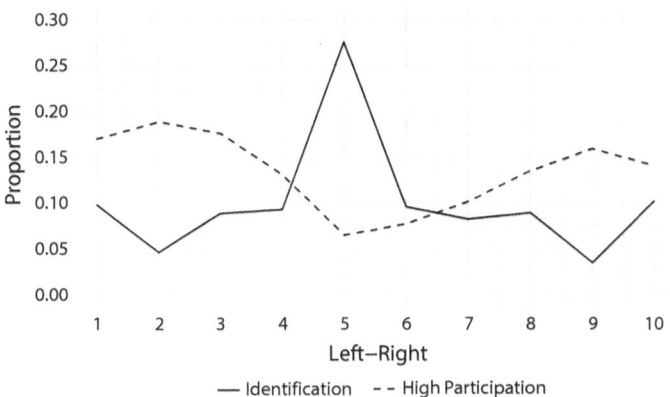

FIGURE 5.6. Ideological self-identification and participation curves. Authors' calculations from LAPOP AmericasBarometer, 2018–2019.

curves. The two curves are the inverse of each other, with ideological self-placement peaking in the center, and participation peaking near both poles. Such asymmetries in rates of political participation may help to explain why partisan and electoral competition appears to be more polarized than public opinion in Latin America. Additional figures for individual countries are provided in the book's appendix (see fig. 5A.1).

To summarize, both expert surveys and public opinion data provide some evidence of deepening polarization and suggest that a "decentering" of politics is well underway. Even if public opinion is not highly polarized in the aggregate, we find that politically engaged citizens are more polarized than public opinion at large. The weakening of centripetal actors, the strengthening of the poles, and the current centrifugal pressures in the electoral arena, therefore, may well have roots in differential levels of political interest, engagement, and participation. We discuss the major observable trends in the electoral arena in the pages that follow.

Electoral Dynamics and Party System Polarization

As we have seen, public opinion in Latin America has progressively moved closer to a tripartite "three-thirds" alignment, with the strengthening of left and right thirds that remain somewhat smaller than the centrist third but provide a significant electoral base for parties located closer to the ideological poles on the left-right axis of competition (see fig. 5.4). Politically engaged citizens, however, are more likely to be located near the left and right poles than the average citizen. It is not surprising, then, that we see polarization in the electoral arena, with the decline of centrist parties, the strengthening of left and right alternatives, and, in some countries, the outflanking of mainstream left and right parties by new alternatives located closer to the ideological poles. This decentering of electoral contestation typically involves heightened contestation of distributive conflicts and the state-market balance on the economic axis and/or the politicization of new axes of conflict related to cultural identities, social norms, and public security considerations. As we note in chapter 1, even if the two axes of contestation tend to overlap in Latin America and most politicization gets mapped onto the left-right axis (Martínez-Gallardo et al. 2023), the different issue dimensions are analytically distinct and susceptible to differentiated levels, patterns, or timings of politicization.

As Meléndez (2022), Luna (2024), and Kessler and Murillo (forthcoming) have shown, political polarization in contemporary Latin America does not necessarily produce cohesive or well-organized rival political blocs. It may, instead, assume more diffuse antiestablishment or antisystemic forms channeled by a wide array of electoral vehicles that fragment party systems and legislative arenas. Fragmentation tends to lower conventional indicators of legislative polarization by reducing the individual party vote shares used to weigh divergent ideological codings. A more accurate assessment of polarization dynamics may thus be gained by examining presidential elections, where institutional rules calling for second-round runoff elections create a binary logic that facilitates the measure-

TABLE 5.2 **Ideological distance polarization in presidential elections**

Country	Pre–left turn	Polarization	Year of left turn	Polarization	Post–left turn	Polarization
Argentina	1995/1999	5.98	2003	8.37	2023	11.96
Bolivia	1993/1997	2.01	2005	12.69	2020	5.25
Brazil	1994/1998	5.31	2002	5.31	2022	13.7
Chile	1989/1993	7.06	1999	10.2	2021	15.3
Ecuador	1998/2002	5.25	2006	13.8	2021	7.08
Uruguay	1994/1999	5.09	2004	6.86	2019	9.59
Venezuela	1989/1993	3.49	1998	12.35	2013	9.85

Source: For mid-1990s baseline, Baker and Greene (2011, 2019), based on Wiesehomeier and Benoit (2009). For year of the left turn, Handlin (2017, 283). For post–left turn, see 2020 Chapel Hill Expert Survey (CHES): Latin America (Martínez-Gallardo et al. 2023), recoded to place the scores on the same 20-point scale used by the aforementioned sources.
Note: For Bolivia, we used the 1993 and 1997 elections to calculate the pre–left turn baseline, since the country's largest spike in volatility occurred in 2002, when the MAS first emerged as one of the two leading contenders for the presidency, a prelude to its election in 2005. Because the 2020 Chapel Hill Expert Survey does not include ideological scores for the new far-right leaders Milei in Argentina and Kast in Chile, we have assigned them the same score as Bolsonaro in Brazil. For Venezuela's post–left turn score, we used the 2013 presidential election, as it was the last election in which the leading opposition candidates were allowed to compete.

ment of change over time in the ideological distance separating the two most competitive political blocs that have a realistic chance of winning executive office.

Building on Handlin (2017, 283), table 5.2 reports simple ideological distance scores between the two leading presidential candidates in each of our seven countries across elections at three different points in time: (1) the pre–left turn period of the Washington Consensus, based on the average polarization scores of the last two elections in each country prior to its left turn; (2) the presidential election in each country that launched its left turn; and (3) the most recent election in each country for which party or candidate ideological scores are available or readily assigned. Ideological scores for the two leading candidates are based on surveys of national experts who coded parties on a twenty-point left-right scale (see Wiesehomeier and Benoit 2009; Martínez-Gallardo et al. 2023).

Table 5.2 provides evidence of significant spikes in ideological polarization during or after the left turn in all seven countries, but it also demonstrates how the timing and dynamics of polarization in the populist-left cases differed from those in the social democratic cases. In the populist-left cases of Bolivia, Ecuador, and Venezuela, polarization surged as the left turn got underway, indicating the polarizing logic of the left turn itself in these countries, as explained in previous chapters. Measured in terms of ideological distance, polarization scores then *declined* in these three countries following the initial left turn, reflecting in part the exodus of Correa in Ecuador and the formation of broad antipopulist fronts in Venezuela and Bolivia that sponsored relatively moderate presidential candidates rather than hard-line conservatives who often took the lead in opposition social and political mobilization. Arguably, in these latter two cases, the most recent scores for ideological polarization in presidential elections significantly understate more fundamental political polarization around regime institutions themselves, as Schedler (2023) would suggest, and as our analysis of the cases in chapter 3 clearly indicates.

By contrast, the largest increase in polarization in the social democratic cases of Brazil and Chile occurred in the aftermath of the left turn with the rise of new major contenders on the far right and, in the Chilean case, a more radical left with movement origins. In Uruguay, as our analysis in chapter 4 suggests, polarization has only moderately and gradually increased over time. In the hybrid case of Argentina, polarization increased moderately at the onset of the left turn and more sharply in the aftermath with the rise of the far-right leader Milei. This reflects the basic realignment of electoral competition between a left Peronist bloc and an increasingly right-wing anti-Peronist bloc, as we explain here.

Looking beyond these aggregate polarization scores, national-level dynamics are highly instructive. The Chilean case is especially dramatic, as electoral competition since the 1990s has produced a steady demise of the center and bilateral polarization toward both ideological poles. The centrist Christian Democratic Party that was electorally dominant during the country's democratic transition in 1989–1990 has suffered a steep decline, while its center-left Socialist Party coalition partner has been overtaken by more radical leftist alternatives—Boric's movement-spawned electoral front in the 2021 elections and a Communist Party candidate in the 2025 presidential primary elections. Likewise, the right-wing parties of the post-transition era were overtaken in 2021 by a new far-right party led by José Antonio Kast that openly embraces the legacy of former military dictator Augusto Pinochet (Díaz, Kaltwasser, and Zanotti 2023).

In Brazil, the center-left Workers' Party (PT) remains the fulcrum of the party system, but leadership of the anti-PT bloc has shifted from the centrist PSDB to more conservative parties and ultimately to the far-right populist Jair Bolsonaro. Drawing on his military past, Bolsonaro relied heavily on the support of religious conservatives mobilized around cultural issues, as well as right-wing sectors nostalgic for military rule. When his reelection bid was defeated by Lula and the PT, Bolsonaro and his supporters tried to block the democratic transfer of power by means of a military intervention and a mob assault on national government buildings (Tanscheit and Barbosa 2023).

In Argentina, the cleavage between Peronists and anti-Peronists remains largely intact, but over the past two decades, it has increasingly polarized along a left-right axis. The Peronist PJ shifted toward left-of-center positions following its adoption of neoliberal reforms in the 1990s and the social backlash against them in the early 2000s. Meanwhile, leadership of the anti-Peronist bloc has gravitated from the centrist UCR to a mainstream conservative party (PRO) and, eventually, the far-right economic libertarian and culturally conservative President Javier Milei (Stefanoni 2021; Semán 2023). Milei characterized himself as an "anarcho-capitalist" and gleefully campaigned with a chainsaw as a symbol of his pledge to attack state spending.

In Venezuela, Bolivia, and Ecuador, mainstream party convergence around neoliberal reforms in the 1990s set the stage for mass social protest, the demise of mainstream centrist and conservative parties, and the rise of new left-wing populist leaders in Venezuela (Hugo Chávez) and Ecuador (Rafael Correa), along with a movement-based leftist party in Bolivia (the MAS of Evo Morales). In Venezuela, Chavismo's institutional and policy reforms combined with its autocratic tendencies to foster a radicalization of opposition forces, which careened between insurgent and institutionalized modes of resistance (Gamboa 2022; Velasco 2022). The populist-left regime resorted to increasingly hard-line authoritarian measures to hold onto power following Chávez's death as opposition strengthened and eventually coalesced behind right-wing political leadership, even when running relatively moderate opposition figures in presidential elections.

In Bolivia, the MAS's organized mass constituencies—especially among the country's historically marginalized but demographically majoritarian indigenous population—allowed the party to dominate the electoral arena. This electoral hegemony, however, combined with Morales's autocratic leadership to radicalize much of the opposition—which itself resorted to undemocratic modes of resistance—and eventually to divide the MAS itself (Molina 2023). In Ecuador, Correa combined an autocratic and polarizing mode of governance with statist development policies that split the left—moving indigenous, environmental, and autonomous civic movements into opposition—while allowing a revival of right-wing neoliberal alternatives following Correa's exodus from power (Ospina Peralta 2023).

Among the seven countries covered here, only in Uruguay did the established parties of the 1990s Washington Consensus era—a two-party conservative bloc and a rising center-left party—remain electorally dominant and alternate in power without experiencing the eruption of more polarizing populist-left, movement-left, or major far-right alternatives in the early twenty-first century (although a smaller far-right party established a presence in recent years). This does not mean that there is no polarization in the country, however. An axis of ideological differentiation separates—or polarizes—the rival party blocs and "sorts" citizens into one or the other based on their interests or preferences (Buquet and Piñeiro 2014; Rossel and Monestier 2021). This basic left-right ideological structuring of partisan competition remained intact through the 1990s era of the Washington Consensus and the early twenty-first century left turn in Uruguay, arguably helping the country avoid the patterns of ideological outflanking that produced more radical far-right and/or populist-left alternatives in neighboring countries.

Conclusion

As this overview of partisan and electoral dynamics suggests, the political polarization in Latin America noted by the V-Dem expert surveys is readily apparent. It is not, however, identifiable across the full range of analytical dimensions along which polarization can be studied. Polarization in the domain of public opinion remains relatively modest, although it has increased over time, and the aggregate measures mask substantially higher levels of polarization among politically engaged citizens. In the partisan sphere, the weakening or collapse of major centrist parties has been common in the cases analyzed here, along with the emergence or strengthening of alternatives closer to the ideological poles. The increasing politicization of cultural dimensions of contestation has clearly contributed to this partisan polarization, as has a series of performance failures that have undermined mainstream parties from across the ideological spectrum. Therefore, despite the region's centrist plurality in public opinion surveys, centrifugal pressures appear to have created a "three-thirds" competitive dynamic—between leftist, centrist, and rightist tendencies—which is highly unstable and prone to polarization in institutional settings where runoff presidential elections impose a bipolar selection process.

In short, in many countries the centrist plurality in public opinion is too weakly articulated or politically fragmented to compete effectively in partisan and electoral arenas. This may be especially problematic for the center in presidential elections when the left and right flanks—energized by more highly engaged citizens—consolidate support around a strong party or leader in first-round elections, surpass centrist alternatives, and face off in highly polarized second-round elections. There is, then, nothing automatic about the mapping of aggregate ideological preferences onto the institutional dynamics of partisan and electoral competition; the latter may well transform moderate levels of social and political polarization into high-stakes, bitterly contested races between staunch ideological rivals.

Conclusion

Polarization, Democracy, and the Leftist Dilemma

The whole history of the progress of human liberty shows that all concessions yet made to her august claims have been born of earnest struggle.... If there is no struggle there is no progress. Those who profess to favor freedom and yet deprecate agitation are men who want crops without plowing up the ground; they want rain without thunder and lightning. They want the ocean without the awful roar of its many waters.... Power concedes nothing without a demand. It never did and it never will. — FREDERICK DOUGLASS, 1857

In a now-classic article that heavily influenced the study of "third wave" democratic transitions (O'Donnell and Schmitter 1986), Dankwart Rustow (1970, 355) suggested that democracy's origins are to be found not in a shared civic culture or a normative consensus regarding the virtues of the regime, but in polarized conflict and political gridlock — what he characterized as a "hot family feud." Democracy's primary purpose was to provide a set of institutional arrangements — such as the rule of law, minority political rights, horizontal checks and balances, and iterative elections that allow for alternation in office — to lower the stakes of political contestation, lengthen actors' time horizons, and regulate political conflicts that might otherwise spiral out of control and lead to political violence. Rustow's formulation provides a useful corrective to nostalgic assumptions that the 1990s era of political and economic convergence should be considered the norm for Latin America. That convergence may have contributed to unprecedented democratic tranquility in the region (Mainwaring and Pérez-Liñán 2014), but it should not be considered a precondition for stable democratic governance. Some measure of polarization is natural, if not inevitable, under democracy; it is, in fact, the raison d'être for liberal democracy — what we have called institutionalized pluralism — as a regime form.

Therefore, as this book shows, it is hardly surprising that the technocratic convergence of the 1990s was not destined to be the end of politics in Latin America—let alone Fukuyama's (1989) famed "end of history." Historical hindsight allows us to recognize the 1990s as an unusually tranquil interregnum between distinct eras of acute political polarization in Latin America—an interregnum that reset the dimensions and boundaries of political contestation without extinguishing its underlying sources of polarization. New democratic regimes in the 1990s could treat revolutionary armed struggle, military coups, socialist development models, labor unrest, and even state capitalism as historical relics belonging to a Cold War museum, and they exuded confidence that their neoliberal reforms bore the imprimatur of economic science, modernity, and international financial institutions. Nevertheless, these regimes inherited societies rigidly divided by class, racial and ethnic hierarchies, and gender inequalities, and the limited forms of democratic inclusion that were compatible with neoliberal technocracy could not prevent societal actors from repoliticizing and challenging entrenched inequalities. Unsurprisingly, these challenges became associated with renewed forms of social and political polarization; after all, power and privilege are not accustomed to relinquishing their hold without a fight.

Polarization and Inequalities

To understand the polarizing dynamics unleashed by these challenges in twenty-first-century Latin America, it is important to recognize that the Washington Consensus, at least as it was implemented in Latin America, was hardly a convergence on centrist space in ideological terms. To the contrary, neoliberal orthodoxy—the progeny of Pinochet and Chile's Chicago Boys—pushed public policy well to the right in Latin America, making moderately left-of-center or redistributive policy platforms markedly different even in the absence of meaningful socialist alternatives. Programmatically speaking, then, neoliberalism itself was polarizing, and a generation of popular and leftist movements made it a focal point of political contestation, even when economic and technocratic elites concurred on the absence of viable alternatives. The "puzzle" of increasing polarization following the collapse of socialism at the end of the Cold War is thus explained in part by capitalism's concomitant rightward drift toward market fundamentalism, and societal resistance to the market insecurities and economic inequalities generated by this transition (see Silva 2009). As explained in chapters 2–4, this societal resistance crystallized politically in the late 1990s and early 2000s in Latin America as the left turn got underway. It found expression in mass protest movements that toppled presidents in Argentina, Ecuador, and Bolivia, the subsequent election of populist-left leaders in these three countries, plus Venezuela, and the strengthening of established social democratic parties that elected their leaders to presidential office in Chile, Brazil, and Uruguay.

If programmatic or spatial polarization on the economic axis of contestation increased as the Washington Consensus faded at the turn of the century, so also did polarization intensify on the vertical axis of sociocultural contestation (see fig. 1.4). Whereas the traditional left prioritized class-based inequalities and labor-based forms of sociopolitical mobilization, new social movements making claims for the rights of women, LGBTQ+ citizens, and Indigenous peoples took aim at gender and racial hierarchies in traditional Latin American social and cultural orders (Hoffman and Centeno 2003). Feminist movement claims for reproductive rights and gender equality challenged patriarchal social structures and spawned vigorous countermobilization from both Catholic and Evangelical religious networks on the right (Smith 2019), often "in the name of the family" (de Souza Santos 2023). Likewise, indigenous movements in the Andean region pressed claims for cultural, economic, environmental, and political rights grounded in ethnic differences, challenging centuries of colonial and postcolonial racial and ethnic domination, as well as more recent neoliberal development models (Yashar 2005; Fontana 2023). Although the political left has varied considerably in its willingness and ability to incorporate such diverse social and cultural claims into a coherent package of policy reforms, in general, these claims have mapped onto and intensified the left-right competitive axis (Martínez-Gallardo et al. 2023). In contrast to Western Europe, where far-right parties often backed away from free-market stands in order to combine economic and cultural appeals to working-class constituencies (Harteveld 2016), the new far right in Latin America has blended staunch support for neoliberal orthodoxy with vigorous defense of the traditional social and cultural order (Mayka and Smith 2021; Payne et al. 2023; Borges et al. 2024). In addition to appeals to cultural and social conservatism, far-right leaders have heavily politicized law and order, crime, and security issues to broaden their potential base of support among popular constituencies who might not otherwise support neoliberal platforms—a potentially formidable response to Ziblatt's (2017) "conservative dilemma" in a region plagued by criminal violence.

As Rustow (1970) suggests, such forms of policy contestation are integral to democratic politics, and they need not be threatening to, or unhealthy for, democratic regimes. Political conflict often provides the impetus for political organization and institution building (Levitsky et al. 2016), and it can help to align partisan competition and strengthen parties' programmatic linkages to mass constituencies (Roberts 2014; Lupu 2016). Polarization is intrinsic to programmatic forms of political representation, and in highly unequal societies such as those in Latin America, at least some polarization is necessary and inevitable for subaltern groups to challenge entrenched social hierarchies. The absence of polarization in such contexts is only a cause for celebration among those who are satisfied with, or the beneficiaries of, the status quo. It likely indicates that inequalities have become so normalized that they encounter little collective resistance, or else that subaltern groups are too politically atomized, fragmented, or controlled by means of clientelist networks to mount effective challenges and defend their basic rights. Latin America during the heyday of the Washington Consensus was an archetype of the latter, indicating that the region's acclaimed democratic tranquility was achieved in part by bounding democratic contestation, insulating technocratic elites from societal pressures, sharply narrowing the programmatic space, and sweeping contentious issues under the rug, so to speak.

It is important to recognize, however, that polarization is a reciprocal, bilateral process. Political mobilization near an ideological pole tends to politicize, or raise the salience of, an entire competitive axis, thus activating opponents and inducing countermobilization processes on the opposite ideological pole as well. Where it does not, it is more proper to speak of radicalization—a unilateral process of spatial distancing—or, perhaps, asymmetrical polarization (Hacker and Pierson 2015; Grossmann and Hopkins 2016) rather than a bilateral process of polarization. The reciprocal character of polarization processes can make political mobilization a two-edged sword; the mobilization of actors who want to make democracy more inclusionary or equitable is routinely countered by those who expect it to reproduce existing social and political hierarchies, and who may thus mobilize to roll back democratic advances that threaten the traditional social order.

Polarization and Democratic Conflict Management

Democratic regimes have well-defined institutional mechanisms to process and regulate political conflict over policy disagreements. In theory, at least, the electoral marketplace is designed to contain polarizing dynamics by forcing parties and leaders to compete for the median voter (Downs 1957). Those who position themselves too far from the median voter—that is, too close to the left or the right ideological pole—are likely to pay a price at the ballot box when public opinion is clustered near the center, as we show it to be in chapter 5. Chapter 5 also suggests, however, that the electoral price paid for ideological radicalism may well be attenuated when voters near the median are less actively engaged in political affairs than those located closer to the ideological poles. The finding that rates of political participation in Latin America vary across the ideological spectrum—peaking near the ideological poles while plunging around the median voter in the center—helps to explain several of the central paradoxes in the study of political polarization in Latin America. It provides insight as to why partisan and electoral politics are often more polarized than what aggregate public opinion trends might suggest, given the added political weight of activist networks near the ideological poles. It also demonstrates why it is misleading to attribute polarizing dynamics entirely to top-down, elite-level political agency; civil society and social movement networks may also contribute an important bottom-up dynamic to polarization processes, even where the mass public itself does not appear to be highly polarized. In our case studies, the rise of polarizing political elites in the electoral arena was often preceded by mass protest movements, both on the left—in Venezuela, Bolivia, Ecuador, and Argentina—and on the right, in Brazil.

These paradoxes illustrate the advantages of analyzing polarization as a multidimensional political process, recognizing that its dynamics are often conditioned by the interaction between different actors at multiple levels of analysis. Indeed, the adoption of a multidimensional perspective makes it readily apparent that polarization involves more than simply ideological or programmatic distancing. Polarization's affective dimensions, for example—that is, the levels of mutual dislike, distrust, and animosity between rival political camps—are unquestionably related to the ideological and programmatic distance that separates them. Negative emotions or affect, however, cannot be reduced to these spatial dimensions, and it has a measure of independence from them. Schedler (2023, 337) recognizes the complementarity between ideological conflict and negative affect (what he calls "social distance"), while arguing that they are sources rather than distinct types or dimensions of polarization. Building on and updating Sartori's (1976) association of polarization with the presence of antidemocratic parties (or leaders), Schedler suggests that the analytical core of polarization is a type of affect with an institutional twist—namely, the fear and distrust of actors who are "perceived enemies of democracy." The "breakdown of basic democratic trust," he says, creates uncertainty about "the ground rules of democratic dispute resolution," and causes democracy to veer "off its equilibrium" (Schedler 2023, 338).

Schedler's conceptualization of polarization is especially instructive, as it reveals the underlying conditionality of Rustow's (1970) account of democracy's origins and equilibrium properties. Rustow believed democracy could be installed by political actors who were not principled democrats— that is, actors who may have preferred some sort of revolutionary or autocratic alternative but accepted democracy as a second-choice institutional compromise when they could not impose their preferred political order on rival actors at acceptable cost. Political gridlock, therefore, and not simply polarized conflict, was a facilitating condition to induce democratic compliance among actors who lacked principled commitments to the regime itself. Initial compliance with the institutional compromise was predicated on strategic self-interest and the absence of viable alternatives; mutual trust and normative commitments to the regime were expected to develop over time endogenously as political learning and habituation transformed actors' preferences and expectations.

In the absence of political gridlock, however, strategic incentives need not induce institutional compliance among actors engaged in polarized conflict. Indeed, major power imbalances exacerbate the "winner's dilemma" under democracy—that is, the challenge of preventing those who emerge victorious in democratic contests from transforming the temporary prerogatives of incumbency into sources of cumulative and permanent competitive advantage (Roberts et al. 2025). Recent studies of democratic erosion or "backsliding" (Bermeo 2016; Levitsky and Ziblatt 2018; Haggard and Kaufman 2021) have explored the myriad ways elected incumbents can exploit opportunities to capture and repurpose democratic institutions, concentrate powers, undermine regime checks and balances, and tilt the democratic playing field to their ongoing advantage. As Schedler (2023) suggests, such patterns of institutional manipulation sow fear and distrust among rival actors, as they dramatically raise the stakes of any electoral defeat (see also Przeworski 2019). They are thus intrinsically polarizing, above and beyond any ideological distance that separates the rival camps. Indeed, they turn Rustow's endogenous process of democratic norm development and trust construction on its head.

Taken together, these works help explain why the recent rise of far-right actors who openly identify with the military dictatorships of the past, and/or contemporary autocratic regimes around the world, has been so polarizing in Latin America. They also, however, illuminate several of the critical differences between the populist-left and social democratic cases examined in this book—in particular, the reasons the former were more intrinsically polarizing than the latter. As explained in chapter 3, populist-left leaders rose to power as outsiders to the political establishment in Venezuela, Bolivia, and Ecuador following the eruption of mass protest movements, in contexts of severe crises that pummeled mainstream party organizations. With backing from strong popular majorities, and facing dramatically weakened elite opposition and institutional constraints, Chávez and Correa were hardly in a situation of political gridlock; they claimed and exercised constitutive powers by plebiscitary means to rewrite constitutions and refound regime institutions under the hegemonic control of their own parties. Power imbalances thus lay at the heart of the autocratic temptations that shaped the left turn in these countries, breeding the types of fear and distrust among opposition sectors that Schedler identified as the essence of polarization. In the Bolivian case, the power imbalance was less extreme, at least early on, and opposition forces retained sufficient institutional leverage to place constraints on Morales and the MAS and force them to compromise on the path to a new constitution.

By contrast, the social democratic parties that came to power in Chile, Brazil, and Uruguay at the beginning of the century were established parties that had experienced military repression in the past and participated in the rebuilding of democratic regimes during the third wave. As seen in chapter 2, they were deeply embedded in regime institutions before their ascension to executive office, and once in office, their freedom to maneuver was restrained by the strength of conservative opposition parties in legislative bodies. Although the Broad Front obtained a narrow legislative majority in Uruguay, the PT in Brazil and the Socialist Party in Chile could govern only through broader multiparty coalitions with centrist and/or conservative allies who could veto any radical reforms or democracy-threatening measures. In short, social democratic lefts governed in contexts where the balance of political power and the vibrancy of institutional checks were much more constraining than in the populist-left cases; they had little capacity to tilt the democratic playing field in ways that would threaten their rivals or generate distrust. Rather than an autocratic temptation, they faced what we call the conformist temptation: the opportunity to achieve political success by internalizing and adopting the behavioral norms of the political order they once sought to transform.

The paradox of these cases is that Chile and Brazil became increasingly polarized over time, even though they experienced very moderate and institutionalized left turns, and their social democratic parties made explicit efforts to build broad coalitions, moderate their programmatic stands, and dampen polarizing tendencies. Both countries experienced the rise of far-right political movements—in Brazil after the PT was weakened by a series of corruption scandals, a faltering economy, and mass protests, and in Chile after the Socialist Party was outflanked on the left by student-led social movements demanding a break with the neoliberal model and a strengthening of social citizenship rights. Within this pairing of social democratic cases, the Brazilian case is especially puzzling. As we show in chapter 2, the PT became as dependent on political patronage and rent-seeking brokerage as other parties in the Brazilian ecosystem, and it was remolded in the image of the system it once vowed to transform. This could have undercut fears on the right of the threatening character of the left—but it did not. The Brazilian case demonstrates that a radical, highly polarizing left is not a precondition for the emergence of a radical right; even the relatively modest forms of social inclusion promoted by the PT in support of women, racial and ethnic minorities, and the poor elicited virulent opposition from far-right quarters, and the latter made little effort to mask their authoritarian leanings under Bolsonaro.

Lessons of the Left Turn

Sifting through these complex dynamics, several important lessons can be drawn from the left turn and the dynamics of polarization that plagued it. First, although the timing, degree, and content of polarization processes vary across countries, some elements of political polarization have been present throughout most of the region since the turn of the century. At the most basic level, this polarization reflects a basic restructuring of partisan and electoral competition along a left-right axis following the neoliberal convergence of the late 1980s and early 1990s. In addition to the countries analyzed here, major elements of this left-right restructuring can also be seen in countries like Colombia, Honduras, Peru, and Mexico. Such a structuring of the political field has not been the norm historically in Latin America, where pre-third-wave party systems in most countries were structured along intraoligarchic divides or a populist-antipopulist cleavage with highly diffuse ideological pillars (Roberts 2014). Contemporary left-right structuring activates economic interests and preferences as well as cultural values and identities; although these are analytically distinct dimensions of contestation, they may largely map onto a single competitive axis, with variation across cases and time periods in their degree of overlap. Polarization, however, is not simply a function of ideological contestation and policy differences. It also reflects an erosion of the "contingent consent" (Schmitter and Karl 1991, 82–83) given by different actors, on both the ideological left and the right, to adhere to core democratic norms and procedures. This erosion generates distrust and animosity toward political actors seen to be acting in violation of democratic principles, and it can dramatically raise the stakes of democratic contestation itself.

Second, although polarization can surely be triggered by the political conflicts spawned by failures or limitations of democracy—for example, failures to generate stable economic growth, reduce inequalities, provide quality public services, and maintain public order and security that pave the way for the rise of antiestablishment leaders (see Kessler and Murillo forthcoming)—it is important to recognize that democratic successes can also become a source of political polarization. The efforts of governments and their allied civic movements to deepen democracy by promoting gender equality, recognizing LGBTQ+ rights, empowering racial and ethnic minorities, or redistributing income may provoke reactions from conservative defenders of traditional social orders. These reactions may seek not only to roll back policy advances but also to restrict the democratic rights and liberties that made such advances possible. Counterintuitively, perhaps, contemporary polarization may be at least in part an unintended consequence of Latin America's "inclusionary turn" in the early twenty-first century (Kapiszewski et al. 2021; Silva and Rossi 2018).

Finally, the study of polarization offers unique insights into the dilemmas of the left in highly unequal societies. Leftist actors can hardly expect to challenge entrenched social and economic inequalities without generating some type of polarization. As this book shows, reconciling that polarization with liberal democracy is no easy matter; indeed, it has been a source of considerable debate and conflict within the left across the Latin American region. Although the region's left turn ultimately included both populist and social democratic trajectories, these trajectories should not be interpreted in essentialist or deterministic ways. "The left" was pluralistic in all of our countries under study, with competing populist, Leninist, radical democratic, and social democratic currents. These currents fought or collaborated with each other in national contexts that provided radically different historical experiences for leftist actors, as well as highly divergent institutional opportunities and constraints during the third wave of democratization. These contextual factors—whether leftist parties had been severely repressed under military dictatorship, whether they had participated in the rebuilding of democratic regimes, whether they emerged out of a social backlash against an existing democratic regime and party system, and whether they were a majoritarian or a minority force—heavily conditioned the political balance between the different leftist currents and the political trajectories they ultimately followed.

The vision of "deepening democracy" resonated across the different leftist currents, but it proved an elusive goal in practice across the full set of cases. Although by no means do we claim that failing to deepen democracy is a necessary condition for polarization, the challenges and limitations faced by the left are integral to the polarizing dynamics we observe today. The Bolivarian or populist-left trajectory fostered new forms of grassroots participation in Venezuela and Bolivia, along with an unprecedented empowerment of the latter country's indigenous majority. In these countries, along with Ecuador, however, democracy itself was distorted—and in Venezuela, destroyed—by the highly polarizing autocratic temptation to fill a crisis-induced power vacuum with a charismatic leader and a hegemonic movement that had little need to share power. Even in contexts where the trends toward inclusivity and the mass empowerment of popular majorities were strong and produced fundamental shifts in domestic power relations—as they did most clearly in Bolivia—sustained progress on the participation dimension often clashed with the dimensions of minority rights and institutionalized contestation. In other words, even where the populist left produced positive legacies and helped to usher in significant social change, it struggled to produce a reconciliation or synergistic reinforcement of Dahl's classic two dimensions of polyarchy (see fig. 1.1). Instead, both dimensions were recurrently in tension with each other and triggered highly destabilizing side effects, including social and political violence.

Deepening democracy was also elusive in the social democratic camp. The social democratic left accomplished significant positive social and political reforms. Distorted by the conformist temptation, however, leftist parties in Brazil and Chile internalized the flaws of their established orders; they contained polarization in the short run, but became vulnerable to outflanking in the longer run. The conformist logic involved tactical concessions to existing power structures in different national settings—playing the "patronage game" in Brazil and reproducing the logic of technocratic neoliberalism in Chile, with considerable short-term success. Nevertheless, this conformism weakened social democratic parties over time by generating fissures on the left, eroding linkages to organized grassroots constituencies, and encouraging debilitating defections—a gradual and cumulative process of political weakening. Ultimately, their "small steps," moderate approach to redistribution and democratic deepening—which was seen as a key to the political sustainability of the social democratic approach—was insufficient to contain polarizing dynamics. In Brazil and Chile, the leftist projects may have ended in a far better place than those of Chávez or Correa, and these differences could be important for the long-term prospects of liberal democracy. However, it is also important to note that mobilizations on the left flank severely challenged and weakened incumbent leftist governments, culminating in disappointment and setting the stage for polarizing dynamics. In Brazil, social protest on the left flank in 2013 migrated toward the right as the PT bore the political costs of the end of the commodity boom and a second major corruption scandal, which severely tarnished the party's historic brand of nurturing a new way of "doing politics." Antipathy toward the PT and the larger political establishment—which the PT initially opposed but eventually became a bedrock of—ultimately fed into the rise of Bolsonaro's brand of far-right antisystem populism. In Chile, iterative cycles of student-led social protest and an ill-fated effort to refound the constitutional order spawned new movement-based alternatives to the left of the mainstream Socialist Party, but also a new far-right alternative staunchly committed to the defense of Pinochet's legacy. In both countries, social democratic parties embraced liberal democratic norms, built multiparty alliances beyond the left, and moderated their programmatic stands—yet still encountered the rise of far-right actors who openly identified with recent authoritarian experiences.

If Brazil and Chile demonstrated that moderation provided no safeguard against the rise of the radical right, the Uruguayan case makes it clear that social democratic moderation does not inevitably culminate in an outflanking to the left by social actors. Uruguay avoided a parallel process of *desgaste* (political attrition) and outflanking, while far-right actors have garnered limited electoral support, making the case especially instructive for comparative purposes. In particular, Uruguay reveals the importance of the relationship between governing left parties and their grassroots activist networks, both inside the party organization and in civil society. Like the PT in Brazil and the Socialist Party in Chile, the Broad

Front in Uruguay embraced liberal democratic institutions, moderated its policy agenda, and sought to contain polarizing dynamics. Unlike its counterparts, however, the FA in office helped empower labor unions, retained stronger organic ties to labor and social movements, and kept open more vibrant channels for grassroots participation in shaping the party's platform and decision-making processes.

To be sure, the Uruguayan case had distinctive properties that may explain its relative success, including a relatively generous welfare state, lower levels of inequality, and the absence of profound ethnic cleavages. The FA also enjoyed greater institutional power than its counterparts as a result of a partisan legislative majority. Nevertheless, the Uruguayan case helps to underscore a key strategic comparative advantage: Preserving close ties to grassroots bases is critical for keeping left parties in power grounded in society and accountable to their popular constituencies. When political, institutional, or market constraints make a process of moderation unavoidable, socially rooted parties are better equipped to incorporate their bases into deliberative and decision-making forums that help to inform their constituencies about the range of strategic choices and their likely consequences and enhance the legitimacy of strategies that are finally chosen. This rootedness, in turn, is important for avoiding some of the most common pitfalls that afflict leftist governments and parties that become detached from their social bases. Where such bonds remained strong, as in Uruguay, the left in power proved the most politically resilient; they also allowed the FA to boast a stronger record of social and political inclusion, creating robust social bases that prevented outflanking on the left. Bolivia exhibited a similar pattern among the populist-left cases, although the relationships between the MAS and social movements have been marked by increasing tensions, particularly as the party failed to prepare for leadership succession.

In the absence of strong social ties, governing leftist parties became politically vulnerable and prone to severe performance failures. In Venezuela and Ecuador, for example, leftist parties that came to power amid severe national crises that dramatically weakened traditional parties never overcame their autocratic birth defects and remained overly dependent on the whims of dominant, charismatic personalities. While Venezuela took a markedly authoritarian turn and descended into economic chaos, Ecuador's governing party ended up politically divided and split by personal rivalries in the midst of a leadership succession. Left parties in Chile and Brazil became increasingly detached from the social movements they once nurtured and became remolded in the image of the political orders they previously sought to transform. While the left in Chile grew overly technocratic, the left in Brazil grew too dependent on corrupt patronage networks to sustain its multiparty coalition and govern effectively. Both faced defections and challenges from the left that were debilitating, and both faced dramatic political defeats and the rise of far-right contenders. Argentina appears to be a consistent hybrid. The strong alliance between the Peronist party and organized labor, including the national labor confederation and organizations representing unemployed workers, enabled some degree of policy radicalism and empowered a broad segment of the popular sectors. This may have helped to prevent large-scale protests against the left, as seen in Chile and Brazil, but it did not preclude debilitating political divisions and economic hardships that culminated in electoral defeats by increasingly right-wing opponents.

Learning from Defeats? The Left's *Autocrítica*

As this book has shown, the left turn's dispiriting demise after 2015 was neither preordained nor inevitable. In their efforts to challenge entrenched social hierarchies, leftist governments in Latin America faced formidable structural obstacles and constraints, and they were at times undermined by forces beyond their control—whether the volatility of global commodity markets, the machinations of political adversaries, or the shifting calculations (or the duplicity and naked opportunism) of former allies, such as those of the PT in Brazil. The economic catastrophe that befell Venezuela was undoubtedly accentuated by US sanctions, even if its origins were homegrown.

However, we hope to have demonstrated that attributing the left's demise solely to misfortune or betrayal offers neither an intellectually satisfying account nor an explanation for its timing and sequencing, even if it helps salve the wounds of political defeat by deflecting responsibility. Our discussion of the autocratic and conformist temptations strongly suggests that leftist parties and leaders in Latin America must shoulder some of the responsibility for their political defeats. Retrospective narratives that emphasize structural constraints and exogenous forces evade accountability for political failings, missteps, and misdeeds. In so doing, they distract from the urgent task of critical self-reflection. Only a vigorous *autocrítica* (self-criticism) can yield meaningful lessons about the political conditions and strategies behind these setbacks and foster the types of political learning and strategic debate needed for a renewal of democratic left alternatives. This renewal is especially urgent today, not only in light of recent leftist electoral victories in countries such as Brazil, Chile, Colombia, Honduras, and Mexico—the latter three having missed out on the early 2000s left turn—but also given the rise and strengthening of conservative forces across much of the region, some of them democratic in character, but others patently reactionary, illiberal, or authoritarian.

Self-criticism is inherently difficult for political actors, and it is routinely lacking in progressive movements and the left-wing camp more generally. When it does occur, it is typically conducted internally, away from public scrutiny, to minimize political vulnerabilities. Yet, as this book has made clear, even if some segments of the Latin American left try to evade it, self-criticism has a rich tradition in the region's leftist movements and parties, and it can clearly be generative. In the late 1970s and early 1980s, as discussed in chapter 2, critical introspection led to a major rethinking of the left's relationship with liberal democracy, and of its role in the polarizing disputes that culminated in democratic breakdowns. In some cases, this introspection produced a significant paradigm shift—an embrace of liberal democracy as a hard-won popular victory, along with more moderate and accommodating redistributive strategies. That down the road some of these "social democratic" experiences ended badly, severely tainting substantial earlier political successes, only underscores the need for further and deeper self-reflection. A crucial question remains, however: To what extent does the social democratic left's adherence to liberal democracy now prevent it from critically examining and potentially enriching its approach to democracy itself, to help it achieve more meaningful forms of popular political expression and empowerment? This is surely a vital debate within leftist thought, especially given the growing strength of illiberal forces in the region.

Perhaps because of its formative experiences and comparatively shorter trajectories, described at length in chapter 3, the populist left has been especially lacking in robust self-criticism, often attributing political defeats to the machinations—and conspiracies—of both domestic and foreign adversaries. While in power, its failure to recognize and correct its own missteps fueled the rise and legitimation of conservative opposition forces. For example, the gradual closure of political space in Bolivia and Ecuador—a by-product of the "autocratic temptation"—not only heightened political tensions but also allowed opposition actors to stoke fears of "Venezuelization," strengthening opposition coalitions and paving the way for the left's political defeat. After defeats, moreover, the continued refusal to engage in meaningful self-criticism further damaged the left's credibility and weakened its political standing. As Svampa (2019, 6) notes, this also "facilitated a series of political arguments in the hands of liberal, conservative, and authoritarian sectors," portraying the left as willing to mobilize against US imperialism but silent when repression, human rights violations, and creeping authoritarianism occur in friendly countries like Venezuela. This perception has undoubtedly reinforced the framing of the populist left as having double standards—a framing that plays directly into the hands of reactionary forces on the right. The populist left is in crisis, even now in Bolivia, where its social bases were the most deeply rooted, densely organized, and capable of autonomous sociopolitical mobilization. If it is to rebuild, the populist left must first acknowledge the reasons for its predicament and the many steps that led to it.

For both the populist and the social democratic lefts, any self-critical process of political renewal is likely to revitalize the imagery of deepening democracy by welding together disparate efforts to secure civil liberties, protect political pluralism, and empower popular constituencies—while also addressing new issues in rapidly changing societies. Reconciling these different and often competing objectives is never easy, and renewed lefts will surely discover that deepening democracy is and will remain a formidable challenge. As this book demonstrates, in highly unequal societies, efforts to empower popular constituencies behind redistributive platforms are notoriously difficult, and like any other challenges to existing power asymmetries, modest or otherwise, they can be intrinsically polarizing. While each of the leftist projects we studied was prone to vulnerabilities and defects that contributed to their inability to carry out and ensure the sustainability of their projects, they were also not immune to the broader "hard facts" of Latin American politics, including structural constraints like the disciplining effects of financial markets on any leftist project (Campello and Zucco 2020). As Hoffman and Centeno (2003, 383–384) noted in their influential article from the early 2000s that continues to resonate today, in contexts of state weakness and high inequality like those that persistently characterize the region,

> the rich can maintain their position through the practice of thuggish violence.... In Latin America, power has a clear face and does not hide itself behind too many institutional walls. Power may be seen in the murder of dissidents, in the assassination of union leaders, and in the killing of street urchins. Most recently, it may also be seen in the threat to withdraw funds to richer havens. This power

need not even be exercised. It is the threat of violence or exit that often makes many policies not viable. The key to Latin American politics seems to be to "not scare the right." As long as the forces that benefit from social misallocation retain this veto, inequality will remain pervasive.

Efforts to deepen democracy during the left turn were probably not a serious threat to the economic status or power resources of economic elites. With the partial exception of Venezuela, none of the leftist projects that we studied engaged in radical redistributive reforms involving expropriations or other measures affecting property rights. But as this book also reveals, leftist projects were *seen* as a threat to entrenched social, economic, and political hierarchies — a challenge to the status and social standing of the guardians of the status quo — and they ultimately elicited a virulent defensive reaction. An ensuing implication is that so long as there are social and political actors committed to deepening democracy and capable of challenging existing power asymmetries, such efforts are sure to antagonize the political right and its social allies. Polarization will likely, then, remain a prominent fixture on the Latin American political landscape.

For anyone expecting this book to provide "solutions" to the "problem" of political polarization in Latin America, reading these pages has undoubtedly proved frustrating, if not futile. Ready-made solutions are nowhere to be found, and we are wary of proscriptions to forestall polarization that would further entrench an unjust status quo. The left cannot abandon struggles to make democracy more equitable and inclusive in Latin America, and such struggles are sure to elicit conservative reactions that are potentially unsettling for democracy itself. But the left can ensure that its transformative agenda is not tainted by autocratic defects that only exacerbate polarization tendencies. Whatever the constraints of its norms and institutions, democracy continues to offer the most promising framework for advancing egalitarian and inclusionary projects in Latin America. Indeed, its conflict-regulating properties offer viable, though hardly foolproof, safeguards to bound and stabilize competition between democratic actors on the left and right, potentially isolating more autocratic contenders. The challenge for the left, then — and for research on it — is to identify more clearly the opportunities and constraints facing reformist projects that are firmly committed to operating within the parameters of liberal democratic institutions, and the conditions that allow them to advance without unsettling democracy itself.

Acknowledgments

This book is the product of a decade-long collaboration. It began in 2016, when we were both based at Tulane University's Center for Inter-American Policy and Research—Santiago as a postdoctoral fellow, and Ken as Greenleaf Distinguished Visiting Chair at the Stone Center for Latin American Studies. The CIPR and its director, Ludovico Feoli, provided crucial institutional support and fostered the kind of collegial environment that proved essential for developing the kernel of an idea that would ultimately launch this project. What started as a blog post—a short comparative reflection on the trajectories in power of four Latin American leftist parties and movements in Bolivia, Brazil, Chile, and Venezuela—gradually evolved into a full-length book manuscript as our research and writing progressed alongside shifting regional political dynamics. We came to realize that, despite different strategic orientations and approaches to politics, each experience in power had ended badly—with the left weakened, politically divided, or tainted by authoritarianism. At the same time, political polarization had intensified in every case—whether under populist or social democratic variants of the "left turn." Yet the timing and patterns of polarization varied considerably across countries. To understand how and why these divergent dynamics emerged, we broadened our scope—bringing Argentina, Ecuador, and Uruguay into the analysis—and delved deeply into comparative historical research and other forms of data collection in search of answers.

In expanding our analysis, Santiago benefited greatly from generous sabbatical support from Dickinson College, and Ken, from Cornell University. We were fortunate that our sabbatical leaves overlapped during the 2021–2022 academic year, allowing us to make significant progress on the theoretical framing and drafting of the four primary cases—Bolivia,

Brazil, Chile, and Venezuela. Santiago spent the year as a visiting scholar at Harvard University's David Rockefeller Center for Latin American Studies, where the collegiality of the visiting fellows, the intellectual engagement with Latin Americanist faculty affiliates and doctoral students, and the outstanding library resources were unparalleled. He is deeply grateful to that community, its staff, and its director Steve Levitsky, with whom both of us had helpful chats and from whom we received incisive feedback on the overall project—both in Cambridge and at a favorite meeting place in Ithaca, Liquid State. Ken spent the 2021–2022 academic year at the Institute for Advanced Study at Princeton, and he benefited enormously from the lively intellectual debates inspired by the research theme on political mobilization and social movements at the institute's School of Social Science. He is especially grateful for the generous support and perceptive insights of Didier Fassin and Wendy Brown, as the leaders of this research theme at the institute. He is also deeply grateful to Donatella della Porta for inviting him to spend a semester as a visiting research fellow in the stimulating environment of the Centre on Social Movement Studies at the Scuola Normale Superiore in Florence; to Robert Fishman for graciously hosting him as a Fulbright visiting scholar at the Universidad Carlos III—Instituto Juan March in Madrid; and to Eduardo Silva for making his time at Tulane both entertaining and intellectually engaging.

Although this book began while we were teaching at different institutions, we were fortunate to complete it as colleagues at Cornell. We are grateful to our department chairs—Shannon Gleeson, in the Department of Global Labor and Work, and Jill Frank in the Department of Government—for their many forms of support as we brought the manuscript across the finish line. Santiago is also thankful to his former department chair at Dickinson College, Sarah Niebler, and to the brilliant and generous colleagues in Dickinson's Department of Political Science and the Latin American, Latinx and Caribbean Studies program. Marcelo Borges, Carolina Castellanos, Maria Bruno, Neil Diamant, Kathryn Heard, Rachel Jacobs, Mariana Past, and Amaury Sosa offered insightful comments during the very early stages of this project.

We are thankful to many colleagues and friends who read portions of the book and gave us excellent comments and suggestions at various stages of the project: Juan Bogliaccini, Fernando Bizzarro, Candelaria Garay, Eric Hershberg, Evelyne Huber, Robert Kaufman, Dorothy Kronick, Steve Levitsky, Francisco Longa, Fernando Mayorga, Rafael Piñeiro, Virginia Oliveros, Verónica Pérez Bentancur, Jessica Rich, Luis Schiumerini,

David Smilde, Eduardo Silva, Sid Tarrow, Talita Tanscheit, Gabriel Vommaro, and Lisa Zanotti.

We have benefited greatly from feedback received at numerous conferences, workshops, and invited lectures at which we presented portions of this work. In the United States, we are grateful for the opportunity to present at the Tuesday Seminar at the David Rockefeller Center for Latin American Studies at Harvard University, the Latin American Working Group at the Massachusetts Institute of Technology, the Center for Inter-American Policy and Research at Tulane University, the Latin American and Caribbean Studies Program at Cornell University, the Frontiers in Political Science Workshop at Duke University, the Institute of Latin American Studies at Columbia University, the Center for Migration and Development at Princeton University, the University of Florida, the University at Buffalo, Florida International University, Wesleyan College, and Carleton College's Foro Latinoamericano. In Latin America, we received valuable feedback from presentations at the Instituto de Estudios Peruanos in Lima, Peru; the Sociedad Argentina de Análisis Político in Buenos Aires; the Universidad Torcuato Di Tella; the Universidad Diego Portales in Santiago, Chile; the Centro de Ética y Democracia at the Universidad Icesi in Cali, Colombia; and the Universidade do Estado do Rio de Janeiro in Brazil. In Europe, we were fortunate to present our work at the London School of Economics, the European University Institute in Florence, the WZB Berlin Social Science Center, Central European University in Budapest, the Swiss School of Latin American Studies in Zurich, the Universidad Complutense in Madrid, the University of Leipzig, the University of Lausanne, and the Americas Center at Warsaw University in Poland.

For organizing and/or providing valuable feedback during these conferences, workshops, and invited lectures, we thank Juan Abal Medina, Moisés Arce, Ernesto Bassi, Michael Bernhard, Sandra Botero, Manuela Caiani, Anna Callis, Miguel Centeno, Kaitlyn Chriswell, Julia Coyoli, Peter Cummings, Jennifer Cyr, Sofía Donoso, Sebastián Etchemendy, Tasha Fairfield, Ludovico Feoli, Patricia Fernández-Kelly, Robert Fishman, Laura Gamboa, Carlos Gervasoni, Natalia González Carrasco, Ezequiel González Ocantos, Fran Hagopian, Jonathan Hartlyn, Alisha Holland, Swen Hutter, Herbert Kitschelt, Hanspeter Kriesi, Steve Levitsky, Juan Pablo Luna, Lindsay Mayka, Oscar Mazzoleni, Al Montero, Lorenzo Mosca, Vicky Murillo, Donatella della Porta, Alejandro Portes, Karen Remmer, Federico Rossi, Cristóbal Rovira Kaltwasser, Ignacio Sánchez-Cuenca, Philippe Schmitter, Emilia Simison, David Smilde, Sue Stokes,

Carlos de la Torre, Madai Urteaga, Paolo Sosa-Villagarcía, Kurt Weyland, and Deborah Yashar. We are also grateful to the many attendees who offered helpful comments during these presentations. Our understanding of polarization and democracy has also been indelibly shaped by varied collaborations and conversations with Suzanne Mettler, Robert Lieberman, Thomas Pepinsky, Rachel Beatty Riedl, David Bateman, Jamila Michener, Gustavo Flores-Macías, Peter Katzenstein, Valerie Bunce, Ronald Herring, Jennifer McCoy, Murat Somer, Ruth Berins Collier, David Collier, Terry Lynn Karl, David Samuels, Raul Madrid, Wendy Hunter, Gerardo Munck, Paolo Moncagatta, Rodolfo Sarsfield, and the late Nicolas van de Walle.

For research assistance on this book, we thank Rocío Salas-Lewin. Rocío assisted with the statistical modeling of polarization dynamics presented in chapter 5, along with the creation of figures and graphs, and she offered valuable feedback on the analysis and interpretation of the results. A version of that chapter was previously published as Santiago Anria, Rocío Salas-Lewin, and Kenneth M. Roberts, "Dinámicas políticas y electorales luego del 'giro a la izquierda,'" in *La era del hartazgo: Líderes disruptivos, polarización y antipolítica en América Latina*, edited by Gabriel Kessler and Gabriel Vommaro (Buenos Aires: Siglo XXI, 2025). We are grateful to Siglo XXI for granting permission to reuse material from that publication.

At the University of Chicago Press, we are especially grateful to Sara Doskow, who provided invaluable encouragement and guidance from the book's inception through every stage of the publication process, including identifying two excellent peer reviewers whose insight significantly improved our manuscript. The rest of her team—Rosemary Frehe, Michaela Luckey, and Adriana Smith—carefully managed the many facets of the book's production process with great attention to detail. We are also grateful to Katherine Faydash for her meticulous copyediting.

Santiago thanks his wife, Anne DeCecco, and his son, Carmelo Anria, whose love, encouragement, and patience have sustained him throughout the long arc of this project. Ken thanks his wife, Angela Cornell, and his children Tasha, Allie, and Tristan, for their boundless dedication and support. We dedicate this book to our mentors—Santiago to Evelyne Huber and John D. Stephens, and Ken to Richard Fagen, Terry Lynn Karl, and Philippe Schmitter—whose commitment to rigorous social science and egalitarian politics has continued to inspire our research on polarization, democracy, and the Latin American left over the years.

Appendix

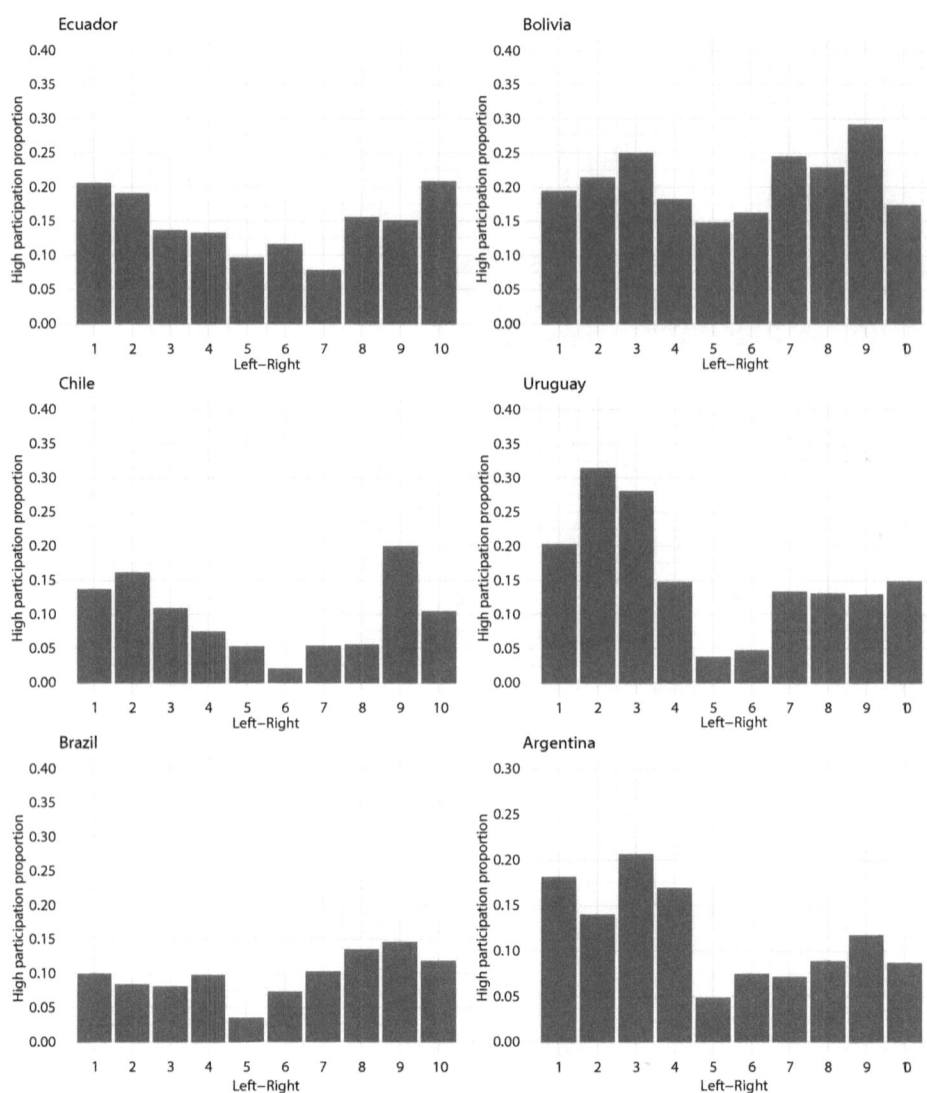

FIGURE 5A.1. Relationship between participation and left-right self-placement (individual countries).

TABLE 5A.1 Ideological self-placement and political engagement (controlling for income)

	DEPENDENT VARIABLE							
	Participation index		Media attention		Interest in politics		Understand political issues	
	(1)	(2)	(3)	(4)	(5)	(6)	(7)	(8)
Left	0.244***	0.243***	0.051*	0.093***	0.219***	0.261***	0.113*	0.129**
	(0.025)	(0.025)	(0.022)	(0.021)	(0.030)	(0.030)	(0.047)	(0.047)
Right	0.213***	0.196***	0.018	0.128***	0.183***	0.245***	0.380***	0.412***
	(0.025)	(0.026)	(0.022)	(0.021)	(0.031)	(0.031)	(0.048)	(0.048)
Male		-0.011		0.056***		0.211***		0.411***
		(0.020)		(0.016)		(0.023)		(0.037)
Age		0.012***		-0.010***		0.001		0.011***
		(0.001)		(0.0005)		(0.001)		(0.001)
Years of education		0.034***		0.050***		0.059***		0.091***
		(0.003)		(0.002)		(0.003)		(0.005)
Income level		0.007**		0.021***		0.019***		0.019***
		(0.002)		(0.002)		(0.003)		(0.004)
Constant	1.323***	0.443***	2.517***	2.193***	2.089***	1.164***	4.118***	2.340***
	(0.012)	(0.044)	(0.011)	(0.036)	(0.014)	(0.052)	(0.023)	(0.082)
Observations	9,345	8,456	9,460	8,543	8,668	7,818	9,308	8,428
R^2	0.014	0.070	0.001	0.177	0.008	0.092	0.007	0.078

Note: Linear regression models with robust standard errors in parentheses.
*$p < 0.05$. **$p < 0.01$. ***$p < 0.001$.

Notes

Introduction

1. The conceptual and analytical distinctions between Latin America's populist and social democratic lefts are explained in chapter 1. For a thoughtful discussion of the distinct dilemmas for the left in power and the left in opposition, see Riofrancos (2020, 168–182).
2. In game theoretic terms, the notion of contingent consent in iterative cycles of democratic contestation is analogous to Axelrod's (2006, 10–11) seminal work on reciprocity and the emergence of cooperative strategies in prisoner's dilemma games with an indefinite number of interactions.
3. Some material appearing in chapter 5 was previously published in Santiago Anria, Rocío Salas-Lewin, and Kenneth M. Roberts, "Dinámicas políticas y electorales luego del 'giro a la izquierda,'" in *La era del hartazgo: Líderes disruptivos, polarización y antipolítica en América Latina*, ed. Gabriel Kessler and Gabriel Vommaro (Buenos Aires: Siglo XXI, 2025).

Chapter One

1. A military coup also removed Honduras' left-leaning populist president Manuel Zelaya in 2009. In contrast to leftist presidents elsewhere in the region, however, Zelaya did not run for office as a candidate of the left, and we believe it would be misleading to characterize him as being part of the left turn.
2. For a discussion on popular sovereignty in terms of constituent power, see Kalyvas (2005).
3. Dahl's horizontal dimension was conceptualized largely in terms of suffrage rights, but it could be extended analytically to incorporate broader notions of majoritarianism and popular sovereignty or empowerment.
4. So elusive, in fact, that Dahl opted to employ the concept of polyarchy rather

than democracy, given the practical impossibility of achieving the latter's exacting standards for governmental responsiveness to citizens' demands (Dahl 1971, 8–9).

5. The institutional context was different in Uruguay, where the FA won legislative majorities and wielded greater political resources once it gained national office. As chapter 4 demonstrates, this meant the FA did not have to find "distasteful" allies to pass legislation, and it could more easily maintain strong ties to labor unions and other popular sector movements.

6. It bears noting that the effects of these institutional contexts are rarely uniform; they are contingent on previously adopted features that condition parties' responses to institutional opportunities and constraints.

7. Argentina's left turn under the PJ often fit uneasily in the existing binary subtypes of leftist governments. As we discuss in chapter 4, its classification is also not clear-cut, given a number of hybrid characteristics. The Peronist Partido Justicialista (PJ) is different from the "new" Bolivarian left in its origins, as it is a long-established party that experienced severe political repression under a bureaucratic-authoritarian regime. Although its rise to power in 2002 followed a protest cycle comparable to that in the populist-left cases, the PJ under Eduardo Duhalde and Néstor Kirchner ultimately took a different path.

8. A version of this argument for the Brazilian case has been made by Samuels and Zucco (2018, 3), who claim that it was Brazil's traditional way of "doing politics" that over time "changed the party far more than the PT had changed Brazil's way of doing politics."

9. Gibson's (1996) sociological notion of "core constituencies" refers to specific sectors that provide financial resources, policymaking support, and guidance to a political party.

Chapter Two

1. See the website of the Partido Socialista de Chile, at https://portal.pschile.cl/el-partido-socialista-sus-origenes-su-historia-y-las-razones-de-su-actual-vigencia/. Rosenblatt (2018, 82) adds that the party was also "born with trauma" given its emergence in the aftermath of the short-lived and violently suppressed "República Socialista."

2. This faction was led in exile by Carlos Altamirano, a former UP Senator and Secretary General of the PSCh who had, ironically, been a leader of the party's revolutionary current under the Allende government (Muñoz Tamayo 2016, 8).

3. Another faction, as Pribble (2013, 122) argues, "remained wedded to the traditional Socialist model." This faction was led by Clodomiro Almeyda, a former minister during the Allende presidency.

4. The notion of prefiguration refers to efforts to embody "within the ongoing political practice of a movement ... those forms of social relations, decision-making,

culture, and human experience that are the ultimate goal" (Boggs 1977, 100). The left's historic struggles over prefigurative politics are chronicled in Renaud (2021).

5. In its founding phase, moreover, the PT had strict requirements for affiliation and demanded a high level of commitment from members (Meneguello 1989, 33). Over time, the PT reduced the barriers of entry to join the party—for example, by introducing collective affiliations during electoral campaigns—and eased membership obligations.

6. This notion of convergence should not be equated with the development of formal organizational ties, or the direct incorporation of those networks of movements as organizational pillars for the party.

7. This faction emerged in 1983 and was initially called Articulation (Articulação). Over the course of the decade, it formed alliances with other moderate segments and formed the Majority Camp, which consolidated itself as a dominant faction (Melo 2021, 20) and steered the party toward important transformations in a centralizing direction and broad alliance-making (Ribeiro 2008, 160; Amaral 2010). It is currently called Building a New Brazil (Construindo um Novo Brasil).

8. While the slogan "PT way of governing" was a branding tool to consolidate the party as distinct, "it was rooted in something real: practical policies that expanded access to education, health, and housing and that improved the quality of services and goods provided" (French and Fortes 2005, 26).

9. For a splendid account of Lula's life trajectory, see French (2022).

10. On this institutional configuration, see Mainwaring (1995).

11. Measured at the legislative level and based on seats. See Michael Gallagher's website "Electoral Systems," at https://www.tcd.ie/Political_Science/about/people/michael_gallagher/ElSystems/index.php/.

12. Perry Anderson (2019, 113–114) argues that the PT had two options upon arriving to power: ally and cut a deal with the PMDB, Brazil's largest party and a master of political brokerage, or stitch together an alliance with myriad smaller parties. The PT opted for the latter until after the Mensalão corruption scandal and Lula's reelection, which then allowed the PMDB to "enter *en bloc* into the government, with a roster of ministries and key posts in Congress." And since that moment, "far from declining, systemic corruption began to escalate" (114).

13. On Brazil's long-standing "patrimonial tradition," see Roett (1999).

14. For a discussion on the Mensalão scheme, see Hunter and Power (2007, 2–3); see also Mainwaring et al. (2018, 194–195).

15. For a review of the major achievements of the PT and the changing economic policies over time, especially during Dilma's presidencies, see Singer (2019).

16. Growth in the minimum wage also meant a parallel increase in the benefits of non-contributory transfers, as they were linked to the minimum wage (Huber and Stephens 2012, 192).

17. Electoral payoffs were spread unevenly, however. As Power and Rodrigues-Silveira (2019, 259) note, "the electoral gains for the PT and allied left parties were

only modest in the more socioeconomically modernized South and Center-South. But sustained pro-poor policies had dramatic effects in the impoverished Northeast, the historical stronghold of conservative machines."

18. On the scandal, see Melo (2016).

19. Mainwaring et al. (2018, 195) vividly note that even before the scandal erupted "the PT was hemorrhaging partisans."

20. A long-standing observer of Brazilian politics, Margaret Keck (2022, 155), notes that "Parts of the upper echelons of Brazilian society have always derided—even sometimes expressed hatred for—both Lula and the PT. But until 2013, supporters and opponents could still be friends. Especially after the campaign to impeach Dilma Rousseff, the famed (though often exaggerated) 'cordiality' of Brazilians broke down, and many Brazilian families could no longer even celebrate holidays together."

21. As Campello (2015) suggests, this combination of low commodity prices and high international interest rates in developing countries tends to aggravate the kinds of constraints that leftist parties in power confront from financial markets. This tends to limit the ability of leftist incumbents to follow their policy preferences, and it may induce policy switches and damage presidential popularity.

22. The impeachment case against Rousseff was not based on charges of corruption but rather on accounting practices in the funding of social programs that were a technical infraction of the Fiscal Responsibility Law. Her predecessors had followed similar accounting practices, albeit on a smaller scale.

23. André Singer (2009, 2012), a former press secretary of the Lula administration and leading public intellectual, offers an alternative explanation of the PT's conformism grounded in political psychology. He argues that the PT accommodated and embraced a long-standing Brazilian tradition of conflict-avoidance, which, he further claims, is deeply grounded in the psychology of the Brazilian poor, a central constituency of Lulismo. In this interpretation, Lula, in particular, was highly sensitive to the impulses of the party's bases and largely adhered to the political culture in the country. In a different publication, Singer (2019, 56) claims that "Lulismo did not intend to confront the ruling classes. But by reducing poverty, it did so unintentionally." This, in his view, helps to partially explain the backlash against the PT.

24. We are indebted to Manuel Antonio Garretón for this term.

Chapter Three

1. Do Alto and Stefanoni (2010) refer to this as the "founding myth" of the MAS.

2. ASP never ran for office under its own name, as leaders failed to register the party in time for the municipal elections of 1995. Instead, they took over the United Left (IU), a defunct leftist party by the mid 1990s, and ran their own can-

didates under the IU label in the municipal elections of 1995 and the national elections of 1997. This story, along with the MAS' eventual legal registration as MAS-IPSP (Movement Toward Socialism—Political Instrument for the Sovereignty of the Peoples), is told in greater detail in Anria (2018, 72–73) and elsewhere (Madrid 2012, 53–54; Bjork-James 2020, 192).

3. Other sponsoring movement organizations included the Syndicalist Confederation of Intercultural Communities of Bolivia (CSCIB) and the Bartolina Sisa National Confederation of Campesino, Indigenous, and Native Women of Bolivia (CNMCIOB-BS).

4. This view is widely shared among founding leaders of the MAS (interviews with Román Loayza, Leonida Zurita, Dionisio Núñez, Juan de la Cruz Villca, and Modesto Condori).

5. This sets the MAS apart from other, more exclusionary indigenous-based parties that emerged during the same period but failed to develop national structures and mass appeal, like the Pachakuti Indigenous Movement (MIP) founded by Aymara leader Felipe Quispe, or the Revolutionary Liberation Movement Tupac Katari (MRTKL).

6. According to Farthing and Becker (2021, 53), moreover, this claim about coca growers applies more broadly to Bolivia's social movements, which tend to "equate democracy with economic and social justice" and not with institutionalized pluralism.

7. For a lengthier discussion about the nuances of these ideological currents, see Zavaleta Mercado (1986), Sanjinés (2004), and Dunkerley (2013).

8. The Grupo Comuna was formed in the context of the anti-neoliberal protest cycle that started in early 2000, and it made an effort to understand the limitations of liberal democracy and theorize an alternative (author's interviews with members of the Grupo Comuna, including Álvaro García Linera, Raúl Prada, and Oscar Vega Camacho).

9. In an influential essay, García Linera (2001, 102–103) claimed that democracy is about "widening the political space, breaking with political monopolies, and the continuous renewal of political institutions so as to widen the political responsibilities of members in a society. . . . A society is more democratic to the extent that more people participate in decision-making." And he went as far as to claim that "in real terms, democratic governments can exist without having an electoral regime" (103).

10. Another new party formed during this period was Solidarity Civic Union (UCS). It was founded in 1989 by beer magnate Max Fernández. Yet another one was the Cochabamba-based party New Revolutionary Force (NFR). See Mayorga (2002).

11. In addition to Evo Morales, Román Loayza, Néstor Guzmán, and Félix Sánchez became deputies for the Chapare. Evo Morales received more than 60 percent of the vote in his district in a crowded electoral field.

12. According to Van Cott (2003, 772), this expulsion was seen by many, including Morales, as "attributed to US pressure."

13. Interview with Marcelo Quezada, La Paz, 11 July 2008.

14. Interview with Román Loayza, La Paz, 22 July 2008.

15. Interview with Antonio Peredo, La Paz, 21 August 2008; also with José Antonio Quiroga, La Paz, 18 July 2008.

16. A change in the party's approach to alliance building happened in the lead-up to the 2005 national election. To a large extent, the refusal to form alliances was seen by MAS leaders as necessary to prevent the fate of parties like CONDEPA and UCS. Both had joined governments led by traditional parties and entered "the system." UCS joined the MNR from 1993 to 1997; CONDEPA joined the MIR, ADN, and UCS in 1997 but left the coalition early in its term. These experiences with joining the system severely undermined their antiestablishment credentials and contributed to their demise. In the lead-up to the 2005 election, the MAS formed an alliance with the center-left and La Paz-based Movement Without Fear (MSM).

17. The MAS finished first in Cochabamba, La Paz, Oruro, and Potosí; it obtained eight senators and twenty-seven deputies in the 2002 elections—a significant boost when compared to 1997 (Van Cott 2003, 764).

18. For excellent accounts of the 2000 mobilizations, see Assies (2003), Silva (2009), and Simmons (2016).

19. Three days before the 2002 election, US ambassador Manuel Rocha warned Bolivians about the risks of voting for a candidate linked to coca-growing activities. Campaign advisers used that statement and Morales's expulsion from Congress earlier that year to fuel feelings of nationalism and anti-Americanism into the campaign.

20. The demand for a constituent assembly predated the MAS; it had been articulated in the historic 1990 March for Territory and Dignity organized by the lowland Confederation of Indigenous Peoples of Bolivia (CIDOB). Additional demands from the 2003–2005 protest cycle included sweeping reforms, such as the nationalization of hydrocarbons and an extensive agrarian reform, leading to what came to be known as the "October Agenda" that the MAS adopted once in power.

21. UNHCR, "Venezuela Humanitarian Crisis," https://www.unrefugees.org/emergencies/venezuela/.

22. Although Morales won the presidential election in a landslide and the MAS captured a majority of seats in the Chamber of Deputies (72 of 130 seats), election results were not enough to guarantee a majority in the Senate, where the MAS obtained 12 of 27 seats. Parties on the right won the additional seats, turning them into a majority in the Senate. The largest of these parties was Social and Democratic Power (PODEMOS), a party closely tied to agribusiness elites, which gained 13 seats.

23. Interview with Álvaro García Linera, La Paz, 4 May 2013.

24. Bolivia's then vice president, Álvaro García Linera, called it a "catastrophic tie" and a "point of bifurcation" (García Linera 2008).

25. Interviews with social movement leaders reveal that they do think they gained agenda-setting capacity (see Anria 2018, chap. 4; also Krausova 2019).

26. This was the case, for example, with CIDOB and CONAMAQ.

27. Data from ECLAC (2020).

28. Electoral opposition to the MAS at local levels of government was more successful, although opposition parties remained largely localized, so organized competition rarely transcended the locality of the opponent in question (Centellas 2018).

29. Several authors attribute the MAS's political decline to a compromising logic that shaped its trajectory. For example, Farthing (2018) and Fabricant and Gustafson (2020, 118) link the political insulation and the weakening of the party's social bases to Morales's shift to the center in economic policies and his reliance on an extractivist growth model. Similarly, drawing on Gramsci's work, Hetland (2023) and McNelly (2023) link the political insulation and demobilization of the MAS's social bases to the national political dynamics of Morales's "passive revolution," arguing that fear of elite opposition prompted a top-down demobilization—and even pacification—of major social allies. Maclean (2022) attributes the MAS's decline—and erosion of its achievements—to a governing logic characterized by political compromises.

30. In a personal interview with Alvaro García Linera, he revealed that regional experiences such as that of the Brazilian Worker's Party (PT) with Lula's hand-picked successor was concerning for MAS leaders (interview with Álvaro García Linera, La Paz, May 4, 2013). In a more recent interview with the Argentine press, he made it clear that the historical precedents of the MNR of the 1950s and 1960s—and other leftist parties in Bolivia—loomed large in the MAS's imaginary and conditioned its approach to leadership renovation (Santucho 2022). After a decade in power following Bolivia's 1952 National Revolution, the MNR splintered in a context of economic instability; it was unable to maintain unity and was removed from power by a military regime (Anria and Cyr 2017).

31. See report by Al Jazeera on Morales's decision, posted at YouTube, at https://www.youtube.com/watch?v=y6Iw6QjQdsM.

32. There is a bitter debate around this point. There is also a growing consensus that the Organization of American States, which monitored the election and audited it upon Morales's request, identified irregularities but did not present compelling evidence of fraud. See Kurmanaev and Trigo (2020).

33. In 2005, Morales won his first presidential election with an unprecedented 54 percent of the vote. In 2008, Morales defeated a recall referendum by winning 67 percent of the vote. In 2009, Bolivian voters approved the country's new constitution by 61 percent of the vote, and Morales was then reelected by a 64 percent landslide. In 2014, he was reelected again—this time with 61 percent of the vote. In the wake of slowing economic growth in 2014, the MAS lost several mayoral and

gubernatorial races, and in 2016 the opposition temporarily united and captured 51.3 percent of a key referendum vote, just enough to defeat Morales's proposed constitutional change that would have allowed him to legally seek a fourth consecutive term.

34. Among other things, the report concludes that "it is appropriate to describe these events as massacres, given the number of people who lost their lives in the same way and at the same time and place, and because the acts in question were committed against a specific group of people. Furthermore, the patterns of injuries that have been recorded point strongly to extrajudicial killing practices." See the press release by the Organization of American States, at http://www.oas.org/en/iachr/media_center/PReleases/2019/321.asp.

35. Elections were postponed twice under the guise of the COVID-19 crisis in the country.

36. Although Morales and the Unity Pact reached an agreement on the presidential ticket, their relationship since then soured. The Unity Pact had proposed its own formula: David Choquehuanca for president and Andrónico Rodríguez for vice president—two leaders with distinct movement bases. While Morales managed to impose Arce over Choquehuanca, the Unity Pact accepted this decision, but not without complaints.

37. Divisions at the grassroots level—and leaders seeking to exacerbate these divisions—are hardly new in Bolivia's popular politics. During Morales's presidencies, major social movements split into "loyalist" and "dissident" factions. Similar fractures in allegiances emerged under the Arce presidency. Morales's core support remained anchored in rural segments, particularly in the Chapare region, where the *cocaleros* were strongly aligned with him and sought to maintain their dominance within the MAS. In contrast, Arce aimed to build support from the largely urban populations that the MAS helped to elevate into the middle class, as well as from movements of the urban poor, many of which are themselves deeply divided. He has also sought to establish connections with rural social movements, especially in Bolivia's eastern region.

38. It does take two to tango, however, and Arce's efforts to challenge Morales's central role and sideline him as a competitor from the electoral arena—especially during a deep economic crisis—only added fuel to the fire.

39. "TSE anula el Congreso del MAS y dispone que se convoque a un nuevo encuentro," Agencia de Noticias Fides, October 31, 2023, https://www.noticiasfides.com/nacional/politica/tse-anula-el-congreso-del-mas-y-dispone-que-se-convoque-a-un-nuevo-encuentro.

Chapter Four

1. On the concept of unrooted parties more generally, see Luna et al. (2022).
2. Later, it also included former guerrilla organizations, such as the Tupamaros,

which, defeated, abandoned armed struggle in the early 1970s and decided to engage in electoral mobilization, forming the Movimiento de Participación Popular (Popular Participation Movement, MPP) (see Rilla and Yaffé 2021, 23; see also Caetano et al. 2021, 199).

3. See the *historial de hojas de votación* for Uruguay, at http://historialhojas.corteelectoral.gub.uy.

4. That Montevideo is the country's largest district and home to about half the electorate means that even though reforms designed to boost participation were not as ambitious as those in Brazil at the local level under the PT, they engaged a proportionally larger population; they were therefore more salient and more consequential in shaping intraparty affairs and party-society linkages.

5. For a fuller discussion, see Sells (2022, 279–280).

6. Álvarez-Rivadulla's (2017) study of land squatting in Montevideo provides a useful window into this issue. Ideological differences around land squatting under democracy were prevalent among different FA factions; divisions deepened when the FA led Montevideo's municipal government. For the Tupamaros, land squatting was a revolutionary act—a way of mobilizing popular classes and expressing "their contempt for 'bourgeois institutions' such as private property" (Álvarez-Rivadulla 2017, 118). Over time, this developed into a major tension line within the Tupamaros; the most radical segments left the FA and clashed with the official party position against land invasions and its increasingly technocratic orientation.

7. Menem received 24.45 percent of the votes, followed by Kirchner with 22.25 percent and Adolfo Rodríguez Saá with 14.11 percent. Menem declined to run in the second round of the election when surveys showed him running far behind Kirchner.

8. On the concept of prefiguration and its relevance for left politics, see Renaud (2021).

9. This was also a consistently ambiguous process. In speeches and official ceremonies, the role of Peronism's radical currents in the violent period preceding the 1976 military coup was minimized, and the Kirchners tried to establish themselves as the real champions of human rights, in contrast to the post-1983 Peronism, which in their view lacked a human rights agenda. They also sought to set themselves apart from the human rights policies under the presidency of Raúl Alfonsín (1983–1989), which were seen as insufficient. The real defense of human rights, in their view, started with Kirchnerism, a "superior phase" in the history of Peronism.

10. The Movimiento Evita, as it is currently called, is Argentina's largest social movement. For an excellent account of its emergence and relationships with the Kirchners and the state, see Longa (2019).

11. We thank Fran Longa for raising this point.

12. This interview with Emilio Pérsico and Fernando "Chino" Navarro is quite telling in this regard, where they both recognize that ignoring the constraints of electoral democracy is often politically perilous. It means that "those at the bottom are the ones who tend to pay the costs." Therefore, social movements "need to try to act

within this liberal democracy, which is not the one we like, but it is rather the one we actually have." See Paula Abal Medina and Mario Santucho, "Puchero a la Evita," *Crisis*, November 13, 2016, https://revistacrisis.com.ar/notas/puchero-la-evita.

13. Annunciata (2023), in contrast, interprets Milei's victory as an electoral expression of "antipolitics" and social discontent, lacking a clear underlying programmatic alignment between voters and Milei.

Chapter Five

1. Barbosa (2023, 6) has similarly identified a high correlation between these two measures.

2. In other contexts, of course, the relationship between elite and mass levels of polarization can be quite different. McCoy et al. (2018, 18) offer an alternative view whereby elite behavior does the heavy lifting in the causal chain. In that account, major underlying divisions in society might exist and be susceptible to politicization from above, but they are not a necessary condition for polarization—elite behavior is. See also McCoy and Somer (2019, 236), where polarization is defined in relational terms and "has the tendency to extend from the partisan world to the realm of everyday social relations."

3. This is, arguably, a right-wing analog to the role that social protest played in shaping the rise of populist-left alternatives during the region's left turn (Silva 2009; Roberts 2014).

4. See, for example, McCoy et al. (2022, 6, 35–37), who discuss the challenges of the V-Dem dataset as well as the methodological innovations used by V-Dem to overcome those challenges.

5. The Latinobarómetro survey is based on a scale of 0 to 10. We code scores of 0–3 as left, 4–6 as center, and 7–10 as right. Moncagatta and Nunes da Silva (2024) report similar results using LAPOP's AmericasBarometer survey data from 2006 to 2018–2019.

6. To make clear, we are not claiming that neoliberalism itself was not polarizing. Neoliberalism drove public policies sharply toward the right pole. The lack of polarization in the electoral arena was largely attributable to the inability of neoliberalism's opponents (i.e., socialism and state-led capitalism) to articulate an alternative. But mounting social protest against neoliberalism (Arce and Bellinger 2007; Silva 2009) suggests that there was already a certain polarizing logic at the societal level as part of the Washington Consensus. See also McCoy et al. (2022) for an argument noting that depolarization events—like the ones observed in the 1980s and 1990s—typically occur in the aftermath of major systemic shocks, such as regime transitions and the end of civil conflicts. For us, it was not only the regime transitions that led to depolarization, but also the technocratic consensus (at the elite level) around the neoliberal model following severe inflationary crises.

7. See, for example, Valenzuela's (1978, 10–11) description of the polarized politics that preceded the coup against Allende in Chile in 1973, where polarization had both elite and mass dimensions that reinforced each other. More recently, McCoy and Somer (2019) have made a similar point.

8. The subsequent LAPOP survey waves, in 2021 and 2023, do not measure left-right self-identification or do not include sufficient participation variables to construct our index, respectively. For that reason, the LAPOP 2018–2019 wave has the most recent data available to carry out the kind of analysis that we are conducting. We excluded Venezuela from the analysis because there is no 2018–2019 survey for the country.

9. We tested the political participation index through a confirmatory factor analysis with a weighted-least-squares (WLSMV) estimator. Because the index includes items of institutional and extrainstitutional participation, we expected that its goodness of fit and reliability would not be perfect (comparative fit index = .899, Tucker–Lewis index = .696, root mean square error of approximation = .062, ordinal α = .52), although the items undoubtedly measure core aspects of political involvement and they obtain good or reasonable loadings: community meetings (λ = .434), protest (λ = .581), retrospective vote (λ = .393), and party sympathy (λ = .452).

10. Raw scores on the response items for media attention were inverted so that higher values indicate higher levels of media attention.

11. We also ran models controlling for income, but including income made us lose too many cases due to nonreporting. Given its .44 correlation with education, we use education alone as a proxy for social class. The models controlling for income are in the Appendix. See table 5A.1.

References

Abers, Rebecca. 2000. *Inventing Local Democracy: Grassroots Politics in Brazil.* Lynne Rienner Publishers.
Acemoglu, Daron, and James A. Robinson. 2009. *Economic Origins of Dictatorship and Democracy.* Cambridge University Press.
Achen, Christopher H., and Larry M. Bartels. 2017. *Democracy for Realists: Why Elections Do Not Produce Responsive Government.* Rev. ed. Princeton University Press.
Adamovsky, Ezequiel. 2024. *Del antiperonismo al individualismo autoritario: Ensayos e intervenciones (2015–2023).* UNSAM Edita.
Aguirre Bayley, Miguel. 2000. *Frente Amplio: "La admirable alarma de 1971": Partido Encuentro Progresista Frente Amplio.* 2nd ed. La República.
Ahumada, Pablo Perez. 2023. *Building Power to Shape Labor Policy: Unions, Employer Associations, and Reform in Neoliberal Chile.* University of Pittsburgh Press.
Alberti, Carla. 2021. "Bolivia's Old and New Illnesses." In *Divisive Politics and Democratic Dangers in Latin America*, edited by Thomas Carothers and Andreas Feldman. Carnegie Endowment for International Peace. https://carnegieendowment.org/2021/02/17/bolivia-s-old-and-new-illnesses-pub-83782.
Albertus, Michael. 2015. *Autocracy and Redistribution: The Politics of Land Reform.* Cambridge Studies in Comparative Politics. Cambridge University Press. https://doi.org/10.1017/CBO9781316227107.
Alenda, Stéphanie. 2003. "Dimensiones de la movilización en torno a conciencia de patria: Hacia un modelo explicativo de un caso de neopopulismo boliviano." *Revista de Ciencia Política* 23 (1): 119–135.
Alonso, Angela, and Ann Mische. 2017. "Changing Repertoires and Partisan Ambivalence in the New Brazilian Protests." *Bulletin of Latin American Research* 36 (2): 144–159. https://doi.org/10.1111/blar.12470.
Alonso, Jimena. 2021. "El frentismo en la izquierda uruguaya." In *Partidos y movimientos políticos en Uruguay: Historia y presente*, edited by José Rilla and Jaime Yaffé, 201–212. Crítica.

Altman, David. 2002. "Popular Initiatives in Uruguay: Confidence Votes on Government or Political Loyalties?" *Electoral Studies* 21 (4): 617–630.

Alvarez, Sonia E. 1990. *Engendering Democracy in Brazil*. Princeton University Press.

Álvarez-Rivadulla, María José. 2017. *Squatters and the Politics of Marginality in Uruguay*. Palgrave Macmillan.

Amaral, Oswaldo E. 2010. "As transformações na orgaização interna do PT entre 1995 e 2009." PhD diss., Instituto de Filosofia e Ciências Humanas, Universidade Estadual de Campinas.

Amaral, Oswaldo E., and Timothy J. Power. 2016. "The PT at 35: Revisiting Scholarly Interpretations of the Brazilian Workers' Party." *Journal of Latin American Studies* 48 (1): 147–171. https://doi.org/10.1017/S0022216X15001200.

Anderson, Cora Fernández. 2020. *Fighting for Abortion Rights in Latin America: Social Movements, State Allies and Institutions*. Routledge.

Anderson, Jon Lee. 2020. "The Fall of Evo Morales." *New Yorker*, March 16. https://www.newyorker.com/magazine/2020/03/23/the-fall-of-evo-morales.

Anderson, Perry. 2019. *Brazil Apart: 1964–2019*. Verso Books.

Andrews-Lee, Caitlin. 2021. *The Emergence and Revival of Charismatic Movements: Argentine Peronism and Venezuelan Chavismo*. Cambridge University Press.

Annunziata, Rocío. 2023. "La antipolítica contemporánea y el fenómeno Javier Milei." In *La antipolítica y los desafíos de la democracia argentina*, edited by Leonardo Avritzer, Enrique Peruzzotti, and Osvaldo Iazzeta. Prometeo Editorial.

Anria, Santiago. 2013. "Social Movements, Party Organization, and Populism: Insights from the Bolivian MAS." *Latin American Politics and Society* 55 (3): 19–46.

Anria, Santiago. 2016. "More Inclusion, Less Liberalism in Bolivia." *Journal of Democracy* 27 (3): 99–108. https://doi.org/10.1353/jod.2016.0037.

Anria, Santiago. 2018. *When Movements Become Parties: The Bolivian MAS in Comparative Perspective*. Cambridge Studies in Comparative Politics. Cambridge University Press.

Anria, Santiago, and Juan Bogliaccini. 2022. "Empowering Inclusion? The Two Sides of Party-Society Linkages in Latin America." *Studies in Comparative International Development* 57: 410–432.

Anria, Santiago, and Jennifer Cyr. 2017. "Inside Revolutionary Parties: Coalition-Building and Maintenance in Reformist Bolivia." *Comparative Political Studies* 50 (9): 1255–1287. https://doi.org/10.1177/0010414016666860.

Anria, Santiago, and Jennifer Cyr. 2022. "Bolivia: Paradoxes of Inclusion and Contestation." In *Challenges to Democracy in the Andes: Strongmen, Broken Constitutions, and Regimes in Crisis*, edited by Maxwell A. Cameron and Grace M. Jaramillo. Lynne Rienner Publishers.

Anria, Santiago, Candelaria Garay, and Jessica A. J. Rich. 2024. "Social Movements and Policy Entrenchment." *Comparative Politics* 57 (1): 113–137.

Anria, Santiago, Verónica Pérez Bentancur, Rafael Piñeiro Rodríguez, and Fernando Rosenblatt. 2022. "Agents of Representation: The Organic Connection Between Society and Leftist Parties in Bolivia and Uruguay." *Politics & Society* 50 (3): 384–412.

Anria, Santiago, and Gabriel Alejandro Vommaro. 2020. "En Argentina, un 'giro a la derecha' que no fue y el improbable regreso del peronismo de centro-izquierda." January. https://ri.conicet.gov.ar/handle/11336/168140.

Arbona, Juan M., and Benjamin Kohl. 2004. "La Paz–El Alto." *Cities* 21 (3): 255–265.

Arce, Moises, and Paul T. Bellinger. 2007. "Low-Intensity Democracy Revisited: The Effects of Economic Liberalization on Political Activity in Latin America." *World Politics* 60 (1): 97–121. https://doi.org/10.1353/wp.0.0003.

Archondo, Rafael. 1991. *Compadres al micrófono: La resurrección metropolitana del ayllu*. Hisbol.

Arigho-Stiles, Olivia. 2024. "A Rift Has Opened in Bolivia's Movement Toward Socialism." *Jacobin*, March. https://jacobin.com/2024/03/bolivia-movement-toward-socialism-arce-morales.

Arnold, Jason, and David J. Samuels. 2011. "Latin America's Left Turn? Evidence from Public Opinion: A Conceptual and Theoretical Overview." In *Latin America's Left Turn*, edited by Steven Levitsky and Kenneth Roberts. Johns Hopkins University Press.

Assies, Willem. 2003. "David Versus Goliath in Cochabamba: Water Rights, Neoliberalism, and the Revival of Social Protest in Bolivia." *Latin American Perspectives* 30 (3): 14–36.

Avritzer, Leonardo. 2002. *Democracy and the Public Space in Latin America*. Princeton University Press.

Avritzer, Leonardo. 2009. *Participatory Institutions in Democratic Brazil*. Woodrow Wilson Center Press, Johns Hopkins University Press.

Axelrod, Robert. 2006. *The Evolution of Cooperation*. Rev. ed. Basic Books.

Baiocchi, Gianpaolo. 2003. *Radicals in Power: The Workers' Party (PT) and Experiments in Urban Democracy in Brazil*. Palgrave.

Baiocchi, Gianpaolo, and Sofia Checa. 2007. "The Brazilian Workers' Party: From Local Practices to National Power." *Working USA* 10 (4): 411–430.

Baker, Andy, and Kenneth F. Greene. 2011. "The Latin American Left's Mandate: Free-Market Policies and Issue Voting in New Democracies." *World Politics* 63 (1): 43–77.

Baker, Andy, and Kenneth F. Greene. 2019. "Latin American Election Results with Party Ideology Scores." https://www.dropbox.com/scl/fo/w9tcfb4202qks0kk7yf8u/AID8tDuZOt9t47YEPn9ce94?dl=0&e=1&preview=readme.docx&rlkey=ge4jd8oxqadz40ketvqpcxvev.

Balán, Manuel, and Françoise Montambeault. 2020. *Legacies of the Left Turn in Latin America: The Promise of Inclusive Citizenship*. University of Notre Dame Press.

Balsa, Javier. 2024. *¿Por qué ganó Milei? Disputas por la hegemonía y la ideología en Argentina*. Fondo de Cultura Económica Argentina.

Barbosa, Pedro. 2023. "Inequality or Redistribution? The Determinants of Severe Polarization in Latin America." Paper presented at the XIII Seminario Discente, Programa de Pós-Graduação em Ciência Política, Universidade de São Paulo.

Barros, Celso Rocha de. 2022. *PT, uma história*. Companhia das Letras.

Beach, Derek, and Rasmus Brun Pedersen. 2013. *Process-Tracing Methods: Foundations and Guidelines*. University of Michigan Press.

Becker, Mark. 2008. *Indians and Leftists in the Making of Ecuador's Modern Indigenous Movements*. Latin America Otherwise. Duke University Press.

Bergquist, Charles W. 1986. *Labor in Latin America: Comparative Essays on Chile, Argentina, Venezuela, and Colombia*. Stanford University Press.

Berman, Sheri. 2006. *The Primacy of Politics: Social Democracy and the Making of Europe's Twentieth Century*. Cambridge University Press.

Berman, Sheri, and Hans Kundnani. 2021. "The Costs of Convergence." *Journal of Democracy* 32 (1): 22–36.

Bermeo, Nancy. 2016. "On Democratic Backsliding." *Journal of Democracy* 27 (1): 5–19.

Bezerra, Carla de Paiva. 2019. "Os sentidos da participação para o partido dos trabalhadores (1980–2016)." *Revista Brasileira de Ciências Sociais* 34 (September). https://doi.org/10.1590/3410016/2019.

Bidegain Ponte, Germán. 2015. "Autonomización de los movimientos sociales e intensificación de la protesta: Estudiantes y mapuche en Chile (1990–2013)." PhD diss., Pontificia Universidad Católica de Chile.

Bittar, Jorge. 1992. *O modo petista de governar*. Teoria & Debate.

Bjork-James, Carwil. 2020. *The Sovereign Street: Making Revolution in Urban Bolivia*. Illustrated ed. University of Arizona Press.

Bjork-James, Carwil. 2024. "When Does Lethal Repression Fail? Unarmed Militancy and Backfire in Bolivia, 1982–2021." *Journal of Latin American Studies* 56 (1): 1–36.

Blanco Muñoz, Agustín (interviewer). 1998. *Habla el Comandante*. 3rd ed. Universidad Central de Venezuela.

Blofield, Merike. 2012. *Care Work and Class: Domestic Workers' Struggle for Equal Rights in Latin America*. Penn State University Press.

Blofield, Merike, Christina Ewig, and Jennifer M. Piscopo. 2017. "The Reactive Left: Gender Equality and the Latin American Pink Tide." *Social Politics* 24 (4): 345–369. https://doi.org/10.1093/sp/jxx016.

Blum, Rachel M. 2020. *How the Tea Party Captured the GOP: Insurgent Factions in American Politics*. University of Chicago Press.

Boggs, Carl. 1977. "Marxism, Prefigurative Communism, and the Problem of Workers' Control." *Radical America* 11 (6): 99–122.

Bogliaccini, Juan. 2024. *Wage Policy as Pre-Distribution: Leftist Approaches to Empowering Labor in Unequal Democracies*. Cambridge University Press.

Bogliaccini, Juan, and Rosario Queirolo. 2017. "Uruguay 2016: Mayorías parlamentarias en jaque y desafíos de revisión para sostener el modelo." *Revista de Ciencia Política* (Santiago) 37 (2): 589–612.

Boix, Carles. 2003. *Democracy and Redistribution*. Cambridge University Press, 2003.

Bonvecchi, Alejandro, and Germán Lodola. 2011. "The Dual Logic of Intergovernmental Transfers: Presidents, Governors, and the Politics of Coalition-Building in Argentina." *Publius: The Journal of Federalism* 41 (2): 179–206.

Borges, André, Ryan Lloyd, and Gabriel Vommaro, eds. 2024. *The Recasting of the Latin American Right: Polarization and Conservative Reactions*. Cambridge University Press.

Borges, André, and Robert Vidigal. 2018. "Do lulismo ao antipetismo? Polarização, partidarismo e voto nas eleições presidenciais brasileiras." *Opinião Pública* 24 (April): 53–89. https://doi.org/10.1590/1807-0191201824153.

Bourne, Richard. 2008. *Lula of Brazil: The Story So Far*. University of California Press. https://muse.jhu.edu/book/25606.

Boyanovsky Bazán, Christian. 2010. *El aluvión: Del piquete al gobierno: Los movimientos sociales y el kirchnerismo*. Sudamericana.

Bradlow, Benjamin H., and Tomás Gold. 2025. "A Processual Framework for Understanding the Rise of the Populist Right: The Case of Brazil (2013–2018)." *Social Forces*. https://academic.oup.com/sf/advance-article/doi/10.1093/sf/soae189/7951993?login=false.

Braver, Joshua. 2016. "Hannah Arendt in Venezuela: The Supreme Court Battles Hugo Chávez Over the Creation of the 1999 Constitution." *International Journal of Constitutional Law* 14 (3): 555–583.

Brewer-Carías, Allan R. 2010. *Dismantling Democracy in Venezuela: The Chávez Authoritarian Experiment*. Cambridge University Press.

Brewer-Carías, Allan R. 2019. "The Collapse of the Rule of Law in Venezuela 1999–2019." *New York University Journal of International Law and Politics* 52: 741.

Brinks, Daniel, Marcelo Leiras, and Scott Mainwaring, eds. 2014. *Reflections on Uneven Democracies*. Johns Hopkins University Press.

Brown, John. 2022. *Deepening Democracy in Post-Neoliberal Bolivia and Venezuela: Advances and Setbacks*. Routledge.

Bull, Benedicte, and Antulio Rosales. 2020. "The Crisis in Venezuela: Drivers, Transitions, and Pathways." *European Review of Latin American and Caribbean Studies* (109). https://doi.org/10.32992/erlacs.10587.

Buquet, Daniel, and Daniel Chasquetti. 2005. "Elecciones Uruguay 2004: Descifrando el cambio." *Revista de Ciencia Política* (Santiago) 25 (2): 143–152. https://doi.org/10.4067/S0718-090X2005000200006.

Buquet, Daniel, and Rafael Piñeiro. 2014. "La consolidación de un nuevo sistema de partidos en Uruguay." *Revista Debates* 8 (1): 127–148. https://doi.org/10.224 56/1982-5269.44774.

Burbano de Lara, Felipe. 2020. "La patria ya es de todos: Pilgrimages, Charisma, Territory, and the Return of the State." In *Assessing the Left Turn in Ecuador*, edited by Francisco Sánchez and Simón Pachano. Palgrave Macmillan, Springer Nature Switzerland.

Burgoa, Carlos, and Modesto Condori. 2011. "El caminar histórico del instrumento político, 1995–2009." Unpublished manuscript, La Paz.

Bustikova, Lenka. 2022. *Extreme Reactions: Radical Right Mobilization in Eastern Europe*. Cambridge University Press.

Buxton, Julia. 2001. *The Failure of Political Reform in Venezuela*. Ashgate.

Buxton, Julia. 2003. "Economic Policy and the Rise of Hugo Chávez." In *Venezuelan Politics in the Chávez Era: Class, Polarization, and Conflict*, edited by Steve Ellner and Daniel Hellinger. Lynne Rienner Publishers.

Caetano, Gerardo, Juan Pablo Luna, Jaime Yaffé, and Rafael Piñeiro. 2003. *La izquierda uruguaya y la hipótesis del gobierno: Algunos desafíos político-institucionales*. Análisis y Propuestas. Friedrich Ebert Stiftung Foundation. https://library.fes.de/pdf-files/bueros/uruguay/01824.pdf

Caetano, Gerardo, Aldo Marchesi, and Vania Markarian. 2021. "Secuencias." In *Partidos y movimientos políticos en Uruguay: Historia y presente*, edited by José Rilla and Jaime Yaffé. Crítica.

Calvo, Ernesto, Gabriel Kessler, María Victoria Murillo, Gabriel Vommaro 2024. "Argentina's New Conservative Coalition." *Americas Quarterly* (blog). https://www.americasquarterly.org/article/argentinas-new-conservative-coalition/.

Calvo, Ernesto, and María Victoria Murillo. 2012. "Argentina: The Persistence of Peronism." *Journal of Democracy* 23 (2): 148–161. https://doi.org/10.1353/jod.2012.0029.

Cameron, Maxwell A. 2018. "Making Sense of Competitive Authoritarianism: Lessons from the Andes." *Latin American Politics and Society* 60 (2): 1–22. https://doi.org/10.1017/lap.2018.3.

Cameron, Maxwell A., and Eric Hershberg. 2010. *Latin America's Left Turns: Politics, Policies, and Trajectories of Change*. Lynne Rienner Publishers.

Cameron, Maxwell A., and Grace Jaramillo. 2022. "The Dilemmas of Democratization in the Andes." In *Challenges to Democracy in the Andes: Strongmen, Broken Constitutions, and Regimes in Crisis*, edited by Maxwell A. Cameron and Grace M. Jaramillo. Lynne Rienner Publishers.

Cameron, Maxwell A., and Kenneth E. Sharpe. 2012. "The Quality and Diversity of Democratic Regimes in the Andes: New Mechanisms of Direct Institutionalized Voice." In *New Institutions for Participatory Democracy in Latin America: Voice and Consequence*, edited by Maxwell A. Cameron, Eric Hershberg, and Kenneth E. Sharpe. Palgrave Macmillan.

Campello, Daniela. 2015. *The Politics of Market Discipline in Latin America: Globalization and Democracy.* Cambridge University Press.

Campello, Daniela, and Cesar Zucco. 2020. *The Volatility Curse: Exogenous Shocks and Representation in Resource-Rich Democracies.* Cambridge University Press.

Canache, Damarys. 2002. "From Bullets to Ballots: The Emergence of Popular Support for Hugo Chávez." *Latin American Politics and Society* 44 (1): 69–90. https://doi.org/10.2307/3177111.

Canel, Eduardo. 2014. *Barrio Democracy in Latin America: Participatory Decentralization and Community Activism in Montevideo.* Penn State University Press.

Canessa, Andrew. 2014. "Conflict, Claim and Contradiction in the New 'Indigenous' State of Bolivia." *Critique of Anthropology* 34 (2): 153–173. https://doi.org/10.1177/0308275X13519275.

Canzani, Agustín. 2024. "Elecciones en Uruguay: Una moneda al aire entre la izquierda y la derecha." *Nueva Sociedad: Democracia y Política en América Latina*, October 31. https://nuso.org/articulo/elecciones-uruguay-izquierda-yamandu-orsi-derecha-multicolor/.

Carothers, Thomas. 2002. "The End of the Transition Paradigm." *Journal of Democracy* 13 (1): 5–21. https://doi.org/10.1353/jod.2002.0003.

Carter Center. 2008. "Report on the Constituent Assembly of the Republic of Ecuador." Quito. https://www.cartercenter.org/resources/pdfs/peace/americas/report_constituent_assembly_ecuador_english_sep_2008_final.pdf.

Cason, Jeffrey. 2000. "Electoral Reform and Stability in Uruguay." *Journal of Democracy* 11 (2): 85–98. https://doi.org/10.1353/jod.2000.0032.

Cason, Jeffrey. 2002. "Electoral Reform, Institutional Change, and Party Adaptation in Uruguay." *Latin American Politics and Society* 44 (3): 89–109. https://doi.org/10.1111/j.1548-2456.2002.tb00215.x.

Castañeda, Jorge. 1993. *Utopia Unarmed: The Latin American Left After the Cold War.* Knopf.

Castañeda, Jorge G. 2006. "Latin America's Left Turn." *Foreign Affairs* 85 (3): 28. https://doi.org/10.2307/20031965.

Castiglioni, Rossana, and Cristóbal Rovira Kaltwasser. 2016. "Challenges to Political Representation in Contemporary Chile." *Journal of Politics in Latin America* 8 (3): 3–24. https://doi.org/10.1177/1866802X1600800301.

Castles, Francis G. 1978. *Social Democratic Image of Society: A Study of the Achievement and Origins of Scandinavian Social Democracy in Comparative Perspective.* Routledge and Kegan Paul.

Casullo, María Esperanza. 2024. "Alerta democrática: Marcadores críticos de riesgo autoritario en el primer año de gestión de Javier Milei." *Asuntos del Sur.* https://asuntosdelsur.org/publicacion/alerta-democratica-marcadores-criticos-de-riesgo-autoritario-en-el-primer-ano-de-gestion-de-javier-milei/.

Centellas, Miguel. 2007. "Democracy on Stilts: Bolivia's Democracy from Stability to Crisis." PhD diss., Western Michigan University. https://scholarworks.wmich.edu/dissertations/843.

Centellas, Miguel. 2013. "Bolivia's New Multicultural Constitution: The 2009 Constitution in Historical and Comparative Perspective." In *Latin America's Multicultural Movements: The Struggle Between Communitarianism, Autonomy, and Human Rights*, edited by Todd Eisenstadt, Michael Danielson, Moisés Jaime Bailón Corres, and Carlos Sorroza Polo. Oxford University Press.

Centellas, Miguel. 2016. "The Santa Cruz Autonomía Movement in Bolivia: A Case of Non-Indigenous Ethnic Popular Mobilization?" *Ethnopolitics* 15 (2): 245–264.

Centellas, Miguel. 2018. "Bolivia in 2017: Headed into Uncertainty." *Revista de Ciencia Politica* 3 (2): 155–179.

CEPAL. 2020. "Bolivarian Republic of Venezuela." *Preliminary Overview of the Economies of Latin America and the Caribbean.* file:///D:/Other%20authors/latin%20america/Venezuela/economic%20crisis.%20cepal%20report.pdf.

Chávez, Hugo, and Marta Harnecker. 2005. *Understanding the Venezuelan Revolution: Hugo Chávez Talks to Marta Harnecker.* Monthly Review Press.

Cherny, Nicolás. 2014. "La relación presidente-partido de gobierno en el kirchnerismo." In *Peronismo y democracia: Historia y perspectivas*, edited by Marcos Novaro and Samuel Amaral. Edhasa.

Ciccariello-Maher, George. 2013. *We Created Chávez: A People's History of the Venezuelan Revolution.* Duke University Press.

Collier, David, ed. 1979. *The New Authoritarianism in Latin America.* Princeton University Press.

Collier, Ruth Berins, and David Collier. 1991. *Shaping the Political Arena: Critical Junctures, The Labor Movement, and Regime Dynamics in Latin America.* University of Notre Dame Press.

Commanding Heights: Ricardo Lagos on PBS. 2002. PBS. https://www.pbs.org/wgbh/commandingheights/shared/minitextlo/int_ricardolagos.html.

Conaghan, Catherine. 2011. "Ecuador: Rafael Correa and the Citizens' Revolution." In *The Resurgence of the Latin American Left*, edited by Steven Levitsky and Kenneth M. Roberts. Johns Hopkins University Press.

Conaghan, Catherine. 2015. "Surveil and Sanction: The Return of the State and Societal Regulation in Ecuador." *European Review of Latin American and Caribbean Studies / Revista Europea de Estudios Latinoamericanos y del Caribe* 98: 7–27.

Conaghan, Catherine. 2018. "From Movements to Governments: Comparing Bolivia's MAS and Ecuador's PAIS." In *Reshaping the Political Arena in Latin America: From Resisting Neoliberalism to the Second Incorporation,* edited by Eduardo Silva and Federico Rossi. Pittsburgh University Press.

Conaghan, Catherine. 2022. "Diminished by Design: Ecuador's Alianza PAIS." In *Diminished Parties: Democratic Representation in Contemporary Latin America,* edited by Juan Pablo Luna, Rafael Piñeiro Rodríguez, Fernando Rosenblatt, and Gabriel Vommaro. Cambridge University Press.

Conniff, Michael L., ed. 2012. *Populism in Latin America*. 2nd ed. University of Alabama Press. https://muse.jhu.edu/book/22550.

Constable, Pamela, and Arturo Valenzuela. 1993. *A Nation of Enemies: Chile Under Pinochet*. 3rd rev. ed. W. W. Norton & Co.

Constitution of the Republic of Ecuador. 2008. Republic of Ecuador.

Coppedge, Michael. 1994. *Strong Parties and Lame Ducks: Presidential Partyarchy and Factionalism in Venezuela*. Stanford University Press.

Coppedge, Michael, John Gerring, Carl Henrik Knutsen, Staffan I. Lindberg, Jan Teorell, David Altman, Fabio Angiolillo, Michael Bernhard, Cecilia Borella, Agnes Cornell, M. Steven Fish, Linnea Fox, Lisa Gastaldi, Haakon Gjerlow, Adam Glynn, Ana Good God, Sandra Grahn, Allen Hicken, Katrin Kinzelbach, Joshua Krusell, Kyle L. Marquardt, Kelly McMann, Valeriya Mechkova, Juraj Medzihorsky, Natalia Natsika, Anja Neundorf, Pamela Paxton, Daniel Pemstein, Josefine Pernes, Oskar Rydén, Johannes von Römer, Brigitte Seim, Rachel Sigman, Svend-Erik Skaaning, Jeffrey Staton, Aksel Sundström, Eitan Tzelgov, Yi-ting Wang, Tore Wig, Steven Wilson and Daniel Ziblatt. 2024. *V-Dem Dataset v14*. Varieties of Democracy (V-Dem) Project. https://doi.org/10.23696/mcwt-fr58.

Cornia, Giovanni Andrea, ed. 2014. *Falling Inequality in Latin America: Policy Changes and Lessons*. WIDER Studies in Development Economics. Oxford University Press. https://doi.org/10.1093/acprof:oso/9780198701804.001.0001.

Coronel, Omar, and Sofia Donoso. 2024. "Olas de protesta, estallidos sociales y partidos políticos en América Latina: Dinámicas y consecuencias." *Desafíos* 36 (1). https://revistas.urosario.edu.co/index.php/desafios.

Corrales, Javier. 2018. *Fixing Democracy: Why Constitutional Change Often Fails to Enhance Democracy in Latin America*. Oxford University Press.

Corrales, Javier. 2021. "The Politics of LGBTQ Rights Expansion in Latin America and the Caribbean." *Elements in Politics and Society in Latin America*, December. https://doi.org/10.1017/9781108993609.

Corrales, Javier, and Michael Penfold. 2011. *Dragon in the Tropics: Hugo Chávez and the Political Economy of Revolution in Venezuela*. Brookings Institution Press.

Corrales, Javier, and Dorothy Kronick. 2025. "How Maduro Stole Venezuela's Vote." *Journal of Democracy* 36 (1): 36–49.

Couto, Cláudio Gonçalves. 1995. *O desafio de ser governo: O PT na Prefeitura de São Paulo, 1989–1992*. Paz e Terra.

Crabtree, John. 2013. "From the MNR to the MAS: Populism, Parties, the State, and Social Movements in Bolivia Since 1952." In *Latin American Populism in the Twenty-First Century*, edited by Carlos de la Torre and Cynthia J. Arnson. Johns Hopkins University Press.

Crabtree, John. 2020. "Assessing Evo's Bolivia: Inclusion, Ethnicity, and Class." *Latin American Research Review* 55 (2): 379–390.

Crabtree, John, Jonas Wolff, and Francisco Durand. 2023. *Business Power and the State in the Central Andes: Bolivia, Ecuador, and Peru in Comparison.* University of Pittsburgh Press.

Crisp, Brian F. 2000. *Democratic Institutional Design: The Powers and Incentives of Venezuelan Politicians and Interest Groups.* Stanford University Press.

Cyr, Jennifer. 2017. *The Fates of Political Parties: Institutional Crisis, Continuity, and Change in Latin America.* Cambridge University Press.

Dahl, Robert A. 1971. *Polyarchy: Participation and Opposition.* Yale University Press.

Dalton, Russell J., and Martin P. Wattenberg, eds. 2000. *Parties Without Partisans: Political Change in Advanced Industrial Democracies.* Oxford University Press.

Delamaza, Gonzalo. 2009. "Sociedad civil y políticas sociales en Chile." In *La "nueva izquierda" en América Latina: Derechos humanos, participación política, y sociedad civil*, edited by Cynthia J. Arnson, Ariel C. Armony, Catalina Smulovitz, Gastón Chillier, and Enrique Peruzzotti, with Giselle Cohen. Woodrow Wilson International Center for Scholars.

Delamaza, Gonzalo. 2010. "La disputa por la participación en la democracia elitista chilena." *Latin American Research Review* 45: 274–297.

de la Torre, Augusto, Simón Cueva, and María Alexandra Castellanos-Vásconez. 2020. "The Macroeconomics of the Commodities Boom in Ecuador: A Comparative Perspective." In *Assessing the Left Turn in Ecuador,* edited by Francisco Sánchez and Simón Pachano. Palgrave Macmillan, Springer Nature Switzerland.

de la Torre, Carlos. 2010. *Populist Seduction in Latin America.* 2nd ed. Ohio University Press.

de la Torre, Carlos, ed. 2015. *The Promise and Perils of Populism: Global Perspectives.* University Press of Kentucky.

de la Torre, Carlos. 2020. "Rafael Correa's Technopopulism in Comparative Perspective." In *Assessing the Left Turn in Ecuador,* edited by Francisco Sánchez and Simón Pachano. Palgrave Macmillan, Springer Nature Switzerland.

De Micheli, David, Jose T. Sanchez-Gomez, and Kenneth M. Roberts. 2022. "Tenuous Pacts and Multiparty Coalitions: The Politics of Presidential Impeachment in Latin America." *Journal of Latin American Studies* 54 (2): 283–311. https://doi.org/10.1017/S0022216X22000219.

DeShazo, Peter. 1983. *Urban Workers and Labor Unions in Chile, 1902–1927.* University of Wisconsin Press.

Dias, Tayrine, Marisa von Bülow, and Danniel Gobbi. 2021. "Populist Framing Mechanisms and the Rise of Right-Wing Activism in Brazil." *Latin American Politics and Society* 63 (3): 69–92. https://doi.org/10.1017/lap.2021.22.

Díaz, Camila, Cristóbal Rovira Kaltwasser, and Lisa Zanotti. 2023. "The Arrival of the Populist Radical Right in Chile: José Antonio Kast and the 'Partido Republicano.'" *Journal of Language and Politics* 22 (3): 342–359. https://doi.org/10.1075/jlp.22131.dia.

Díaz-Cuellar, Vladimir. 2019. "Requiem para el 'Proceso de Cambio.'" *Control Ciudadano* 13 (32): 1–16.

Díez, Jordi. 2015. *The Politics of Gay Marriage in Latin America: Argentina, Chile, and Mexico.* Cambridge University Press.

Do Alto, Hervé, and Pablo Stefanoni. 2010. "El MAS: Las ambivalencias de la democracia corporativa." In *Mutaciones en el campo político boliviano.* UNDP.

Doglio, Natalia, Luis Senatore, and Jaime Yaffé. 2004. "Izquierda política y sindicatos en Uruguay (1971–2003)." In *La izquierda uruguaya: Entre la oposición y el gobierno,* edited by Jorge Lanzaro. Editorial Fin de Siglo.

Donoso, Sofia. 2013. "Dynamics of Change in Chile: Explaining the Emergence of the 2006 Pingüino Movement." *Journal of Latin American Studies* 45 (1): 1–29. https://doi.org/10.1017/S0022216X12001228.

Donoso, Sofia, and Marisa von Bülow, eds. 2017. *Social Movements in Chile: Organization, Trajectories, and Political Consequences.* Palgrave Macmillan.

Downs, Anthony. 1957. *An Economic Theory of Democracy.* Harper and Row.

Drake, Paul W. 1978. *Socialism and Populism in Chile, 1932–52.* University of Illinois Press.

Drake, Paul W. 1996. *Labor Movements and Dictatorships: The Southern Cone in Comparative Perspective.* Johns Hopkins University Press.

Drake, Paul W., and Eric Hershberg. 2006. *State and Society in Conflict: Comparative Perspectives on Andean Crises.* University of Pittsburgh Press.

Dunkerley, James. 2013. "The Bolivian Revolution at 60: Politics and Historiography." *Journal of Latin American Studies* 45 (2): 325–350. https://doi.org/10.1017/S0022216X13000382.

Eaton, Kent. 2007. "Backlash in Bolivia: Regional Autonomy as a Reaction Against Indigenous Mobilization." *Politics & Society* 35 (1): 71–102. https://doi.org/10.1177/0032329206297145.

Eaton, Kent. 2011. "Conservative Autonomy Movements: Territorial Dimensions of Ideological Conflict in Bolivia and Ecuador." *Comparative Politics* 43 (3): 291–310. https://doi.org/10.5129/001041511795274896.

Eaton, Kent. 2016. "Challenges of Party-Building in the Bolivian East." In *Challenges of Party-Building in Latin America,* edited by Steven Levitsky, James Loxton, Brandon Van Dyck, and Jorge I. Domínguez. Cambridge University Press.

ECLAC. Various years. *Statistical Yearbook on Latin America and the Caribbean.* UN Economic Commission on Latin America and the Caribbean.

"Ecuador's Congress Sacks Judges." 2007. *BBC,* April 24. http://news.bbc.co.uk/2/hi/americas/6590245.stm.

Eisenstadt, Todd A., and Karleen Jones West. 2019. *Who Speaks for Nature? Indigenous Movements, Public Opinion, and the Petro-State in Ecuador.* Studies in Comparative Energy and Environmental Politics. Oxford University Press.

Elkins, Zachary, Tom Ginsburg, and James Melton. 2016. "Constitution Rankings." https://comparativeconstitutionsproject.org/ccp-rankings.

Ellner, Steve. 2008. *Rethinking Venezuelan Politics: Class, Conflict, and the Chávez Phenomenon*. Lynne Rienner Publishers.

Ellner, Steve. 2014. *Latin America's Radical Left: Challenges and Complexities of Political Power in the Twenty-First Century*. Rowman & Littlefield.

Ellner, Steve. 2020a. "Class Strategies in Chavista Venezuela: Pragmatic and Populist Policies in a Broader Context." In *Latin America's Pink Tide: Breakthroughs and Shortcoming*, edited by Steve Ellner. Rowman & Littlefield.

Ellner, Steve. 2020b. "Latin America's Pink Tide Governments: Challenges, Breakthroughs, and Setbacks." In *Latin America's Pink Tide: Breakthroughs and Shortcomings*, edited by Steve Ellner. Rowman & Littlefield.

Ellner, Steve, ed. 2021. *Latin American Extractivism: Dependency, Resource Nationalism, and Resistance in Broad Perspective*. Rowman & Littlefield.

Ellner, Steve, ed. 2022. "The April 2002 Coup Through Time." *NACLA Report on the Americas* 54 (1): 16–19.

Esberg, Jane. 2018. "The Audience of Repression: Killings and Disappearances in Pinochet's Chile." SSRN Scholarly Paper ID 3246120. Social Science Research Network. https://doi.org/10.2139/ssrn.3246120.

Escóbar, Filemón. 2008. *De la revolución al Pachakutí: El aprendizaje del respeto recíproco entre blancos e indios*. Garza Azul.

Espejo, Paulina Ochoa. 2011. *The Time of Popular Sovereignty: Process and the Democratic State*. Penn State University Press.

Estimación de la Pobreza por el Método del Ingreso, Año 2017. 2018. Instituto Nacional de Estadística (Uruguay).

Etchemendy, Sebastián. 2011. "El sindicalismo argentino en la era pos-liberal (2003–2011)." In *La política en tiempos de los Kirchner*, edited by Andrés Malamud and Miguel de Luca. Eudeba.

Etchemendy, Sebastián. 2019. "The Rise of Segmented Neo-Corporatism in South America: Wage Coordination in Argentina and Uruguay (2005–2015)." *Comparative Political Studies* 52 (10): 1427–65. https://doi.org/10.1177/0010414019830729.

Etchemendy, Sebastián, and Candelaria Garay. 2011. "Argentina: Left Populism in Comparative Perspective, 2003–2009." In *The Resurgence of the Latin American Left*, edited by Steven Levitsky and Kenneth M. Roberts. Johns Hopkins University Press.

Exeni Rodríguez, José L. 2024. "La crisis boliviana y el tiempo de las cosas pequeñas." *Nueva Sociedad: Democracia y Política en América Latina*, September 4. https://nuso.org/articulo/bolivia-y-el-tiempo-de-las-cosas-pequenas/.

Fabricant, Nicole, and Bret Gustafson. 2020. "The Fall of Evo Morales." *Catalyst* 4 (1): 104–131.

Faguet, Jean-Paul. 2013. *Decentralization and Popular Democracy: Governance from Below in Bolivia*. University of Michigan Press.

Fairfield, Tasha. 2015. *Private Wealth and Public Revenue in Latin America: Business Power and Tax Politics.* Cambridge University Press.

Farthing, Linda. 2018. "An Opportunity Squandered? Elites, Social Movements, and the Government of Evo Morales." *Latin American Perspectives* 46 (224): 212–229.

Farthing, Linda, and Thomas Becker. 2021. *Coup: A Story of Violence and Resistance in Bolivia.* Haymarket Books.

Farthing, Linda, and Kathryn Ledebur. 2004. "The Beat Goes On: The U.S. War on Coca." *NACLA Report on the Americas* 38 (3): 34–41. https://doi.org/10.1080/10714839.2004.11724506.

Feinmann, José Pablo. 2010. *Peronismo: Filosofía política de una persistencia argentina.* Planeta.

Fernandes, Sujantha. 2010. *Who Can Stop the Drums? Urban Social Movements in Chavez's Venezuela.* Duke University Press.

Fernández de Kirchner, Cristina. 2019. *Sinceramente.* Sudamericana.

Figueroa, Valentín. 2021. "Political Corruption Cycles: High-Frequency Evidence from Argentina's Notebooks Scandal." *Comparative Political Studies* 54 (3–4): 482–517. https://doi.org/10.1177/0010414020938102.

Fishman, Robert M. 2018. "What Made the Third Wave Possible? Historical Contingency and Meta-Politics in the Genesis of Worldwide Democratization." *Comparative Politics* 50 (4): 607–626. https://doi.org/10.5129/001041518823565614.

Flores-Macías, Gustavo A. 2012. *After Neoliberalism? The Left and Economic Reforms in Latin America.* Oxford University Press.

Fontana, Lorenza B. 2023. *Recognition Politics: Indigenous Rights and Ethnic Conflict in the Andes.* Cambridge Studies in Comparative Politics. Cambridge University Press. https://doi.org/10.1017/9781009265515.

Fowler, Anthony, Seth J. Hill, Jeffrey B. Lewis, Chris Tausanovitch, Lynn Vavreck, and Christopher Warshaw. 2023. "Moderates." *American Political Science Review* 117 (2): 643–660. https://doi.org/10.1017/S0003055422000818.

Foxley, Alejandro. 1983. *Latin American Experiments in Neoconservative Economics.* University of California Press.

Frank, Jason. 2010. *Constituent Moments: Enacting the People in Postrevolutionary America.* Duke University Press.

Frank, Jason. 2017. "Populism and Praxis." In *The Oxford Handbook of Populism*, edited by Cristóbal Rovira Kaltwasser, Paul Taggart, Paulina Ochoa Espejo, and Pierre Ostiguy. Oxford University Press.

French, John D. 2009. "Lula, the 'New Unionism,' and the PT: How Factory Workers Came to Change the World, or At Least Brazil." *Latin American Politics and Society* 51 (4): 157–169. https://doi.org/10.1111/j.1548-2456.2009.00067.x.

French, John D. 2020. *Lula and His Politics of Cunning: From Metalworker to President of Brazil.* University of North Carolina Press.

French, John D., and Alexandre Fortes. 2005. "Another World Is Possible: The Rise of the Brazilian Workers' Party and the Prospects for Lula's Government." *Labor* 2 (3): 13–31. https://doi.org/10.1215/15476715-2-3-13.

Fuentes, Claudio. 2015. "Shifting the Status Quo: Constitutional Reforms in Chile." *Latin American Politics and Society* 57 (1): 99–122. https://doi.org/10.1111/j.1548-2456.2015.00258.x.

Fukuyama, Francis. 1989. "The End of History?" *National Interest*, no. 16, 3–18.

Gamallo, Leandro A. 2014. "Usando a Gramsci: El debate acerca de la hegemonía kirchnerista." *Sudamérica: Revista de Ciencias Sociales* 3 (December): 173–196.

Gamarra, Eduardo A. 1997. "Hybrid Presidentialism in Bolivia." In *Presidential Institutions and Democratic Politics*, edited by Kurt von Mettenheim. Johns Hopkins University Press.

Gamboa, Laura. 2017. "Opposition at the Margins: Strategies Against the Erosion of Democracy in Colombia and Venezuela." *Comparative Politics* 49 (4): 457–477.

Gamboa, Laura. 2022. *Resisting Backsliding: Opposition Strategies against the Erosion of Democracy*. Cambridge University Press. https://doi.org/10.1017/9781009164085.

Garay, Candelaria. 2007. "Social Policy and Collective Action: Unemployed Workers, Community Associations, and Protest in Argentina." *Politics & Society* 35 (2): 301–328. https://doi.org/10.1177/0032329207300392.

Garay, Candelaria. 2016. *Social Policy Expansion in Latin America*. Cambridge University Press.

Garcés, Fernando. 2011. "The Domestication of Indigenous Autonomies in Bolivia: From the Pact of Unity to the New Constitution." In *Remapping Bolivia: Resources, Territory, and Indigeneity in a Plurinational State*, edited by Nicole Fabricant and Bret Gustafson. School for Advanced Research Press.

García Linera, Álvaro. 2001. "¿Qué es la democracia?" In *Pluriverso: Teoría política boliviana*, edited by Álvaro García Linera, Raquel Gutiérrez, Raúl Prada, and Luis Tapia. Muela del Diablo.

García Linera, Álvaro. 2006. "El evismo: Lo nacional-popular en acción." *Revista OSAL: Observatorio Social de América Latina* (19): 25–32.

García Linera, Álvaro. 2008. "Empate catastrófico y punto de bifurcación." *Crítica y Emancipación: Revista Latinoamericana de Ciencias Sociales* 1 (1): 23–33.

García Linera, Álvaro. 2019. "El odio al indio." *CELAG* (blog), November 16. https://www.celag.org/el-odio-al-indio/.

García Linera, Álvaro, Marxa Chávez León, and Patricia Costa Monje. 2004. *Sociología de los movimientos sociales en Bolivia*. Plural Editores.

García Yapur, Fernando, Marizol Soliz Romero, Alberto García Orellana, Rodrigo Rosales Rocha, and Mariana Zeballos Ibáñez. 2015. *No somos del MAS, el MAS es nuestro": Historias de vida y conversaciones con campesinos indígenas de Bolivia*. PNUD Bolivia.

García-Guadilla, María Pilar. 2018. "The Incorporation of Popular Sectors and Social Movements in Venezuelan Twenty-First Century Socialism." In *Reshaping the Political Arena in Latin America: From Resisting Neoliberalism to the Sec-*

ond Incorporation, edited by Eduardo Silva and Federico Rossi. University of Pittsburgh Press.

Garretón, Manuel Antonio. 1987. "En qué consistió la renovación socialista? Síntesis y evaluación de sus contenidos." In *La renovación socialista: Balance y perspectivas de un proceso vigente*. Ediciones Valentín Letelier.

Gates, Leslie C. 2010. *Electing Chávez: The Business of Anti-Neoliberal Politics in Venezuela*. University of Pittsburgh Press.

George, Alexander L., and Andrew Bennett. 2005. *Case Studies and Theory Development in the Social Sciences*. MIT Press.

Gervasoni, Carlos. 2011. "La política provincial es política nacional: Cambios y continuidades subnacionales del menemismo al kirchnerismo." In *La política en tiempos de los Kirchner*, edited by Andrés Malamud and Miguel de Luca. Eudeba.

Gibson, Edward L. 1996. *Class and Conservative Parties: Argentina in Comparative Perspective*. Johns Hopkins University Press.

Gilbert, Jonathan. 2013. "Voters, in Midterm Elections, Give New Momentum to the Opposition in Argentina." *New York Times,* October 28. https://www.nytimes.com/2013/10/29/world/americas/opposition-party-makes-gains-in-argentine-elections.html.

Gillespie, Charles G. 1985. "Uruguay's Return to Democracy." *Bulletin of Latin American Research* 4 (2): 99–107. https://doi.org/10.2307/3338320.

Gillion, Daniel Q. 2020. *The Loud Minority: Why Protests Matter in American Democracy*. Princeton University Press.

Giorgi, Ana Laura de. 2011. *Las tribus de la izquierda en los 60: Bolches, latas y tupas: Comunistas, socialistas y tupamaros desde la cultura política*. Editorial Fin de Siglo.

Giusti-Rodríguez, Mariana. 2023. "From Social Networks to Political Parties: Indigenous Party-Building in Bolivia." *American Political Science Review* 118 (4): 1803–1823. https://doi.org/10.1017/S0003055423001272.

Goldfrank, Benjamin. 2011a. *Deepening Local Democracy in Latin America: Participation, Decentralization, and the Left*. Penn State University Press.

Goldfrank, Benjamin. 2011b. "The Left and Participatory Democracy: Brazil, Uruguay, and Venezuela." In *The Resurgence of the Latin American Left*, edited by Steven Levitsky and Kenneth M. Roberts. Johns Hopkins University Press.

Goldfrank, Benjamin. 2020. "Participatory Democracy in Latin America: Limited Legacies of the Left Turn." In *Legacies of the Left Turn in Latin America: The Promise of Inclusive Citizenship*, edited by Manuel Balán and Françoise Montambeault. University of Notre Dame Press.

Gómez Bruera, Hernán. 2013. *Lula, the Workers' Party and the Governability Dilemma in Brazil*. Routledge.

Gott, Richard. 2000. *In the Shadow of the Liberator: Hugo Chávez and the Transformation of Venezuela*. Verso.

Green Rioja, Romina, Elisa Roncón, and Alondra Carrillo Vidal. 2022. "Transforming Chile from the Ground Up." *NACLA Report on the Americas* 54 (4): 382–388.

Grisaffi, Thomas. 2019. *Coca Yes, Cocaine No: How Bolivia's Coca Growers Reshaped Democracy.* Duke University Press.

Grossmann, Matt, and David A. Hopkins. 2016. *Asymmetric Politics: Ideological Republicans and Group Interest Democrats.* Oxford University Press.

Guidry, John A. 2003. "Not Just Another Labor Party: The Workers' Party and Democracy in Brazil." *Labor Studies Journal* 28 (1): 83–108. https://doi.org/10.1177/0160449X0302800105.

Guzman-Concha, Cesar. 2012. "The Students' Rebellion in Chile: Occupy Protest or Classic Social Movement?" *Social Movement Studies* 11 (3–4): 408–415. https://doi.org/10.1080/14742837.2012.710748.

Haagh, Louise. 2002. "The Emperor's New Clothes: Labor Reform and Social Democratization in Chile." *Studies in Comparative International Development* 37 (1): 86–115. http://dx.doi.org/10.1007/BF02686339.

Habermas, Jürgen. 1991. *The Structural Transformation of the Public Sphere: An Inquiry into a Category of Bourgeois Society.* 5th ed. MIT Press.

Hacker, Jacob S., and Paul Pierson. 2015. "Confronting Asymmetric Polarization." In *Solutions to Political Polarization in America,* edited by Nathaniel Persily. Cambridge University Press. https://doi.org/10.1017/CBO9781316091906.003.

Haggard, Stephan, and Robert R. Kaufman. 2016. *Dictators and Democrats: Masses, Elites, and Regime Change.* Princeton University Press.

Haggard, Stephan, and Robert R. Kaufman. 2021. *Backsliding: Democratic Regress in the Contemporary World.* Cambridge University Press. https://www.cambridge.org/core/elements/backsliding/CCD2F28FB63A56409FF8911351F2E937.

Hagopian, Frances. 1990. "Democracy by Undemocratic Means? Elites, Political Pacts, and Regime Transition in Brazil." *Comparative Political Studies* 23 (2): 147–170. https://doi.org/10.1177/0010414090023002001.

Hagopian, Frances. 2016. "Brazil's Accountability Paradox." *Journal of Democracy* 27 (3): 119–128. https://doi.org/10.1353/jod.2016.0043.

Han, Hahrie, Elizabeth McKenna, and Michelle Oyakawa. 2021. *Prisms of the People: Power & Organizing in Twenty-First-Century America.* Chicago Studies in American Politics. University of Chicago Press. https://press.uchicago.edu/ucp/books/book/chicago/P/bo68659118.html.

Handlin, Samuel. 2017. *State Crisis in Fragile Democracies: Polarization and Political Regimes in South America.* Cambridge University Press. https://doi.org/10.1017/9781108233682.

Handlin, Samuel, and Ruth Berins Collier. 2011. "The Diversity of Left Party Linkages and Competitive Advantages." In *The Resurgence of the Latin American Left,* edited by Steven Levitsky and Kenneth M. Roberts. Johns Hopkins University Press.

Harteveld, Eelco. 2016. "Winning the 'Losers' but Losing the 'Winners'? The Electoral Consequences of the Radical Right Moving to the Economic Left." *Electoral Studies* 44: 225–234. https://doi.org/10.1016/j.electstud.2016.08.015.

Hawkins, Kirk A. 2010a. *Venezuela's Chavismo and Populism in Comparative Perspective*. Cambridge University Press. https://doi.org/10.1017/CBO9780511730245.

Hawkins, Kirk A. 2010b. "Who Mobilizes? Participatory Democracy in Chávez's Bolivarian Revolution." *Latin American Politics and Society* 52 (3): 31–66. https://doi.org/10.1111/j.1548-2456.2010.00089.x.

Healy, Kevin. 1991. "Political Ascent of Bolivia's Peasant Coca Leaf Producers." *Journal of Interamerican Studies and World Affairs* 33 (1): 87–121. https://doi.org/10.2307/166043.

Heiss, Claudia. 2021. "Latin America Erupts: Re-Founding Chile." *Journal of Democracy* 32 (3): 33–47. https://doi.org/10.1353/jod.2021.0032.

Hellinger, Daniel. 2018. "The Second Wave of Incorporation and Political Parties in the Venezuelan Petrostate." In *Reshaping the Political Arena in Latin America: From Resisting Neoliberalism to the Second Incorporation*, edited by Eduardo Silva and Federico M. Rossi. University of Pittsburgh Press.

Hernández, Virgilio E, and Fernando Buendía. 2011. "Ecuador: Avances y desafíos de Alianza PAÍS." *Nueva Sociedad* 234: 129–142.

Hetland, Gabriel. 2023. *Democracy on the Ground: Local Politics in Latin America's Left Turn*. Columbia University Press.

Hipsher, Patricia L. 1996. "Democratization and the Decline of Urban Social Movements in Chile and Spain." *Comparative Politics* 28 (3): 273–297. https://doi.org/10.2307/422208.

Hite, Katherine. 2000. *When the Romance Ended*. Columbia University Press.

Hoffman, Kelly, and Miguel Angel Centeno. 2003. "The Lopsided Continent: Inequality in Latin America." *Annual Review of Sociology* 29 (December): 363–390.

Holloway, John. 2019. *Change the World Without Taking Power: The Meaning of Revolution Today*. 4th ed. Pluto Press.

Hora, Roy. 2024. "Javier Milei y el incierto experimento libertario." *Nueva Sociedad: Democracia y Política en América Latina*, December 20. https://nuso.org/articulo/javier-milei-y-el-incierto-experimento-libertario/.

Huber, Evelyne, Dietrich Rueschemeyer, and John D. Stephens. 1997. "The Paradoxes of Contemporary Democracy: Formal, Participatory, and Social Dimensions." *Comparative Politics* 29 (3): 323–342. https://doi.org/10.2307/422124.

Huber, Evelyne, and John D. Stephens. 2012. *Democracy and the Left: Social Policy and Inequality in Latin America*. University of Chicago Press.

Human Rights Watch. 2022. "Venezuela: Events of 2021." *World Report 2022*. https://www.hrw.org/world-report/2022/country-chapters/venezuela.

Hummel, Calla. 2017. "Disobedient Markets." *Comparative Political Studies*, January, article 0010414016679177. https://doi.org/10.1177/0010414016679177.

Hunter, Wendy. 1995. "Politicians Against Soldiers: Contesting the Military in Post-authorization [sic] Brazil." *Comparative Politics* 27 (4): 425–443. https://doi.org/10.2307/422228.

Hunter, Wendy. 2007. "The Normalization of an Anomaly: The Workers' Party in Brazil." *World Politics* 59 (3): 440–475.

Hunter, Wendy. 2010. *The Transformation of the Workers' Party in Brazil, 1989–2009*. Cambridge University Press.

Hunter, Wendy. 2011. "Brazil: The PT in Power." In *The Resurgence of the Latin American Left*, edited by Steven Levitsky and Kenneth M. Roberts. Johns Hopkins University Press.

Hunter, Wendy, and Timothy J. Power. 2005. "Lula's Brazil at Midterm." *Journal of Democracy* 16 (3): 127–139. https://doi.org/10.1353/jod.2005.0046.

Hunter, Wendy, and Timothy J. Power. 2007. "Rewarding Lula: Executive Power, Social Policy, and the Brazilian Elections of 2006." *Latin American Politics & Society* 49 (1): 1–30.

Hunter, Wendy, and Timothy J. Power. 2019. "Bolsonaro and Brazil's Illiberal Backlash." *Journal of Democracy* 30 (1): 68–82. https://doi.org/10.1353/jod.2019.0005.

Huntington, Samuel P. 1991. *The Third Wave: Democratization in the Late Twentieth Century*. University of Oklahoma Press.

Hylton, Forrest, and Sinclair Thomson. 2007. *Revolutionary Horizons: Past and Present in Bolivian Politics*. Verso.

Idrobo, Nicolás, Dorothy Kronick, and Francisco Rodríguez. 2022. "Do Shifts in Late-Counted Votes Signal Fraud? Evidence from Bolivia." *Journal of Politics* 84 (4): 2202–2215.

Ignazi, Piero. 1992. "The Silent Counter-Revolution." *European Journal of Political Research* 22 (1): 3–34. https://doi.org/10.1111/j.1475-6765.1992.tb00303.x.

International Labour Organization. 1998. *Latin America and the Caribbean 1998 Labour Overview*. ILO.

Iraola, Jerónimo Guerrero. 2011. "Apuntes sobre hegemonía: Disquisiciones acerca de la construcción de sentido del 'kirchnerismo.'" *Question/Cuestión* 1 (31). https://perio.unlp.edu.ar/ojs/index.php/question/article/view/1195.

Iyengar, Shanto, Gaurav Sood, and Yphtach Lelkes. 2012. "Affect, Not Ideology: A Social Identity Perspective on Polarization." *Public Opinion Quarterly* 76 (3): 405–431.

Jackisch, Carlota. 1997. "Peronismo y dictadura militar (1973–1983): Un ciclo anómico en la reciente historia argentina." *Ibero-Amerikanisches Archiv* 23 (3–4): 439–462.

Jiménez, Maryhen. 2021. "Contesting Autocracy: Repression and Opposition Coordination in Venezuela." *Political Studies* 71 (1): 47–68.

Jobet, Julio César. 1987. *Historia del Partido Socialista de Chile*. Ediciones Documentas.

Justiniano, Lourdes Montero, ed. 2022. *La paridad más allá de la paridad: Participación política de las mujeres en el largo camino hacia la democracia paritaria intercultural en Bolivia.* Oxfam en Bolivia.

Kadivar, Mohammad Ali, Adaner Usmani, and Benjamin H. Bradlow. 2020. "The Long March: Deep Democracy in Cross-National Perspective." *Social Forces* 98 (3): 1311–1338.

Kalmoe, Nathan P., and Lilliana Mason. 2022. *Radical American Partisanship: Mapping Violent Hostility, Its Causes, and the Consequences for Democracy.* Chicago Studies in American Politics. University of Chicago Press. https://press.uchicago.edu/ucp/books/book/chicago/R/bo163195227.html.

Kalyvas, Andreas. 2005. "Popular Sovereignty, Democracy, and the Constituent Power." *Constellations* 12 (2): 223–244. https://doi.org/10.1111/j.1351-0487.2005.00413.x.

Kapiszewski, Diana, Steven Levitsky, and Deborah J. Yashar, eds. 2021. *The Inclusionary Turn in Latin American Democracies.* Cambridge University Press. https://doi.org/10.1017/9781108895835.

Karl, Terry Lynn. 1987. "Petroleum and Political Pacts: The Transition to Democracy in Venezuela." *Latin American Research Review* 22 (1): 63–94.

Karl, Terry Lynn. 1990. "Dilemmas of Democratization in Latin America." *Comparative Politics* 23 (1): 1–21. https://doi.org/10.2307/422302.

Karl, Terry Lynn. 1997. *The Paradox of Plenty: Oil Booms and Petro-States.* University of California Press.

Katz, Richard S., and Peter Mair. 1995. "Changing Models of Party Organization and Party Democracy: The Emergence of the Cartel Party." *Party Politics* 1 (1): 5–28. https://doi.org/10.1177/1354068895001001001.

Keck, Margaret E. 1992. *The Workers' Party and Democratization in Brazil.* Yale University Press.

Keck, Margaret E. 2022. "On Lula and His Politics of Cunning." *Latin American Politics and Society* 64 (1): 151–155. https://doi.org/10.1017/lap.2021.60.

Kessler, Gabriel, and María Victoria Murillo. Forthcoming. *The Social Underpinnings of Political Discontent in Latin America.* Cambridge University Press.

Kessler, Gabriel, and Gabriel Vommaro. 2024. "¿Cómo se organiza el descontento en América Latina?" *Nueva Sociedad,* March–April, 92–105.

Kestler, Thomas. 2022. "Radical, Nativist, Authoritarian—Or All of These? Assessing Recent Cases of Right-Wing Populism in Latin America." *Journal of Politics in Latin America* 14 (3): 289–310. https://doi.org/10.1177/1866802X221117565.

Kirchheimer, Otto. 1966. "The Transformation of the Western European Party Systems." In *Political Parties and Political Development,* edited by Joseph LaPalombara and Myron Weiner. Princeton University Press.

Kitschelt, Herbert. 2000. "Linkages Between Citizens and Politicians in Democratic Polities." *Comparative Political Studies* 33 (6–7): 845–879.

Kohl, Benjamin. 2003. "Democratizing Decentralization in Bolivia: The Law of Popular Participation." *Journal of Planning Education and Research* 23 (2): 153–164. https://doi.org/10.1177/0739456X03258639.

Komadina, Jorge, and Celine Geffroy. 2007. *El poder del movimiento político: Estrategia, tramas organizativas e identidad del MAS en Cochabamba (1999–2005)*. CESU, DICYT-UMSS, and Fundación PIEB.

Kozloff, Nikolas. 2009. *Revolution! South America and the Rise of the New Left*. St. Martin's Griffin.

Krausova, Anna. 2019. "Just Another Protest Cycle? Bolivia's Indigenous Peasant Movement and 'Their' Government." In *Revolutions in Bolivia*, edited by Into A. Goudsmit, Kate MacLean, and Winston Moore. Anglo-Bolivian Society.

Kronick, Dorothy, Barry Plunkett, and Pedro Rodríguez. 2021. "Backsliding by Surprise: The Rise of Chavismo." Unpublished manuscript.

Kurmanaev, Anatoly, and Maria Silvia Trigo. 2020. "A Bitter Election: Accusations of Fraud, and Now Second Thoughts." *New York Times*, June 7. https://www.nytimes.com/2020/06/07/world/americas/bolivia-election-evo-morales.html.

Lacerda, Alan D. 2002. "O PT e a unidade partidária como problema." *Dados* 45 (1): 39–76.

Laclau, Ernesto. 2005. *On Populist Reason*. Verso.

Lanzaro, Jorge Luis. 2004. "La izquierda se acerca a los uruguayos y los uruguayos se acercan a la izquierda: Claves de desarrollo del Frente Amplio." In *La izquierda uruguaya entre la oposición y el gobierno*. Editorial Fin de Siglo.

Lanzaro, Jorge Luis. 2011. "Uruguay: A Social Democratic Government in Latin America." In *The Resurgence of the Latin American Left*, edited by Steven Levitsky and Kenneth M. Roberts. Johns Hopkins University Press.

Lanzaro, Jorge Luis. 2014. *Social democracias tardías*. Centro de Estudios Políticos y Constitucionales.

LAPOP. 2023. "Who Perceives Well-Protected Basic Rights in the Americas?" AmericasBarometer Insights Series No. 159, LAPOP.

LAPOP. 2018–2019. *AmericasBarometer, 2018/19*. Center for Global Democracy. www.vanderbilt.edu/lapop.

Laruta, Carlos Hugo. 2008. "Organizaciones y movimientos sociales en el proceso político actual — Diciembre 2005 a junio 2008." In *Los actores políticos en la transición boliviana*, edited by Horst Grebe López. Instituto Prisma.

Latinobarómetro. 2006. *Latinobarómetro Opinión Pública Latinoamericana*. Corporación Latinobarómetro. https://www.latinobarometro.org/latOnline.jsp.

Latinobarómetro. 2007. *Latinobarómetro Opinión Pública Latinoamericana*. Corporación Latinobarómetro. https://www.latinobarometro.org/latOnline.jsp.

Latinobarómetro. 2016. *Latinobarómetro Opinión Pública Latinoamericana*. Corporación Latinobarómetro. https://www.latinobarometro.org/latOnline.jsp.

Lavinas, Lena. 2013. "21st Century Welfare." *New Left Review* 84 (December): 5–40.

Lehoucq, Fabrice. 2020. "Bolivia's Citizen Revolt." *Journal of Democracy* 31 (3): 130–144.
Levendusky, Matthew. 2009. *The Partisan Sort: How Liberals Became Democrats and Conservatives Became Republicans.* University of Chicago Press.
Levine, Daniel H. 1973. *Conflict and Political Change in Venezuela.* Princeton University Press.
Levitsky, Steven. 2003. *Transforming Labor-Based Parties in Latin America: Argentine Peronism in Comparative Perspective.* Cambridge University Press.
Levitsky, Steven. 2018. "Latin America's Shifting Politics: Democratic Survival and Weakness." *Journal of Democracy* 29 (4): 102–113. https://doi.org/10.1353/jod.2018.0066.
Levitsky, Steven, and James Loxton. 2013. "Populism and Competitive Authoritarianism in the Andes." *Democratization* 20 (1): 107–136.
Levitsky, Steven, James Loxton, Brandon Van Dyck, and Jorge I. Domínguez, eds. 2016. *Challenges of Party-Building in Latin America.* Cambridge University Press.
Levitsky, Steven, James Loxton, and Brandon Van Dyck. 2016. "Introduction: Challenges of Party-Building in Latin America." In *Party-Building in Latin America,* edited by Steven Levitsky, James Loxton, Brandon Van Dyck, and Jorge Domínguez. Cambridge University Press.
Levitsky, Steven, and María Victoria Murillo. 2003. "Argentina Weathers the Storm." *Journal of Democracy* 14 (4): 152–166. https://doi.org/10.1353/jod.2003.0081.
Levitsky, Steven, and María Victoria Murillo. 2008. "Argentina: From Kirchner to Kirchner." *Journal of Democracy* 19 (2): 16–30. https://doi.org/10.1353/jod.2008.0030.
Levitsky, Steven, and Kenneth M. Roberts. 2011a. "Introduction: Latin America's 'Left Turn': A Framework for Analysis." In *The Resurgence of the Latin American Left,* edited by Steven Levitsky and Kenneth M. Roberts. Johns Hopkins University Press.
Levitsky, Steven, and Kenneth M. Roberts, eds. 2011b. *The Resurgence of the Latin American Left.* Johns Hopkins University Press.
Levitsky, Steven, and Daniel Ziblatt. 2018. *How Democracies Die.* Crown.
Lieberman, Robert C., Suzanne Mettler, and Kenneth M. Roberts, eds. 2021. *Democratic Resilience: Can the United States Withstand Rising Polarization?* Cambridge University Press. https://doi.org/10.1017/9781108999601.
Linz, Juan J. 1978. *The Breakdown of Democratic Regimes: Crisis, Breakdown and Reequilibration—An Introduction.* Johns Hopkins University Press.
Lissidini, Alicia. 2001. "Las paradojas de la democracia directa: Plebiscitos y referendos en el Uruguay (1917–1994)." In *Seducción y desilusión: La política latinoamericana contemporánea,* edited by Susana Mallo and Miguel Serna. Ediciones Banda Oriental.

Lissidini, Alicia. 2012. "Direct Democracy in Uruguay and Venezuela: New Voices, Old Practices." In *Institutions for Participatory Democracy in Latin America: Voice and Consequence*, edited by Maxwell A. Cameron, Eric Hershberg, and Kenneth E. Sharpe. Palgrave Macmillan.

Longa, Francisco. 2017. "La etapa kirchnerista: Nuevo 'momento constitutivo' entre movimientos sociales y Estado en Argentina." *Sociohistórica* 39: e023–e023. https://doi.org/10.24215/18521606e023.

Longa, Francisco. 2019. *Historia del Movimiento Evita*. Siglo Veintiuno Editores.

López Maya, Margarita. 2003. "Hugo Chávez Frías: His Movement and His Presidency." In *Venezuelan Politics in the Chávez Era: Class, Polarization, and Conflict*, edited by Steve Ellner and Daniel Hellinger. Lynne Rienner Publishers.

López Maya, Margarita. 2005. *Del Viernes Negro al referendo revocatorio*. Alfadil Ediciones.

López Maya, Margarita. 2011. "Venezuela: Hugo Chávez and the Populist Left." In *The Resurgence of the Latin American Left*, edited by Steven Levitsky and Kenneth M. Roberts. Johns Hopkins University Press.

López-Calva, Luis Felipe, and Nora Lustig. 2010. *Declining Inequality in Latin America: A Decade of Progress?* Brookings Institution Press.

Lucero, José. 2008. *Struggles of Voice: The Politics of Indigenous Representation in the Andes*. University of Pittsburgh Press.

Luengo, Néstor Luis, and María Gabriela Ponce. 1996. "Lectura oblicua del proceso electoral de 1995." *Politeia* 19: 63–80.

Luna, Juan Pablo. 2007. "Frente Amplio and the Crafting of a Social Democratic Alternative in Uruguay." *Latin American Politics and Society* 49 (4): 1–30. https://doi.org/10.1111/j.1548-2456.2007.tb00390.x.

Luna, Juan Pablo. 2014. *Segmented Representation: Political Party Strategies in Unequal Democracies*. Oxford University Press.

Luna, Juan Pablo. 2016. "Delegative Democracy Revisited: Chile's Crisis of Representation." *Journal of Democracy* 27 (3): 129–138. https://doi.org/10.1353/jod.2016.0046.

Luna, Juan Pablo. 2024. "Disjointed Polarization in Chile's Enduring Crisis of Representation." *Latin American Politics and Society* 66 (2): 72–101.

Luna, Juan Pablo, and David Altman. 2011. "Uprooted but Stable: Chilean Parties and the Concept of Party System Institutionalization." *Latin American Politics and Society* 53 (2): 1–28. https://doi.org/10.1111/j.1548-2456.2011.00115.x.

Luna, Juan Pablo, and Fernando Filgueira. 2009. "The Left Turns as Multiple Paradigmatic Crises." *Third World Quarterly* 30 (2): 371–395.

Luna, Juan Pablo, and Rodrigo M. Medel. 2023. "Uneven States, Unequal Societies, and Democracy's Unfulfilled Promises: Citizenship Rights in Chile and Contemporary Latin America." *Latin American Politics and Society* 65 (2): 170–196. https://doi.org/10.1017/lap.2022.59.

Luna, Juan Pablo, Rafael Piñeiro Rodríguez, Fernando Rosenblatt, and Gabriel Vommaro, eds. 2022. *Diminished Parties: Democratic Representation in Contem-*

porary Latin America. Cambridge University Press. https://doi.org/10.1017/978 1009072045.
Luna, Juan Pablo, and Cristóbal Rovira Kaltwasser, eds. 2014. *The Resilience of the Latin American Right*. Johns Hopkins University Press.
Luna, Juan Pablo, and Cristóbal Rovira Kaltwasser. 2021. "Castigo a los oficialismos y ciclo político de derecha en América Latina." *Revista Uruguaya de Ciencia Política* 30 (1): 135–156. https://doi.org/10.26851/rucp.30.1.6.
Luna, Juan Pablo, Elizabeth J. Zechmeister, and Mitchell A. Seligson. 2010. *Cultura política de la democracia en Chile, 2010: Consolidación democrática en las Americas en tiempos difíciles*. Latin American Public Opinion Project, Vanderbilt University.
Lupu, Noam. 2016. *Party Brands in Crisis: Partisanship, Brand Dilution, and the Breakdown of Political Parties in Latin America*. Cambridge University Press.
Lupu, Noam, Virginia Oliveros, and Luis Schiumerini. 2021. "Derecha y democracia en América Latina." *Población y Sociedad* 28 (2): 80–100. https://doi.org/10.19137/pys-2021-280205.
Maclean, Kate. 2023. *Cash, Clothes, and Construction: Rethinking Value in Bolivia's Pluri-Economy*. University of Minnesota Press.
Madison, James. 1787. *Federalist Papers No. 10*. https://billofrightsinstitute.org/primary-sources/federalist-no-10.
Madrid, Raúl L. 2008. "The Rise of Ethnopopulism in Latin America." *World Politics* 60 (3): 475–508. https://doi.org/10.1017/S0043887100009060.
Madrid, Raúl L. 2010. "The Origins of the Two Lefts in Latin America." *Political Science Quarterly* (Academy of Political Science) 125 (4): 587–609.
Madrid, Raúl L. 2011. "Bolivia: Origins and Policies of the Movimiento al Socialismo." In *The Resurgence of the Latin American Left*, edited by Steven Levitsky and Kenneth M. Roberts. Johns Hopkins University Press.
Madrid, Raúl L. 2012. *The Rise of Ethnic Politics in Latin America*. Cambridge University Press.
Madrid, Raúl L. 2025. *The Birth of Democracy in South America*. Cambridge University Press.
Mahoney, James, and Dietrich Rueschemeyer. 2003. *Comparative Historical Analysis in the Social Sciences*. Cambridge University Press.
Mainwaring, Scott. 1995. "Brazil. Weak Parties, Feckless Democracy." In *Building Democratic Institutions: Party Systems in Latin America*, edited by Scott Mainwaring and Timothy Scully. Stanford University Press.
Mainwaring, Scott. 2018. "Party System Institutionalization in Contemporary Latin America." In *Party Systems in Latin America: Institutionalization, Decay, and Collapse*, edited by Scott Mainwaring. Cambridge University Press.
Mainwaring, Scott, Ana María Bejarano, and Eduardo Pizarro Leongómez. 2006. *The Crisis of Democratic Representation in the Andes*. Stanford University Press.
Mainwaring, Scott, and Aníbal Pérez-Liñán. 2014. *Democracies and Dictatorships in Latin America: Emergence, Survival, and Fall*. Cambridge University Press.

Mainwaring, Scott, Timothy J. Power, and Fernando Bizzarro. 2018. "The Uneven Institutionalization of a Party System: Brazil." In *Party Systems in Latin America: Institutionalization, Decay, and Collapse,* edited by Scott Mainwaring. Cambridge University Press. https://doi.org/10.1017/9781316798553.007.

Mair, Peter. 2013. *Ruling the Void: The Hollowing of Western Democracy.* Verso.

Mamani, Pablo, ed. 2020. *Whiphalas, luchas y la nueva nación: Relatos, análisis y memorias de octubre-noviembre de 2019 desde El Alto, Cochabamba y Santa Cruz.* Círculo de Estudios Estratégicos de El Alto.

Mantúfar, César. 2020. "State-Organized Crime: A Hypothesis on the Institutionalization of Corruption During the Revolución Ciudadana." In *Assessing the Left Turn in Ecuador,* edited by Francisco Sánchez and Simón Pachano. Palgrave Macmillan, Springer Nature Switzerland.

Marchesi, Aldo. 2018. *Latin America's Radical Left: Rebellion and Cold War in the Global 1960s.* Cambridge Latin American Studies. Cambridge University Press. https://doi.org/10.1017/9781316822968.

Marshall, Thomas Humphrey. 1950. *Citizenship and Social Class: And Other Essays.* Indiana University Press.

Martínez-Gallardo, Cecilia, Nicolás de la Cerda, Jonathan Hartlyn, Liesbet Hooghe, Gary Marks, and Ryan Bakker. 2023. "Revisiting Party System Structuration in Latin America and Europe: Economic and Socio-Cultural Dimensions." *Party Politics* 29 (4): 780–792. https://doi.org/10.1177/13540688221090604.

Martínez Novo, Carmen. 2020. "Intellectuals, NGOs, and Social Movements under the Correa Regime: Collaborations and Estrangements." In *Assessing the Left Turn in Ecuador,* edited by Francisco Sánchez and Simón Pachano. Palgrave Macmillan, Springer Nature Switzerland.

Martuccelli, Danilo, and Maristella Svampa. 1997. *La plaza vacía: Las transformaciones del peronismo.* Editorial Losada.

Mason, Lilliana. 2018. *Uncivil Agreement: How Politics Became Our Identity.* University of Chicago Press.

Massetti, Astor, Ernesto Villanueva, and Marcelo Gómez, eds. 2010. *Movilizaciones, protestas e identidades políticas en la Argentina del Bicentenario.* Nueva Trilce.

Mayka, Lindsay. 2019. *Building Participatory Institutions in Latin America: Reform Coalitions and Institutional Change.* Cambridge University Press.

Mayka, Lindsay, and Amy Erica Smith. 2021. "Introduction: The Grassroots Right in Latin America: Patterns, Causes, and Consequences." *Latin American Politics and Society* 63 (3): 1–20. https://doi.org/10.1017/lap.2021.20.

Mayorga, Fernando. 2002. *Neopopulismo y democracia: Compadres y padrinos en la política boliviana (1988–1999).* Centro de Estudios Superiores Universitarios, Centro de Planificación y Gestión, and Plural Editores.

Mayorga, Fernando. 2011. *Dilemas.* CESU/Plural Editores.

Mayorga, Fernando. 2019. "Bolivia: Ciclo electoral 2014–2015 y mutaciones en el campo político." In *Elecciones y legitimidad democrática en América Latina*, edited by Fernando Mayorga. CLACSO. https://doi.org/10.2307/j.ctvt6rkct.11.

Mayorga, Fernando. 2020a. "Derrota política del MAS y proyecto de restauración oligárquico-señorial." In *Crisis y cambio político en Bolivia: Octubre y noviembre de 2019: La democracia en una encrucijada*, edited by Fernando Mayorga. CESU-UMSS/Oxfam.

Mayorga, Fernando. 2020b. *Mandato y contingencia: Estilo de gobierno de Evo Morales*. CLACSO.

Mayorga, Fernando. 2022. *Resistir y retornar: Avatares del proceso decisional en el MAS-IPSP (2019–2021)*. FES Bolivia.

Mayorga, René Antonio. 2006. "Outsiders and Neopopulism: The Road to Plebiscitary Democracy." In *The Crisis of Democratic Representation in the Andes*, edited by Scott Mainwaring, Ana M. Bejarano, and Eduardo Pizarro Leongómez. Stanford University Press.

McAdam, Doug, and Karina Kloos. 2014. *Deeply Divided: Racial Politics and Social Movements in Postwar America*. Oxford University Press.

McAdam, Doug, John D. McCarthy, and Mayer N. Zald, eds. 1996. *Comparative Perspectives on Social Movements: Political Opportunities, Mobilizing Structures, and Cultural Framings*. Cambridge University Press.

McAdam, Doug, and Sidney Tarrow. 2010. "Ballots and Barricades: On the Reciprocal Relationship Between Elections and Social Movements." *Perspectives on Politics* 8 (2): 529–542. https://doi.org/10.1017/S1537592710001234.

McAdam, Doug, Sidney Tarrow, and Charles Tilly. 2001. *Dynamics of Contention*. Cambridge University Press.

McCoy, Jennifer. 2023. "Latin American Democratic Resilience and Political Polarization in Comparative Perspective." APSA Preprints. https://doi.org/10.33774/apsa-2023-m75f3.

McCoy, Jennifer, Tahmina Rahman, and Murat Somer. 2018. "Polarization and the Global Crisis of Democracy: Common Patterns, Dynamics, and Pernicious Consequences for Democratic Polities." *American Behavioral Scientist* 62 (1): 16–42. https://doi.org/10.1177/0002764218759576.

McCoy, Jennifer, and Murat Somer. 2019. "Toward a Theory of Pernicious Polarization and How It Harms Democracies: Comparative Evidence and Possible Remedies." *Annals of the American Academy of Political and Social Science* 681 (1): 234–271. https://doi.org/10.1177/0002716218818782.

McCoy, Jennifer, Murat Somer, and Ozlem Tuncel. 2022. "Reducing Pernicious Polarization: A Comparative Historical Analysis of Depolarization." Carnegie Endowment for International Peace. https://carnegieendowment.org/2022/05/05/reducing-pernicious-polarization-comparative-historical-analysis-of-depolarization-pub-87034.

McGuire, James. 1997. *Peronism Without Perón: Unions, Parties, and Democracy in Argentina*. Stanford University Press.

McKenna, Elizabeth. 2020. "Taxes and Tithes: The Organizational Foundations of Bolsonarismo." *International Sociology* 35 (6): 610–631. https://doi.org/10.1177/0268580920949466.

McNelly, Angus. 2019. "Bolivia in Crisis: How Evo Morales Was Forced Out." *The Conversation*, November 12. http://theconversation.com/bolivia-in-crisis-how-evo-morales-was-forced-out-126859.

McNelly, Angus. 2023. *Now We Are in Power: The Politics of Passive Revolution in Twenty-First-Century Bolivia*. University of Pittsburgh Press.

Meléndez, Carlos. 2022. "The Post-Partisans: Anti-Partisans, Anti-Establishment Identifiers, and Apartisans in Latin America." *Elements in Politics and Society in Latin America*. https://doi.org/10.1017/9781108694308.

Melo, Carlos Ranulfo. 2021. "Participação, pluralismo e autonomia das lideranças: Partido dos Trabalhadores, Frente Ampla e Partido Socialista do Chile em perspectiva comparada." *Dados* 64 (3): 1–39. https://doi.org/10.1590/dados.2021.64.3.243.

Melo, Marcus André. 2016. "Latin America's New Turbulence: Crisis and Integrity in Brazil." *Journal of Democracy* 27 (2): 50–65. https://doi.org/10.1353/jod.2016.0019.

Meneguello, Rachel. 1989. *PT: A formação de um partido, 1979–1982*. Paz e Terra.

Michels, Robert. (1911) 1962. *Political Parties: A Sociological Study of the Oligarchical Tendencies of Modern Democracy*. Free Press.

Mische, Ann. 2009. *Partisan Publics: Communication and Contention across Brazilian Youth Activist Networks*. Princeton Studies in Cultural Sociology. Princeton University Press.

Molina, Fernando. 2007. *Conversion sin fe: El MAS y la democracia*. Ediciones Eureka.

Molina, Fernando. 2019. "Bolivia; 'Es la economía, estúpido.'" *Nueva Sociedad*, October. https://nuso.org/articulo/bolivia-es-la-economia-estupido/.

Molina, Fernando. 2020. "La rebelión de los blancos: Causas raciales de la caída de Evo Morales." In *Crisis y cambio político en Bolivia octubre y noviembre de 2019: La democracia en una encrucijada,* edited by Fernando Mayorga. CESU-UMSS/Oxfam.

Molina, Fernando. 2021. *Racismo y poder en Bolivia*. Oxfam.

Molina, Fernando. 2023. "Evistas Versus Arcistas." *Nueva Sociedad* 307: 4–13.

Moncagatta, Paolo, Carlos Espinosa Fernández de Córdova, and Mateo Pazmiño. 2023. "Ganar perdiendo: Oportunidades y limitaciones de una coalición antipopulista en Ecuador." *América Latina Hoy* 93 (November): e29747–e29747. https://doi.org/10.14201/alh.29747.

Moncagatta, Paolo, and Pedro Nunes da Silva. 2024. "Recent Trends in Ideological Polarization in Latin America." *Latin American Politics and Society* 66 (2): 24–46.

Morais, Fernando. 2024. *Lula: A Biography*. Verso.

Mouffe, Chantal. 2018. *For a Left Populism.* Verso.
Muñoz Tamayo, Víctor. 2016. "El Partido Socialista de Chile y la presente cultura de facciones: Un enfoque histórico generacional (1973–2015)." *Izquierdas*, no. 26 (January): 1–31. https://journals.openedition.org/izquierdas/681.
Murillo, María Victoria. 2021. "Protestas, descontento y democracia en América Latina." *Nueva Sociedad* 294 (July-August): 4–13.
Murillo, María Victoria. 2022. "Latin America: Not as Polarized as You Think." *Americas Quarterly* (blog). https://www.americasquarterly.org/article/latin-america-not-as-polarized-as-you-think/.
Murillo, María Victoria, Virginia Oliveros, and Milan Vaishnav. 2010. "Electoral Revolution or Democratic Alternation?" *Latin American Research Review* 45 (3): 87–114.
Murillo, María Victoria, and Virginia Oliveros. 2024. "Argentina 2023: La irrupción de Javier Milei en la política argentina." *Revista de Ciencia Política* (Santiago) 44 (2): 161–185. https://doi.org/10.4067/s0718-090x2024005000116.
Natanson, José. 2012. *¿Por qué los jóvenes están volviendo a la política? De los indignados a la cámpora.* Penguin Random House Grupo Editorial Argentina.
Negri, Antonio. 1999. *Insurgencies: Constituent Power and the Modern State.* University of Minnesota Press.
Nicas, Jack. 2024. "Bolsonaro and Allies Planned a Coup, Brazil Police Say." *New York Times,* February 8. https://www.nytimes.com/2024/02/08/world/americas/brazil-police-raid-bolsonaro-attempted-coup-investigation.html.
Nicolau, Jairo Marconi. 2020. *O Brasil dobrou à direita: Uma radiografia da eleição de Bolsonaro em 2018.* Editora Azahar.
O'Donnell, Guillermo. 1973. *Modernization and Bureaucratic-Authoritarianism.* Institute of International Studies.
O'Donnell, Guillermo. 1994. "Delegative Democracy." *Journal of Democracy* 5 (1): 55–69. https://doi.org/10.1353/jod.1994.0010.
O'Donnell, Guillermo A., and Philippe C. Schmitter. 1986. *Transitions from Authoritarian Rule: Tentative Conclusions About Uncertain Democracies.* Johns Hopkins University Press.
OECD. 2004. *Reviews of National Policies of Education: Chile.* Organisation for Economic Cooperation and Development.
OHCHR. 2018. *Human Rights Violations in the Bolivarian Republic of Venezuela: A Downward Spiral with No End in Sight.* Office of the UN Commission on Human Rights.
Oikonomakis, Leonidas. 2019. "From the Rainy Place to the Burnt Palace: How Social Movements Form Their Political Strategies. The Case of the Six Federations of the Tropic of Cochabamba." *Bulletin of Latin American Research* 38 (5): 654–669.
Ollier, María Matilde. 2015. "El ciclo de presidencias dominantes: Néstor y Cristina Kirchner (2003–2013)." In *10 años de kirchnerismo, la década ganada?* Debate.

Ondetti, Gabriel. 2008. *Land, Protest, and Politics: The Landless Movement and the Struggle for Agrarian Reform in Brazil.* Penn State University Press.

Ospina Peralta, Pablo. 2023. "Las paradojas del triunfo de la derecha en Ecuador." *Nueva Sociedad: Democracia y Política en América Latina*, October 19. https://nuso.org/articulo/el-triunfo-de-la-derecha-en-ecuador/.

Ostiguy, Pierre. 2022. "The Voice and Message of Hugo Chávez: A Rhetorical Analysis." In *Populist Rhetorics: Rhetoric, Politics, and Society*, edited by Christian Kock and Lisa Villadsen. Palgrave Macmillan.

Ostiguy, Pierre, and Aaron Schneider. 2018. "The Politics of Incorporation: Party Systems, Political Leaders and the State in Argentina and Brazil." In *Reshaping the Political Arena: From Resisting Neoliberalism to the Second Incorporation*, edited by Eduardo Silva and Federico Rossi. University of Pittsburgh Press.

Oxhorn, Philip. 1995. *Organizing Civil Society: The Popular Sectors and the Struggle for Democracy in Chile.* Penn State University Press.

Oxhorn, Philip. 2011. *Sustaining Civil Society: Economic Change, Democracy, and the Social Construction of Citizenship in Latin America.* Penn State University Press.

Panebianco, Angelo. 1988. *Political Parties: Organization and Power.* Cambridge University Press.

Panizza, Francisco. 2014. "'Everybody Out,' 'We Are Fantastic:' The Politics of Financial Crises in Argentina and Uruguay 2001–2003." In *Moments of Truth: The Politics of Financial Crises in Comparative Perspective*, edited by Francisco Panizza and George Philip. Routledge.

Partido dos Trabalhadores. 1998. *Partido dos Trabalhadores: Resoluções de encontros e congressos.* A Secretaria, Editora Fundação Perseu Abramo.

Paschel, Tianna S. 2016. *Becoming Black Political Subjects: Movements and Ethno-Racial Rights in Colombia and Brazil.* Princeton University Press.

Payne, Leigh A., Julia Zulver, and Simón Escoffier, eds. 2023. *The Right Against Rights in Latin America.* Proceedings of the British Academy. Oxford University Press.

Pereira, Carlos, Frederico Bertholini, and Eric D. Raile. 2016. "All the President's Men and Women: Coalition Management Strategies and Governing Costs in a Multiparty Presidency." *Presidential Studies Quarterly* 46 (3): 550–568. https://doi.org/10.1111/psq.12296.

Perelmiter, Luisina. 2016. *Burocracia plebeya: La trastienda de la asistencia social en el Estado argentino.* UNSAM Edita de Universidad Nacional de General San Martín.

Pérez Bentancur, Verónica. 2023. "La izquierda uruguaya se prepara para volver al poder." *Nueva Sociedad: Democracia y Política en América Latina*, March 31. https://www.nuso.org/articulo/Uruguay-Frente-Amplio/.

Pérez Bentancur, Verónica, Rafael Piñeiro Rodríguez, and Fernando Rosenblatt. 2019. *How Party Activism Survives: Uruguay's Frente Amplio.* Cambridge University Press.

Pérez Bentancur, Verónica, Rafael Piñeiro Rodríguez, and Fernando Rosenblatt. 2022. *Cómo sobrevive la militancia partidaria: El Frente Amplio de Uruguay.* Ediciones Túnel.

Perochena, Camila. 2022. *Cristina y la historia: El kirchnerismo y sus batallas por el pasado.* Crítica Argentina.

Piñeiro Rodríguez, Rafael, and Fernando Rosenblatt. 2020. "Stability and Incorporation: Toward a New Concept of Party System Institutionalization." *Party Politics* 26 (2): 249–260. https://doi.org/10.1177/1354068818777895.

Piscopo, Jennifer M., and Peter M. Siavelis. 2023. "Chile's Constitutional Chaos." *Journal of Democracy* 34 (1): 141–155.

Poertner, Mathias. 2024. *Creating Partisans: The Organizational Roots of New Parties in Latin America.* Cambridge University Press.

Polga-Hecimovich, John. 2020. "Reshaping the State: The Unitary Executive Presidency of Rafael Correa." In *Reshaping the State: The Unitary Executive Presidency of Rafael Correa,* edited by Francisco Sánchez and Simón Pachano. Palgrave Macmillan, Springer Nature Switzerland.

Policzer, Pablo. 2009. *Rise and Fall of Repression in Chile.* University of Notre Dame Press.

Postero, Nancy. 2007. *Now We Are Citizens: Indigenous Politics in Postmulticultural Bolivia.* Stanford University Press.

Postero, Nancy. 2010. "Morales's MAS Government." *Latin American Perspectives* 37 (3): 18–34.

Postero, Nancy. 2017. *The Indigenous State: Race, Politics, and Performance in Plurinational Bolivia.* University of California Press.

Power, Timothy J. 2022. "Lula, Lifelong Learner?" *Latin American Politics and Society* 64 (1): 162–167. https://doi.org/10.1017/lap.2021.62.

Power, Timothy J., and Rodrigo Rodrigues-Silveira. 2019. "The Political Right and Party Politics." In *Routledge Handbook of Brazilian Politics,* edited by Barry Ames. Routledge.

Pribble, Jennifer. 2013. *Welfare and Party Politics in Latin America.* Cambridge University Press.

Pribble, Jennifer, and Evelyne Huber. 2011. "Social Policy and Redistribution: Chile and Uruguay." In *The Resurgence of the Latin American Left,* edited by Steven Levitsky and Kenneth M. Roberts. Johns Hopkins University Press.

Przeworski, Adam. 1991. *Democracy and the Market: Political and Economic Reforms in Eastern Europe and Latin America.* Cambridge University Press.

Przeworski, Adam. 2019. *Crises of Democracy.* Cambridge University Press. https://doi.org/10.1017/9781108671019.

Przeworski, Adam, and John Sprague. 1988. *Paper Stones: A History of Electoral Socialism.* University of Chicago Press.

Pucciarelli, Alfredo, and Ana Castellani. 2019. *Los años del kirchnerismo: La disputa hegemónica tras la crisis del orden neoliberal.* Siglo XXI Editores.

Queirolo, Rosario. 2013. *The Success of the Left in Latin America: Untainted Parties, Market Reforms, and Voting Behavior.* University of Notre Dame Press.

Queirolo, Rosario, Cecilia Rossel, Eliana Álvarez, and Lorena Repetto. 2019. "Why Uruguay Legalized Marijuana? The Open Window of Public Insecurity." *Addiction* 114 (7): 1313–1321.

Remmer, Karen L. 1980. "Political Demobilization in Chile, 1973–1978." *Comparative Politics* 12 (3): 275–301. https://doi.org/10.2307/421927.

Remmer, Karen L. 1989. *Military Rule in Latin America.* Westview Press.

Renaud, Terence. 2021. *New Lefts: The Making of a Radical Tradition.* Princeton University Press.

Rennó, Lucio. 2023. *La ultraderecha en Brasil: De Bolsonaro al bolsonarismo.* Fundación Friedrich Ebert. https://library.fes.de/pdf-files/bueros/chile/20672.pdf.

República de Ecuador. 1998. Constitución de 1998. https://pdba.georgetown.edu/Constitutions/Ecuador/ecuador98.html#mozTocId933133.

Resmini, Fabio, and Eduardo Silva. 2024. "The Durability of Pink Tide Era Interest Intermediation Regimes: Parties, Popular Sector Organizations, and the Legacies of Their New Incorporation." Paper presented at the annual meeting of the American Political Science Association (APSA), Philadelphia.

Rhodes-Purdy, Matthew. 2017. *Regime Support Beyond the Balance Sheet: Participation and Policy Performance in Latin America.* Cambridge University Press.

Rhodes-Purdy, Matthew, and Fernando Rosenblatt. 2023. "Raising the Red Flag: Democratic Elitism and the Protests in Chile." *Perspectives on Politics* 2 (21): 241-253. https://doi.org/10.1017/S1537592721000050.

Rial, Juan. 1985. "Las reglas del juego electoral en el Uruguay y sus implicaciones." *Revista Mexicana de Sociología* 47 (2): 85–110. https://doi.org/10.2307/3540537.

Rilla, José, and Jaime Yaffé. 2021. "Partidos y movimientos políticos en Uruguay: Historia y presente." In *Partidos y movimientos políticos en Uruguay: Historia y presente,* edited by José Rilla and Jaime Yaffé. Crítica.

Ribeiro, Pedro. 2008. "Dos sindicatos ao governo: A organização nacional do PT de 1980." PhD diss., Universidade Federal de São Carlos.

Ribeiro, Pedro. 2014. "An Amphibian Party? Organisational Change and Adaptation in the Brazilian Workers' Party, 1980–2012." *Journal of Latin American Studies* 46 (1): 87–119.

Rich, Jessica. 2019. *State-Sponsored Activism: Bureaucrats and Social Movements in Democratic Brazil.* Cambridge University Press.

Rich, Jessica, Liam Bower, and Elise Massard. 2024. "What Makes Bureaucracies Politically Resilient? Evidence from Brazil's Covid-19 Vaccination Campaign." *Comparative Politics* 57 (1): 25–48.

Riofrancos, Thea. 2020. *Resource Radicals: From Petro-Nationalism to Post-Extractivism in Ecuador.* Duke University Press.

Rivera, Soledad Valdivia. 2019. *Political Networks and Social Movements: Bolivian State–Society Relations Under Evo Morales, 2006–2016.* Berghahn Books.

Rivera, Soledad Valdivia. 2024. "Vínculos entre movimientos sociales y partidos políticos, y su impacto electoral en el contexto del estallido social en Bolivia, 2019–2020." *Desafíos* 36 (1). https://doi.org/10.12804/revistas.urosario.edu.co/desafios/a.13220.

Roberts, Kenneth M. 1998. *Deepening Democracy? The Modern Left and Social Movements in Chile and Peru*. Stanford University Press.

Roberts, Kenneth M. 2014. *Changing Course in Latin America: Party Systems in the Neoliberal Era*. Cambridge Studies in Comparative Politics. Cambridge University Press.

Roberts, Kenneth M. 2021. "Populism and Polarization in Comparative Perspective: Constitutive, Spatial and Institutional Dimensions." *Government and Opposition*, June, 1–23. https://doi.org/10.1017/gov.2021.14.

Roberts, Kenneth, Valerie J. Bunce, Thomas Pepinsky, and Rachel Beatty Riedl. 2025. "Global Challenges to Democracy: Backsliding, Resiliency, and Democratic Theory." In *Global Challenges to Democracy: Comparative Perspectives on Backsliding, Autocracy, and Resilience*, edited by Valerie J Bunce, Thomas Pepinsky, Rachel Beatty Riedl, and Kenneth M. Roberts. Cambridge University Press.

Rodríguez, Francisco. 2024. "Scorched Earth Politics and Venezuela's Collapse." Paper presented at Conference on Venezuelan Politics, Becker Friedman Institute for Economics, University of Chicago. https://franciscorodriguez.net/2024/11/15/scorched-earth-politics-and-venezuelas-collapse/.

Rodríguez, Francisco. 2025. *The Collapse of Venezuela: Scorched Earth Politics and Economic Decline, 2012–2020*. University of Notre Dame Press.

Rodríguez, Juan M., Beatriz Cozzano, Graciela Mazzuchi, and María E. González. 2016. "Las relaciones laborales en 2016 y perspectivas para 2016." Working paper, Series Instituto de Relaciones Laborales, Universidad Católica del Uruguay. https://ucu.edu.uy/sites/default/files/facultad/fce/i_rrll/2015/Informe_anual_de_Relaciones_Laborales_2015.pdf.

Rodríguez García, Gabriel. 2024. "Bolivia in Its Labyrinth." NACLA. https://nacla.org/bolivia-its-labyrinth.

Roett, Riordan. 1999. *Brazil: Politics in a Patrimonial Society*. 5th ed. Praeger.

Romero, Carlos, Carlos Böhrt Irahola, and Raúl Peñaranda. 2009. *Del conflicto al diálogo: Memorias del Acuerdo Constitucional*. FES-ILDIS y fBDM.

Rosaldo, Manuel. 2016. "Revolution in the Garbage Dump: The Political and Economic Foundations of the Colombian Recycler Movement, 1986–2011." *Social Problems* 63 (3): 351–372. https://doi.org/10.1093/socpro/spw015.

Rosales, Antulio, and Maryhen Jiménez. 2021. "Venezuela: Autocratic Consolidation and Splintered Economic Liberalization." *Revista de Ciencia Política* (Santiago) 41 (2): 425–447. https://doi.org/10.4067/S0718-090X2021005000113.

Rosenblatt, Fernando. 2018. *Party Vibrancy and Democracy in Latin America*. Oxford University Press.

Rossel, Cecilia, Denise Courtoisie, and Magdalena Marsiglia. 2014. "Programas de transferencias, condicionalidades y derechos de la infancia: Apuntes a partir del caso del Uruguay." November. https://repositorio.cepal.org/handle/11362/37328.

Rossel, Cecilia, and Felipe Monestier. 2021. "Uruguay 2020: El despliegue de la agenda de centro derecha en contexto de pandemia." *Revista de Ciencia Política* 41 (2): 401–424. https://doi.org/10.4067/S0718-090X2021005000119.

Rossi, Federico M. 2017. *The Poor's Struggle for Political Incorporation: The Piquetero Movement in Argentina.* Cambridge University Press.

Rovira Kaltwasser, Cristóbal. 2019. "La (sobre)adaptación programática de la derecha chilena y la irrupción de la derecha populista radical." *Colombia Internacional*, no. 99 (July): 29–61. https://doi.org/10.7440/colombiaint99.2019.02.

Rueschemeyer, Dietrich, Evelyne Huber Stephens, and John D. Stephens. 1992. *Capitalist Development and Democracy.* University of Chicago Press.

Russo, Sandra. 2013. *Fuerza propia: La Cámpora por dentro.* Penguin Random House Grupo Editorial Argentina.

Rustow, Dankwart A. 1970. "Transitions to Democracy: Toward a Dynamic Model." *Comparative Politics* 2 (3): 337–363. https://doi.org/10.2307/421307.

Sader, Emir, ed. 2013. *10 anos de governos pós-neoliberais no Brasil: Lula e Dilma.* Boitempo Editorial.

Saferstein, Ezequiel, and Analía Goldentul. 2022. "La batalla cultural de las 'nuevas derechas.'" *Revista Anfibia* (blog), May 23. https://www.revistaanfibia.com/javier-milei-la-batalla-cultural-de-las-nuevas-derechas/.

Samuels, David J. 2004. "From Socialism to Social Democracy: Party Organization and the Transformation of the Workers' Party in Brazil." *Comparative Political Studies* 37 (9): 999–1024. https://doi.org/10.1177/0010414004268856.

Samuels, David J., and Cesar Zucco. 2018. *Partisans, Antipartisans, and Nonpartisans: Voting Behavior in Brazil.* Cambridge University Press.

Samuels, David J., and Karine Belarmino. 2024. "Partisan Dehumanization in Brazil's Asymmetrically Polarized Party System." *Journal of Politics in Latin America,* August, 1866802X241268648. https://doi.org/10.1177/1866802X241268648.

Sánchez, Francisco, and Simón Pachano, eds. 2020. *Assessing the Left Turn in Ecuador.* Palgrave Macmillan.

Sánchez-Sibony, Omar. 2021. "Competitive Authoritarianism in Morales's Bolivia: Skewing Arenas of Competition." *Latin American Politics and Society* 63 (1): 118–144. https://doi.org/10.1017/lap.2020.35.

Sandbrook, Richard, Marc Edelman, Patrick Heller, and Judith Teichman. 2007. *Social Democracy in the Global Periphery: Origins, Challenges, Prospects.* Cambridge University Press.

Sanjinés, Javier. 2004. *Mestizaje Upside-Down: Aesthetic Politics in Modern Bolivia.* Illuminations. University of Pittsburgh Press.

Santos, Fabiano, Talita Tanscheit, and Tiago Ventura. 2020. "The Workers' Party and Participatory Institutions: The Influence of Intra-Party Dynamics in the Adop-

tion of Participatory Budgeting." *Dados* 63 (3): 1–35 . https://doi.org/10.1590/dados.2020.63.3.202.
Santucho, Mario. 2022. "Entrevista con Álvaro García Linera: Bolivia no tiene escrito su destino." *Revista Crisis*, October 22. https://revistacrisis.com.ar/notas/bolivia-no-tiene-escrito-su-destino.
Sarlo, Beatriz. 2011. *La audacia y el cálculo: Kirchner 2003–2010.* Sudamericana.
Sarsfield, Rodolfo, Paolo Moncagatta, and Kenneth M. Roberts. 2024. "Introduction: The New Polarization in Latin America." In "The New Polarization in Latin America: Sources, Dynamics, and Implications for Democracy," special issue, *Latin American Politics and Society* 66: 1–23. https://doi.org/10.1017/lap.2024.15.
Sartori, Giovanni. 1976. *Parties and Party Systems: A Framework for Analysis.* Cambridge University Press.
Sauer, Sérgio, and George Mészáros. 2017. "The Political Economy of Land Struggle in Brazil Under Workers' Party Governments." *Journal of Agrarian Change* 17 (2): 397–414. https://doi.org/10.1111/joac.12206.
Sawyer, Suzana. 2004. *Crude Chronicles: Indigenous Politics, Multinational Oil, and Neoliberalism in Ecuador.* Duke University Press.
Schedler, Andreas. 2023. "Rethinking Political Polarization." *Political Science Quarterly* 138 (3): 335–359. https://doi.org/10.1093/psquar/qqad038.
Schipani, Andrés. 2019. "Strategies of Redistribution: The Left and the Popular Sectors in Latin America." PhD diss., University of California at Berkeley.
Schlotterbeck, Marian E. 2018. *Beyond the Vanguard: Everyday Revolutionaries in Allende's Chile.* University of California Press.
Schmitter, Philippe C., and Terry Lynn Karl. 1991. "What Democracy Is . . . and Is Not." *Journal of Democracy* 2 (3): 75–88. https://doi.org/10.1353/jod.1991.0033.
Secco, Lincoln. 2011. *História do PT, 1978–2010.* Ateliê.
Seidman, Gay W. 1994. *Manufacturing Militance: Workers' Movements in Brazil and South Africa, 1970–1985.* University of California Press.
Selçuk, Orçun. 2024. *The Authoritarian Divide: Populism, Propaganda, and Polarization.* University of Notre Dame Press.
Sells, Cameron. 2022. "The Life of the Party: Grassroots Activists and Mass Partisanship in Latin America." Unpublished manuscript.
Semán, Pablo. 2023. *Está entre nosotros: ¿De dónde sale y hasta dónde puede llegar la extrema derecha que no vimos venir?* Siglo XXI Editores.
Servetto, Alicia. 2010. *73/76: El gobierno peronista contra las provincias montoneras.* Siglo Veintiuno Editores.
Shakow, Miriam. 2014. *Along the Bolivian Highway: Social Mobility and Political Culture in a New Middle Class.* University of Pennsylvania Press.
Siavelis, Peter. 2000. *The President and Congress in Postauthoritarian Chile: Institutional Constraints to Democratic Consolidation.* Penn State University Press.
Silva, Eduardo. 1996. *The State and Capital in Chile: Business Elites, Technocrats, and Market Economics.* Westview Press.

Silva, Eduardo. 2009. *Challenging Neoliberalism in Latin America.* Cambridge University Press.

Silva, Eduardo. 2017. "Reorganizing Popular Sector Incorporation." *Politics & Society* 45 (1): 91–122. https://doi.org/10.1177/0032329216683166.

Silva, Eduardo, and Federico Rossi, eds. 2018. *Reshaping the Political Arena in Latin America: From Resisting Neoliberalism to the Second Incorporation.* University of Pittsburgh Press.

Silva, Luiz Inácio Lula da. 2002. "Carta ao povo brasileiro." International Institute for Social History. http://www.iisg.nl/collections/carta_ao_povo_brasileiro.pdf.

Simmons, Erica S. 2016. *Meaningful Resistance: Market Reforms and the Roots of Social Protest in Latin America.* Cambridge University Press.

Singer, André. 2009. "Raízes sociais e ideológicas do lulismo." *Novos Estudos CEBRAP* 85: 83–102. https://doi.org/10.1590/S0101-33002009000300004.

Singer, André. 2012. *Os sentidos do Lulismo: Reforma gradual e pacto conservador.* Ciências Humanas e Sociais. Companhia das Letras.

Singer, André. 2019. "From a Rooseveltian Dream to the Nightmare of a Parliamentary Coup." In *The Brazilian Left in the 21st Century: Conflict and Conciliation in Peripheral Capitalism,* edited by Vladimir Puzone and Luis Felipe Miguel. Palgrave Macmillan.

Singer, André. 2024. "Lulismo 3.0: A Mid-Term Diagnosis." *New Left Review* 150 (November–December): 39–54.

Sivak, Martin. 2010. *Evo Morales: The Extraordinary Rise of the First Indigenous President of Bolivia.* Palgrave Macmillan.

Skocpol, Theda, and Vanessa Williamson. 2016. *The Tea Party and the Remaking of Republican Conservatism.* Oxford University Press.

Slater, Dan, and Erica Simmons. 2013. "Coping by Colluding: Political Uncertainty and Promiscuous Powersharing in Indonesia and Bolivia." *Comparative Political Studies* 46 (11): 1366–1393. https://doi.org/10.1177/0010414012453447.

Smilde, David, and Daniel Hellinger, eds. 2011. *Venezuela's Bolivarian Democracy: Participation, Politics, and Culture under Chávez.* Duke University Press.

Smilde, David, Verónica Zubillaga, and Rebecca Hanson, eds. 2022. *The Paradox of Violence in Venezuela: Revolution, Crime, and Policing During Chavismo.* University of Pittsburgh Press.

Smith, Amy Erica. 2019. *Religion and Brazilian Democracy: Mobilizing the People of God.* Cambridge Studies in Social Theory, Religion and Politics. Cambridge University Press. https://doi.org/10.1017/9781108699655.

Somma, Nicolás M. 2012. "The Chilean Student Movement of 2011–2012: Challenging the Marketization of Education." *Interface: A Journal for and About Social Movements* 4 (2): 296–309.

Somma, Nicolás M., Matías Bargsted, Rodolfo Disi Pavlic, and Rodrigo M. Medel. 2021. "No Water in the Oasis: The Chilean Spring of 2019–2020." *Social Movement Studies* 20 (4): 495–502. https://doi.org/10.1080/14742837.2020.1727737.

Soruco, Ximena, Daniela Franco Pinto, and Mariela Durán Azurduy. 2014. *Composición social del estado plurinacional: Hacia la descolonización de la burocracia*. Centro de Investigaciones Sociales.

Souza, Isabel Ribeiro de Oliveira Gómez de. 1988. *Trabalho e política: As origens do Partido Dos Trabalhadores*. Vozes.

Souza Santos, Andreza Aruska de. 2023. "'In the Name of the Family': The Evangelical Caucus and Rights Rollbacks in Brazil." In *The Right Against Rights in Latin America*, edited by Leigh A. Payne, Julia Zulver, and Simón Escoffier. Oxford University Press.

Stefanoni, Pablo. 2020. "Las lecciones que nos deja Bolivia." *Nueva Sociedad*. https://nuso.org/articulo/Bolivia-Evo-Morales-elecciones/.

Stefanoni, Pablo. 2021. *¿La rebeldía se volvió de derecha? Cómo el antiprogresismo y la anticorrección política están construyendo un nuevo sentido común*. Siglo XXI Editores.

Stefanoni, Pablo, and Hervé Do Alto. 2006. *Evo Morales: De la coca al palacio: Una oportunidad para la izquierda indígena*. Malatesta.

Stokes, Susan C. 2001. *Mandates and Democracy: Neoliberalism by Surprise in Latin America*. Cambridge University Press.

Stott, Michael, and Benedict Mander. 2019. "Chile President Sebastián Piñera: 'We Are Ready to Do Everything to Not Fall into Populism.'" *Financial Times*, October 17. https://www.ft.com/content/980ec442-ee91-11e9-ad1e-4367d8281195.

Stoyan, Alissandra. 2014. "Constituent Assemblies, Presidential Majorities, and Democracy in Latin America." PhD diss., University of North Carolina at Chapel Hill.

Svampa, Maristella. 2013. "La década kirchnerista: Populismo, clases medias y revolución pasiva." *LASA Forum* 44 (4): 14–16.

Svampa, Maristella, and Sebastián Pereyra. 2003. *Entre la ruta y el barrio: La experiencia de las organizaciones piqueteras*. Editorial Biblos.

Svolik, Milan W. 2019. "Polarization Versus Democracy," *Journal of Democracy* 30 (3): 20–32.

Tanscheit, Talita, and Pedro Barbosa. 2023. "Una batalla de dos presidentes: Lula vs. Bolsonaro en las elecciones brasileñas de 2022." *Revista de Ciencia Política* (Santiago) 43 (2): 167–191. https://doi.org/10.4067/s0718-090x2023005000111.

Tarlau, Rebecca. 2019. *Occupying Schools, Occupying Land: How the Landless Workers Movement Transformed Brazilian Education*. Global and Comparative Ethnography. Oxford University Press.

Tarrow, Sidney G. 2010. "The Strategy of Paired Comparison: Toward a Theory of Practice." *Comparative Political Studies* 43 (2): 230–259. https://doi.org/10.1177/0010414009350044.

Tarrow, Sidney G. 2021. *Movements and Parties: Critical Connections in American Political Development*. Cambridge University Press.

Tarrow, Sidney G. 2022. *Power in Movement. Social Movements and Contentious Politics.* 4th ed. Cambridge University Press.

Taylor, Matthew M. 2020. *Decadent Developmentalism: The Political Economy of Democratic Brazil.* Cambridge University Press.

Teichman, Judith. 2024. "Populist Rhetoric and Political Polarization: Insights from Venezuela." *Latin American Perspectives* 51 (6): 166–184. https://doi.org/10.1177/0094582X241298581.

Tinker Salas, Miguel. 2009. *The Enduring Legacy: Oil, Culture, and Society in Venezuela.* Duke University Press.

Trejo, Guillermo, and Fernando Bizzarro. 2015. "Religious Competition and the Rise of Leftist Parties: Why the Catholic Church Provided the Mass Base for the Workers' Party in Brazil." SSRN Scholarly Paper ID 3148471. Social Science Research Network. https://doi.org/10.2139/ssrn.3148471.

Tremlett, Giles. 2014. "José Mujica: Is This the World's Most Radical President?" *The Guardian,* September 18. https://www.theguardian.com/world/2014/sep/18/-sp-is-this-worlds-most-radical-president-uruguay-jose-mujica.

Trinkunas, Harold A. 2011. *Crafting Civilian Control of the Military in Venezuela: A Comparative Perspective.* University of North Carolina Press.

UN Development Programme. 2015. *Auditoría a la democracia: Más y mejor democracia para un Chile inclusivo.* UNDP.

Urbinati, Nadia. 2017. "Populism and the Principle of Majority." In *The Oxford Handbook of Populism,* edited by Cristóbal Rovira Kaltwasser, Paul Taggart, Paulina Ochoa Espejo, and Pierre Ostiguy. Oxford University Press.

Valenzuela, Arturo. 1978. *The Breakdown of Democratic Regimes, Chile.* Johns Hopkins University Press.

Van Cott, Donna Lee. 2000. *The Friendly Liquidation of the Past: The Politics of Diversity in Latin America.* University of Pittsburgh Press.

Van Cott, Donna Lee. 2003. "From Exclusion to Inclusion: Bolivia's 2002 Elections." *Journal of Latin American Studies* 35 (4): 751–775.

Van Cott, Donna Lee. 2005. *From Movements to Parties in Latin America: The Evolution of Ethnic Politics.* Cambridge University Press.

Van Cott, Donna Lee. 2007. "Latin America's Indigenous Peoples." *Journal of Democracy* 18 (4): 127–142.

Van Cott, Donna Lee. 2008. *Radical Democracy in the Andes.* Cambridge University Press.

Van Dyck, Brandon. 2014. "The Paradox of Adversity: New Left Party Survival and Collapse in Latin America." PhD diss., Harvard University.

Van Dyck, Brandon. 2016. "The Paradox of Adversity: New Left Party Survival and Collapse in Brazil, Mexico, and Argentina." In *Challenges of Party-Building in Latin America,* edited by Steven Levitsky, James Loxton, Brandon Van Dyck, and Jorge I. Domínguez. Cambridge University Press.

Van Dyck, Brandon. 2021. *Democracy Against Parties: The Divergent Fates of Latin America's New Left Contenders.* University of Pittsburgh Press.

Velasco, Alejandro. 2022. "The Many Faces of Chavismo." *NACLA Report on the Americas* 54 (1): 20–73.

Velasco Guachalla, V. Ximena, Calla Hummel, Sam Handlin, and Amy Erica Smith. 2021. "Latin America Erupts: When Does Competitive Authoritarianism Take Root?" *Journal of Democracy* 32 (3): 63–77. https://doi.org/10.1353/jod.2021.0034.

Vergara, Camila. 2020. *Systemic Corruption: Constitutional Ideas for an Anti-Oligarchic Republic*. Princeton University Press.

Viera-Gallo, José Antonio. 1976–1977. "Reflexiones para la formulación de un proyecto democrático para Chile." *Chile-América* 25–27: 50–65.

Villanueva Rance, Amaru. 2022. "Firefly Dynamics." *ReVista*. https://revista.drclas.harvard.edu/firefly-dynamics/.

Vommaro, Gabriel. 2023. "Conservatives Against the Tide: The Rise of the Argentine PRO in Comparative Perspective." *Cambridge Elements in Politics and Society in Latin America,* June. https://doi.org/10.1017/9781009418256.

Vommaro, Gabriel, and Mariana Gené. 2023. *El sueño intacto de la centroderecha y sus dilemas después de haber gobernado y fracasado.* Siglo Veintiuno Editores.

Walters, Jonah. 2019. "Bolivia's Path to Camacho (Interview)." NACLA. 2019. https://nacla.org/news/2019/11/13/bolivia-path-camacho-interview-morales.

Walton, John, and David Seddon. 1994. *Free Markets and Food Riots: The Politics of Global Adjustment.* Blackwell.

Wampler, Brian. 2007. *Participatory Budgeting in Brazil: Contestation, Cooperation, and Accountability.* Pennsylvania State University Press.

Wasow, Omar. 2020. "Agenda Seeding: How 1960s Black Protests Moved Elites, Public Opinion and Voting." *American Political Science Review* 114 (3): 638–659. https://doi.org/10.1017/S000305542000009X.

Webber, Jeffery R. 2010. "Carlos Mesa, Evo Morales, and a Divided Bolivia." *Latin American Perspectives* 37 (3) (172): 51–70.

Webster, Steven W., and Alan I. Abramowitz. 2017. "The Ideological Foundations of Affective Polarization in the U.S. Electorate." *American Politics Research* 45 (4): 621–647. https://doi.org/10.1177/1532673X17703132.

Weeks, Gregory, and Silvia Borzutzky. 2012. "Michelle Bachelet's Government: The Paradoxes of a Chilean President." *Journal of Politics in Latin America* 4 (3): 97–121. https://doi.org/10.1177/1866802X1200400304.

Wenman, Mark. 2013. *Agonistic Democracy: Constituent Power in the Era of Globalisation.* Cambridge University Press. https://doi.org/10.1017/CBO9780511777158.

Weyland, Kurt. 1997. "'Growth with Equity' in Chile's New Democracy?" *Latin American Research Review* 32 (1): 37–67.

Weyland, Kurt. 2001. "Clarifying a Contested Concept: Populism in the Study of Latin American Politics." *Comparative Politics* 34 (1): 1–22. https://doi.org/10.2307/422412.

Weyland, Kurt. 2002. *The Politics of Market Reform in Fragile Democracies: Argentina, Brazil, Peru, and Venezuela.* Princeton University Press.

Weyland, Kurt. 2013. "The Threat from the Populist Left." *Journal of Democracy* 24 (3): 18–32. https://doi.org/10.1353/jod.2013.0045.

Weyland, Kurt. 2014. *Making Waves: Democratic Contention in Europe and Latin America Since the Revolutions of 1848*. Cambridge University Press. https://doi.org/10.1017/CBO9781107045279.

Weyland, Kurt. 2024. *Democracy's Resilience to Populism's Threats: Countering Global Alarmism*. Cambridge University Press.

Weyland, Kurt G., Raúl L. Madrid, and Wendy Hunter. 2010. *Leftist Governments in Latin America: Successes and Shortcomings*. Cambridge University Press.

Weyland, Kurt, Raúl L. Madrid, and Wendy Hunter. 2010. *Leftist Governments in Latin America: Successes and Shortcomings*. Cambridge University Press.

Wickham-Crowley, Timothy P. 1993. *Guerrillas and Revolution in Latin America*. Rev. ed. Princeton University Press.

Wiesehomeier, Nina, and Kenneth Benoit. 2009. "Presidents, Parties, and Policy Competition." *Journal of Politics* 71 (4): 1435–1447. https://doi.org/10.1017/S0022381609990193.

Williamson, John. 1990. *Latin American Adjustment: How Much Has Happened?* Institute for International Economics.

Winn, Peter. 1986. *Weavers of Revolution: The Yarur Workers and Chile's Road to Socialism*. Oxford University Press.

Winters, Matthew S., and Rebecca Weitz-Shapiro. 2014. "Partisan Protesters and Nonpartisan Protests in Brazil." *Journal of Politics in Latin America* 6 (1): 137–150. https://doi.org/10.1177/1866802X1400600105.

Wolff, Jonas. 2007. "(De-)Mobilising the Marginalised: A Comparison of the Argentine Piqueteros and Ecuador's Indigenous Movement." *Journal of Latin American Studies* 39 (1): 1–29.

Wolff, Jonas. 2018. "Ecuador After Correa: The Struggle over the 'Citizens' Revolution.'" *Revista de Ciencia Política* 38 (2): 281–302.

Wolford, Wendy. 2010. *This Land Is Ours Now: Social Mobilization and the Meanings of Land in Brazil*. Duke University Press.

Wolford, Wendy, and John D. French. 2016. "Deconstructing the Post-Neoliberal State Intimate Perspectives on Contemporary Brazil." *Latin American Perspectives* 43 (2): 4–21.

Yaffé, Jaime. 2005. *Al centro y adentro: La renovación de la izquierda y el triunfo del Frente Amplio en Uruguay*. Linardi y Risso.

Yaffé, Jaime. 2013. "Competencia interna y adaptación partidaria en el Frente Amplio de Uruguay." *Perfiles Latinoamericanos* 21 (41): 71–94.

Yashar, Deborah J. 2005. *Contesting Citizenship in Latin America: The Rise of Indigenous Movements and the Postliberal Challenge*. Cambridge University Press.

Zanotti, Lisa, and Kenneth M. Roberts. 2021. "(Aún) la excepción y no la regla: La derecha populista radical en América Latina." *Revista Uruguaya de Ciencia*

Política 30 (1): 23–48. https://www.colibri.udelar.edu.uy/jspui/handle/20.500.12008/28132.

Zavaleta Mercado, René. 1986. *Lo nacional-popular en Bolivia*. Siglo XXI.

Zegada, María, Claudia Arce, Gabriela Canedo, and Alber Quispe Escobar. 2011. *La democracia desde los márgenes: Transformaciones en el campo político boliviano*. Muela del Diablo.

Zegada, María Teresa, and Jorge Komadina. 2014. *El espejo de la sociedad: Poder y representación en Bolivia*. CERES/Plural.

Ziblatt, Daniel. 2017. *Conservative Parties and the Birth of Democracy*. Cambridge Studies in Comparative Politics. Cambridge University Press.

Zuazo, Moira. 2008. *¿Cómo nació El MAS? La ruralización de la política en Bolivia: Entrevistas a 85 parlamentarios del partido*. Fundación Ebert.

Zúquete, José Pedro. 2008. "The Missionary Politics of Hugo Chávez." *Latin American Politics and Society* 50 (1): 91–121. https://doi.org/10.1111/j.1548-2456.2008.00005.x.

Index

Page numbers in italics refer to figures.

AAA (Argentine Anticommunist Alliance), 158
abortion rights, 39, 72, 153
accountability: democratic, 6, 113; popular, 107; societal, 120
Acosta, Alberto, 136–37
activism: civic, 43; revolutionary, 48; right-wing, 68, 70, 182; by students, 78–79
acute polarization, 2
AD (Democratic Action), 17, 89–90, 92, 100, 109
ADN (Nationalist Democratic Action), 96
adversity, 53
affective polarization, 176, 182
Alencar, José, 67
Allende, Salvador, 17, 47–49, 51, 62, 64, 76–77, 233n7
alliance building, 145
Alliance for Jobs, Justice, and Education (Argentina), 160
alliance making, 60
Almeyda, Clodomiro, 224n3
Alonso, Angela, 70
Altamirano, Carlos, 224n2
alternative democratic imaginaries, 22–31, *25*
Altman, David, 78
Álvarez-Rivadulla, María José, 231n6
American Popular Revolutionary Alliance (APRA) (Peru), 42
AmericasBarometer (LAPOP), 155, 188
anarcho-capitalism, 171
Anderson, Perry, 66, 225n12

Andrews-Lee, Caitlin, 166
Áñez, Jeanine, 125, 127
antigovernment protests, 104
anti-incumbent voting, 20
antisystem parties, 5
AP (Proud and Sovereign Homeland Alliance), 131, 136, 138, 140
APRA (American Popular Revolutionary Alliance), 42
Arauz, Andrés, 141
Árbenz, Jacobo, 17
Arce, Luis, 126
Arévalo, Bernardo, 19
Argentina: AAA, 158; Alliance for Jobs, Justice, and Education, 160; CC, 167; CGT, 164, 170; CTA, 170–71; Dirty War, 158, 171; FPV, 162, 167, 169; FR, 170; Frente de Todos, 170; FREPASO, 160; JP, 165; MDT Evita, 165, 231n10; MRP, 159; Peronism in, 127, 129, 157–72; PJ, 158, 159, 161, 163, 164, 224n7; presidential elections, *18*; "El Proceso," 158; "La Renovación," 159; UCR, 159, 171–72; Unión por la Patria, 171
Argentine Anticommunist Alliance (AAA), 158
Argentine Workers' Central Union (CTA) (Argentina), 170–71
Articulation (Articulação) (Brazil), 225n7
Assembly for the Sovereignty of the People (ASP) (Bolivia), 94, 102, 226n2
asymmetrical polarization, 201
authoritarian centralization, 122

authoritarianism, 19, 23, 64, 86–87, 128, 139, 145, 159
autocratic temptation, 11, 30, 87, 104–27, 129–30, 211
autocrítica (self-criticism), 210–13
autogolpe (presidential coup), 73
autonomous social mobilization, 120
Axelrod, Robert, 223n2
Aylwin, Patricio, 61, 63, 74

Bachelet, Michelle, 69, 73–80, 179
backsliding (democratic erosion), 1, 3, 8, 15, 122, 139, 175, 203
Base Committees, 151, 153
base nuclei (*núcleos de base*), 52
basismo, 52, 57
Batlle, Jorge, 150
Becker, Thomas, 227n6
Bermeo, Nancy, 139
Blanco Party, 143, 146–48, 150, 153, 155–56
Bogliaccini, Juan, 152
Bolívar, Simón, 90
"Bolivarian circles," 99, 109
Bolivarian Republic of Venezuela, 107
Bolivarian Revolution, 114
Bolivia: ADN, 96; AP, 131, 136, 138, 140; ASP, 94, 102, 226n2; CIDOB, 228n20; CR, 131, 141, 142; CSUTCB, 94–95; EBR-200, 90–91; Half Moon, 117; IU, 102, 226n2; March for Territory and Dignity, 228n20; MAS, 31, 82, 94–98, 101–5, 116–27, 195, 226n2; MBR-200, 91–93, 99; MNR, 96, 127; National Revolution (1952), 96, 97; PP, 99
Bolivian Workers' Central (COB) (Bolivia), 95, 124
Bolsa Família (family allowance) (Brazil), 68
Bolsonaro, Jair, 71–72, 73, 182, 185, 187, 194, 205
Boric, Gabriel, 82, 84, 185, 187, 194
Brazil: Articulation, 225n7; Bolsa Família, 68; Building a New Brazil, 225n7; Chamber of Deputies, 54; Constituent Assembly, 56, 59; Diretas Já, 54; MST, 53, 57, 68. *See also* Workers Party (PT) (Brazil)
Brazilian Democratic Movement (MDB), 53
Brazilian Democratic Movement (PMDB), 57, 71
Brazilian Social Democratic Party (PSDB), 59, 60, 65, 194

Broad Front (FA) (Uruguay), 29, 80, 82, 129, 142–57, 204, 208–9, 224n5
Brown, John, 122
Bucaram, Abdalá, 132
Building a New Brazil (Construindo um Novo Brasil), 225n7
business opposition, 108–9

Caetano, Gerardo, 145
Caldera, Rafael, 92, 100
Cambiemos (Let's Change) (Argentina), 170
Campello, Daniela, 226n21
campesino movements, 104
Campo Majoritário, 56–57, 225n7
Cámpora, La (youth organization) (Argentina), 168
capital, private, 74
capitalism, 39, 59; anarcho-, 171; market fundamentalism and, 199
Caracazo (popular uprising) (Venezuela), 90–91
Cárdenas, Francisco Arias, 93
Cardoso, Fernando Henrique, 59–60, 65, 68
Carmona, Pedro, 109
Carothers, Thomas, 175
Carrió, Elisa, 167
Carter Center, 136
Castro, Fidel, 108
Catholic religious networks, 200
Cavallo, Domingo, 160
CC (Civic Coalition), 167
Centeno, Miguel Angel, 212
Central Bank, 75
CEPAL, 114
CGT (General Labor Confederation), 164, 170
Chamber of Deputies (Brazil), 54
Chávez, Hugo, 28, 39, 88–93, 99–101, 128, 195, 204, 208
Chavismo, 101, 105–16
checks and balances, 9, 24–26, 29, 41, 105, 114, 122
Chicago Boys, 62, 199
Chile: CONFECH, 80; CUT, 80; DINA, 49; MIR, 49, 96; New Majority, 80, 82; PCCh, 48, 61, 80, 82, 84, 194; PDC, 50, 55, 61, 63, 74, 79–80, 83, 147, 194; PPD, 61; PRO, 170; Radical Party, 48; UDI, 74; UP, 48–49. *See also* Socialist Party (PSCh) (Chile)

Choquehuanca, David, 230n36
Christian Democratic Party (PDC) (Chile), 50, 55, 61, 74, 79–80, 83, 147, 194
Christianity, 124
CIDOB (Confederation of Indigenous Peoples of Bolivia), 228n20
Citizens Council, 75
Citizens' Revolution Movement (CR) (Bolivia), 131, 141, 142
citizenship rights, 96–97, 135
civic activism, 43
Civic Coalition (CC) (Argentina), 167
civic engagement, 77
Civic Union (Uruguay), 146
civil rights, 55
civil society organizations, 106
civil warfare, 31–32
coalition politics, 60–65
COB (Bolivian Workers' Central), 95, 124
cocalero (coca growers) movement, 94–95, 102, 120
Cold War, 32, 64, 199
collective action, 6
Collier, Ruth Berins, 154
Collor, Fernando, 59
Colombia, 19, 89, 205, 211
Colorado Party, 143–44, 147–48, 150, 153, 156
Commission of Judicial Emergency, 107
commodity boom (post-2003), 18, 36, 76–77, 110, 137, 139, 167
commodity prices, 18
Communist Party (PCCh) (Chile), 48, 61, 80, 82, 84, 194
competition: democratic, 4; institutionalized, 26
Conaghan, Catherine, 137
CONAIE (Confederation of Indigenous Nationalities of Ecuador), 130, 132, 138, 141
Concertación, 61–64, 74–75, 79
Concertación de Partidos por el No (Chile), 61
CONDEPA (Conscience of the Fatherland), 102
Confederation of Chilean Students (CONFECH), 80
Confederation of Indigenous Nationalities of Ecuador (CONAIE), 130, 132, 138, 141
Confederation of Indigenous Peoples of Bolivia (CIDOB), 228n20

Confederation of Workers of Venezuela (CTV), 109, 110
conflict: democratic management of, 201–5; distributive, 8; extraordinary, 53; political, 7–8; regulating mechanisms, 41
conformism, 129
conformist temptation, 46, 65–84, 329
Conscience of the Fatherland (CONDEPA), 102
conservative autonomy movements, 117
conservative dilemma, 40
conservative political backlashes (countermovements), 7, 19
Constituent Assembly (Bolivia), 117
Constituent Assembly (Brazil), 56, 59
constituent moments, 28, 99, 116, 137
Constitutional Assembly (Ecuador), 134–36
Constitutional Council, 83
Constitutional Court (Ecuador), 134
Constitutional Tribunal, 74
constitutive authority, 105
constitutive powers, 82–83
Construindo um Novo Brasil, 225n7
contentious politics, 5, 43
contextualized comparisons, 13
contingent consent, 8, 206, 223n2
Contreras, Manuel, 49
convergence, 225n6
COPEI (Independent Political Electoral Organization Committee), 89–90, 92, 100, 109
core constituencies, 40, 224n9
Correa, Rafael, 28, 129–42, 172, 179, 195, 204, 208
Correismo, 141
corruption scandals, 11
Costa Rica, 17, 18, 19, 89
countermovements (conservative political backlashes), 7, 19
COVID-19 pandemic, 81, 141, 171
CR (Citizens' Revolution Movement), 131, 141, 142
CSUTCB (Unified Confederation of Rural Laborers of Bolivia), 94–95
CTA (Argentine Workers' Central Union), 170–71
CTV (Confederation of Workers of Venezuela), 109, 110
Cuba, 17
Cuban Revolution, 3, 32, 48, 143

cultural identities, 40
cultural issues, 40
culture war, 171
Cunha, Eduardo, 71
CUT (United Workers Central), 80

Dahl, Robert A., 25, 207, 223n3, 223n4
De Gennaro, Víctor, 165
de la Rúa, Fernando, 160–61, 162
debt crisis (1980s), 27, 33, 64
"deepening" democracy, 19, 25, 50, 60, 84, 123, 207
democracia de los acuerdos, la ("the democracy of agreements"), 75, 77, 83
democracy: accountability, 6, 113; alternative imaginaries, 22–31, 25; centralism, 52; competition, 4; conflict management, 201–5; conflict-regulating mechanisms of, 41; contestation, 44, 124; "deepening," 19, 25, 50, 60, 84, 123, 207; delegative forms of, 35; direct, 111, 149; dual transitions to, 16; essential institutional arrangements of, 7; imaginaries, 16, 22–31; as institutionalized pluralism, 23–25, 27, 50, 84; liberal, 45, 110; mechanisms, 107; origins of, 198; pacted, 96, 101, 103; paradox of polarization and, 4–12; protagonistic, 112; transitions to, 33
Democratic Action (AD) (Venezuela), 17, 89–90, 92, 100, 109
Democratic Coordinator, 109
democratic erosion (backsliding), 1, 3, 8, 15, 122, 139, 175, 203
Democratic Unity Roundtable (MUD) (Venezuela), 113–15
democratization, 23, 32–33, 54; social democratic left and, 55–65; third wave of, 3–4
depolarization, 34, 35, 43
desgaste (political attrition), 208
Dias, Tayrine, 68
DINA (Directorate for National Intelligence), 49
direct democracy, 111, 149
Directorate for National Intelligence (DINA) (Chile), 49
Diretas Já (Direct Elections Now) protest movement (Brazil), 54
Dirty War (Argentina), 158, 171
discursive polarization, 42
disjointed polarization, 41

distributive conflicts, 8
Do Alto, Hervé, 97
"doing politics," 29, 58, 66, 69, 208
domestic workers' rights, 70
Dominican Republic, 19
Douglass, Frederick, 198
drugs, war on, 94, 102
drug-trafficking cartels, 142
dual militancy arrangement, 61
dual transitions, 33–34; to democracy, 16
Duhalde, Eduardo, 158, 161, 162, 164, 224n7

EBR-200 (Revolutionary Bolivarian Army-200), 90–91
Ecological Action (Ecuador), 136
economic crisis, in Venezuela, 114
economic recovery, 63
Ecuador, 131–42; CONAIE, 130, 132, 138, 141; Electoral Tribunal, 134; Pachakutik, 130, 132–33, 141; UNES, 141
education system, 79
El Salvador, 1, *18*, 19, 23
electoral abstention, 93
electoral hegemony, 138
electoral participation, 56
electoral payoffs, 225n16
Electoral Tribunal (Ecuador), 134
elite bargaining, 65
elite polarization, 42
"end of history," 199
Etchemendy, Sebastián, 152
Evangelical religious networks, 200
Everyone's Front, 170
executive aggrandizement, 122, 139
extractive industries, 120
extractivism, 137–38
extraordinary conflict, 53

FA (Broad Front), 29, 80, 82, 129, 142–57, 204, 208–9, 224n5
Facebook, 188
Faguet, Jean-Paul, 102
family allowance, 68
farmers' rebellion, 167
Farthing, Linda, 227n6
Fatherland for All (PPT) (Venezuela), 100
Fedecámaras, 109, 110
Federation of the Tropics, 95
feedback mechanisms, 31, 113
feminist movements, 200

Fernandes, Sujantha, 112
Fernández, Max, 227n10
Fernández de Kirchner, Cristina, 157–58, 163, 166–71
Fifth Republic Movement (MVR) (Venezuela), 86, 93, 98–99, 105, 109, 161
Finance Ministry, 76
Financial Times, 81
Fiscal Responsibility Law, 226n22
FPV (Front for Victory), 162, 167, 169
FR (Renewal Front), 170
Frank, Jason, 28
free-market (neoliberal) development models, 4
free-market reforms, 20
free-trade agreements, 75
Frei Ruiz-Tagle, Eduardo, 63, 74, 79
French, John D., 52, 60
Frente de Todos (Everyone's Front) (Argentina), 170
frentista coalitional politics, 54
Front for a Country in Solidarity (FREPASO) (Argentina), 160
Front for Victory (FPV) (Argentina), 162, 167, 169
Fukuyama, Francis, 199

García Linera, Álvaro, 98, 227n9, 229n24, 229n30
gas wars, 131
gender, 36, 121, 199, 200, 206
General Labor Confederation (CGT) (Argentina), 164, 170
Gibson, Edward L., 224n9
Gillespie, Charles G., 144
Gini index of income inequality, 36, 37, 121
González, Luisa, 142
González Urrutia, Edmundo, 115
Gott, Richard, 91
Goulart, João, 17
governability, 46
grassroots, 53, 57, 230n37; Base Committees, 151, 153; *basismo*, 52; "Bolivarian circles," 99, 109; Chavismo, 111–12; civic networks, 92; *cocalero* and, 95; mobilization, 25; participatory channels, 10; popular power, 49; right-wing activism, 68, 182; shantytown youth and, 51
Greek philosophy, 23
Grisaffi, Thomas, 97

gross domestic product, 114
"growth with equity" strategy, 63
Grupo Comuna, 98, 227n7
Guaidó, Juan, 115
Guatemala, 1, 17, 19
guerrilla movement, urban, 144
Gutiérrez, Lucio, 132

Haggard, Stephan, 8, 38
Half Moon (Media Luna) (Bolivia), 117
Handlin, Samuel, 26, 38, 154, 193
hegemonic temptation, 168
Hetland, Gabriel, 118
Hoffman, Kelly, 212
Honduras, 1, 19, 205, 211, 223n1
Huber, Evelyne, 6, 152
human rights, 115, 164, 171, 231n9
humanitarian crisis, in Venezuela, 114
Hunter, Wendy, 55
hydrocarbon rents, 117
hyperinflation, 35, 160
hyperinflationary pressures, 4
hyperpolarization, 112

identities, cultural, 40
ideological distancing, 5
ideological moderation, 34
ideological radicals, 186
import substitution industrialization (ISI), 148, 152
inclusion, political and social, 143
income distribution, 64
income inequality, Gini index of, 36, 37, 121
Independent Democratic Union (UDI) (Chile), 74
Independent Political Electoral Organization Committee (COPEI) (Venezuela), 89–90, 92, 100, 109
indigenismo, 97
indigenous communities, 195, 227n5; movements, 11, 36, 86, 94–96, 116–17, 120, 137; rights for, 9, 72, 79, 83, 140; uprisings, 132
informal powers, 134
in-groups, 41
institutional polarization, 37, 176
institutionalized competition, 26
institutionalized pluralism, 47, 111, 123, 128, 146; democracy as, 23–25, 27, 50, 84; PT and, 57, 67

Inter-American Commission on Human Rights, 124
interlocking rules, 62
internal pluralism, 46
International Monetary Fund, 33, 93, 160, 170
ISI (import substitution industrialization), 148, 152
IU (United Left), 102, 226n2

Jara, Jeannette, 84
JP (Peronist Youth), 165
June Journeys (2013) (Brazil), 69
Justicialist Party (PJ) (Argentina), 158–59, 161, 163–64, 224n7

Karl, Terry Lynn, 8
Kast, José Antonio, 82–83, 185, 187, 194
Katarista Aymara nationalism, 97
Kaufman, Robert R., 8, 38
Keck, Margaret, 182, 226n20
Kessler, Gabriel, 192
Kirchner, Néstor, 157–58, 162–67, 169, 171, 224n7
Kirchnerist radicals (*radicales K*), 167

labor: organized, 52–53; PIT-CNT, 146, 150–52; unions, 3, 40, 126, 170
Lacalle Pou, Luis, 143, 155, 156
Laclau, Ernesto, 23, 166
Lagos, Ricardo, 61, 65, 73–76, 151
land reform, 68, 117
land squatting, 231n6
Landless Workers' Movement (MST) (Brazil), 53, 57, 68
Lanzaro, Jorge Luis, 21
LAPOP. *See* Latin American Public Opinion Project (LAPOP)
Lasso, Guillermo, 140, 141
Latin American Public Opinion Project (LAPOP), 14, 233n8; Americas-Barometer, 155, 188
Latinobarómetro, 133, 183, 232n5
Lavín, Joaquín, 74
Law on the Expiration of the Punitive Claims of the State (Ley de Caducidad), 147
LCR (Radical Cause), 91, 92
left turn, 1, 16–22, 205–10
left-wing nationalism, 97

legal scaffolding, 74
Leninism, 54
Let's Change (Cambiemos), 170
"Letter to the Brazilian People" (Lula da Silva), 60
Levitsky, Steven, 53, 158, 161, 164, 172
Ley de Caducidad (Law on the Expiration of the Punitive Claims of the State), 147
LGBTQ+ rights, 39, 72, 168
liberal democracy, 45, 110
Liberal Party (PL) (Brazil), 67
Longa, Francisco, 165
Lozada, Sánchez de, 104
Lula da Silva, Luiz Inácio, 65–73, 182, 185, 187, 194, 225n12, 226n23; election of, 59; imprisonment of, 53; "Letter to the Brazilian People," 60; trade unions and, 52
Luna, Juan Pablo, 41, 78, 147, 192
Lupu, Noam, 184

Machado, María Corina, 115
Macri, Mauricio, 19, 170–71
Madison, James, 24
Madrid, Raúl L., 96
Maduro, Nicolás, 114–15, 139
Mahuad, Jamil, 132
Mainwaring, Scott, 4
Majority Camp (Campo Majoritário), 56–57, 225n7
Manini Ríos, Guido, 156
Mantúfar, César, 139
March for Territory and Dignity (1990) (Bolivia), 228n20
market fundamentalism, 199
market liberalism, 89
market liberalization, 18, 23
market orthodoxy, 67
market reforms, 96, 170
marriage, same-sex, 168
Martínez, Daniel, 155
Marxism, 45, 143, 162
MAS. *See* Movement Toward Socialism (Bolivia)
mass empowerment, 163
Massa, Sergio, 169–71, 185, 187
MBR-200 (Revolutionary Bolivarian Movement-200), 91–93, 99
McAdam, Doug, 5, 102
McCoy, Jennifer, 4, 6, 232n2

INDEX 281

McKenna, Elizabeth, 70
MDB (Brazilian Democratic Movement), 53
MDT Evita (Movement of Unemployed Workers Evita), 165, 231n10
Media Luna (Half Moon), 117
median voters, 185, 187, 202
Meléndez, Carlos, 192
Menem, Carlos, 160–62, 231n7
Mensalão vote-buying scandal (2004–2005), 68, 225n12
Mesa, Carlos, 104, 123
Mexico, 19, 205, 211
Michels, Robert, 151
middle class, urban, 121, 123
Milei, Javier, 157, 171–72, 185, 187, 194–95
militant unionism (*novo sindicalismo*), 51
military coups, 32, 49, 91–92, 158
military repression, 4, 22, 50
minimum wage, 152, 225n16
minority political rights, 26
MIR (Movement of the Revolutionary Left), 49, 96
Mische, Ann, 70
MNR (Nationalist Revolutionary Movement), 96, 127
Molina, Fernando, 97
Montesquieu, 24
Montoneros, 159, 165
Morales, Evo, 28, 31, 95–104, 116–25, 128, 195, 228n22, 229n33, 230n36
Moreno, Lenín, 140, 141
Movement of the Revolutionary Left (MIR) (Chile), 49, 96
Movement of Unemployed Workers Evita (MDT Evita), 165, 231n10
Movement Toward Socialism (MAS) (Bolivia), 31, 82, 94–98, 101–5, 116–27, 195, 226n2
MPP (Popular Participation Movement), 149, 230n2
MRP (Revolutionary Peronist Movement), 159
MST (Landless Workers' Movement), 53, 57, 68
MUD (Democratic Unity Roundtable), 113–15
Mujica, José "Pepe," 142, 154
Multicolor Coalition (Uruguay), 156
multiculturalism, 36
Murillo, María Victoria, 161, 164, 192

MVR (Fifth Republic Movement), 86, 93, 98–99, 105, 109, 161

National Liberation Party (PLN) (Costa Rica), 17
national party systems, 28
National Revolution (1952) (Bolivia), 96, 97
nationalism: left-wing, 97; resource, 137
Nationalist Democratic Action (ADN) (Bolivia), 96
Nationalist Revolutionary Movement (MNR) (Bolivia), 96, 127
nationalization, 120
natural resource extraction, 135
Naval Club Pact, 146
Navarro, Fernando "Chino," 165
negative partisanship, 42
negative popular majorities, 84
neoliberal (free-market) development models, 4
neoliberalism, 34, 63, 95, 130, 136, 232n6; "by surprise," 90; orthodoxy, 16, 38, 40, 64, 199; political contestation of, 38; political convergence around, 35; reforms, 27, 33, 35, 59; restructuring, 62; savage, 99; shock treatments, 33
New Majority (Nueva Mayoría) (Chile), 80, 82
"new" polarization, 174–75; conclusion, 196–97; electoral dynamics and, 192–96, *193*; multiple faces of, 176–96; party system polarization and, 192–96, *193*; polarization dynamics and public opinion in, 183–86, *184*; public opinion, numbers versus intensities, 187–92, *190*, *191*; tracking through expert surveys, 177–83, *178*, *180*, *181*
New Revolutionary Force (NFR) (Bolivia), 227n10
Nicaragua, 1, 17, *18*, 19, 23, 31
Noboa, Álvaro, 133, 142
Noboa, Daniel, 142
novo sindicalismo (militant unionism), 51
núcleos de base (base nuclei), 52
Nueva Mayoría (New Majority), 80, 82

October Agenda, 228n20
O'Donnell, Guillermo, 3, 127
oil prices, 92
oil rents, 110

OPEC (Organization of Petroleum Exporting Countries), 108
Open Cabildo (Uruguay), 156
opposition groups, 24
Organisation for Economic Co-operation and Development, 78
Organization of Petroleum Exporting Countries (OPEC), 108
organized labor, 52–53
Orsi, Yamandú, 156
Ortega, Daniel, 31
out-groups, 41

Pachakutik (Ecuador), 130, 132–33, 141
Pacheco Areco, Jorge, 144
pacted democracy, 96, 101, 103
Pacto de Puntofijo, 89
Palenque, Carlos, 102
Panama, 19, 91
Paraguay, *18*, 23
partidocracia (partyarchy), 94, 108, 131, 133
partisanship, negative, 42
Party for Democracy (PPD) (Chile), 61
Party for the Victory of the People (PVP) (Uruguay), 149
Party of the Venezuelan Revolution (PRV) (Venezuela), 91
partyarchy (*partidocracia*), 94, 108, 131, 133
party-system polarization, 38
passive revolution, of Morales, 118
Patriotic Pole (PP) (Bolivia), 99
PCCh (Communist Party), 48, 61, 80, 82, 84, 194
PCV (Venezuelan Communist Party), 100
PDC (Christian Democratic Party), 50, 55, 61, 74, 79–80, 83, 147, 194
PDVSA (Petroleum of Venezuela), 109, 110
penguin (*pingüino*) rebellion, 78–79
Peredo, Antonio, 103
Pérez, Carlos Andrés, 90–92
Pérez, Yaku, 141
Pérez Bentancur, Verónica, 151
Pérez Jiménez, Marcos, 89
Pérez-Liñán, Aníbal, 4
pernicious polarization, 6
Perochena, Camila, 166, 168
Perón, Juan, 158
Perón, María Estela (Isabel) Martínez de, 158
Peronism, 42, 127, 129, 157–72, 195, 231n9

Peronist Youth (JP) (Argentina), 165
Pérsico, Emilio, 165
Peru, 1, 17, 19, 42, 91, 205
Petrobras, 70
Petrolão, 70
Petroleum of Venezuela (PDVSA), 109, 110
Piñera, Sebastián, 79, 80–81
pingüino (penguin) rebellion, 78–79
Pinochet, Augusto, 43, 61–63, 80–83, 146, 194, 199, 208; Bachelet and, 77; "deepening" democracy and, 50, 60; military dictatorship of, 10
piqueteros (street picketers), 162
PIT-CNT (the national labor confederation), 146, 150–52
PJ (Justicialist Party), 158–59, 161, 163–64, 224n7
PL (Liberal Party), 67
Plan Bolívar, 108
Plano Real currency stabilization, 59
PLN (National Liberation Party), 17
pluralism, internal, 46. *See also* institutionalized pluralism
PMDB (Brazilian Democratic Movement), 57, 71
polarization, 4–5
policy radicalism, 157
political attrition (*desgaste*), 208
political conflict, 7–8
political contestation, 38, *39*
political inclusion, 143
political learning, 47–55
political polarization, 177, *178*, 179, *181*, 182
political rights, 26, 55
polyarchy, 25, *25*, 35, 207, 223n4
popular accountability, 107
popular consultation, 136
popular councils, 56
popular empowerment, 42
popular front coalition, 48
popular mobilization, 33
Popular Participation Movement (MPP) (Uruguay), 149, 230n2
popular power, 49, 58
popular rebellion, 61
popular sovereignty, 23, 27, 61, 74, 87, 104–27, 174
Popular Unity (UP) (Chile), 48–49
popular uprisings, 132

populism, 23–24, 76, 166
populist left, 2, 9–10, 14, 21–22, 26, 28, 30, 86–87; conclusion, 127–28; in Ecuador, 130–42; formative processes and, 88–98; historical experiences and, 88–98; institutional contexts of, 104–27; roads to power and, 98–104
positive democratic majority, 84
poverty, 63–64, 92, 121, 160
power: asymmetries of, 29; concentration of, 30; consolidation of, 108; constitutive, 82–83; informal, 134; popular, 49, 58; promiscuous powersharing, 96, 101; roads to, 55–65
Power, Timothy J., 225n16
PP (Patriotic Pole), 99
PPD (Party for Democracy), 61
PPT (Fatherland for All), 100
prefiguration, 224n4
presidential coup. See *autogolpe* (presidential coup)
Pribble, Jennifer, 76, 152, 224n3
private capital, 74
private property, 63
PRO (Republican Proposal), 170
"Proceso, El" (Argentina), 158
progressive movements, 7
promiscuous powersharing, 96, 101
protagonism, 107
protagonistic democracy, 112
protest movements, 3, 5, 46, 49, 69–70, 81, 161; antigovernment, 104; criminalizing, 139; cycles of, 77; Diretas Já, 54; social, 35; violent repression of, 124–25
Proud and Sovereign Homeland Alliance (AP) (Bolivia), 131, 136, 138, 140
PRV (Party of the Venezuelan Revolution), 91
PSCh. *See* Socialist Party (PSCh) (Chile)
PSDB (Brazilian Social Democratic Party), 59, 60, 65, 194
PSUV (United Socialist Party of Venezuela) (PSUV), 86, 111, 113, 115
PT. *See* Workers Party (PT) (Brazil)
public opinion: numbers versus intensities, 187–92, *190*, *191*; polarization dynamics and, 183–86, *184*
Puntofijo system, 89, 93, 101
PVP (Party for the Victory of the People), 149

que se vayan todos (throw everyone out), 161, 165
Quiroga, José Antonio, 103
Quispe, Felipe, 103

racism, 97
Radical Cause (LCR) (Venezuela), 91, 92
Radical Civic Union (UCR) (Argentina), 159, 171–72
Radical Party (Chile), 48
radicales K (Kirchnerist radicals), 167
redistributive policies and reforms, 6, 17, 121, 122, 174
redistributive welfare states, 9
reformism, 67
regime reconstitution, 105
regime transitions, 64
religious networks, 200
Renewal Front (FR) (Argentina), 170
"Renovación, La" (Argentina), 159
reproductive rights, 200
Republican Proposal (PRO) (Argentina), 170
resource nationalism, 137
"Respect the Vote," 123
retrospective economic voting, 18
revolutionary activism, 48
Revolutionary Bolivarian Army-200 (EBR-200) (Venezuela), 90–91
Revolutionary Bolivarian Movement-200 (MBR-200) (Venezuela), 91–93, 99
revolutionary Marxists, 45
revolutionary movements, 33
Revolutionary Peronist Movement (MRP) (Argentina), 159
Rhodes-Purdy, Matthew, 76
rights: abortion, 39, 72, 153; citizenship, 96–97, 135; civil, 55; for domestic workers, 70; equal, 9; human, 115, 164, 171, 231n9; indigenous, 9, 72, 79, 83, 140; LGBTQ+, 39, 72, 168; minority political, 26; political, 26, 55; reproductive, 200; social citizenship, 2, 11, 62, 68, 108, 169; of women, 9, 39
right-wing activism, 68, 70, 182
right-wing self-identification, 183
Roberts, Kenneth M., 158
Rocha, Manuel, 228n19
Rodrigues-Silveira, Rodrigo, 225n16
Rodríguez, Andrónico, 230n36

Rodríguez, Francisco, 114
Rodríguez Saá, Adolfo, 162, 231n7
Römer, Henrique Salas, 100
Rosenblatt, Fernando, 148
Rousseff, Dilma, 43, 46, 68–70, 72, 179, 182, 226n22
Rustow, Dankwart, 7–8, 198, 200, 203

Sáez, Irene, 100
Salary Councils, 152
same-sex marriage, 168
Samuels, David J., 72, 224n8
San Francisco Syndicate, 95
Sartori, Giovanni, 5, 38, 185, 202
savage neoliberalism, 99
Schedler, Andreas, 38, 41, 194, 202–4
Schmitter, Philippe C., 3, 8
Scioli, Daniel, 170
self-criticism (*autocrítica*), 210–13
self-determination, 23
self-identification, 183, 186, 187
self-placement, 189, *190*, *191*, 220, *221*
self-reflection, 49–50, 51
self-rule, 23
Sells, Cameron, 149
Seregni, Líber, 145–46
Serra, José, 60
sex education, 72
sexuality, 36
shantytown youth, 51
shock treatments, 33
Simmons, Erica S., 96
Sinceramente (Fernández de Kirchner), 167
sindicalismo (union organizing), 94
Singer, André, 226n23
Slater, Dan, 96
social citizenship rights, 2, 11, 62, 68, 108, 169
social collectives, 80
social democratic left, 2, 10, 14, 21, 26, 45–46; conclusion, 84–85; conformist temptation and, 65–84; democratization and, 55–65; formative processes of, 47–55; historical experiences of, 47–55; political learning and, 47–55; PSCh development and, 48–51; PT founding and, 51–55; roads to power and, 55–65
social distance, 202
social *estallidos* (social explosions), 1, 82
social hierarchies, 39

social inclusion, 42, 143
social media, 188
social mobilization, 5, 36, 49, 58, 64, 117, 124, 157; autonomous, 120; for equal rights, 9
social movements, 45, 52, 60, 69, 119
social polarization, 177, 179, *180*, 182
social policy initiatives, 63
social protest, 35
social technocracy, 77
socialism, 33, 39–40, 48, 60, 66, 113, 138
Socialist Party (PSCh) (Chile), 19, 29–31, 45–47, 62–65, 82–85, 143, 194, 204–5; development of, 48–51; rise and eclipse of, 73–84
socialist renovation, 49–50
societal accountability, 120
Solidarity Civic Union (UCS) (Bolivia), 227n10
Soviet Union, 32
soybean exports, 167
spatial distancing, 201
spatial polarization, 5, *37*, 41, 176, 182
state repression, 96
status quo, 46, 116, 166, 213
Stefanoni, Pablo, 97
Stephens, Jones D., 6
Stokes, Susan C., 90
street picketers (*piqueteros*), 162
structural adjustment policies, 35
student activism, 78–79
Supreme Tribunal of Justice (Venezuela), 115, 116
Svampa, Maristella, 168, 212
Svolik, Milan W., 6

Tarrow, Sidney G., 43, 102
Teichman, Judith, 108
Temer, Michel, 71
term limits, 122, 160
third wave of democratization, 3–4; democratic transitions, 7, 198
TIPNIS crisis, 120
Torrijos, Omar, 91
trade unions, 52
Transitions from Authoritarian Rule (O'Donnell and Schmitter), 3
Trotskyism, 54
Tupamaros, 144, 230n2
"two lefts," 22–31, *25*, 45

UCR (Radical Civic Union), 159, 171–72
UCS (Solidarity Civic Union), 227n10
UDI (Independent Democratic Union), 74
unemployment, 160
UNES (Union for Hope), 141
Unified Confederation of Rural Laborers of Bolivia (CSUTCB), 94–95
Union for Hope (UNES) (Ecuador), 141
union organizing (*sindicalismo*), 94
Unión por la Patria (Union for the Homeland) (Argentina), 171
unions: labor, 3, 40, 126, 170; movement, 63; representation, 52; trade, 52; unionization, 63
United Left (IU) (Bolivia), 102, 226n2
United Socialist Party of Venezuela (PSUV), 86, 111, 113, 115
United States, 32
United Workers Central (CUT) (Chile), 80
Unity Pact, 104, 117, 230n36
University of Chicago, 62
University of Illinois, 131
UP (Popular Unity), 48–49
urban guerrilla movement, 144
urban middle class, 121, 123
Uruguay, 2, 10, 12, 14, 19–21, 27, 36, 172–73; FA, 29, 80, 82, 129, 142–57, 204, 208–9, 224n5; MPP, 149, 230n2; presidential elections, *18*; PVP, 149

Van Dyck, Brandon, 53, 144
Vargas, Getúlio, 52
Varieties of Democracy (V-Dem), 14, 34, 177, 179, 182, 196
Vázquez, Tabaré, 142, 150–54, 156
V-Dem, 14, 34, 177, 179, 182, 196
Velasco, Alejandro, 106, 108
Velasco Alvarado, Juan, 17, 91

Venezuela: AD, 17, 89–90, 92, 100, 109; Caracazo, 90–91; COPEI, 89–90, 92, 100, 109; CTV, 109, 110; LCR, 91, 92; MUD, 113–15; MVR, 86, 93, 98–99, 105, 109, 161; PDVSA, 109, 110; PPT, 100; PRV, 91; PSUV, 86, 111, 113, 115; Supreme Tribunal of Justice, 115, 116
Venezuelan Communist Party (PCV), 100
violence, transcended political, 144
violent repression, 124–25, 144, 158
volatility, 1
voter fraud, 110
voter registration, 78
voting: anti-incumbent, 20; median voters, 187, 202; Mensalão vote-buying scandal, 68, 225n12; "Respect the Vote," 123; retrospective economic, 18

wars: civil warfare, 31–32; Cold War, 32, 64, 199; culture, 171; Dirty War, 158, 171; on drugs, 94, 102; gas, 131; water, 103, 131
Washington Consensus, 18, 33, 35, 38–39, 186, 196, 200–201, 232n6; Chavismo and, 89; ideological hegemony of, 4
water wars, 103, 131
Webber, Jeffery R., 104
welfare states, redistributive, 9
Weyland, Kurt, 74
WhatsApp, 188
women, rights for, 9, 39
Workers Party (PT) (Brazil), 29–31, 45–47, 85, 144, 182, 194, 225n5, 229n30; founding of, 51–55; rise and fall of, 66–73; road to power for, 56–60

Zelaya, Manuel, 223n1
Ziblatt, Daniel, 172, 200
Zucco, Cesar, 72, 224n8

www.ingramcontent.com/pod-product-compliance
Lightning Source LLC
Chambersburg PA
CBHW022039290426
44109CB00014B/918